Working Songs

Industrial ballads and poems from Britain and Ireland, 1780s-1980s

ROY PALMER

HERRON PUBLISHING
www.herronpublishing.co.uk

First published September 2010 by
David Herron Publishing, Wellington Rd.,
Todmorden, Yorkshire OL14 5DY

This paperback edition published 2010

ISBN 978-095-4068257

Music set by Alison Burns
Designed and typeset by Bryan Ledgard
Printed in Great Britain by Henry Ling & Co.

Contents

Epigraphs

I was an offspring of the pioneers of the Industrial Revolution, the weavers and the spinners who took the blitz of the machines that came out of space to them on the chin; and now they lie under the sod. They haunt me, the spirits of those men and women and even children who had to take this terrible invasion of the machinery into their lives. Those weavers and spinners haunt me, the millwrights and engineers and early pioneers of the Industrial Revolution who carried on almost ignored by the rest of the world...
William Holt of Todmorden, West Yorkshire, quoted in Glyn Hughes, *Millstone Grit* (1975)

Folk Song in its classic form has certainly not been the music, the great popular music, of the industrial proletariat in England, although in certain areas and certain industries, alongside their reception of what was provided for them by stage professionals and so on, the workers maintained a certain enthusiasm for producing their own song material, especially at critical moments like strikes or mine disasters or such, but not only at those critical moments, for fun too. They maintained rather well right up to the present time a certain capacity for song making.
A.L. Lloyd, interviewed in 1970 by Mark Gregory

Introduction

'The Industrial Revolution marks the most fundamental transformation of human life in the history of the world recorded in written documents', wrote Eric Hobsbawm.[1] Among those documents, not only written but also sometimes oral, were the songs and poems – often ignored or even despised – of workers and their allies. And they reflected, recorded and at times influenced industrial attitudes and events, not only during the Industrial Revolution in Britain, but also during the succeeding centuries. Accordingly, they illustrate the cycle of working life, with struggles over pay and conditions a major feature. The volume of ballads arising from strikes is astonishing, and I do not think in emphasising it I am merely indulging in a penchant for class conflict.

Music While You Work

'One thing of which we can be certain is that singing was ubiquitous in pre-industrial society', writes Vic Gammon, and then quotes the Elizabethan writer on music, John Case:

> And hence it is, that wayfaring men, solace themselves with songs, and ease the wearisomeness of their journey . . . the manual labourers and mechanical artificers of all sorts, keep such a chaunting and singing in their shops, the tailor on his baulk, the shoemaker at his last, the mason at his wall, the ship boy at his oar, the tinker at his pan, and the tiler on the house-top . . . every troublesome and laborious occupation useth Music for a solace and recreation.[2]

Most of these instances involved, to borrow the title of a series of radio programmes broadcast during the Second World War, 'music while you work'. These were aimed mainly at keeping up the morale of (predominantly women) factory workers, who sang along as they listened. Songs continued to fill their time-honoured role of lightening labour by lifting the workers' spirits and helping them to pass the weary hours. The lyrics were entirely diversionary, not to say escapist, and the rhythms employed had no direct connection with the work done, which was of many different kinds.

By contrast, certain songs were designed for particular tasks, or

adapted to suit them. Although boundaries may be blurred, it is clear that work songs proper were widely used to accompany certain kinds of collective and individual hand labour. Indeed there is a theory that the needs of communal work in stimulating and co-ordinating the efforts of those involved, helped in the distant past to give rise to song in the first place. Different rhythms were designed to suit particular tasks, and work songs were once a ubiquitous feature of group labour.

Until the late twentieth century, many work songs (though no longer sung to accompany tasks) were remembered in the Hebrides, especially those for 'waulking'. The common English surname, Walker, indicated in Old English a person who trod or walked cloth in a trough as part of the fulling process, though this was later mechanised in walk-mills where a waterwheel turned a camshaft which operated a wooden drop hammer. There, as with foot-walking, the cloth was soaked in urine collected for the purpose from local households. In Wales at one time 'They paid a penny a bucket, twopence if you were a Methodist because it would be alcohol free'.[3]

No songs from the hand (or foot) walking era in England have survived. Scotland, and in particular the Hebrides and parts of the Highlands, is a different matter. Individually woven lengths of tweed or blankets were collectively waulked. Six or eight women sat round a board in a shed or barn or house, and pounded and pulled at cloth which had been soaked in sour urine, heated and mixed with flakes of soap. The activity lasted for several hours in an evening, accompanied by exuberant songs in which a soloist's narrative, one line at a time, was punctuated with chorused vocals, as in this case:

> Faill ù hill ò hillinn is ò
> Faill ù hill ò ho ro éileadh
> Is moch an diugh a rinn mi gluasad [Early today I set out]
> Faill ù hill ò ho ro éileadh
> Faill ù hill hillinn is ò
> Faill ù hill ò ho ro éileadh.

There are twenty-five more single-line verses, each accompanied by the panoply of vocables.[4] The imaginative sweep of the tale they tell of a lost lover is far removed from thoughts of the singers' gruelling task. Hamish Henderson has described the genre as 'a surging, pounding maelstrom of song, into which has been drawn material from the most disparate sources: love songs, hunting songs, flytings, eulogies, laments, and even swatches of versified folk narratives'. He adds:

'at the waulking-board, where the surge and the beat of the song often reaches a pitch which one can only call ecstatic'

> Here, at the waulking-board, where the surge and beat of the song often reaches a pitch which one can only call ecstatic, the whole inner life of the women seems to come to the surface in uninhibited self-expression: desire, scorn, reproach, desolation – all the sexual joys and agonies of the women come pouring out like a burn in spate. One feels, at times, that all this emotion is only bearable because it is confined between the banks of traditional formulaic utterance.[5]

The only work songs, which compare in vivacity and variety with the (women's) waulking repertoire, are the (men only) sailors' shanties. With some exceptions, they, too, were only sung to accompany shipboard tasks - hauling on ropes, heaving at windlass, capstan, and pumps. R.R. Terry (1864-1938), who, influenced by his Northumbrian roots, collected and studied shanties, wrote in 1920:

> A shanty was a labour song, sung by sailors aboard the old sailing ships. Each class of work had its own class of shanty by which the labour was lightened. Sailors sang shanties only when at work; never by way of recreation. Shanties were moreover confined to the merchant service; they were never used aboard men-o'-war, where the work was carried out in silence, - the orders being given to the pipe of the bosun's whistle.[6]

Later commentators were rather less watertight with their categories. A.L. Lloyd suggested that 'many shanties might be used indiscriminately for both hauling and heaving jobs', though he conceded that 'others were shaped for specific uses, for long hauls or short, for hoisting yards, sweating up or bunting, for heaving on the jerky brake-windlass or smoothly shoving the capstan round'.[7]

Shanties were entirely subordinate to the tasks they accompanied. The command 'belay' (known as 'the shanty full stop'), or 'avast heaving', put an instant end to both task and song. The rambling and chaotic corpus of shanties might also be described as 'a maelstrom of song.' Texts and tunes were appropriated and adapted from a huge range of sources. Lyrics, often coarse, sometimes obscene ('Rabelaisian' was how Terry preferred to put it), frankly reflected the vicissitudes of the sailor's life, ashore and afloat. At times, too, they approached the emotional power of waulking songs; and at times, as with 'Stormalong' and 'Shallow Brown' they could be almost unbearably beautiful. Percy Grainger recorded versions of these at Dartmouth in 1908 from his 'genius sea chanty singing man', John Perring.[8]

'The advent of screw steamers', wrote Terry, 'sounded the death knell of the shanty'.[9] The change, of course, did not happen overnight: the shanty was a long time a-dying, and the waulking song even longer, in the remote Hebrides.

The heavy and noisy machinery required for the mass production characteristic of the Industrial Revolution not only removed the need for work songs like these, but also often obliterated the possibility of singing at all. Indeed, some employers such as Ambrose Crowley (1658-1713) forbade workers to sing, and made deductions from the wages of those who disobeyed (see chapter 1).

Early in the twentieth century, despite high levels of noise, 'In the mills of Blackburn weavers rehearsed the *Messiah* and *Elijah* over the roar of their looms';[10] and at about the same time, fifteen miles to the east as the crow flies, William Holt, speaking of the cotton mills of the Calder Valley, where he became a weaver in 1910 at the age of thirteen, said that 'The noise of the machinery of weaving is a monotonous roar so loud that you can't hear your own voice even if you shout'; but even so: 'Sometimes all the weavers sang in unison. It was just possible to hear the high notes above the roar of the machinery'.[11]

'Cotton was the fibre of the industrial revolution', wrote John Styles;[12] and coal, one could add, provided its motive power. The sheer difficulty and strenuousness of mining largely precluded singing, though the odd exception proves the rule. A visitor of 1784, appalled by the series of wet and rickety ladders which provided access to a Cornish tin mine, remarked: 'I had no idea of the difficulty and danger attending such an undertaking and only wonder that accidents are not more frequent among the miners, who run up and down these slippery places like lamp-lighters, singing and whistling all the day'. He was amazed to encounter 'figures that hardly wore the appearance of human beings, *singing at their work*' (his italics).[13]

In factories, as we have seen, the problem was either management prohibition or sheer volume of noise. However, while songs, which accompanied work, declined and disappeared, songs about work continued to flourish. They have been variously known as occupational songs and labour songs, but in this book I have called them working songs. It is paradoxical that whereas work songs overwhelmingly avoided the subject of work, working songs - sung in a public house, round the fireside at home, at a social gathering or during an outing, at a union meeting, during a demonstration or picket - dealt with little else.

Working Songs

Long before the Industrial Revolution (and for that matter, long after) there was a vigorous tradition of featuring the worker in songs, which praised his or her skill. The notion of the handloom weaver's pre-eminence, at least as expressed in song, survived beyond industrialisation. 'The Wark o' the Weavers', written by David Shaw to be sung at the annual meeting of the Forfar Weavers' Friendly Society, became widely known in Scotland and remained in oral circulation until at least the middle of the twentieth century.[14] During the 1840s Shaw and his two daughters attended Chartist meetings during which they were called upon to sing between speeches.[15] One hopes that 'The Wark o' the Weavers' featured:

> An' it werena the weavers what wad we do?
> We wadna get claith made o' our 'oo [wool];
> We wadna get a coat, either black or blue,
> An' it werena for the honourable weavers.

There are miners' songs with the same kind of optimism. 'A New Song, in Praise of the Coal-miners',[16] dating from the eighteenth century, mentions casualties:

> 'You Coalminers of *England* your Skill is so pure,
> You excel all other Callings, that is to be sure:
> For those that despise you are highly to blame,
> For the Good of the Country there's many one slain'.
> Yet it is unhesitatingly acquiescent:
> 'But us poor Coal-miners we stand to their Test,
> With Fendings and Bargains we still do make Shift,
> We go to our Labour with joy and Content
> We live on the portion that Heav'n hath us sent'.

Even at the beginning of the nineteenth century, the song 'Colliers of Wear & Tyne,'[17], alludes to low earnings:

> 'A collier works hard for his living, and that too by night and by day,
> And rears up a brood of young colliers, and that on his poor penny pay'

However, it appeals only for charitableness:

> 'Sure those that are crop full of riches, A little indulgence should give,
> And take up a brotherly maxim, And that is to "live and let live"'.

Only when the subject of Napoleon comes up does any asperity arise:

A truce with all peevish complaining,
Or on the right head let it fall
They say it's a madman call'd Boney
That makes the poor earning so small
If I had him dead I assure you
I'd cover him heavy with stones
And living if I could but catch him
I'd sharpen my pick on his bones.

It is remarkable that contemporary with 'Colliers of Wear & of Tyne' was a powerful and uncompromising song, first published in 1793, and known to be popular in 1815:

The Colliers Rant[18]

As me and my marrow was ganning to wark,
We met with the devil, it was in the dark;
I up with my pick, it being in the neit,
I knock'd off his horns, likewise his club feet.
Follow the horses, Johnny my lad oh!
Follow them through, my canny lad oh!
Follow the horses, Johnny my lad oh!
Oh lad ly away, canny lad oh!

Oh! marrow, oh! marrow, this is wor pay week,
We'll get penny loaves and drink to our beek;
And we'll fill up our bumper, and round it shall go,
Follow the horses, Johnny lad oh!
Follow the horses, &c.

There is my horse, and there is my tram:
Twee horns full of grease will make her to gang!
There is my hoggars, likewise my half shoon,
And smash my heart, marrow, my putting's a' done.
Follow the horses, etc

(Marrow: workmate; putting: conveying coal; tram: low truck; low: light; drift: underground passage; hoggars: footless stockings; half-shoon: old shoes with the toes cut off).

These first known appearance of this text was in *The Northumberland Garland; or Newcastle Nightingale: A Matchless*

Collection of Famous Songs, edited by the Stockton-on-Tees-born scholar, Joseph Ritson (1752-1803), and issued in Newcastle by the broadside printers, Hall and Elliot. Ritson's source, whether oral or printed, is not given.[19] The song may have lingered in oral circulation in the north-east of England, and there is a story, which may be apocryphal, that it was sung 'by massed choirs of miners on vesting day in 1947 to mark the nationalisation of the pits'.[20] It turned up in the repertoire of a celebrated family of Durham miners, the Elliotts of Birtley, and from them spread widely in the folk revival of the 1950s and onwards.[21]

The assurance and power of 'The Collier's Rant' are characteristic of many of the ballads - and also poems - with which working people and their allies responded to industry in general and the Industrial Revolution in particular. Often there is no indication of authorship: a song in oral circulation is assumed to be common currency, collective property. In the case of manuscript or printed material, ascription tends to be minimal.

However, in Dave Harker's anthology, *Songs and Verse of the North-east Pitmen, c. 1780-1844*, of the 121 items, predominantly

Engraving of Joseph Ritson. Courtesy of John Wardroper

broadsides, half have known authors, many of whom proudly identify themselves as miners, sometimes giving their place of work, either in the heading or at the foot of a sheet.[22] Women authors, including a collier's wife, are also occasionally cited.[23] In many cases, little more is known of such writers than these minimal details, though sometimes further information has come to light. William Mitford (1788-1851), was a singing shoemaker turned publican, some of whose compositions in a lighter vein remained popular in the North-East for generations: for example, 'The Pitman's Courtship', set to the perhaps surprising tune of 'The Night before Larry was Stretched'.[24] Even better known as a songwriter was Joseph Philip Robson (1808-1870), 'the bard of the Tyne and minstrel of the Wear'. Robson supplemented his earnings as a schoolmaster by writing songs for the music hall, some of which, like 'The Pawnshop Bleezin''[25] remained in the repertoire until well into the twentieth century. He also wrote for *The Miner's Advocate* a series of poems on the dangers of pit work, including 'The Miner's Doom' and 'The Trapper-Boy's Dream'.[26]

Fugacious Literature

Large numbers of songs relating to industrial matters have survived, thanks to having been printed on single-sheet broadsides, and these have been one of the principal sources for this book. In an article of 1839 entitled 'Songs of the Working Classes', John Harland of Manchester wrote of 'the "fugacious literature" exhibited in rows upon the dead walls of our large towns, where a few yards of twine, and here or there a nail driven into the mortar of the wall, form the bookstand and reading desk of the lover of song amongst the industrious population'. He believed it to be 'of some importance to know the character of that class of ballads which are manufactured for the marker of the poorer classes, - of those songs which, in order to find favour and a ready sale, must reflect the feelings, opinions, and wishes, the likings and the hates, the prejudice and the passions, of the operatives, whose only poetry they constitute'.[27]

Many ballads were written by a worker or group of workers, who simply paid a printer to produce copies, but Harland's point about commercial operators is unexceptionable. He goes on of 'the songs of our own operatives' that: 'They have all a political character, and the subjects are generally the so-called evils of the present times, as compared with the fancied blessings of olden times, the state of trade and wages, the new poor law, and taxation'. Another commentator takes a more sympathetic view: 'For all their limitations the broadsides can be seen as a positive cultural tool which helped much of the working class to adapt to the industrial age'.[28]

The Poetry of the People

Harland may have used this phrase somewhat patronisingly but it certainly applies, not only to the broadside ballads, but also to a range of material covered by this book. Its authors are numerous, and mainly unknown, so for the most part their work has to speak for itself. Some of it, perhaps, with phrases like 'Blush! at the Murder'd Innocent', 'the tyrant's yoke', 'last dread trumpet', and 'cruel death hath been severe', veers towards the conventionally emotive. The best is both direct and striking. Figures of speech are few. There are occasional similes such as 'sly as a mouse', 'black as a sloe', 'voices like trumpets', and the occasional striking image, for example, the weaver complaining that 'I've woven myself to th' fur end'. The extended sexual metaphor was particularly favoured, as with the woman steam-loom weaver's encounter with an engine driver:

> She said my loom is out of fettle,
> Can you right it – yes or no? –
> You say you are an engine driver,
> Which makes the steam so rapid flow,
> My lambs and jacks are out of order,
> My laith in motion has not been,
> So work away without delay,
> And quickly muster up the steam.[29]

The passage also illustrates the joy and ease in manipulating technical terms, which occur in a number of songs.

The listener or reader is quickly drawn in at the beginning of a piece by such invitations as 'Good people I pray you give ear', 'You North Country people', 'Ye working men of Britain', 'You power loom weavers far and near' and 'Now come all you jolly collier lads'. Alternatively, we are plunged into the action with openings like 'As me and my marrow was ganning to work', 'It wis in November en aw nivor will forget', 'At the docks there is a strike that the company don't like', 'The Rego girls are marching with spirits all aglow', and 'Oh, we are two motor trade workers, We're labelled as loafers and shirkers'.

Harland's accusation of 'doggrel' (as he spells it) cannot always be rejected, but much of the material is not only straightforward and effective but also powerful, and at times wonderfully memorable. A worker's experience of early factory life is resumed in four lines of (with one exception) monosyllables:

You have just got time to eat & sleep
A man is set your time to keep;
And if you chance to come too late,
You'r mark'd on paper or on slate.[30]

That the simplest words can count is demonstrated by this expression early in the nineteenth century of a Lancashire hand weaver's resentment at his 'mester' and his despair of making a decent living:

To think that we mun work to keep them and awth set,
All the days o' my life and still be in their debt;
So I'll give o'er trade an work with a spade,
Or go and break stones upoth road.[31]

A hundred years after this women in the jute mills of Dundee were still singing:

Oh dear me, the world's ill divided:
Them that work the hardest are the least provided,
But I'll just bide contented, dark days or fine,
But there's no much pleasure living affen ten and nine.[32]

The singer here, Mary Brooksbank, did not in fact 'bide contented', since she was involved in strike action as early as the age of fifteen.
Strike ballads, at the heart of this book, provide a remarkable insight into the creativity and wit of working people, as well as their anger. According to a broadside of 1853:

In Liverpool, the Postmen struck and sent word to their betters,
Begging them to recollect that they were men of letters;
They asked for three bob more a week, and got it in a crack
And although each man has got his bag, they have not got the sack.[33]

In the same year the cotton weavers of Preston excoriated their employers in a blizzard of ballads, including verses such as this:

The working people such as we,
Pass their time in misery,
While they live in luxury,
The Cotton Lords of Preston.
They're making money every way,

And building Factories every day,
Yet when we ask them for more pay,
They had the impudence to say,
To your demands we'll not consent,
You get enough to be content,
But we will have our Ten per Cent,
From the Cotton Lords of Preston.[34]

The invective in strike songs sometimes became vitriolic, as in:

May every Durham colliery owner that is in the fault,
Receive nine lashes with the rod, then be rubbed with salt;
May his back end be thick with boils, so that he cannot sit,
And never burst until the wheels go round at every pit.[35]

The writer here, Tommy Armstrong, also expresses high emotion with the most sparing of means. Two lines in a piece on a pit disaster - 'Let us think of Mrs Burnett, Once had sons but now has none' - uses the simplest of words to tremendous effect.[36]

An elegiac element occurs in some ballads of pit disaster, as it does in the commemoration in a recent composition of a picket's death:

The snow may melt and the frost depart,
But the breath of winter is on my heart.
The flowers may rise with the soft spring sun,
But the fairest flower of all is dead and gone.[37]

Oral Tradition

A new song might well have been ephemeral, rapidly falling from favour after serving its purpose in publicising a strike, raising money after a disaster or complaining at working conditions - or the lack of work. Alternatively, it might have continued in oral tradition, sung at a family gathering, a convivial evening in pub or club, or latterly a folk festival or gathering. One has to admit that industrial songs surviving orally in this country have not been plentiful. Examples may of course have slipped into oblivion for want of a sympathetic observer. The oral tradition was regarded as a rural phenomenon by folk song collectors such as Sabine Baring Gould, Lucy Broadwood, Ralph Vaughan Williams and Cecil Sharp, who overwhelmingly avoided urban centres. An exception was Frank Kidson, who obtained a good deal of material from Leeds, though even he found nothing relating to large-scale industry.

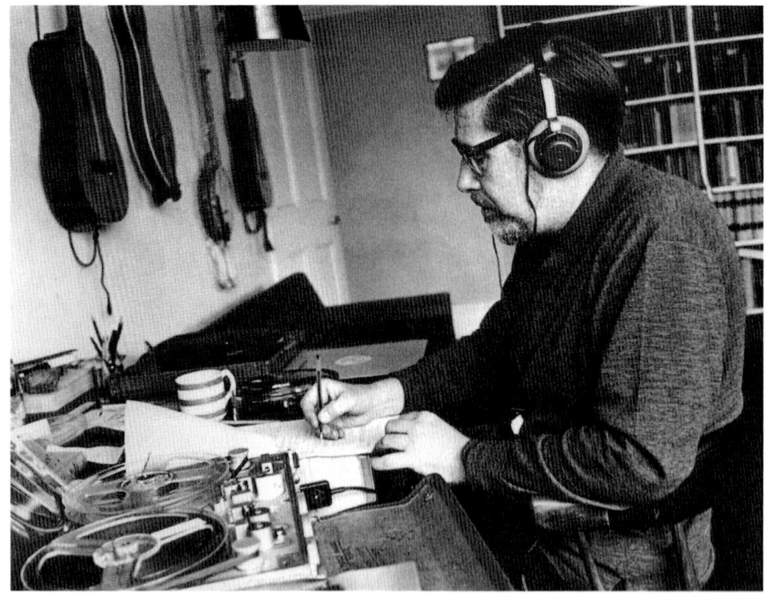

Ewan MacColl at work. Courtesy of Peggy Seeger

One family of traditional singers, whose repertoire included industrial songs, was the Elliotts of Birtley in County Durham, the subject of a collective biography in 2008 by Pete Wood. The family came to wider notice only in the late 1950s and early 60s, thanks to the emergence of folk song clubs, and of visits by Ewan MacColl, Peggy Seeger and A.L. Lloyd. 'Like Sam Larner, Jack Elliott was exactly the type of figure MacColl might have invented had he not existed in the flesh', wrote Ben Harker.

'Broad-shouldered, handsome, irrefutably working class, politically militant, Jack Elliott was a singing collier … Song and storytelling remained part of everyday life for Jack Elliott, his wife Emily and their extended family. … The family were embraced by the folk revival, and embraced it in turn'.[38]

From nine hours of recordings made in the Elliotts' kitchen, MacColl and Seeger selected songs, stories and reminiscences from Jack Elliott, his wife, Em, and his brother, Reece, together with various other family members, for a pioneering LP record, *The Elliots* [sic] *of Birtley. A Musical Portrait of a Durham Mining Family*, issued by Folkways of New York in 1962, and again seven years later by Transatlantic in London. Alongside mainstream material from the oral tradition such as versions of 'Seven Nights Drunk' and 'Henry, My Son' there were seven songs connected with mining which ranged from the venerable 'Collier's Rant' and 'Bonnie Pit Laddie' to the exuberant 'Celebrated Working Man', deriving from a Pennsylvania original of 1892, and 'Little Chance', unique to the Durham coalfield:

Ye're gan ower the Busty Fields te gan doon the pit,
Ye get your lamp oot, ye gan inbye, an there ye sit at the kist.
The deputy says, 'Thi place is holed, thoo'll ha' te gan straight on'.
I says to him, 'What's the matter wi mi aan?' He says, 'she canna gan on'.

Aa filled fifteen oot of a jud, titty fa la titty fa lay,
Eh by hell she was good, titty fal la titty fa lay.
Aa came oot te get a shaft, when the timmer it gie a crack,
When a stone fell on mi back, titti fa la titty fa lay,
Tra tra la la la la, ower the wall's oot.[39]

The Elliotts, as Pete Wood has pointed out, were far from being a typical family. Yet there is further strong evidence of a singing tradition among miners in A.L. Lloyd's anthology, *Come All Ye Bold Miners*,[40] with some 170 songs and versions of which 45 are from oral sources (see below). On the other hand, slightly more came from printed street ballads, though it is worth repeating that print and orality could and did readily undergo mutual osmosis.

Lloyd and Ewan MacColl, who were at the forefront after the Second World War of the traditional song revival in Britain, pioneered a new interest in industrial balladry. Indeed, Lloyd (1908-1982), expressed the view in the 1950s that folk creativity had 'passed almost entirely into the scope of the industrial working class'.[41]

'The Singing Englishman'
Author's own collection

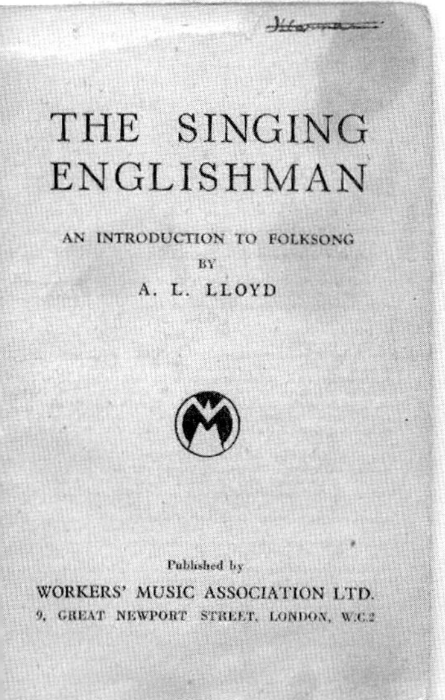

THE SINGING ENGLISHMAN

AN INTRODUCTION TO FOLKSONG
BY
A. L. LLOYD

Published by
WORKERS' MUSIC ASSOCIATION LTD.
9, GREAT NEWPORT STREET, LONDON, W.C.2

Having been sent to Australia at the age of sixteen as an assisted migrant, he became intrigued by the wry and gritty songs of 'the sheep- and cattle-hands, shearers, and itinerant swagmen'[42] with whom he worked. Returning to unemployment in the England of the 1930s, he made two voyages aboard whaling ships where traditional song was less prolific, but still yielded versions of 'Greenland Bound', 'The Bonny Ship the Diamond', 'The Baleana' and 'Off to Sea Once More'[43] Towards the end of the Second World War, during which he served in the army, Lloyd published the 69-page, green-covered booklet, *'The Singing Englishman. An Introduction to Folksong'* (1944), in which industrial song is poorly represented.

However, less then half a dozen years later he conceived the idea of making a collection of mining songs. On the occasion of the Festival of Britain in 1951 he persuaded *Coal* magazine and the filmed *Mining Review* to fund a competition for 'any songs of miners' life, pastimes, disasters or union struggles in the coalfields'. Lloyd primed the pump with an article in *Coal* quoting or

'A. L. 'Bert' Lloyd'. Photo courtesy of Rod Stradling

mentioning such songs as 'The Bonny Pit Laddie', 'The Collier's Rant' and 'The Lure of the Mines' (better known as 'Dark as a Dungeon'). The response was good, and the resulting anthology, which Lloyd edited, *Come All Ye Bold Miners. Ballads and Songs of the Coalfields* (1952), was enthusiastically received. (I still treasure the copy, bought at the time, for which I paid 7s. 6d.). Of the 66 items, 16 with tunes, three were contributed by Ewan MacColl: 'Fourpence a Day' (see page 58), 'The Gresford Disaster' (see page 108) and his own song, 'The Plodder Seam'.[44]

Like Lloyd, MacColl (1915-1989) was an autodidact who took advantage of the leisure afforded by unemployment to improve his knowledge. In both cases their experiences led to their becoming Communists. They did not meet until the beginning of the 1950s, when they became for a time 'a singing Marxist double act'[45] with a repertoire of sea shanties and industrial songs. They were very different in approach: Lloyd was very much the quiet scholar-singer, while MacColl, with a background in experimental and alternative theatre, combined consummate performing skills with prolific and inventive song writing.

They collaborated on occasion, while each pursued his own projects. In 1956 Lloyd assembled a group of singers and instrumentalists for a pioneering LP, *The Iron Muse. A Panorama of Industrial Folk Song,* on which he commented: '"Classical" folk song, music hall song, pop song, art song have all contributed to the home-made lyrical creations of industrial workers, but at heart the matter has remained astonishingly true to the tradition that, for want of a better name, we call "folk song"'[46] For his part, with the formidable contribution of his wife, the virtuoso instrumentalist and singer, Peggy Seeger, MacColl issued, with the same company, Topic Records, *Steam Whistle Ballads* (1958), which included mining and railway songs.

The pioneering 'Iron Muse' © Courtesy of Topic Records

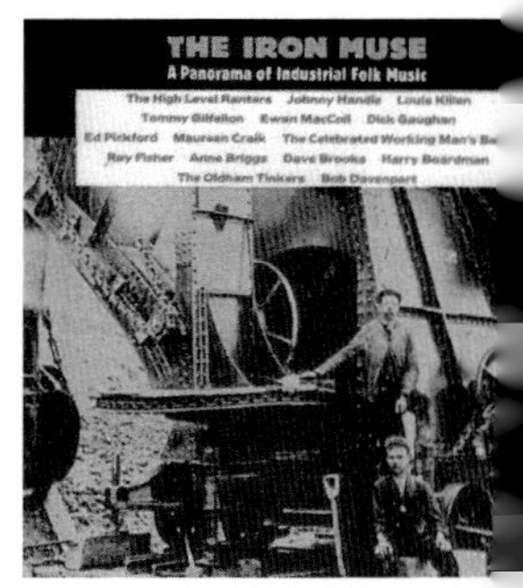

The Wide Midlands. Author's own collection

The Seeger-MacColl partnership also produced, not to speak of a very large number of live performances, radio and television broadcasts and also LP records, what was probably the most creative and significant achievement on the British folk scene of the second half of the twentieth century, the radio-ballads. These were hour-long programmes on railwaymen, fishermen, miners and others. Their essential features were the recorded speech (and sometimes singing) of working people, songs specially written by Ewan MacColl, inspired musicianship and direction by Peggy Seeger, strategic planning by MacColl and Seeger, and meticulous production by Charles Parker. (There were other singers and instrumentalists involved, including in some cases A.L. Lloyd).

The result was eight enthralling kaleidoscopes of speech, sound and song broadcast by the BBC between 1958 and 1964. They were later issued as LPs by Decca, and in 1999 as CDs by Topic Records, and then re-released in 2008, a testimony to their lasting appeal.[47] The form was revived in 2006 by John Tams and others to cover six themes: AIDS and HIV, hunting with hounds, internecine strife in Northern Ireland and the decline of the steel and shipbuilding industries. A further programme followed in 2009 to mark the twenty-fifth anniversary of the miners' strike of 1984-85.[48]

It was my great good fortune during the 1960s, as well as attending a considerable number of performances by Lloyd and MacColl, to have participated in many hours of seminars and workshops by them, run by an organisation as yet unchronicled, the Birmingham and Midland Folk Centre, of which I was for a time the chairman. I have remained deeply indebted to Lloyd and MacColl, and also the Folk Centre, ever since. One of Lloyd's talks in Birmingham was later the basis for a article, in which he observed:

> It is well known that the coming of industrialisation broke up many of the old rural communities; it is not always realised that the growth of industry brought about new group awareness. The solidarity of mining communities is proverbial; also, quite clearly in the Industrial Revolution the establishment of large factories employing hundreds of spinners or weavers under one roof meant an enlargement of communal feeling among textile workers. ... For the makers and bearers of industrial folklore, the great virtues are a combination of solidarity and independence, at once a sense of class pride and personal pride, a strong feeling for the homely kin but also for the working community. The workers' folk songs – those created from within the industries on behalf of the community of 'insiders' – reflect this synthesis.[49]

The workforce outside Bell Mill in Stanley near Perth. Courtesy of Perth Museum & Art Gallery

1 Stop that clock

Time for work

Did William Blake *sing* 'Jerusalem'? Late in life, according to his first biographer, he did sing, 'in a voice tremulous with age, sometimes old ballads, sometimes his own songs, to melodies of his own'.[1] Even if the poem, written between 1804 and 1808, had to wait to be sung for Parry's setting of 1916, the words made their impact long before, with one powerful phrase, 'dark satanic mills', coming to epitomise (though it was probably not meant literally) the working environment created by the Industrial Revolution. Grim though they might be, the new factories drew people in by the thrill of novelty and the spur of necessity. The owners imposed a rigorous, not to say oppressive, code of discipline which, as E.P. Thompson demonstrated in an influential essay, 'Time, Work-discipline and Industrial Capitalism'[2], was an essential requisite for the establishment of the system. New attitudes to work were imposed, as Thompson explains, by 'the division of labour; the supervision of labour; fines; bells and clocks; money incentives; preachings and schoolings; the suppression of fairs and sports'[3].

The new style of employer is exemplified by Ambrose Crowley, whose iron-manufacturing firm, the biggest of its kind in Europe, was worth £100,000 and employed 1,000 men. By 1707–09 Crowley owned two slitting mills, two forges, four steel furnaces, many warehouses, and a large number of smithies in County Durham alone. The Stourbridge-born industrialist was gently satirised by Richard Steele in *The Tatler* as Sir Arthur de Bradly and by Joseph Addison as Jack Anvil, alias Sir John Enville, in *The Spectator*. Although he made some welfare provision for his employees he insisted on rigorously regulating them at work. His 'Law Book', a 100,000 word document now in the British Library, instituted a working day from 5 am till 8 pm, with half an hour from 8 am for breakfast and an hour from noon for dinner: 'There will then be thirteen hours and a half neat service'. A sheet for each worker, accurate to the minute, recorded times of 'Come' and 'Run'. Deductions from wages were made for 'playing, sleeping, smoaking, singing, reading of news history, quarelling, contention, disputes or anything foreign to my business', together with 'any way loytering' (slacking). The sole arbiter of time was the official watch, kept under lock and key, 'that it may not be in the power of any person to alter the same', by the warden, who also rang the bell to mark when work began and ended. Crowley died in 1713, laden with honours, including a knighthood. His firm 'lasted well into the reign of Queen Victoria, prospering from all the wars in the century following his death'.[4]

Crowley's departure from the old patterns and rhythms of work, and his removal of scope for individual variation, set a pattern which became widespread. The success of Josiah Wedgwood (1730–1795) at his famous Burslem and Etruria works depended on the rigorous regime laid down in his 'Potters' Instructions' of 1780, which required workers' specialisation (a forerunner of the subsequent production line), a clocking-in system and a range of fines. Replacing the earlier horn, a factory bell governed the day.[5] This style of factory system continued through Victorian times and indeed, well beyond.

NOTICE!

On the 1st of January, 1872, the following alterations in hours of WORK and MEAL TIMES will take place :--

45 minutes will be allowed for Breakfast.

The Works will Open at 6 a.m. and Close at 6 p.m. on every working day except Saturday, when the Works will close at Half-past 12 as usual. To state in full detail:--

The Bell will ring on Monday, Tuesday, Wednesday, Thursday and Friday, as follows :--

In at 6-0 a.m.
Out at 8-0 " for Breakfast.
In at 8-45 "
Out at 12-30 p.m. for Dinner.
In at 1-30 "
Out at 6-0 "

The Bell will ring on Saturday :--

In at 6-0 a.m.
Out at 8-0 " for Breakfast.
In at 8-45 "
Out at 12-30."

57 hours will constitute 6 days.
9½ " " " 1 day.

The Gates will be closed immediately the Bell stops ringing, and all late-time will be strictly deducted.

No preparations for Meals will be allowed in working hours. Every person must be ready for work when the Bell stops ringing IN, and must not prepare to leave before the Bell commences ringing OUT.

BROAD OAK PRINT WORKS. **F. W. Grafton & Co.**

J. EDWARDS, MACHINE PRINTER, 11, ABBEY-ST., ACCRINGTON.

At Waterfoot Mill near Haslingden in Lancashire the twenty-one rules which governed the workforce in 1851 included this: 'Anyone found away from their usual place of work, except for necessary purposes . . . will be fined 2d. for each offence.' I wondered what exactly these necessary purposes were until I saw another rule: 'If two persons are known to be in one Necessary together they shall be fined 3d. each; and if any Man or Boy go into the Women's Necessary he shall be dismissed instantly.'[6]

At much the same time, Samuel Bastow's employees in the Cliff House Iron Works at Hartlepool may have been working a mere ten hours 'neat' (to use Crowley's term) per day, but the list of twenty-four 'Rules and Regulations' they were required to observe would have been entirely familiar to their predecessors. They include:

- Work to commence at 6 o'clock in the Morning, and to end at 6 o'clock at Night, except on Saturdays, when the Days of Work shall end at 4 o'clock, and on the Pay Saturday [alternate weeks] at 2 o'clock, no Dinner hour being allowed (IV).
- Meal Hours to be from 8 to ½ past 8 o'clock, for Breakfast; and 12 to 1 o'clock, for Dinner. No Dinner Hour being allowed on Pay Saturdays (V).
- Time to be kept by the *Hour*. 10 Working Hours to be a day's work (VI).
- The Door shall be closed every Morning when the Bell Rings, at 6 o'clock; but, should any Workman over-sleep himself, he may be admitted at 10 minutes past 6 o'clock, forfeiting ½ an hour . . . (VII).
- Any Workman making preparations to leave his Work, before the Bell Rings, to pay a Fine of 2s. 6d. men, - and 1s. boys (XV).[7]

Although many forsook farming for factory work because of the better pay, some cast regretful glances over their shoulders to the relative freedom they had left behind. Like churches and schools, factories summoned people by a bell:

The Factory Bell[8]

Oh happy man, O happy thou
While toiling at thy spade and plough,
While thou amidst thy pleasures roll,
All at thy labour uncontroll'd

While at the mills in pressing crowds
Where high built chimneys puff black clouds
And all around the slaves do dwell,
Who are called to labour by a Bell.

You have just got time to eat & sleep
A man is set your time to keep;
And if you chance to come too late,
You'r mark'd on paper or on slate
No matter e'er what be the cause,
You must abide by their own laws.
And at the time you draw your wage
For coming late there's so much charged.

And if a word chance to be spoke,
Some catches it that wears a cloak
Be it right or wrong be it truth or lies,
It quickly to the master flies.
But Masters, they are not to blame,
The men are worst, you know the same,
For man to make himself a king,
Cares not who sink if he but swim

Some wheedling foreman every hour
Makes big himself with stolen power;
He hectering [sic] goes in every place,
Few know his heart who see his face
But a time will come that will forsooth,
And show that man that wears a cloak;
Altho' well clothed long time ere past
He must be naked stript at last.

This printed ballad, 'The Factory Bell', probably dates from December 1840 or soon afterwards. The anonymous writer concludes with the pious hope that 'We all in golden days shall live, ... And die in peace when life is o'er'.

Another ballad on the same theme, 'Factory Bells of England', parodies a music hall song, 'The Merry Bells of England', issued at the time of the Crimean War. It comments rather more flippantly:

Oh, the bell of that 'ere factory,
I wish it was not hung!
It wakes me from my slumbers,
When the morning is but young!
It startles all the sleepers
For half a mile around!
Oh, the bell of that 'ere factory,
I wish it would not sound!

Oh, the bell of that 'ere factory,
I hate to hear it clink,
When seated arter dinner,
Just trying to get a wink!
My dreams of joy and happiness,
Are scattered in the air:
Oh, the bell of that 'ere factory,
I wish it was not there![9]

In 'The Factory Bell', a poem by the Lancashire writer Edwin Waugh (1817–90), or 'Ned Woff', as he was affectionately known, a father tenderly advises his young son:

The Factory Bell[10]

Come, Billy, come; dost yer [hear] yon bell?
Thou'll ha' yon mill agate [started]
Afore thou'rt up! Do stir thisel',
Or else thou'll be too late:
I know thou'rt tire't, my lad – I know;
What can a body do?
It's very cowd; but, frost or snow,
Thou knows thou'll ha' to goo!

Billy obediently gets up and runs off through the snow, carrying 'his dinner in a can' and eating 'a bit o' oon-cake [ovencake]' as he goes. The mood sharply changes in the final verse:

Some folk can lie till th' clock strikes eight;
Some folk may sleep till ten,
Then rub their e'en an' yawn a bit,
An' turn 'em o'er again;
Some folk can ring a bell i' bed,
Till th' sarvant brings some tay;

But weet or dry, a factory lad
Mun jump at break o' day!

A further protest comes in a sheet headed 'A Dialouge [sic] between Owd Carder Joan o' th' Mumps, an' Tom o' lung Harrys i' Owdham'. (The Mumps is a district in Oldham, which once had its own railway station.) After the dialogue, a discussion of Sadler and the Ten Hours movement (see also next chapter), these verses follow:

A Dialouge [sic] between Owd Carder Joan o' th' Mumps, an' Tum o' lung Harrys i' Owdham.[11]

Hark! The Factory Bell is ringing;
Yes I hear the dismal sound:
Thousands at its call its bringing,
Long before daylight comes round.

Listen to the Victims Wailing,
As they pass your Dwellings by,
When 'tis freezing snowing raining,
Or Thunder rolling through the sky.

No excuse for non-attendance,
At The Lordly Tyrants call,
Though they do live at a distance,
Nay should the very Heavens fall.

Come they must, or pay the forfeit,
Feel the Strap or turned away;
If by it they should get a surfeit,
That attends them to their dying day.

Then for thirteen hours together,
At their frames they're forced to stay,
With not a moment time of Leisure,
But just to eat and then away.

Call ye this a Land of Freedom,
Where such Slavery does abound;
No! cursed be the very Kingdom,
Where such things are to be found.

Tell me not of Negro Slavery,
Where Afric's sons are bought and sold;
Nor ever boast of British bravery,
Whilst Childrens BLOOD is spilt for GOLD1

Where Factory Lords do strut in splendour,
Wrung from the labours of the Poor,
Protected in the unholy plunder,
By the Tyrants now in Power.

The bell installed in 1803 at the Royal Worcester porcelain factory, and used until the 1930s, is now preserved in the works museum, where it has outlasted any production on the adjacent site. At Stanley, near Perth, the towering Bell Mill of 1786–87, so called because of its crowning belfry, still stands. By 1795, 350 people, of whom 300 were either women or children under sixteen, worked in the mill complex at Stanley, which is now in the care of Historic Scotland.[12] Richard Arkwright's design for the Bell Mill included indoor lavatories on each floor. How enlightened, one thinks, but then one discovers that the intention was to minimise the time workers spent on 'necessary' absences, and to maximise supervision.

The Bell Mill at Stanley as it stands today.
Photo: Pat Palmer

Resentment at the imperious summons of the factory bell, or the whistle or hooter which succeeded it, was expressed in epigrammatic songs such as:

The morn is black as a raven, the streets are wet and cold;
The mill is mournfully telling it's time that I should go.
Another day at the loom, my lass, where shuttles they do fly;
The noise is like to screaming when some they come to die.

And:

Oh the whistle is a-blowing, sleep my bonny bairn;
Oh the whistle is a-blowing, it's time for me to go.
Oh the wheels they are turning and the noise it makes thee scream;
There's a racing and a going and the hissing of the steam.[13]

Faced with the threat of losing wages or being sacked for lateness, working people had to organise time-keeping for themselves. Until well into the twentieth century, those without clocks or watches were 'knocked up' (awakened) at the right time for work, either by a friend, perhaps returning from the night shift, or by a professional 'knocker-up', who for a small fee went round and tapped with a pole on bedroom windows. One early film captured precisely this activity. A Belfast man, born in 1900, who started work in the mills at the age of 14, said that few homes had an alarm clock (which at the time cost 3s. 6d.): 'So the horn screeched out at half-past five in the morning ... And if you didn't get in for six o'clock, you were shut out, and you were fined three pence.' For some, the horn had to be supplemented by the summons of the 'knocker-up' or 'rapper-up' in the person, so far as one neighbourhood of Belfast was concerned, of a sailor with one arm who tapped on doors with his stick until he heard the

'Come, Get up wi' thi'!' Knocker Up. Courtesy of Burnley Community History Library

response of 'Right'. In another area of the city an old woman called Sally used a long cane to tap on windows, and was paid sixpence a week by each of her customers for doing so.[14]

William Woodruff (1916–2008), in the classic account of his childhood, *The Road to Nab End*, makes the astonishing remark, reflecting the total dominance over people's lives of the mills where they worked, that 'To escape time in Blackburn you had to go into the country'. He recalled that 'Mr Smalley, whom we called t' knocker-up man, came with his wire-tipped pole in the dark six mornings a week to shake our window until our father stirred and shouted loud enough to be heard in the street below, "We're up!".' [15] In Salford at the same time, Betsy Miller, mother of the future Ewan MacColl, disliked the practice: 'She prided herself that *her* family didn't need the services of the local knocker-up who rattled on the terrace windows to wake slumbering neighbours for work.'[16]

The word knocker-up was first recorded by the *OED* only in 1861. Twenty years before that, William Dodd, lodging in Manchester during his investigative tour of the mill towns, was warned not to be alarmed by a knocking at the window in the morning, and to acknowledge it:

> At about *half past four o'clock* (mark the time), a rattling noise was heard at the window, which was answered, as agreed upon, from within. The watchman, or person who performs this duty (for which he gets *3d.* per head, per week, from all he calls up in the mornings), then went to the next house, and so on through the streets, disturbing the whole neighbourhood, till the noise of his 'infernal machine' died away in the distance. This machine was made for the purpose of making a great noise on the glass windows without breaking them, and is somewhat similar to a shepherd's crook, only longer in the handle, to enable the person using it to reach the upper windows.[17]

In the coalfields of the north-east of England, the 'caller' went round twice, first to wake the early shift men and later to wake the boys and day shift men. At one time, after knocking he gave the ritual summons: 'Wake up and go to work, in the name of God.'[18] Until the mid-nineteenth century at least, policemen in London – and perhaps elsewhere – supplemented their wages by charging a few pence to wake early workers. Timothy Cavanagh, who joined the Metropolitan Police in 1855, was lucky enough to find himself on a beat with forty such calls, on which he commented:

> A 'call' meant that a man (and here they mostly belonged to the Borough Market) wanted calling at four or five, or even earlier, in the morning, for which service he paid on Saturday night with great regularity the sum of sixpence. Should he, however, fail to pay up, matters were soon put right by failing to call him on Monday morning, when, in consequence of losing half a day's work, he was certain to be in the way with the stipulated 'tanner' the next night.[19]

Songs from Yorkshire singers which reflect the practice of rousing workers include:

The Knocking Up Song[20]

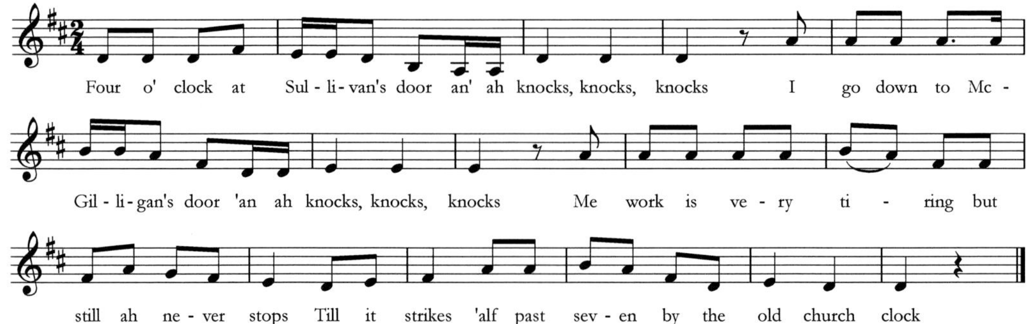

Four o'clock at Sullivan's doors, an' ah knocks, knocks, knocks.
I go down to McGilligan's door an' ah knocks, knocks, knocks.
Me work is very tiring but still ah never stops
Till it strikes 'alf-past seven by the old church clock.

And:

A pal of mine once said to me,
'Will you knock me up at half-past three?'
And so promptly at half-past one
I knocked him up and said, 'Oh, John,
I've just come round to tell you,
I've just come round to tell you,
I've just come round to tell you,
You've got two more hours to sleep.'[21]

The playful treatment recurs in an item from the north-east of England:

'Wake up, wake up, my love, we've slept the clock through;
The bus has flown, the men are gone.'
Well, didn't he glower as he turned ower:
'You bloody fool,' he said, 'it's Sunday morn.'[22]

Building workers from the Midlands joked about arresting the passage of time. I recorded this slightly surrealistic song in 1966 from Mrs E.M. Turner of Wednesbury in Staffordshire, hence the Black Country flavour. She was born in a pub in the town, seventy-seven years earlier, and as a child picked up the song from the customers.

Stop That Clock[23]

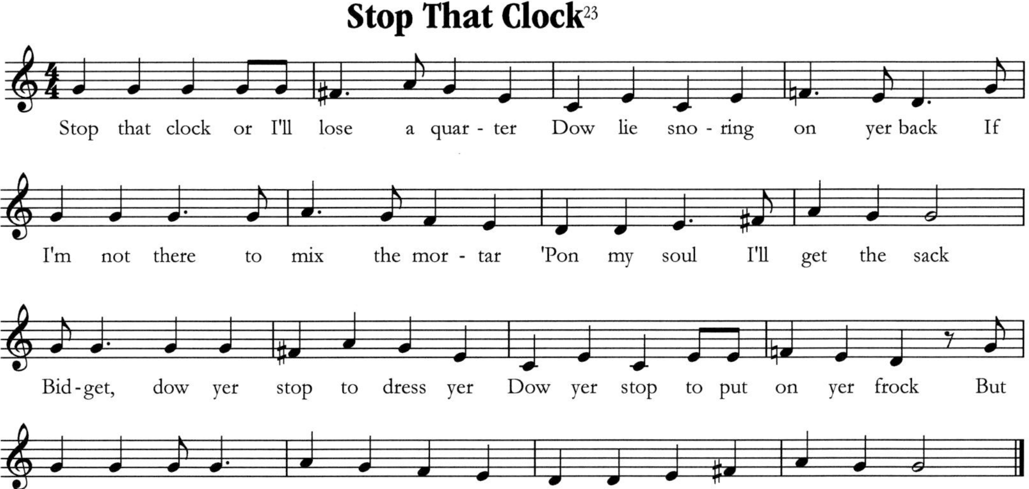

Stop that clock or I'll lose a quarter,
Dow [don't] lie snoring on yer back;
If I'm not there to mix the mortar,
'Pon my soul I'll get the sack.
Bridget, dow yer stop to dress yer,
Dow yer stop to put on yer frock,
But while I'm pullin' up me trousers,
Yo go down and stop that clock.

The inexorable pressure of time inspired Cyril Tawney (1930–2005), better known perhaps for songs reflecting his time in the Royal Navy as a submariner, to write:

On a Monday Morning[24]

Too soon to be out of me bed,
Too soon to be back at this 'bus queue caper,
Or fumbling for change for me picture paper
On a Monday morning.

Wrong end of the week for a smile,
Wrong end of the day for being civil;
There's many a saint would be a devil
On a Monday morning.

Where is the weekend now?
Where is the whisky and beer I tasted?
Gone the same way as the pay I've wasted
On a Monday morning.

If only the birds would booze,
If only the sun was a party-giver;
If I could just lend someone else me liver
On a Monday morning.

My lover she lies asleep,
My lover is warm and her heart is mellow;
I'd trade you the world just to share her pillow
On a Monday morning.

It was the lack of absolute compulsion to be out of the house at a specific time on Monday or any other morning which appealed to the handloom weavers of the Calder Valley in Yorkshire, where until the 1830s (even later for some) 'There was no bell to ring them up at four or five o'clock in the morning nor again at noon, nor were they bound to stay late at night; there was freedom to start and stay away as they craved. Some weavers had smallholdings, and many, gardens. They could choose to spend an hour or two in their gardens at the appropriate time of the year, or they could take a day off to go to a wedding or a wake.'[25]

Thomas Beggs (1789–1847) was a bleacher in the Belfast area, where by 1833 there were already ten steam-powered flax mills. He contrasted, perhaps in too idyllic a fashion, the spinner at home with her sisters in the factory:

The mountain lass, at her wee bit wheel,
How blithe was her e'e, an' how rosy her cheek!
Her bosom was white, an' her heart was leal,
Her mien it was modest, her manner was meek;
But now the pert maidens, wha ply in the mill,
How wan is their visage, how dim is their e'e,
For the ban they maun bide is enough to chill
The spring o' the heart au' to deaden their glee:
To toil for men that are hard to please,

In a hot-bed rank wi' vice an' disease.
An' when they speak, it maun be wi a squeal;
They maun rise an' rin' at the toll o' the bell,
An' brook the insult o' a tyrant an' de'il,
An' the jargon they hear is the language o' hell.
To breed a bit lassie in sic a vile place,
Instead o' her ain father's cot on the green,
It puts the puir thing in a pitifu' case –
Ah! black was the day when they made the machine,
It has added mair pelf to the hoards o' the great
And left those that were low in a far lower state.[26]

Young women with their nimble fingers and perceived adaptability were welcomed in factories; older men, set in their ways and considered intractable, were not. Handloom weavers, renowned for their independence, suffered from a lack of female company. 'Where are the girls?' one of them asked in a song:

Where are the girls? I'll tell you plain.
The girls have gone to weave by steam,
And if you'd find 'em you must rise at dawn
And trudge to the mill in the early morn.

This is from 'The Weaver and the Factory Maid', in which the narrator even offers to relinquish his independence and go into a factory:

The Weaver and the Factory Maid[27]

I am a hand weaver to my trade,
I fell in love with a factory maid;
And if I could but her favour win
I'd stand beside her and weave by steam.

My father to me scornful said,
'How could you fancy a factory maid,

When you could have girls fine and gay,
And dressed like to the Queen of May?

'As for your fine girls, I do not care;
And could I but enjoy my dear,
I'd stand in the factory all the day,
And she and I'd keep our shuttles in play'.

I went to my love's bedroom door,
Where oftentimes I had been before;
But I could not speak nor yet get in
To the pleasant bed my love laid in.

'How can you say it's a pleasant bed,
When nowt lies there but a factory maid?,
'A factory lass although she be,
Blest is the man that enjoys she'.

Oh, pleasant thoughts come to my mind
As I turned down the sheets so fine,
And I seen her two breasts standing so,
Like two white hills all covered with snow.

Where are the girls? I'll tell you plain,
The girls have gone to weave by steam;
And if you'd find 'em you must rise at dawn
And trudge to the mill in the early morn.

The song, which had pre-industrial origins, was noted as late as 1951 by A.L. Lloyd from oral tradition, through the person of William Oliver of Widnes.

Apart from losing the girls, weavers who stayed out of the factories suffered progressive reductions in earnings, thanks to the superior productivity of power-looms. On the other hand, those who went in would have to leave the flexibility of home or the small workplace ('loom-shop') and accept subjection not only to fixed hours of employment but to rhythms of activity determined by machines:

If you go into a loom-shop, where there's three or four pair of looms,
They are all standing empty, incumbrances of the rooms;
And if you ask the reason why, the old mother will tell you plain,

My daughters have forsaken them, and gone to weave by steam.
So, come all you cotton-weavers, you must rise up very soon,
For you must work in factories from morning until noon:
You mustn't walk in your garden for two or three hours a-day,
For you must stand at their command, and keep your shuttles in play.

These are the last two verses of 'Hand-loom *v.* Power-loom', from John Harland's *Ballads and Songs of Lancashire*.[28] The expression 'pair of looms' indicates, paradoxically, a single loom. Harland (1806–1868), antiquarian, historian and *Manchester Guardian* journalist, wrote in 1839 that the steam engine, which then powered the factories, was known as 'Owd Ned'. He quotes a song ('a tolerably good specimen of the Lancashire dialect') in which a wide-eyed visitor from the country tours the town and marvels at what he sees:

To a factory next I went, and ne'er had been t' one afore,
There twisting thrums and reels and straps, I'm sure were mony a score;
They said owd Ned turn'd every wheel, and every wheel a strap,
By gum, thowt I t' myself, owd Ned's a rare strong chap.[29]

The song, 'Owd Ned's a Rare Strong Chap', must date from after 1825, when the gas-lit clock mentioned in another verse was installed at the hospital in Manchester's Piccadilly. By the same year, according to Harland, 30,000 power-looms were working in the town. Oddly enough, the earliest extant broadside version seems to be that by W. Wright of Birmingham. Manchester printings followed. Later, with suitable changes of terminology, Yorkshire variants circulated, under the title of 'The Wensleydale Lad', with Leeds being the town visited. Indeed they continued to do so until towards the end of the twentieth century.[30]

As late as the 1850s the novelty of steam power still excited the admiration shown in 'Oldham Workshops'[31] by a visitor to the town's factories. He found some of them idle, thanks to a 'turnout' (strike) in one case and a drinking bout in another, but one was very much at work:

Some chaps ot they cawd smiths, great bellows they had got,
Like foos they blowed cowd wind to make the iron hot;
But then owd Neddy engine I think he beats the whole,
He's fond o summut warm sure, for they feed him up o' coal.

Familiarity with steam power here leads, not to contempt, but to affection and a humanising nickname. A plethora of ballads toyed with the comic possibilities of steam arms, boots, carriage, cigar, coach, (tailor's) goose, jaw, pills, tongue and washing. The opportunity for sexual metaphor was eagerly exploited in:

Steam-Loom Weaver[32]

One morn for pleasure I did ramble,
In the pleasant month of June.
The birds did sing the lambkins play,
Two lovers walking in their bloom.
The lassie was a steam-loom weaver,
The lad an engine driver keen,
And all their discourse was about weaving,
And the getting up of steam.

She said my loom is out of fettle,
Can you right it – yes or no. –
You say you are an engine driver,
Which makes the steam so rapid flow,
My lambs and jacks are out of order,
My laith in motion has not been,
So work away without delay,
And quickly muster up the steam.

I said fair maid you are determined,
No longer for to idle be,
Your healds and laith I'll put in motion,
Then work you can without delay,
She said young man a pair of pickers,
A shuttle too I want you ween,
Without these three I cannot weave,
So useless then would be the steam.

Dear lass these things I will provide,
But when to labour you will begin,
As soon my lad as things are ready,
My loom shop you can enter in,
A shuttle too and pickers too,
This young man did provide amain,
And soon her loom was put in tune,
So well it was supplied with steam.

Her loom work'd well, the shuttle flew,
Her pickers played, the tune nick-nack,
Her laith did move with rapid motion,
Her temples, healds, long-lambs and jacks,
Her cloth beam roll'd the cloth up tight,
The yarn beam emptied soon it seems,
The young man cry'd your loom works well,
And quickly then shot off the steam.

She said young man another web,
Upon the beam let's get, don't strike,
But work away while yet it's day,
This steam-loom weaving well I like.
He said, good lass, I cannot stay,
But if a fresh warp you will beam,
If ready when I come this way,
I'd strive for to get up the steam.

The exuberant use of technical terms implies that writer, singer and listener were not merely familiar with the factory environment but completely at home in it.

Enthusiasm for the literal powers of the steam engine remained strong, as indeed it still does among the ranks of railway enthusiasts. A song of the early 1870s, variously known as 'A Country Life', 'Eggs for Breakfast' and 'When the old cock crows', has these lines:

> I like to hear the old cock crow early in the morning,
> I like to stroll through the bright green fields just as the day is dawning;
> I like to hear the little birds sing their merry lay:
> Hurrah for the life in the country,
> And a ramble in the new-mown hay.[33]

In the hands of an ingenious parodist they became:

> I like to be there when the engine starts early in the morning;
> I like to sit me down at breakfast time, just when the engine's roaring;
> And I like to see the piecers as on the floor they lay
> Then hurrah for the life in the factory,
> While we're waiting for the judgment day.

This was obtained in the 1930s by Joan Littlewood, of Theatre Workshop fame, from an Oldham weaver, Eliza Bolton.[34] A piecer, first recorded by the *OED* in 1835 as 'piecener', was 'a child or young person employed in a spinning-mill to keep the frames filled with rovings, and to join together the ends of threads which break while being spun or wound'. The latter task was often accomplished by crawling on the floor beneath the moving frames.

One has the suspicion that the parody's expression of pleasure may have been tongue-in-cheek. William Dodd (quoted earlier) describes the working day of a Manchester factory girl who rises at five:

> Then, for the first time, the girl becomes conscious of the necessity for haste; and having slipped on her clothes, and (if she thinks there is time) washed herself, she takes a drink of cold coffee, which has been left standing in the fireplace, a mouthful of bread (if she can eat it), and having packed up her breakfast in her handkerchief, hastens to the factory. The bell rings as she leaves the threshold of her home. Five minutes more, and she is in the factory, *stripped and ready for work.* The clock strikes half-past five; the engine starts, and her day's work commences.
>
> At half-past seven, and in some factories at eight, the engine slacks its pace (seldom stopping) for a short time, *till the hands have cleaned the machinery,* and swallowed a little food. It then goes on again, and continues at full speed till twelve o' clock, when it stops for dinner. Previously to leaving the factory, and in her dinner-hour, she has her machines to clean. The distance of the factory is about

> five minutes' walk from her home. I noticed every day that she came in at half-past twelve, or within a minute or two, and once she was over the half-hour; the first thing she did, was to wash herself, then get her dinner (which she was seldom able to eat), and pack up her drinking for the afternoon. This done, it was time for her to be on her way to work again, where she remains, without one minute's relaxation, till seven o' clock; she then comes home, and throws herself into a chair exhausted. This repeated *six* days in the week (save that on Saturdays, she may get back a little earlier, say an hour or two), can there be any wonder at their preferring to lie in bed till dinner-time, instead of going to church on the *seventh*?[35]

By contrast, high spirits are to the fore in a ballad of the 1880s, written by one Sextus Adams of Garibaldi Street, Everton, 'Author of some of the most popular Comic Songs, and Duets, sung by the Principal Artistes in the Profession'. As with 'I like to be there', 'The Factory Lad' is based on an urban song of country life, in this case 'Jim the Carter Lad', of which the tune is given below. Nevertheless, the text makes an important reference to a strike for better pay and conditions, which reveals a glimpse of the reality of working life.

The Factory Lad[36]

Behold in me a factory lad, a factory lad am I,
I'm always happy, never sad, and never will say die,
I rise with the lark, then to work I go, so jolly, blythe and gay,
But how I toil you little know, with the lads in the Factory.

Chorus
For they call me Joe, in the factory,
There's none so blythe as me you see,
Working away all the day,
With the lads in the Factory.

I was born in Manchester, in Ancoats Lane was reared,
And brought up as a factory lad, I was upon my word;
I never fret for what I can't get, you will never find me sad,
I know there's many a one worse off than me, the honest Factory lad.

We factory lads have been on strike, to get nine hours a day,
Not only that, but we require – a little extra pay;
And then to work we'll proudly go, each one will feel so glad,
I'm sure none can feel more so – than the little factory lad.

Although I lead a jolly life, I always like to see,
My friends around, good tempered like, and just the same as me;
Then merrily we'd jog along, without a care I know,
No one could lead a happier life, than little Factory Joe.

Tune: 'Jim the Carter Lad'

Many people, even young boys, were attracted to the workplace because they wanted the status which went with working. Some of the children obliged to work before elementary education became compulsory – and this was not definitively the case until 1880 – might well have preferred school. Perversely, their successors could not soon enough exchange the classroom for the workplace:

Down the pit we want to go Away from school with all its woe,
Working hard as collier's butty, make us all so very happy!
Did you ever see, did you ever see,
Did you ever see such a funny thing before?

The song, to the well-known tune of 'Y Mochyn Du' ('The Black Pig', better known as 'Cosher Bailey'), was remembered by Walter Haydn Davies (1903–84), who left school at the age of thirteen to go down the pit at Bedlinog, Glamorgan. He writes:

> To a schoolboy there was a prestige about entering this man's world. Off to the pit on his 'first morning' he felt just as elated as the new pupil proceeding to his Grammar school, for he considered wearing a collier's red muffler more desirable than wearing a school tie, the

wearing of a miner's moleskin trousers as distinctive as wearing the school uniform, carrying the miner's lamp as more significant than that of carrying a school satchel. These were some of the visible attractions of entering a miner's workaday world, extolled by all for these were symbols of the act of stepping out of a boy's world into that of a man.[37]

A diametrically opposed view of pit work for children is expressed by the Scottish miner and poet, David Wingate (1828–1892), in 'The Collier's Ragged Wean':

He's up at early morning, howe'er the win' may blaw,
Lang before the sun comes roun' to chase the stars awa';
And 'mang a thousan' dangers, unkent in sweet daylight,
He'll toil until the stars again keek through the chilly night.

Miners at the end of a long shift. Only the pit boys seem to be smiling!

See the puir wee callan' 'neath the cauld clear moon:
His knees oot through his troosers, an his taes oot through his shoon,
Wading through the freezing snaw, and thinking ower again
How happy every wean maun be that's no' a collier's wean.[38]

Pit boys, because of their small stature, were employed as trappers and pony drivers. Trappers were stationed by doors, which they opened for traffic to pass, and closed to assure the necessary circulatory system for ventilation. In 1841, as many as 5,000 children between five and ten years old were working underground in this capacity.[39] One of them, John Saville, aged seven, from near Sheffield, made this statement in 1842 to the Parliamentary commissioners enquiring into children's employment:

> I've worked in the pit about two weeks. I stand and open and shut the door all day. I'm generally in the dark and sit me down against the door. I like it very well. It doesn't tire me. I never see daylight now except on Sundays. They don't ill use or beat me. I fell asleep one day and a corve ran over my leg and made it smart. When I go home I wash myself and get my drinking and sit me down on the house floor. I've tea and bread and butter to my drinking. I've sometimes dry bread and cheese and sometimes red herring and potatoes to my dinner in the pit. I know my letters. I've never been to school at all. I go to Park Sunday School and they teach me writing. I go to chapel every Sunday. I don't know who made the world. I've never heard of God.[40]

Thomas Burt (1837–1922), the future Liberal MP, started work as a trapper at Haswell Pit, County Durham, immediately after his tenth birthday, sitting in darkness for twelve-hour shifts, the time counting not 'from bank to bank', but at the workings. He was delighted to be transferred after a few weeks to donkey driving: 'This, surely, was swift and real promotion. My pay rose at a bound from tenpence to the full round sum of a shilling a day.'[41] A pitman poet, the shaft sinker Alexander Barrass, writing in the 1890s, described such work in 'The Driver':

The Driver[42]

There was ne sign o' schuel boards when Aa was a lad.
Aa went inte the pit when but nine summers aad,
To keep a trap door on an aad rolley way,
For the wonderful wage of a shillin a day.
But aalways bein wishful te cut an' contrive,
To better me wages Aa started te drive;

An' oh, ye should 'a' heard how Aa whustled an' sang
As Aa rattled the full uns an' chum [empty] uns alang.

[Chorus]
Siss, siss! [Go]. Baa, baa! [Stop].
That's hoo we drive them doon belaa.

Aa remember the very first morning Aa yoked.
Hoo the landin lads laughed an' the putters aal joked.
But a shift or two myed me se used to the wark,
Aa could yoke 'em or lowse 'em or drive in the dark,
For Aa knew ev'ry curve, ev'ry way-end an' switch,
Where te grape [grope] for the dregs when Aa come tiv a hitch
[sudden gradient],
Hoo te splice a good whup, hoo te use a one tee!
Eh, we did not do badly, aad Smiler an' me.

Aa confess that Aa liked a bit fun te create,
An' Aa've jolloped the drivers that's stolen me bait,
Had me hand in at fondies an' all such as that,
But Aa'd never let putters wait-on at the flat.
When sets would get off, or the horses would kick,
An' the drivers would promise the weight of a stick,
Aa could aalways contrive te keep well oot the way,
When the overman ettled [intended] the piper te pay.

When the men had ne coals or there'd been a big fall,
Aa've swapped midgies an' played 'Droppy candle' an' aal,
An' wi' lads like meself when nowt else could be deun,
Aa've tossed up me pit cap an' Aa've fitten [fought] foor fun.
But it's useless for me to reflect on the past –
The bit pluck Aa had then'll be mine till the last,
An' whatever God sends us Aa'm willin' te bear,
But Aa'm certain that Aa'll never drive ony mair.

A version of these words was sung to the tune of 'The Mountains of Mourne' by Reece Elliott of Birtley, County Durham, who retired in 1960 after fifty-two years as a miner.[43]

A briefer and more plaintive reflection on the same theme was recorded in 1966 by the folklorist A.E. Green from William Hill, a miner from Castleford in Yorkshire who had started work as a pony driver at the age of fifteen. It was then that he learned this song, which the drivers would

A pit pony pulling tubs along the 'road'. The first five pony-stalls in the 'standing' were 'invariably as follows: Tom, King, Shot, Dick, Turpin.'

sing to their ponies, sitting on the five- and seven-hundredweight coal-tubs with their feet on the swingletrees. A 'doggy' was an overman who was responsible for maintaining the rails on which the tubs ran; it was not unusual for the tubs to go off the 'road', and it was then that the doggy's job was to get them back on – if he was to be found. The 'pass-by' was a section of double track where tubs could pass, most of the road being single track. The 'standing' in verse 3 is a pony-stall. Mr Hill says that in every pit he ever worked, the stalls were marked with the ponies' names, and the first five were invariably as follows: Tom, King, Shot, Dick, Turpin. The business of going off the road (especially if, as here, the pony was 'rubbing', i.e. catching its back on the roof, causing an unpleasant sore), was clearly very trying to a young lad on his first job.

The Pony Driver[44]

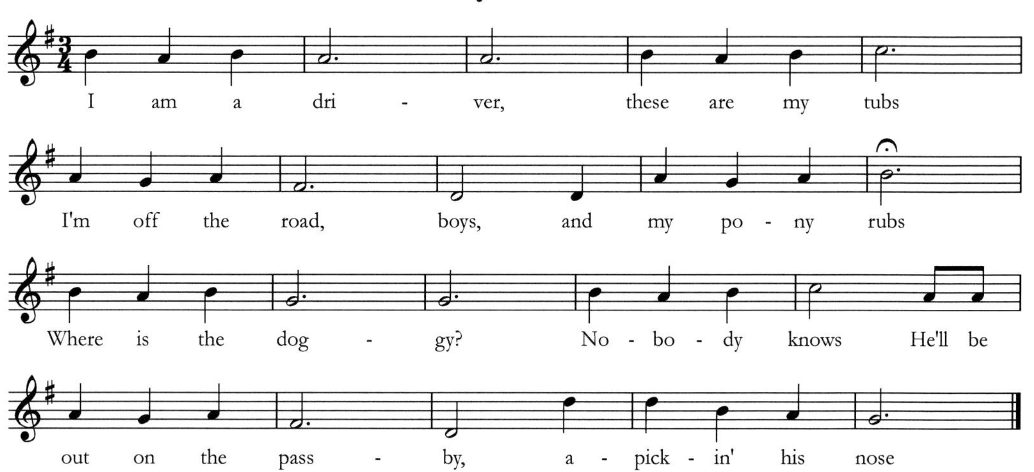

I am a driver, these are my tubs.
I'm off the road, boys, and my pony rubs.
Where is the doggy? Nobody knows;
He'll be out on the pass-by, a-pickin' his nose.

I shall be glad when this shift is done,
Then I'll be up there, out in the sun.
Tha'll be dahn 'ere, boy, in this dark 'oil,
Still gruntin' and groanin', pullin' this coil [coal].

Corn's in the manger, water's in t'trough;
Tha'll shove thi nose out when tha's 'ad enough.
I'll tek thee in t'standin' and drop off thi gear;
When I come back, lad, I know tha'll be 'ere.

A rather more perky attitude emerges in 'The Best Little Doorboy',[45] which Alan Lomax recorded from a Jeff Randall, presumably in Wales, in the 1950s. The tune is the well- known 'Villikins':

The Best Little Doorboy[45]

The workmen in the Rhondda are wonderful boys,
They get to their work without any noise;
They say through the Rhondda you never will see
A merrier lot than in Tipperary.
Tooraloo, tooralay,

The best little doorboy that's under Jim Grey.

Old William, the lampman, and Dan with his horse,
And Daniel, the sawyer, is always so cross.
They say, &c.

Two girls from Treorchy pull out a full tram.
They've holes in their stockings, they don't care a damn!
They say, &c.

Oh talk about hauling – it's nothing but fun,
To do her on the level as well as the run,
To hook her and sprag her and holler 'Gee-way!'
I'm the best little doorboy that's under Jim Grey.

And so the trapper, the piecer, the children of the poor in their thousands embarked – barring accident, breakdown of health, strike and lockout, or unemployment – on a lifetime of work.

2 Idle, useless and burdensome

At the age of seven, the boy who became known as Jack the Giant Killer was sent out into the fields by his father to tend his oxen. Cinderella had to work as a kitchen maid until she found her prince. Little Bo-Peep lost her sheep and Little Boy Blue failed to blow his horn and therefore to keep the cow out of the corn. Many another child features as a drudge in traditional tales and rhymes, which reflect the unremarkable reality of child labour.

Women and children first

Daniel Defoe, best known for *Robinson Crusoe* and other novels, was also a pamphleteer and essayist. Having remarked in 1728 on the low wages paid to the agricultural labourer, he approvingly added:

> But if this man's wife and children can at the same time get employment, if at next door, or at the next village, there lives a clothier or a bay [baize] maker or a stuff or drugget weaver: the manufacturer sends the poor woman comb'd wool or carded wool every week to spin, and she gets eightpence or ninepence a day at home; the weaver sends for her two little children, and they work by the loom, winding, filling quills [bobbins], &c., and the two bigger girls spin at home with their mother, and there earn threepence or fourpence a day each: so that put it together, the family at home generally gets as much as the father abroad and generally more.[1]

'The Half-timer', oil painting (1906) by Patti Mayor (1872-1962). The model was Annie Hill, who had just started work as a half-time tenter in a Preston mill at 2s. 9d. a week. The picture was greatly admired by George Bernard Shaw. Courtesy of the Harris Museum & Art Gallery, Preston.

Defoe shared the commonplace view of his day that it was hugely beneficial for both women and children – 'the most idle, useless and burthensome part of our People' – to work, and he welcomed their employment as lacemakers, who, as it happens, did sing at their work to help pass the monotonous hours.[2] In his celebrated book, *A Tour Thro' the whole Island of Great Britain*, published 1724–26, Defoe commented admiringly that at Halifax:

> among the manufacturers' houses are likewise scattered an infinite number of cottages or small dwellings, in which … the women and children … are always busy carding, spinning, &c. so that no hands being unemployed, all can gain their bread, even from the youngest to the ancient; hardly anything above four years old, but its hands are sufficient to itself.[3]

Small children from poor families were routinely employed in the fields as bird scarers or cattle minders. They worked both at home and in outside establishments as spinners and weavers, and also as assistant nail and chain makers. In the mines they were hurriers and trappers, and it is no surprise that their labour was welcomed in the new factories. However, some parents resisted. As Cole and Postgate observed:

> Up to the early years of the nineteenth century … the factory owners constantly complained of an actual shortage of child labour. This was partly because the early factories employed an even larger proportion of children than the factories after 1815. It was also because there had not yet been time for the industrial towns to grow in response to the demand, and because parents, until they were driven by sheer economic necessity, were often unwilling to send young children to face the hardships of factory labour.[4]

Even so, as E.P. Thompson has pointed out, 'there was a drastic increase in the intensity of exploitation of child labour between 1780 and 1840'. He continues: 'In the mills, the child and juvenile labour force grew yearly; and in several of the outworker or "dishonourable" trades the hours of labour grew longer and the work more intense.'[5] According to Sidney Pollard:

> In the predominantly youthful population of the time, the proportion of young workers was high. In the Cumberland mines, for example, children started work at the age of between five and seven, and as late as 1842, two hundred to two hundred and fifty of the 1,300–1,400 workers in the Lonsdale mines were under eighteen. At Alloa collieries, 103 boys and girls of under seven were employed in 1780. … Josiah Wedgwood, in 1816, had 30 per cent of his employees under eighteen, 3.3 per cent under ten years of age. The greatest problems, however, were encountered in the textile mills. The silk mills were dependent almost exclusively on child labour, and there the children started particularly young, at the

> ages of six or seven, compared with nine or ten in the cotton mills. Typically from two-thirds to three-quarters of the hands were under eighteen but in some large mills, the proportion was much higher ... In the cotton industry the proportion of children and adolescents under eighteen was around 40–45 per cent.[6]

Testimonies abound, both against child labour and in favour. Dr Andrew Ure, a fierce advocate of the factory system (and *bête noire* of Marx and Engels), wrote in 1835 in his book, *Philosophy of Manufactures*:

> Of all the common prejudices that exist with regard to factory labour, there is none more unfounded than that which ascribes to it excessive tedium and irksomeness above other occupations, owing to its being carried on with the 'unceasing motion of the steam-engine'. In an establishment for spinning or weaving cotton, all the hard work is performed by the steam-engine, which leaves for the attendant no hard labour at all, and literally nothing to do in general; but at intervals to perform some delicate operation, such as joining the threads that break, taking the cops off the spindles, &c. ... These remarks apply more especially to the labour of children in factories. Three-fourths of the children so employed are engaged in piecing at the mules. 'When the carriages of these have receded a foot and a half or two feet from the rollers,' says Mr Tufnell, 'nothing is to be done, not even attention is required from either spinner or piecer.' Both of them stand idle for a time, and in fine spinning, particularly, for three quarters of a minute or more. Consequently, if a child remains at this business twelve hours daily, he has nine hours of inaction.[7]

By contrast with such specious reasoning, an anonymous Sunday-school teacher interviewed by William Dodd in Bradford in 1841 knew the reality rather than the theory of child labour:

> We had many scholars of from eight or nine to thirteen or fourteen years of age, who worked in the factories during the week. When I first became acquainted with them, their appearance to me was healthy and strong, and as fresh and blooming as the flowers in May; and continued so for a short time. But this did not continue long; for, in the short space of three years, I saw many of them sink into the grave; the factory system having worn out their very vitals.[8]

A large number of street ballads featured the plight of factory children. 'The White Slave; or, The Factory Girl's Last Day', issued in the 1830s by Thomas Ford of Chesterfield, begins portentously:

The Factory Girl's Last Day[9]

'Twas on a winter's morning, the weather wet and mild,
Three hours before the dawning, the father roused his child;
Her daily morsel bringing, the darksome room he paced,
And cried, 'The bell is ringing, my hapless darling, haste!'

At the end of a long day during which the child is beaten by the overlooker, she collapses on the way home. Her fellow workers carry her to her father, and then:

All night, with tortur'd feeling, he watched his speechless child;
And close beside her kneeling, she knew him not nor smil'd,
Again the factory's ringing, her last perceptions tried;
When from her straw-bed springing, '*'Tis time!*' she shrieked,
and died!

A final verse contrasts the concern of 'the daughters of her master' for 'Negro wrongs' with their indifference to the plight of the dying 'white slave … Who gain'd their father's gold!'

In 'The Factory Girl' Robert Dibb of Dewsbury levels a charge of murder against a cruel overlooker and a rapacious employer when another child dies exhausted on her way home. His emotive and unashamedly propagandist ballad, sold at 1d., with '*The profits arising therefrom to go towards forwarding the TEN HOURS BILL!!!*', concludes:

Ye! who alone on Gold are bent,
Blush! at the Murder'd Innocent,
Let not Old England's glorious pride
Be stain'd by black Infanticide!!
But let Humanity's bright Ray
Protect from greedy Tyrant's sway
The poor defenceless Factory Girl![10]

A note on the sheet informs us that 'The Factory Child's Complaint', by Miss A. Strickland, was forwarded to the printer by George Strickland, MP for the West Riding. This must have been before 1841, when Strickland began to represent Preston. Since he and his wife were childless, the author of the lachrymose piece could have been their niece.

THE

FACTORY CHILD'S

COMPLAINT.

BY MISS A. STRICKLAND,

Received from George Strickland, Esq., M.P. for the West-Riding.

I hear the blithe voices of Children at play,
And the sweet birds rejoicing on every green spray;
On all things the bright beams of Summer have smil'd,
But they smile not on me, the poor Factory Child.

The gay sports of childhood to me they deny,
And the fair paths of learning I never must try—
A companion of creatures whom guilt has defiled,
Oh! who does not pity the Factory Child?

Oh! who would not mourn for a victim like me?
A young heart-broken slave in the land of the free;
Hardly tasked and oft beaten, oppressed and reviled—
Such, such is the lot of the Factory Child.

In the dead of the night, when you take your sweet sleep,
Through the dark dismal streets to my labours I creep;
To the din of the loom, till my poor brain seems wild:
I return—an unfortunate Factory Child.

The bright bloom of health has forsaken my cheek,
My spirits are gone, and my young limbs grown weak;
Oh! ye Rich and ye Mighty! let Sympathy mild,
Appeal to your hearts for the Factory Child.

Oh! pity my suff'rings, ere yet the cold tomb
Succeed my loath'd prison, its tasks, and its gloom;
And the clods of the valley untimely are piled,
O'er the pale wasted form of the Factory Child.

The Factory Child's Complaint. Source: West Yorkshire Archive Service

The Factory Child's Complaint[11]

I hear the blithe voices of Children at play,
And the sweet birds rejoicing on every green spray;
On all things the bright beams of Summer have smil'd,
But they smile not on me, the poor Factory Child.

The gay sports of childhood to me they deny,
And the fair paths of learning they never must try –
A companion of creatures whom guilt has defiled,
Oh! Who does not pity the Factory Child?

Oh! Who would not mourn for a victim like me?
A young heart-broken slave in the land of the free;
Hardly tasked and oft beaten, oppressed and reviled –
Such, such is the lot of the Factory Child.

In the dead of the night, when you take your sweet sleep,
Through the dark dismal streets to my labours I creep;
To the din of the loom, till my poor brain seems wild:
I return – an unfortunate Factory Child.

The bright bloom of health has forsaken my cheek,
My spirits are gone, and my young limbs grow weak;
Oh! Ye Rich and ye Mighty! Let Sympathy mild,
Appeal to your hearts for the Factory Child.

Oh! Pity my suff'rings, ere yet the cold tomb
Succeed my loath'd prison, its tasks, and its gloom;
And the clods of the valley untimely are piled,
O'er the pale wasted form of the Factory Child.

Even without the effective endorsement of a Member of Parliament, one would have been acutely conscious that this was not a child worker's voice, but that of a middle-class spokeswoman.

Nevertheless, those with first-hand experience of labour did express themselves in verse and song. In 1874, burning with anger, Joseph Burgess (1853–1934) wrote 'There's Nowt Loike Shoddy',[12] which might have become nationally known, were it not for the density of the vernacular employed. After looking back at his own work in the mill as a child, Burgess made these extraordinary statements:

An' if aw'm e'er so lucky as to have a little lad,
To coam at neet to meet me, tak' mi hont an' co' me 'Dad!'
Afore he'st piece on shoddy, an' stew i' th' mill o' day,
Aw'll ax the Gentle Shepherd to tak' His lamb away.

And:

An' ere a choilt o' mine 'at striven o' it cud,
To add to th' mesthu's profit by makkin' bad work good,
Should be trayted loike a slave i' freedom's native isle,
Aw cud lay it in its grave an' feel relievt enoof to smile.

Shoddy, shredded cotton or wool mixed with new wool, was hard on both spinner and weaver, and its floating fibres could be inhaled and cause 'shoddy fever'.

Burgess, who became a journalist in later life, started work at Failsworth, Lancashire, as a piecer earning 1s. 6d. for a sixty-hour week. Long as they were, these hours were extended, essentially by cheating:

Aw've seen when aw've bin wakkent at foive o'clock i' th' dark,
On bitter frosty mornin's, an' packt off to mi' wark,
An' if, ere th'engine started, aw had no' eylt mi tops,
Mi moinder 'ud a cusst me, an' cleawted me i' th' chops,
An' what wi' th'engine chettin' abeawt ten minnits then,
An' runnin' o'er at breakfast toime at leeust another ten,
Wi' seven or eight at six o' clock, an' full fifteen at noon,
It wer' very, very seldom as aw geet theer too soon.

Thirty years earlier, a Chartist weaver, Samuel Leach, wrote a book, *Stubborn Facts from the Factories by a Manchester Operative*, which greatly impressed Frederick Engels. Leach, who mentioned a typical rule that 'Every operative detected speaking to another, singing or whistling, will be fined 6d.', observed that workers 'often find the factory clock moved forward a quarter of an hour and the doors shut, while the clerk moves about with the fines book inside, noting the many names of the absentees'. He claimed 'to have counted ninety-five operatives thus shut out, standing before a factory whose clock was a quarter of an hour slower than the town clocks at night, and a quarter of an hour faster in the morning'.[13]

Burgess's poem concludes:

Why! a fact'ry's loike a prison, yo' con noather see nor yer
(When yo'n getten insoide it) owt 'at's passin' eawt o' th' dur,
For they're filled wi' frosted windows, an' built insoide a yard,

Wi' a wall yo' conno' get o'er, an' a dur 'at's allus barred.
So aw'm beawn to save mi oddie [money] 'at when aw get upgroon,
Aw con bid good-bye to shoddy an' top workin' beat mi shoon,
An' hopin' yo' as yer me'll think aw'm doin' reet,
An' clap me lawd an' heartily, aw'll weesh yo' o' good-neet.

That this was indeed sung is not only implied in the last line, but emphasised by a remark elsewhere: 'Aw'm a shoddy piecer 'at's singin' yo' this sung.' A century later, Harry Boardman (1930–1987) valiantly performed it on his LP record, *A Lancashire Mon*.[14]

Personal revulsion at child labour could be transformed into political action, and one campaigner, the Tory Radical Richard Oastler (1789–1861), earned himself the title of 'king of the factory children'. He was a failed businessman who in 1820 succeeded his father as the steward of a big estate at Fixby, near Huddersfield. There, he 'became quite the squire *manqué*. He revived old manorial customs such as rent day and harvest fair. He rode the fields, got to know the tenants, and carefully disbursed alms among the cottagers.'[15] From 1830, as a former slave trade abolitionist, he began to campaign on working conditions in factories, starting in Bradford where 'thousands of our fellow creatures and fellow subjects, both male and female, ... are this very moment existing in a state of slavery *more horrid* than are the victims of that hellish system –

Little piecers at Mons Mill, Todmorden. Piecers used to crawl beneath the looms to join the ends of broken threads. Photo: Roger Birch

OASTLER

And the Factory Children's Rights

FOR EVER!!

Come all you tender parents, give hear unto my song,
And when you've heard my verses through you cannot say they're wrong;
Concerning of a GENTLEMAN, a man of noble fame,
And if you wish to know this man, " 'Squire OASTLER is his name.

CHORUS.

So drink success to OASTLER, boys, and cheer him 3 times 3,
He will protect our " children's rights," from " bondage" set them free.

OASTLER supports the Factory Bill, to protect our children's rights,
We are well assur'd that all such men in honesty delights;
Back'd by the Duke of Sussex, let's hope he will prevail,
In a cause of such humanity, we trust he'll never fail.
So drink, &c.

'Squire OASTLER is a Christian, and a friend unto the poor,
And it is his wish to send a cheap loaf to the door;
With energy and eloquence he supports the Children's cause,
So rally round his standard, boys, and give him great applause.
So drink, &c.

The slave that's in the Indies, work but 9 hours each day,
While Children here work 16 hours, and gets but little pay;
We hope that all such slavish trades will soon be done away,
Let the poor be paid for labour, aloud the Nation cries.
So drink, &c.

There are many thousands in this land, you very well do know,
That never knew what it was a hard day's work to do;
But let them try a week or two, with half a belly full,
How soon they'd strike, their fingers bite, what long faces they would pull.
So drink, &c.

See what OLD ENGLAND has come too, for want of alteration,
Can any man in senses not see its situation;
To see the useless " Sinecures" and " Taxes" wich we pay,
And in what a shameful manner it is squandered away.
So drink, &c.

So to conclude and end my song, we'll fear no person's taunts,
Addition to our "UNIONS' STRENGTH,", substraction to our ,' WANTS;"
Multiplication to our " BLESSINGS," division to our " FOES,"
Reduction of our " DEBTS," my boys, our " RENTS" and " TAXES" too.
So drink, &c.

J. LISTER, PRINTER, A LITTLE ABOVE THE GAS WORKS, NEAR HALIFAX.

'colonial slavery.'[16] Oastler also excoriated the new Poor Law of 1834.

He was a big man, over six feet tall, with a stentorian voice and tremendous power as an orator, who became identified with the demand for a Ten Hour Day in textile mills. Factory owners in Yorkshire and Glasgow recoiled in horror, and in 1838 Oastler's employer, Thomas Thornhill, not only sacked him but instituted proceedings for the recovery of debts, which led to his being imprisoned for three and a half years. Friends, principally John Fielden, MP for Oldham, eventually raised over £3,000 to secure his release in 1844.

The huge, cheering crowds which turned out to greet Oastler sang ballads such as 'The King of the Factory Children', which went to the exuberant tune (see p.194) of 'The King of the Cannibal Islands':

The King of the Factory Children

To limit the hours of Factory toil,
He stood undaunted 'midst the broil,
Of those who strove the work to foil,
Of the King of the Factory Children.
But infants' labour was curtail'd,
And petty tyrants writh'd and wail'd,
With oaths and curses they assail'd
The King of the Factory Children.
But gratitude the chain has broke,
Which bound him to the tyrant's yoke,
The prison-house no more's the walk
Of the King of the Factory Children.

Other ballads gleefully took up the celebrations. According to 'A New Song on the Liberation of Richard Oastler!!',[17] 'The little children in the streets his praises they do sing, "Long Life attend poor Oastler, our noble Factory King".' A further sheet, 'Oastler and the Factory Children's Rights for Ever!!',[18] called for readers and singers to 'drink success to Oastler, boys, and cheer him 3 times 3', and claimed that "e will protect our "children's rights", from "bondage" set them free'.

However, ill and depressed after his release from prison, Oastler took little further part in the movement to limit factory hours. Yet his efforts undoubtedly contributed to the change in the climate of opinion which brought about the passing in 1847 of the Ten Hours' Act, overriding mill owners' objections that they could not make a profit on a working day of that length, and setting a precedent for future regulatory legislation. By prohibiting women and children from working more than ten hours a day in textile mills the law had the effect of similarly restricting men. In response, mill owners devised a system by which women worked in relays over the period from 5.30 am to 8.30 pm, thus enabling men to be retained at will between those times. Further acts in 1850 and 1853 forbade the relay system and restricted factories to twelve hours a day but lengthened the permissible working week for women from 58 to 60 hours (ten and a half on weekdays, seven and a half on Saturdays). Even Lord Palmerston, then Home Secretary, thought it right to intervene in Parliament during the discussion of the 1853 Act:

> He really thought that to have little children from eight to twelve years of age brought out on a drizzling winter's morning at five, or half-past five, ... was a practice which must entail such evils that

> no one could be surprised at the extreme mortality among the children of factory operatives. . . . It was said that to limit the number of hours . . . for the employment of children, would indirectly tend to limit the employment of persons of more advanced age; but all he could say was, he thought it so essential to protect these children from being overtasked that he could not consider the results which it might be imagined would flow from it.[19]

The clear ten-hour day was not secured until 1874, and it is richly ironic that this was the pre-industrial norm of a century earlier, when the customary working stint for craftsmen was from six in the morning until six in the evening, with a two-hour break in the middle.

Child labour persisted well into the twentieth century, in the form of the half-time system. The Factory Act of 1833, which applied to textile mills, excluded children under 9, and as well as limiting those aged from 9 to 13 to nine hours a day, insisted that they have two hours' schooling daily. For this, the first enactment of compulsory education in England and Wales, each child had to pay 2d. a week or have it stopped from wages. A further Act of 1844, covering all factories, lowered the qualifying age to 8 but limited children's working day to six and a half hours, and insisted on three hours' schooling, after 8 am and before 6 pm. Between 1874 and 1899 a series of education acts successively raised the minimum age for half-timers to 12. There was opposition to such restrictions, which 'were widely resented as imposing burdens upon the poor in the shape of loss of earnings and the payment of fees, so that both masters and operatives connived at their evasion'.[20] The qualifying labour certificate required from 1903 was administered by local school boards, some of which insisted only on a Standard 1 level of education. In 1906–07, nationally, there were 47,360 half-timers working, of whom 30,800 (65%) were in Lancashire and Yorkshire. The half-time system was abolished in 1918 under the Fisher Education Act, which established full-time schooling for all up to the age of 13.[21]

Among the many who remembered their days as half-timers was Harry Pollitt (born in 1890), who walked the three miles from Droylsden to Ashton-under-Lyne with a crowd of other children aged twelve to sit for the examination which would permit those who passed to work for a year as half-timers, with one week in the mill from 6 am (with a half hour for breakfast) until 12.30 pm, then from 2 till 4 pm in school, and the next week in the mill from 1.30 until 5 pm, with the morning in school, and so on. Pollitt was worried about the examination, but later reflected: 'The mill-owners who controlled the educational bodies took precious good care that the biggest dunce in the school could pass it. . . . They wanted cheap labour, and intended to see that they got it.' He was delighted to be starting work, though his mother 'bitterly regretted the step which had to be taken, but it saved her from paying half a crown a week to some other half-timer to help her with her four looms'. 'At last,' wrote Pollitt, who in due course was to become the general secretary of the Communist Party of Great Britain:

> The night that seemed eternal came to an end, and I walked proudly up the village street with my mother to Benson's Mill. Of course, I had been inside many times before when the looms were working, but I imagined it would be quite different when I helped work the looms myself. The roar of the machinery started, and I was quite deafened. I soon got used to the routine. I was the only lad in the weaving shed, all the other half-timers being girls. They all made a great fuss of me, and told me 'I had a little face as round as an apple'. On Fridays, when I was on afternoon turns, I must have got many more toffees than were good for either my teeth or my digestion. The usual tricks played on a learner were played on me, but the weavers, being a cut above the cardroom operatives (as they thought) played only polite, ladylike tricks on me. It was left to the buxom girls and women in the cardroom to break me in by taking my trousers down and daubing my unmentionable parts with oil and packing me up with cotton waste.[22]

When William Holt (1897–1976) became a half-timer in a Todmorden shirt factory he felt that he had 'become a man'. Dressed in 'cloth cap, jacket and waistcoat, fustian breeches, and clogs with heavy Colne shods, or irons', he went on errands for the owner. One day, after seeing him running, his Uncle Tom stopped him to give 'socialist' advice: 'Thou should never run for a boss. . . .He willn't pay thee ony more for running.' At thirteen Holt became a full-timer weaver, working a 52-hour week.[23] His eventful life included soldiering in the First World War, organising a branch of the National Unemployed Workers' Movement and serving nine months' imprisonment for 'unlawful assembly and incitement' during a demonstration against the undue rigour of the Means Test, a period as a Communist councillor in Todmorden, and a flourishing career as an inveterate traveller and a prolific journalist and writer.

Less spectacular reminiscences inspired this song of the 1970s:

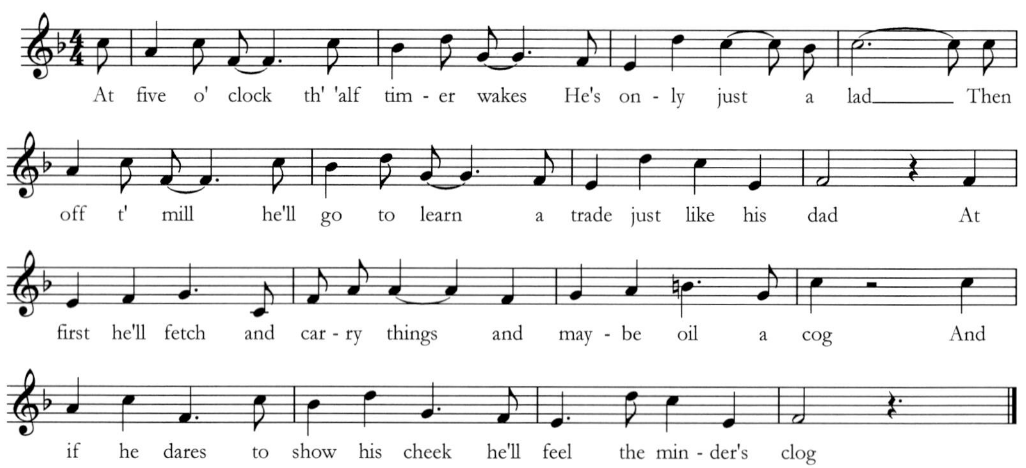

At five o'clock th' 'alf timer wakes – he's only just a lad –
Then off t' mill he'll go to learn a trade just like his dad.
At first he'll fetch and carry things and maybe oil a cog,
And if he dares to show his cheek he'll feel the minder's clog.

At dinner time he takes his bread and sits down on the stool.
His head it nods but he daresn't sleep, or he'll be late for school.
Th' 'alf timer sits at t' back o' t' class, his head cupped in his hands,
His eyes they close and then he feels the back of teacher's hand.

And so he's kept in after school to learn his ABC,
A telling-off, some lines to write, then home to have some tea:
A clout round th' ear for being late but t' lad he doesn't weep,
Cos all t' 'alf timer wants to do is go and have some sleep.

And then he's off up wooden hill and in his prayers he'll say
'God bless the family and give us strength to face another day';
And through his sleep he'll 'appen dream of things to come, and when,
Just as a gaffer he's become, it's five o' clock again.

So far as the mines were concerned, a series of Parliamentary enquiries between 1841 and 1843 had dramatic effects. 'Victorian society was clearly moved by the stories of harsh labour among the children,' writes Anthony Burton, 'but they were profoundly shocked by the prospect of wholesale immorality underground. There was a thrill of horror as they considered

NOTICE.

NO FEMALES

Permitted, on any account, to work under ground at this Colliery; and all such is STRICTLY PROHIBITED, by Orders from His Grace the Duke of Hamilton.

JOHN JOHNSTON, Overseer.

REDDING COLLIERY, 4th March, 1845. J. Duncan, Printer, Falkirk.

the prospect of men and women working together naked in the dark places under the earth.'[25] As a consequence, from 1842 women and girls were prohibited from working underground, as were boys under ten. According to the census of the previous year, of the 118,000 coalminers at work in Britain, 2,350 were women, mainly in Lancashire, the West Riding and Scotland. After 1842 some women continued to work – on the surface – though it is clear from a notice of three years later (see illustration) that some may have carried on for a time underground.

A striking evocation of child labour in the mines comes from a ballad printed by John Harkness of Preston, probably in 1843. The anonymous author, using simple language, builds a dignified but powerful statement.

The Collier Lass[26]

My name is Polly Parker, I'm come o'er from Worsley,
My father and mother work in the coal mine,
Our family's large, we have got seven children,
So I am obliged to work in the same mine,
And as this is my fortune I know you feel sorry,
That in such employment my days I should pass,
But I keep up my spirits, I sing and look merry,
Although I am but a poor Collier lass.

By the greatest of dangers each day I'm surrounded,
I hang in the air by a rope or a chain,
The mine may fall in, I may be kill'd or wounded,
May perish by damp or the fire of a [powder] train,
And what would you do if it were not for our labour,
In wretched starvation your days you would pass,
While we could supply you with life's greatest blessing
Then do not despise the poor Collier Lass.

All the day long you may say we are buried,
Depriv'd of the light and warmth of the sun,
And often at night from our beds we are hurried,
The water is in, and bare footed we run;
And though we go ragged and black are our faces,
As kind and as free as the best will be found,
And our hearts are as white as your lords' in fine places
Although we're poor Colliers that work under ground.

I am now growing up fast some how or other,
There's a collier lad strangely runs in my mind,
And in spite of the talking of father or mother,
I think I should marry if he was inclin'd,
But should he prove surley [sic] and will not befriend me,
Another and better chance may come to pass,
And my friends here I know, to him will recommend me
And I'll be no longer a collier Lass.

It is entirely possible that the writer of the ballad was inspired by the first report of the Parliamentary commission on the employment of children, which came out in 1842. Patience Kershaw, a 17-year-old Halifax girl earning 8s. 6d. a week at Joseph Stock's Booth Town Pit, gave this evidence:

> My father has been dead about a year; my mother is living and has ten children, five lads and five lasses; the oldest is about thirty, the youngest is four; three lasses go to mill; all the lads are colliers, two getters and three hurriers; one lives at home and does nothing; mother does nought but look after home. . . .
> All my sisters have been hurriers, but three went to the mill. Alice went because her legs swelled from hurrying in cold water when she was hot. I never went to day-school; I go to Sunday-school, but I cannot read or write; I got to pit at five o'clock in the morning and come out at five in the evening; I get my breakfast of porridge and milk first; I take my dinner with me, a cake, and eat it as I go; I do not stop or rest at any time for the purpose; I get nothing else till I get home, and then have potatoes and meat, not every day meat. I hurry in the clothes I now have now got on, trousers and ragged jacket; the bald place upon my head is made by thrusting the corves; my legs have never swelled, but sisters' did when they went to the mill; I hurry the corves a mile and more under ground and back; they weigh 300 cwt [3 hundredweight, 3 x 112 lbs]; I hurry 11 a-day; I wear a belt and chain at the workings to get the corves out;

> the getters that I work for are *naked* except their caps; they pull off all their clothes; I see them at work when I go up; sometimes they beat me, if I am not quick enough, with their hands; they strike me upon my back; the boys take liberties with me sometimes, they pull me about; I am the only girl in the pit; there are about 20 boys and 15 men; all the men are naked; I would rather work in mill than in coal-pit.

The inspector merely commented: 'This girl is an ignorant, filthy, ragged, and deplorable-looking object, and such an one as the uncivilised natives of the prairies would be shocked to look upon.'[27]

Rather more sympathy was evinced well over a century later by Frank Higgins of Liverpool in his song:

The Testimony of Patience Kershaw[28]

It's good of you to ask me, sir,
To tell you how I spend the day.
Well, in a coal black tunnel, sir,
I hurry corves to earn my pay.
The corves are full of coal, kind sir,
I push them with my hands and head.
It isn't lady-like but, sir,
You've got to earn your daily bread.

An illustration from the 1842 Parliamentary Commission report on the employment of children

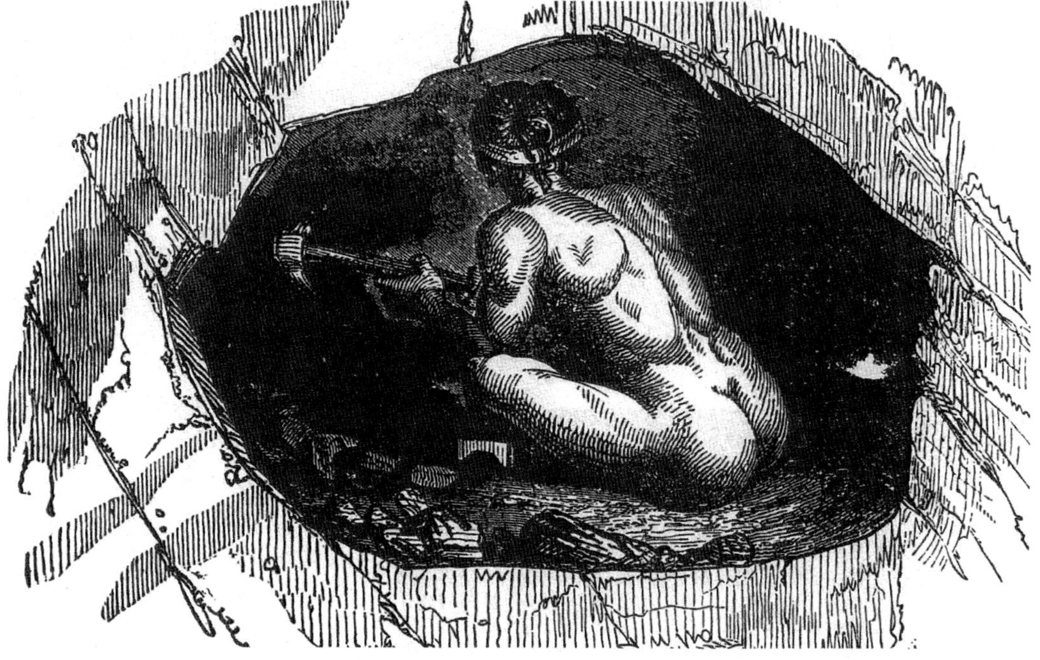

Only after the Education Acts of 1880 and 1891, which made attendance at elementary schools first compulsory, then free, did large-scale child labour decline. The progressive raising of the leaving age – to fourteen in 1918, fifteen in 1944 and sixteen in 1972 – completed the process. Even so, traditional songs on the subject of child labour survived well into the twentieth century. Joan Littlewood found herself in 1947 at Middleton-in-Teesdale, County Durham, where she made a remarkable discovery. 'Teesdale,' she wrote, 'was new to me, disused lead mines, all the farmhouses painted white, as decreed by some forgotten seigneur. I amused myself collecting fragments of an old song and got Jimmie [Miller] a job completing it.' She quotes only one verse:

> Fourpence a day, me lads and verra hard to work
> With never a pleasant look from a scruffy-looking Turk
> His heart it may fail his conscience may give way
> And he'll raise us our wages to ninepence a day.[29]

According to Jimmie Miller, better known subsequently as Ewan MacColl, the fragment, which he filled out, came from John Gowland, a retired lead miner.

Fourpence a Day[30]

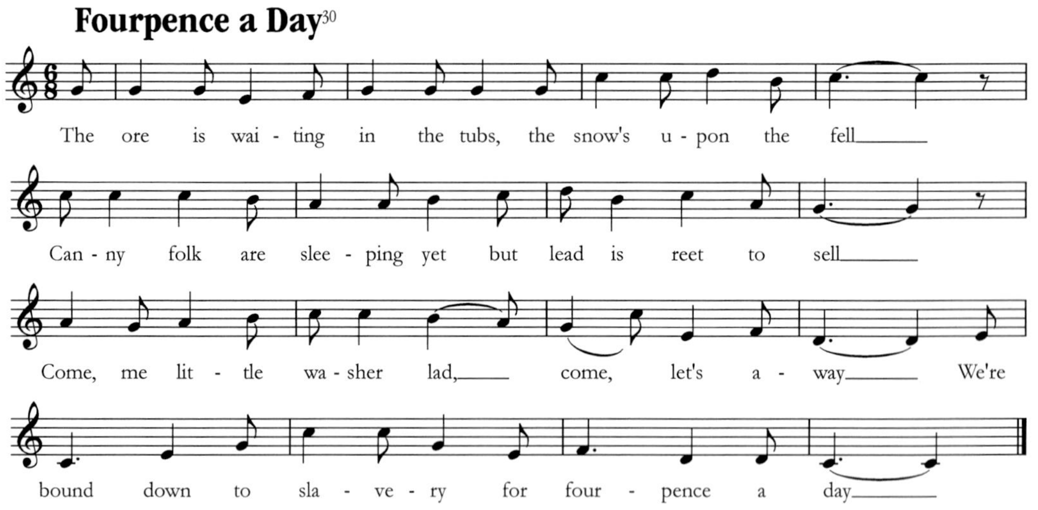

> The ore is waiting in the tubs, the snow's upon the fell;
> Canny folk are sleeping yet but lead is reet to sell.
> Come, me little washer lad, come, let's away,
> It's very hard to work for fourpence a day.

> It's early in the morning, we rise at five o'clock,
> And the little slaves come to the door to knock, knock, knock.
> Come, me little washer lad, come, let's away,
> It's very hard to work for fourpence a day.
>
> My father was a miner and lived down in the town;
> 'Twas hard work and poverty that always kept him down.
> He aimed for me to go to school but brass he couldn't pay,
> So I had to go to the washing rake for fourpence a day.
>
> My mother rises out of bed with tears on her cheeks,
> Puts my wallet on my shoulders, which has to serve a week.
> It often fills her great big heart when she unto me does say,
> 'I never thought thou would have worked for fourpence a day.'
>
> Fourpence a day, me lad, and very hard to work,
> And never a pleasant look from a gruffy looking Turk.
> His conscience it may fail and his heart it may give way,
> Then he'll raise us our wages to ninepence a day.

The original authorship of the song has been attributed to Thomas Raine, lead miner and writer, also from Teesdale. Raine, who originally came from Barnards Castle in County Durham, is an elusive figure, and I have been able to trace only one item of his in print: 'The Birkdale Shepherds or An Account of the sufferings of W. Ritson and death of J. Allinson' (1836).[31] The poem tells in thirty-six verses of how William Ritson and John Allinson set out from near Cauldron Spout to bring in a sheep but lost their bearings during a snowstorm. Allinson was eventually found dead but Ritson survived after being found in a drift and carried home. A lugubrious couplet concluded:

> Now shepherds all who tend your flocks, who ramble void of care,
> A warning be this unto you that you for death prepare.

Despite the hardships, a washer lad or a young shepherd might have been better off than a boy sent to work down the mine:

> Mother wept, and father sighed with delight a-glow
> Cried the lad, 'Tomorrow,' cried, 'To pit I go.'
>
> Up and down the place he sped, greeted old and young,
> Far and wide the tidings spread, clapt his hands and sung.

Came his cronies some to gaze wrapt in wonder; some
Free with counsel; some with praise; some with envy dumb.

'May he,' many a gossip cried, 'Be from peril kept';
Father hid his face and sighed, Mother turned and wept.[32]

So wrote Joseph Skipsey, who within weeks of his birth in March 1832 lost his own father, an overman at Percy Main Colliery near North Shields, shot dead by a special constable during a strike. The boy started work as a trapper at the age of seven, and during his sixteen-hour days he found time to teach himself to read by conning discarded playbills and advertisements. He graduated to the Bible, Pope's version of the *Iliad*, then Milton and Shakespeare, Burns and Blake. As a pitman he moved up through the ranks from putter to hewer, then to deputy, but reverted to hewer to escape what he deemed an undue burden of responsibility. He remained a pitman until his retirement, except for interludes in other roles such as, bizarrely, curator of Shakespeare's birthplace at Stratford. Several volumes of his own poems were published, and attracted the attention of such figures as Burne-Jones, Browning, Tennyson, Rossetti and William Morris. Skipsey died in 1903. According to a recent commentator: 'His best lyrics, about mining life, bring written poetry close to nineteenth-century traditional oral dialect ballads.'[33]

Pick and shovel at the coalface

The plain words, 'Mother wept', chillingly evoke the dangers of mining, as does the simple language of this poem, also by Skipsey:

Get Up[34]

'Get up,' the caller calls, 'get up!'
And in the dead of night,
To win the bairns their bite and sup,
I rise a weary wight.

My flannel dudden [clothes] donn'd, thrice o'er
My birds are kissed, and then,
I with a whistle shut the door,
I may not ope again.

As the children became young adults they inevitably looked for life-partners among both workmates and those in other industries.

Factory girls and collier lads

There is a time-honoured tradition of songs which extol or at least evaluate different tradesmen and women as possible sexual or marital partners. Thomas Lanfiere, the author of 'The Clothiers Delight' (see p.73), also wrote 'The Taunton Maids delight, or, Hey for the honest Woosted-Comber'.[35] The eponymous maid successively rejects:

'a Barbor brave' ('Your Rayzer and Washing balls truly, for my Bacon is not fit'),
'a miller ('When 'tis my fortune to be wedd, it shall not be with a Thief'),
'a Smith that was cole-black' ('A Blacksmith's hammer never shall, Upon my Anvill smight'),
'a prick-louse [prickless]' taylor ('I told him that Cabbage [the word is used both with its normal meaning – implying poverty – and that of pieces of cloth filched by tailors or taken as perquisites] I did hate, with my body 'twould not agree') and
'a cold Shoemaker' ('Quoth I, march off with Sir Hugh's bones [St Hugh of Lincoln was the patron of shoemakers], your suite [sic] it is in vain').

Then came 'An honest Weaver, . . . a handsome, proper Lad', but even he could not measure up to a comber:

Taunton Maids Delight *or* Hey for the Honest Woosted-Comber[35]

Of all sorts of Tradesmen that are dwelling in Taunton town,
None with a Comber can compare, for valour and renown:
He is both courageous and stout, in Battel to fight he is free,
To his enemy he'l face about, he scornes a Coward to be.

When he with his comrades doth meet, his money he'l freely spend,
With good strong Beer his heart he'l cheer, to the Ale-Wife he's a good friend:

And when he hath spent an hour or twain in merry company,
At the Come-pot [?] again with might & maine, his work he then doth ply.

Somertimes in the fields with his true-love a progress he doth take,
With kisses sweet he doth her greet, and much of her doth make:

On the green grass the time they pass in sweet felicity,
With heart and mind their loves they bind, ne'er parted for to be.

And thus the Woosted-Comber's praise I have declared to you,
In every part is his desert, I have described true,
He is the man that I esteem, above Rubies or Pearle,
I'de rather chuse to lie by him then by a Lord or Earle

God bless the Combers and Weavers both that in Taunton doth dwell,
Unto them all both great and small I heartily wish well;
To those in Milverton so brave I also do commend,
Good trading I wish they still may have, and so I make an end.

[Chorus]
They hey for the Woosted-Comber brave I love him as my life,
If ever I a Husband have I will be a Comber's wife.

The unequivocal rejection of 'a Lord or Earle' is a straw, one of many, showing a powerful wind of change, which would intensify with the Industrial Revolution.

One way in which the new factory workers entered balladry was by their taking and adapting existing rural pieces. 'The Farmer's Boy', with its well-loved refrain, 'To plough and sow and reap and mow, And be a farmer's boy, and be a farmer's boy', which lingered in oral tradition until the end of the twentieth century, gave rise to the much less long-lived, 'Lucky Factory Boy', with the much less affectionately-remembered refrain, 'To strip and grind, or weave or wind, Or be a factory boy'.[36] In 'The Pretty Ploughboy', widespread on broadsides and in oral tradition, a rich man, infuriated when his daughter falls in love beneath her station, has the offending ploughboy removed by a pressgang; but the spirited girl follows, disguised as a man, and secures his release. Only a short step was needed to substitute for the pretty ploughboy 'The Pretty Factory Boy':

It's of a brisk young factory lad was going to his work,
As the factory bell was ringing amain.
His road was in a grove and his eyes did beam with love
When he met with the pretty lady Jane.[37]

On a Harkness ballad sheet, 'The Pretty Factory Boy' is paired with 'The Factory Girl',[38] of which it is necessary to add the opening words ('All you that love a merry jest') to distinguish it from other items with the same title. The former is indistinguishable from its model, save for the substitution of factory boy for ploughboy, and its language is rather high-flown. The latter is good-humoured and relaxed, hugely at ease in its industrial context, its idiom demotic. It has one priceless line – 'It would revive a nobleman to see her curl her hair' – and these down-to-earth verses:

> Always use them [factory girls] tenderly when you are so inclined,
> And they will please you to the heart, according to your mind,
> But should you be obstropelus [sic], and make their bellies swell,
> Then weekly wages you must pay unto the Factory Girl.
>
> If you attempt to run away and cannot pay the brass,
> Maidens they will beat you as neatly as you can cast,
> The overseer will send you unto the tread mill,
> And make you pay, or else consent to wed the Factory Girl.

In 'Mary and the Handsome Factory Boy', the eponymous Mary is confined to a cellar 'For ten long months on bread and water' by her father, the squire, who then conveniently dies, leaving her his 'factory and fortune'. She promptly marries the object of her father's ire, William, the handsome factory boy.[39] We swing back the other way with 'The (Fortunate) Factory Girl',[40] which probably dates from the 1830s. Versions were issued by numerous ballad printers, including Birt, Catnach, Disley, Hill, Hodges, Pitts and Taylor in London, Pratt and Russell in Birmingham, Harkness in Preston, Jacques in Manchester and Keys in Devonport. 'One fine summer's morning', just after sunrise, with birds singing from the bushes, lads and lasses are on the way to 'large buildings' where 'their labour begins'. The male narrator then sees 'a fair damsel, far brighter than Venus, ... [a] lovely young goddess, a factory girl'. He immediately accosts her and offers to make her a lady. She responds:

> Go marry a lady and you will do well:
> So let me alone, sir, the bell is a ringing,
> I am only a hard working factory girl.

After threatening to waste his life 'in some foreign land' if she will not agree to be his bride, he repeats the offer:

> Your beauty upon me it has cast a spell:
> I'll marry you speedy, and make you a lady,
> If you will become mine, dear factory girl.

At this, 'She gave her consent, when a licence was purchas'd', and they were married. To conclude:

> Now this loving couple live happy together,
> She blesses the day that she met with her swain,
> So this factory girl she is made a great lady,
> And married to a squire of honour and fame.

Despite – or perhaps thanks to – the extremity of wishful thinking, the ballad continued in oral tradition in England for upwards of a hundred years, and later still in Ireland (north and south), where outstanding traditional singers such as Margaret Barry, Elizabeth Cronin and Sarah Makem all had versions.[41]

Expressions of the desirability of factory girls and their sterling qualities as good wives are not merely a literary convention in this context; they at times reflect deeply held conviction, as in this highly partisan street ballad:

The Factory Lasses of Aberdeen[42]

You may brag of your boarding school lasses
And sewsters so dandy and fair;
But the factory girls them surpasses,
With them they will never compare.
Though not dress'd in a fine silken beaver,
With ribbons all tucked up in beaux [sic];
For poverty ne'er would I leave her,
For beauty consists not in clothes.

[Chorus]
In Glasgow there are bonny lasses,
Likewise in the auld town o' Ayr;
But the Aberdeen girls them surpasses,
With them they can never compare.

If you marry a wife that has riches,
In the end she will make you a sot;
For if once she gets hold of the breeches,
She'll soon get the vest and the coat.
With her friends and her money to back her
She will keep you as quiet as a mouse;
And if once you offer to whack her,
They will chase you away from the house.

They will walk wi' their leghorn bonnets,
For a poor man their care not a fig,
They think they're the finest of china,
And us like a coarse patterton pig.
Though our coats in the elbow be worn,
Yet we always will stand by the truth,
We are not like your gentlemen born,
With a silver spoon stuck in their mouth.

Then away wi' your dandies an' misses,
To a tradesman they are of no use,
There's none like the factory lasses,
To keep meat and fire in the house.
On Sunday when wi' their lads walking,
Wi' their mantles and bonnets so fine,
So its heedless for me to be talking,
For the rest of the girls they outshine.

'And sewsters so dandy and fair' A remarkably light and airy room for the times. Courtesy of the Hebden Bridge Local History Society Archive.

Apart from the mention of the factory bell in one of these ballads, there are no details of working life here; but in a further song from Northern Ireland, 'Campbell's Mill',[43] 'a fine well-looking gentleman' invites a factory girl to 'come with me no more to roam, So early to the spinning mill'. She, though, is committed to 'a heckler lad':

> So fare ye well, I must away,
> For the last whistle said its will,
> I must go back to my young man
> Who works with me in Campbell's Mill.

Again from Northern Ireland, the song 'The Flower of Corby Mill'[44] remains in oral circulation even now. It is a warm, lyrical song, which lavishes praise on 'a mill girl to her trade', 'the blooming rose of Antrim, the flower of Corby Mill'. However, it seems to derive from a rather sterner ballad, 'The Handsome Factory Lass',[45] which introduces both industrial strife and the well-loved theme of the broken token normally used to identify a lover long unseen. Once again, a male narrator 'down by the factory' comes across 'a blooming maid', but this time he is disconcerted because she is crying:

> Her cheeks were as red as any rose, the tears were falling fast,
> She's the blooming rose of England is the handsome factory lass.

She tells him she is weeping for her 'bonny factory lad', who left her eight months earlier to travel through Ashton (in Lancashire) and vowed to 'prove faithful'. The young man tells her that he has news:

Your lover was my comrade and he in the turnout [strike] fell,
A soldier's sword made him to fall and gave him a deadly gash,
And he begg'd me to protect his handsome factory lass.

She avers that she wishes only to share her lover's fate, whereupon the young man (in defiance of any similitude) identifies himself as that same lover. The reunited pair are quickly married:

Now on a pleasant evening, the lovers often walk,
A crossing of the fields so gay, they in contentment talk,
In a little cottage they reside, where happiness to pass,
Young William of the factory, and his handsome factory lass.

The strike injury here replaces the battlefield wound of the conventional broken token song, and we are still no nearer the authentic flavour of a factory courtship. Perhaps this is achieved in this street ballad issued by J.O. Bebbington of Manchester between 1856 and 1861.

Dashing Steam Loom Weaver[46]

One day I got on the spree, I fell out with my mother,
She says we can't agree, you'd better find another;
I said yo need not fret, for I's i' th' humour o' starting,
So straightway I did set, on purpose to seek my fortune.
[Chorus] Rite to-loo-ra-loo, &c.

I came to Bolton town, I met all things satisfactory,
I tried at mony a loom, til I geet to weave at factory;
I had not been long i' th' shade, before my merit took, sir,
I geet so weel on with trade, they made me Overlooker.

I dress'd myself up fine, thinks I – I'll cut a dash-on,
I geet a sweetheart, too, fear I should be out o' th' fashion;
Hoo [she] talked to me so fine – sed hoo wur no deceiver,
For weel off we should be, for hoo wur a dashing steam-loom weaver.

One night I came to town, and didn't happen bring her,
I scarcely had set down, to harken t' Star Inn singer,
When a chap, works side o' me, I didn't think him that deceiver,
He walk'd, and sit by me – side of him my steam-loom weaver.

I thought to let him sup [drink], but he put me in such fettle,
So to him I bristles up, to show I had a bit of mettle:
Thou'll leave that lass of mine, or I'll gi' thy chops a driver;
He says, Dunna thee come it so fine, for hoo's my dashing steam-loom weaver.

Next day to her I went, to see if hoo'd a cruel conscience,
Hee sed, Lad, rest thyself content, for it's nought but a bit of nonsense;
I met this chap next day, gin him o'er his chops a driver,
We fought a full hour up and down, thro' my dashing steam-loom weaver.

When we were on the ground, as hard as we could batter,
This girl came walking round, to see what wur the matter,
I purr'd him o'er his mug, hoo run at him in a fever,
Hoo pelted at him with her clog, so I won my steam-loom weaver.

We very soon geet friends, geet wed on Easter Sunday,
Wedding kept among our friends, all day on Easter Monday;
I geet good wage you see, what brass I mean to save, sir,
We are as content as aught can be, is me and my steam-loom weaver.

Women undoubtedly had the dominant share in romantic songs featuring factory workers, but in mining there was no contest, even before women were excluded from underground work in 1842. 'I do not know a blither old song than this,' wrote Robert Burns in 1792, when he sent these words, possibly having worked them over himself, to James Johnson in 1792 for his *Scots Musical Museum*:

My Collier Laddie[47]

Whare live ye, my bonie lass, and tell me how they ca' ye?
My name, she says, is Mistress Jean, and I follow the Collier laddie.
My name, she says, is Mistress Jean, and I follow the Collier laddie.
See you not yon hills and dales the sun shines on sae brawlie?
They a' are mine and they shall be thine,
gin ye'll leave your Collier laddie.
They a' are mine and they shall be thine,
gin ye'll leave your Collier laddie.

Ye shall gang in gay attire, weel buskit [dressed] up sae gaudy;
And ane to wait on every hand, gin ye'll leave your Collier laddie.
And ane to wait on every hand, gin ye'll leave your Collier laddie.
Tho' ye had a' the sun shines on, and the earth conceals sae lowly;
I wad turn my back on you and it a', and embrace my Collier laddie.
I wad turn my back on you and it a', and embrace my Collier laddie.

I can win my five pennies in a day an' spen 't at night fu' brawlie;
And make my bed in the Collier's neuk [corner], and lie down wi' my Collier laddie.
And make my bed in the Collier's neuk, and lie down wi' my Collier laddie.

Loove for love is the bargain for me, tho' the wee Cot-house should haud me;
And the warld before me to win my bread, and fair fa' [blessings on] my collier laddie!
And the warld before me to win my bread, and fair fa' my Collier laddie!

No earlier history of the song has emerged, but coal mining had begun in Ayrshire by 1790, and went back much earlier in Fife. 'My Collier Laddie' circulated orally well into the twentieth century, and adapted as 'The Plooman Laddie' was sung in farm workers' bothies until at least the 1930s.[48] The remaining verse of what was probably a fragmentary version, first published in 1769, is determinedly unsentimental:

My mither sent me to the well, she had better gane hersell,
I got the thing I dare nae tell, whistle o'er the lave owt.[49]

Some forty years later, when John Bell heard the same song sung in the streets of Newcastle-on-Tyne, it included this verse:

Sailor Lads gets Gold and Silver, soldier Lads gets nought but brass
I will have my Sailor lad because I am a Sailor lass.[50]

And at some stage the rivals became colliers and potters (1930s):

Colliery lads make gold and silver
Pottery lads make brass
'Oo would marry a Buslem [Burslem] thrower
When there's plenty of collier lads?[51]

Then colliers and factory lads in general, or weavers in particular (1950s):

Collier lads bring gold and silver,
Factory lads bring owt [anything] but brass,
Who'd be bothered with a two-loom waiver,
When there's plenty collier lads?[52]

Mary Thomason (1863-1937) of Leigh in Lancashire, an elementary teacher from the age of 13, and also a Co-operator and Wesleyan, wrote poems in both standard English and local dialect on religious and patriotic themes, but also on textile workers (tacklers, piecers, weavers) and colliers, dealing with strikes and unemployment as well as leisure and love. Some of these betray a familiarity with traditional lyrics:

Mother sent me for some water for some water to the well
Laughing there and waiting for me was that rascal Willie Bell,
Willie Bell's a forward rascal, coming there and courting me
And he kiss, kiss, kisses, kisses till I promise his to be.[53]

Thomason's poems can be a touch sentimental, but she unashamedly writes of the finer feelings of ordinary folk, as in:

A Factory Lassie[54]

I am just a factory lassie and lowly my estate,
But my fortune I'd not change with the greatest of the great.

Oh, I a priceless treasure have, a lover good and kind,
I would not barter his true love for all the gold e'er mined.

Love, love, Johnnie's love, love that's true and kind,
Love, love, true love, all the gold e'er mined
Is not worth my Johnnie's love, true and kind.

More money many maidens have, but these I envy not;
Wealth would have frightened my true love, then sad had been my lot.

My lover is a collier lad, a lad both good and kind,
I would not barter his true love for all the gold e'er mined.

Love, love, Johnnie's love, love that's good and kind,
Love, love,true love, all the gold e'er mined
Is not worth my Johnnie's love, true love and kind.

Another song entitled 'Collier Lads', sometimes more distinctively given as 'Brave Collier Lads' or 'The Gloucestershire Colliers', was widely popular, as a street ballad in Birmingham, Cheltenham, London, Manchester and Newcastle.[55] As in some of the factory girl ballads, the milkmaid and the collier meet in an idyllic setting reminiscent of an eighteenth-century pastoral, save that she promptly asks him whether he belongs to the union. He does not immediately reply; they kiss; and then he calls on 'noble gentlemen' not to 'pull down' miners' wages, 'nor break their unity'. This immediately wins over the milkmaid, who expresses the hope that the miners will 'win the day', and promises she will 'ever take your part'.

The Brave Collier Lads[56]

As I walk'd out one summer morn, all in the month of June
The flowers they were springing and the birds were in full tune
I overheard a lovely maid and this was all her theme,
Success attend the Collier Lads, for they are lads of fame.

I stepped up to her and bending of my knee,
I asked her pardon for making with her so free.

Your pardon it is granted young collier she said,
Pray do you belong to the brave union boys.

You may see I'm a collier as black as a sloe,
And all the night long I was working down below,
I do love a collier as I do love my life,
My father was a pitman all the days of his life.

Come now young collier and rest here awhile,
And when I have done milking I'll give you a smile,
He kissed her sweet lips while milking her cow,
And the lambs they were sporting all in the morning

Come all you noble gentlemen wherever that you be,
Do not pull down their wages to break their unity,
You see they hold like brothers, like sailors on the sea,
They do their best endeavours for their wives and families.

Then she claspt her eyes around him like Venus round the vine
You are my pretty collier lad you've won this heart of mine
And if that you do win the day as you have won my heart,
I'll crown you with honour and for ever take your part,

The colliers are the best of boys their work lies under ground,
And when they to the ale-house go they value not a crown,
They spend their money freely and pay before they go,
They work under ground while the stormy winds do blow.

So come all you pretty maidens where ever you may be,
A collier lad do not despise in any degree,
For if you use them well the same they'll do to thee,
There is none in the world like a pit-boy for me.

The sterner struggles which lay ahead for collier and factory worker inevitably involved sweethearts and wives, and also children.

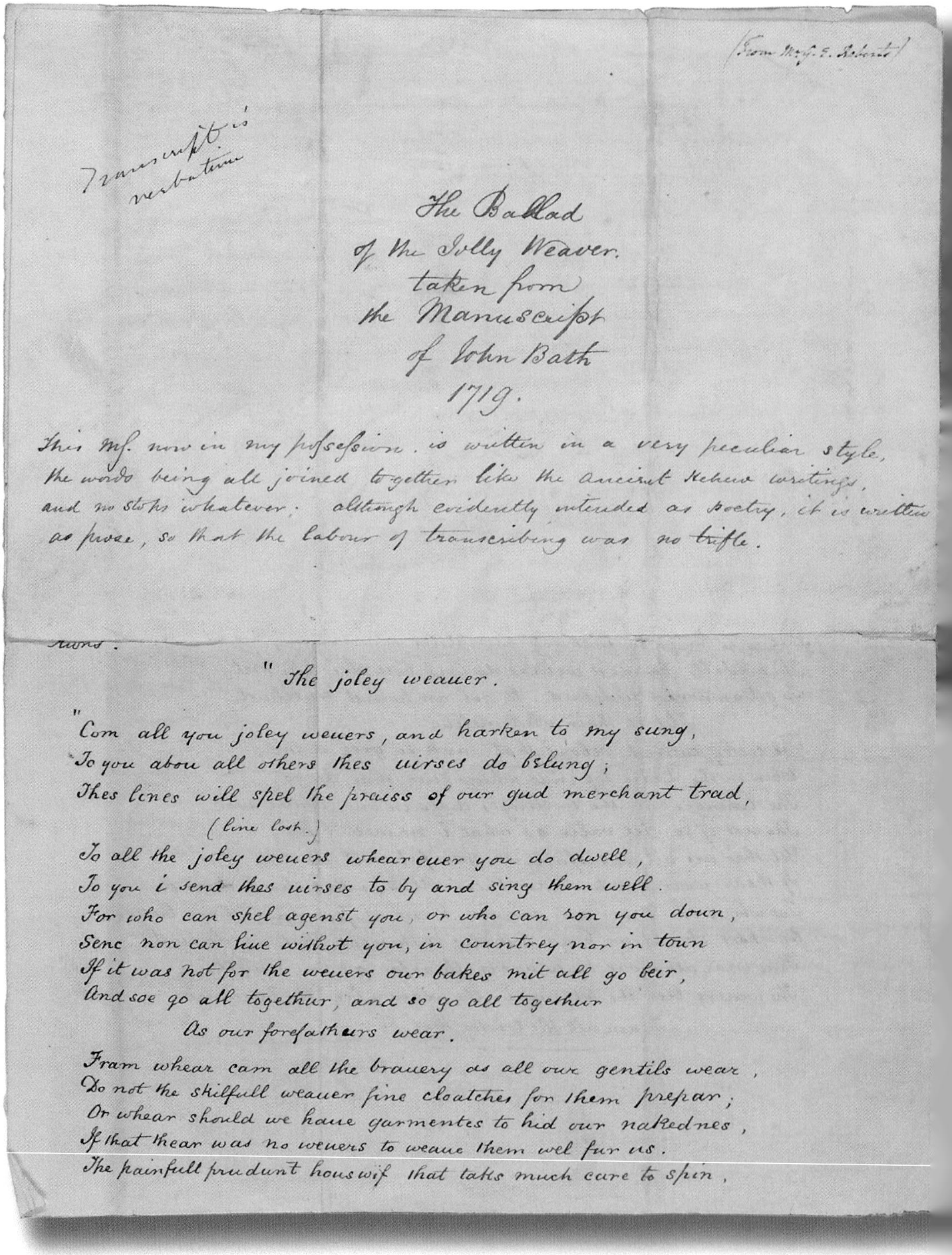

(From Mr J. E. Roberts)

Transcript is verbatim

The Ballad
of the Jolly Weaver.
taken from
the Manuscript
of John Bath
1719.

This MS. now in my possession, is written in a very peculiar style, the words being all joined together like the ancient Hebrew writings, and no stops whatever; although evidently intended as poetry, it is written as prose, so that the labour of transcribing was no trifle.

tions.

"The joley weauer.

"Com all you joley weuers, and harken to my sung,
To you abou all others thes uirses do bslung;
Thes lines will spel the praiss of our gud merchant trad,
(line lost.)
To all the joley weuers whear euer you do dwell,
To you i send thes uirses to by and sing them well.
For who can spel agenst you, or who can son you doun,
Senc non can liue withot you, in countrey nor in toun
If it was not for the weuers our bakes mit all go beir,
And soe go all togethur, and so go all togethur
As our forefathers wear.
Fram whear cam all the brauery as all our gentils wear,
Do not the skilfull weauer fine cloatches for them prepar;
Or whear should we haue garmentes to hid our nakednes,
If that thear was no weuers to weaue them wel fur us.
The painfull prudunt houswif that taks much care to spin,

'The Ballad of the Jolly Weaver', manuscript of 1719. 'Non can live without you, in countrey nor in town'. Courtesy of Worcestershire Record Office

3 The bitter cry of labour

Wages too small

Me thought I saw how wealthy men did grind the poor men's faces,
And greedily did prey on them, not pittying their cases:
They make them toyle and labour sore for wages too, too small;
The rich men in the taverns rore, but poor men pay for all'.

So runs a ballad of 1630 entitled 'The Poor Man Payes for All'.[1] The vehemence of its sentiments are echoed in other sheets of the same century such as 'All things be dear but poor Mens Labour; Or, The sad Complaint of Poor People' and 'The Troubles of this World; Or, Nothing Cheap but Poor Mens Labour'.[2] The various authors, as in many if not most ballads, are unknown. Sometimes we have a name and a little information.

Thomas Lanfiere, who came from Watchet in Somerset, wrote on the West Country clothing trade with a bitter cry of labour against capital', adding that 'a great part' of the history of the common people was 'to be learned only from their ballads'.[3]

'The Clothiers Delight: OR, The Rich Mens Joy, and the Poor Mens Sorrow. Wherein is exprest the craftiness and subtility of many Clothiers in England, by beating down their Work-mens wages', to give it its full title, was printed in London between 1674 and 1679 for F. Coles, T. Vere, J. Wright and J. Clarke.[4] Of the three possible tunes prescribed, 'Monk hath confounded', 'Jenny, come tie my cravat' and 'Packington's Pound', the relentless rhythm of the last perfectly matches the ballad's remorseless text:

The Clothiers Delight[4]

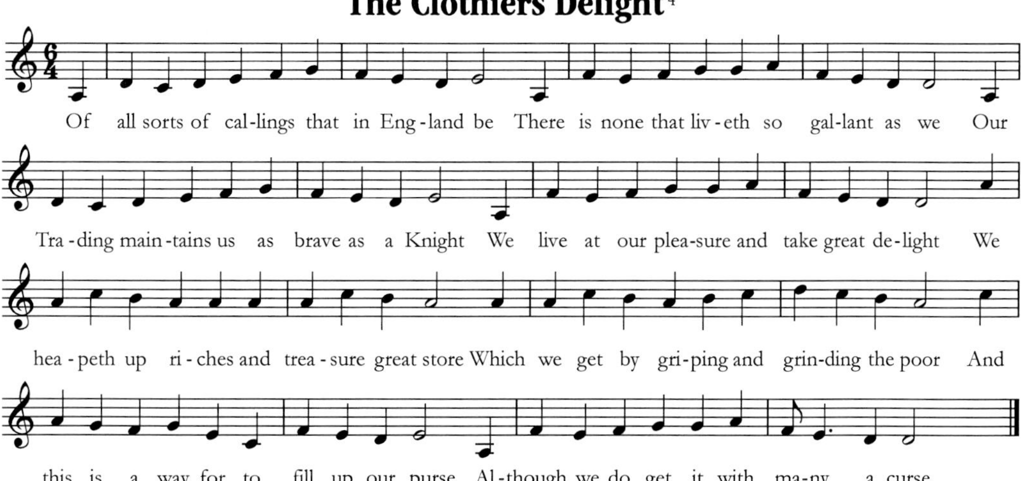

Of all sorts of callings that in England be,
There is none that liveth so gallant as we:
Our Trading maintains us as brave as a Knight,
We live at our pleasure and taketh delight:
We heapeth up riches and treasure great store,
Which we get by griping and grinding the poor.

[Chorus]
And this is a way for to fill up our purse,
Although we do get it with many a curse.

Throughout the whole Kingdom, in Country and Town,
There is no danger of our Trade going down,
So long as the Comber can work with his Comb,
And also the Weaver weave with his Lomb;
The Tucker [fuller] and Spinner that spins all the year,
We will make them earn their wages full dear.

In former ages we us'd to give,
So that our Work-folks like farmers did live;
But the times are altered, we will make them know,
All we can for to bring them under our Bow;
We will make them to work hard for Six pence a day,
Though a shilling they deserve if they had their just pay.

And first for the Combers we will bring them down
From Eight groats a score unto Half a Crown: [that is over 50%]
If at all they murmur, and say 'tis too small,
We bid them cho[o]se whether they will work at all.
We'l make them believe that Trading is bad,
We care not a pin, though they are ne'r so sad.

We'l make the poor Weavers work at a low rate,
We'l find fault where no fault, and so we will bate:
If Trading grows dead, we will presently shew it:
But if it grows good, they never shall know it;
We'l tell them that Cloath beyond Sea will not go,
We care not whether we keep cloathing or no.

The arguments are amazingly familiar even today. To increase profit, wages are reduced, on the pretext that trade is poor and exports are down.

Workers who object are invited to leave; those who stay are further penalised by the operation of a truck system: payment in kind rather than in cash: 'We have Bread and Bacon, and Butter that's good, With Oatmeal and Salt that is wholesome for food; We have Sope and Candles whereby to give light, That you may work by them so long as you have light.' It is richly ironic that out-workers must buy candles at inflated prices in order to keep on earning at reduced rates. The result of the employers' parsimony is:

> And thus we do gain all our Wealth and Estate,
> By many poor men that works early and late;
> If it were not for those that do labour full hard,
> We might go and hang ourselves without regard:
> The Combers, and Weavers, and Tuckers also,
> With the Spinners that worketh for Wages full low.
>
> Then hey for the Cloathing Trade, it goes on brave,
> We scorn for to toyl and moyl, nor yet to slave.
> Our Work-men do work hard, but we live at ease,
> We go where we will, and come when we please:
> We hoard up our bags of Silver and Gold;
> But conscience and charity with us is cold:
> By poor peoples labour we fill up our purse;
> Although we do get it with many a curse.

The ballad refers to 'our Work-men', but the spinners at least (threatened, according to one verse, with being obliged to process three pounds of wool for the price of two) would have been women. Women's labour would be at a premium in factories, which in time drew in Lanfiere's combers, spinners, weavers and many other outworkers.

Keep your shuttles in play

By the mid-nineteenth century factories were a routine part of the physical and mental landscape, but only a generation earlier employers were still struggling to impose the system. Workers were wary both of the buildings, which bore an uncanny resemblance to workhouses and gaols (the Round Mill at Belper deliberately followed the pattern of a Benthamite Panopticon prison, and an overseer at the centre had a clear view of what went on in all the eight segments), and of the harsh discipline enforced by beatings and fines, sacking and blacklisting. A powerful ballad, 'The Weavers' Crime',[5] reflects the transition from

John Heathcoat's Mill at Loughborough, which was attacked by armed Luddites in 1816 (see p. 124). Picture courtesy of Malcolm Hornsby.

domestic to factory working and reproves the new regime. It was printed in Manchester, by G. Jacques, between 1840 and 1845. The 'crime' was presumably the offences for which weavers (and other workers) could be fined or disciplined. John Harland gave the awkward and unconvincing title of 'Hand-loom *v.* Power-loom' (see p. 30) to the version 'sung by John Grimshaw, better known by his sobriquet of "Common", of Gorton, near Manchester'[6]. One wonders whether the nickname was to distinguish Grimshaw from his namesake, Robert, the burning down of whose unpopular factory in Gorton was celebrated in a ballad quoted in Chapter 4, p. 21. John Grimshaw's singing was also the source of 'The Hand-loom Weavers' Lament',[7] which bears the marks of having been circulating before 1815:

> You say that Bonyparty he's been the spoil of all,
> And that we have got reason to pray for his downfall;
> Now Bonyparty's dead and gone, and it is plainly shown
> That we have bigger tyrants in Boneys of our own.

Grimshaw's version of 'Hand-loom *v.* Power-loom' may well predate the Jacques broadside, which extends its appeal from weavers to all factory workers, and adds a curious and enigmatic final verse:

Weavers' Crime[5]

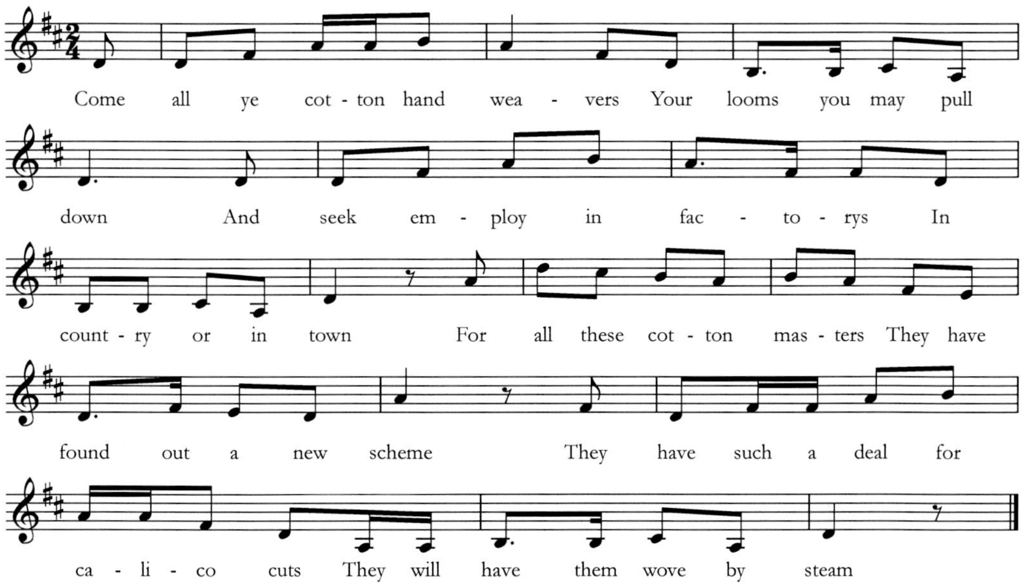

Come all ye cotton hand weavers,
Your looms you may pull down,
And seek employ in factorys
In country or in town.
For all these cotton masters
They have found out a new scheme,
They have such a deal for calico cuts
They will have them wove by steam.

You may go into a loom shop,
See three or four pairs of looms
There moulderin standing empty,
More cumbrance to the room
And if you ask the reason why,
The old mother will tell you plain,
My daughters they have forsaken them,
And gone to work by steam.

There sow makers and dressers,
And some are making warps,
While these pincop spinners
Must mind their flats and sharps,
For if one end slips under,

And that by chance it may,
The weaver cries, my piece is marred,
You have one shilling to pay.

Then comes the gurly [?surly] winder,
He says my twist is marred,
It's full of snarls and soft bad ends,
I have roved out many yards,
I shall certainly tell the master,
Or the Jos when he comes in,
They will daub you down one shilling to pay
And money comes rolling in.

Next comes on is the weaver's turn,
For they must not escape,
To enlarge their master's fortune,

They do in every shape,
Bad edges and thin places,
One end out or afloat,
Which causes them to scribe you down,
Two, three [pence], or a groat.

Come all you factory workmen,
You must rise up very soon,
And be confined in factory,
From morning until noon,
You must not walk out in your garden,
By two or three hours a day,
But you must stand at their command,
And keep their shuttles in play.

The interior of Spring Mills, Llanidloes. Notice the overhead system of pulleys and drive belts to power the looms. (John Thomas Collection) By permission of The National Library of Wales.

There will be good times for work, folks,
When Old England is at an end,
For combined laws and steam engines,
They make poor people bend,
There is no redress here to be found,
That every workman sees,
For we are used like galley slaves
[All] in West Indies.

The writer clearly expected readers (or hearers) of the ballad to be familiar with technical terms such as 'sow' (size), which 'dressers' applied to the warp threads. (The dressers were doomed to disappear as the dressing frame invented in 1803 gradually spread through the industry.) 'Pincops' were pear-shaped cops or rolls of yarn of appropriate dimensions for the weft in power-looms. The 'Jos' (or joss) was the head man, who imposed fines for various faults, including a 'float' – a flaw caused when the shuttle passed over the threads of the warp instead of in between them.

There were also penalties for lateness. Thomas Dodd described seeing, 'early in the morning, at Stockport and other places, from fifty to a hundred men, women, and children, standing at the door of a factory, locked out for being *half a minute* [his italics] too late', and discovering after they were let in that it would take them until 10 or 11 am to earn their respective fines of 3d., 2d. and 1d. apiece.[8] As late as 1911 workers at a weaving factory in Ulster were fined 2d. for being late in the morning, and 3d. for being late after a meal break.

There were also a series of penalties for other operatives, including deductions from the wages of 'WEAVERS where a beam of yarn is not evenly and well woven into good cloth and taken only at cut marks, and is not free from crammed or empty splits, dropped warp, yarn out, weft slubs or ravels, floats, catches, shires, rough selvages, wrong drafts, broken shots, broken patterns, dirt stains, and all other imperfections that a worker can be reasonably expected to avoid.'[9]

By contrast, there were those who revelled in factory work: this had been the case since the earliest days of the Industrial Revolution. John Trafford Clegg (1857–1895) worked for a time in a cotton mill at Glossop owned by his father. His exuberant response to factory life in his 'Weighver's Song' could no doubt have been shared by ordinary workers, at least on a good day:

Weighver's Song[10]

Deawn i' th' shed on a summer's day,
Th' owd sun shinin through th' white-weshed top;
Brids on th' slate are chirpin away,
An' aw whistle a tune to every cop;
Clattherin loom an' whirlin' wheel,
Flyin' shuttle an' steady reed –
This is wark to make a mon feel
There's wur jobs nor weighvin i' time o' need. . . .

Lads an' lasses stonnin i' rows,
Wortchin away fro morn to neet;
Tenters – Bobs, Sals, Bettys, an' Joes –
Runnin abeaut o' their nimble feet,
Keepin time to a steady tune
Played bi th' engine fro leet to dark
Keepin time to a steady tune
Played bi th' engine fro leet to dark
(Feed him wi waything an coal, beaut spoon,
An' he's olez reet for another day's wark).[10]

At Blackburn, William Woodruff's father, had he known the poem, would have appreciated its sentiments: 'I think he loved the mills; he loved the humming, clattering machinery, the oil and the dirt. He started each week with a clean, collarless cotton shirt, buttoned at the neck, and cheap, blue overalls. The sleeves of his shirt were rolled up to the elbow. When he was a tackler, he wore a natty red neckerchief and a fustian waistcoat, which we thought dandy.'[11]

Some women, too, were high-spirited in their responses to working life. 'The Factory Girl'[12] shows a lively and independent attitude:

The Factory Girl[12]

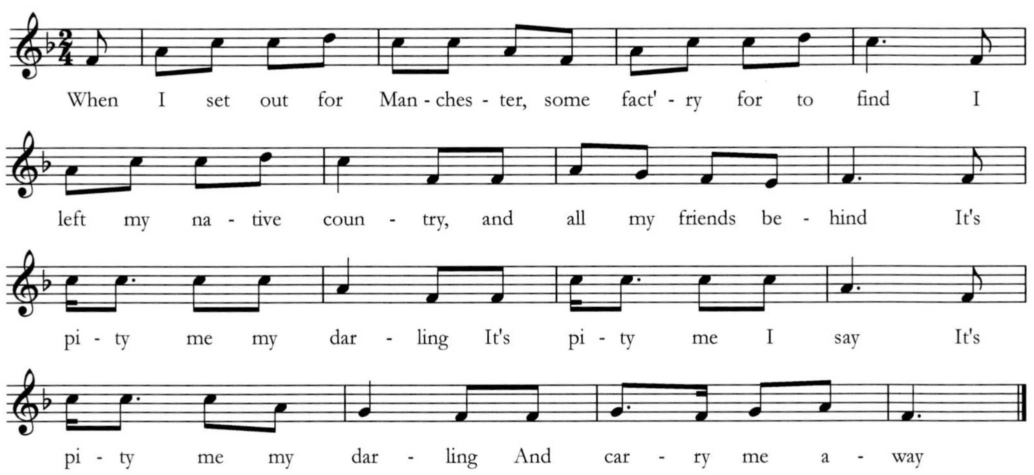

When I set out for Manchester, some factory for to find,
I left my native country, and all my friends behind.
Chorus – Sing ter re a re I re O.

But now I am in Manchester, and summoned by the bell,
I think more of the factory girls than of my native dell.

The factory bell begins to ring, and we must all obey,
And to our old employment go, or else be turned away.

My overseer has cut my wages down to ten-and-six a week,
And before I'll work for that, my true love's heart I'll seek.

So far, we are clearly with an Irish exile in Lancashire, but the next stanza whisks us to the USA:

I do not like my overseer, I do not mean to stay,
I mean to hire some depot cab to carry me away.

It is possible that the song started life in the English Manchester, where wages in 1835 averaged 11s. for a 69-hour week, and moved to one of the two American Manchesters (those in Connecticut and New Hampshire – there are thirteen others) which in the nineteenth century were mill towns where immigrants from the north-west of England undoubtedly helped to establish the textile industry. The ballad narrator carries on to make a spirited and extended valediction to factory life:

No more I'll oil my picker rod, no more I'll brush my loom,
No more I'll scour my nasty floor, all in the weaving-room.

No more I'll draw the thread All through the harness eye,
No more I'll say, "My work goes so, O dear me, I shall die".

No more they'll come to me and say, "Your ends they are all down",
While I am in the middle of the room, or acting out the clown.

No more I'll go to the overseer to come and fix my loom;
No more I'll go to him and say, "May I stay out till noon?"

Despite similarly exacting work, women in the linen mills of Northern Ireland displayed a similar vivacity. Their lore and has been explored in a fine book by Betty Messenger, *Picking up the Linen Threads*, which is full of lively banter and anecdote, jokes and songs. Of the last, one woman said: 'You stood all day at your work and sung them songs. . . . We had no pay hardly, but we were happy'. Songs often expressed rivalry between different workers:

You Will Easy Know a Weaver[13]

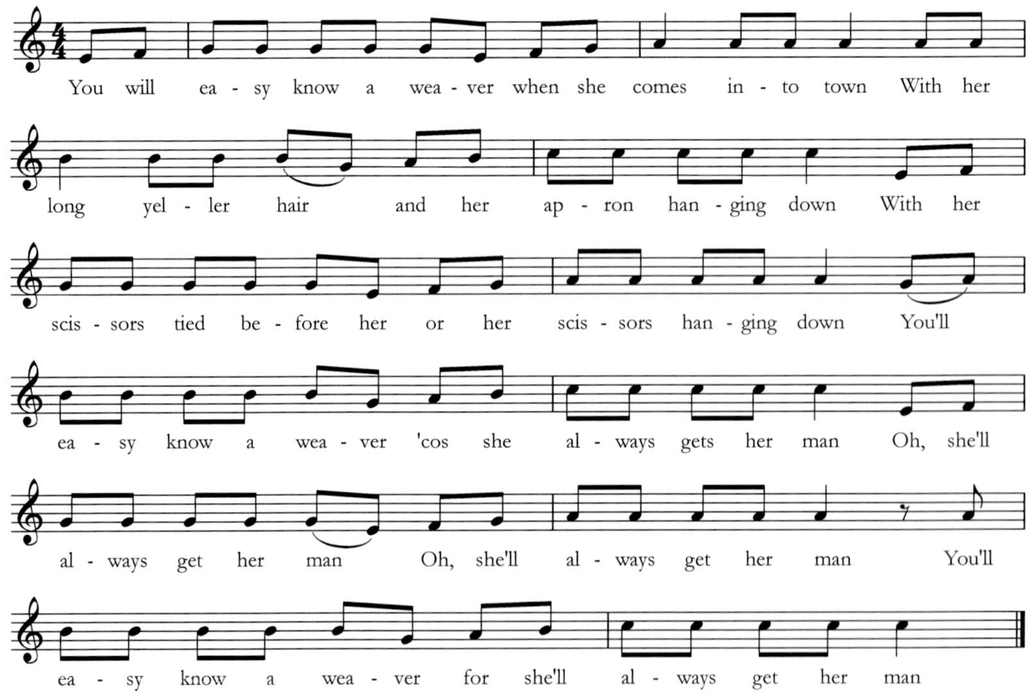

You will easy know a weaver when she goes down to town,
With her long yeller hair and her apron hanging down,
With her scissors tied before her or her scissors in her hand,
You'll easy know a weaver for she'll always get her man.

Using the same tune, this was re-worked by doffers, both negatively:

> You will easy know a weaver when she comes into town,
> With her oul' tatty hair, and her stockin's hangin' down,
> And her apron tied before her, and her scissors in her hand,
> You will easy know a weaver, for she'll never get a man.

and positively:

> You will easy know a doffer, when she comes into town,
> With her long yeller hair, and her ringlets hangin' down,
> And her rubber tied before her, and her picker in her hand,
> You will easy know a doffer, for she'll always get her man.[13]

Doffers worked in a spinning room, within which:

> [There] was a *spinning master*, who spent much of his time walking up and down the pass seeing that all was functioning smoothly. Also acting as supervisors were *doffing mistresses*. They saw to it that full bobbins of spun yarn were *doffed* from each machine and replaced with empty bobbins to be filled. Those who did the actual doffing were children, most of whom began work under the half-time system, dividing the workweek between school and mill. Although this method of employment in textile industries, which persisted until after the First World War, was essentially the same as that legalized by the English Factory Act of 1833 and regularized in 1844, some important modifications had been made… For example, by 1901, the legal starting age had been raised from eight to twelve years, and, in Ireland, alternate days in school and mill had replaced the practice of having children work half a day and attend school the other half.[14]

I know of no study like that of Messenger on mill workers in England, but it is clear that a sub-culture existed, judging from rare examples like 'The Doffers of Old Whittam's Mill', recorded in 1975 from John Gregson of Burnley, who commented:

> Everybody knew that – … it's only a ditty … Whittam's is the one down there by the gate with the clock. Well, doffers in Burnley, well, doffers anywhere was the lowest textile workers you got. A very dirty job, and they had to work in their stockinged feet. Bare feet, I should say. Weavers would know – weavers didn't congregate with doffers, did they? [N]or [did] winders. Winders and weavers were the elected cotton people.

The Doffers of Old Whittam's Mill[15]

Oh the doffers of old Whittam's Mill,
They laugh as they work at their till [toil],
And the blouses they wear and the style of their hair
Is enough to make anyone ill.
Their stockings are full of big holes,
Their clogs are worn down to the soles,
And when out in the street little children will shout:
'Hello, the doffers of old Whittam's Mill.'

The tune here seems to be a variation on 'In the Shade of the Old Apple Tree', a music hall piece of 1905. The Belfast doffers, like the soldiers of the First World War, drew extensively both on hymns and music hall songs as vehicles for their own lyrics.

The plight of handloom weavers left outside the factory system created an undertow of gloom, which persisted for many decades. In 1823, a writer observed that, thanks to the dressing frame, 'a boy or girl, 14 or 15 years of age, can manage two steam looms, and with their help can weave three and a half times as much as the best hand weaver'.[16] The problems of such weavers in Lancashire were compounded by the depression which followed the end of the Napoleonic Wars: during the period between 1814 and 1832 their average weekly earnings fell from between 18 and 24s. to only 5 or 6s. The song, 'Jone o' Grinfield', evokes with grim humour both the deep distress of a handloom weaver and the resulting bitter anger - which in due course would contribute to the rise of Chartism.

Jone o'Grinfield[17]

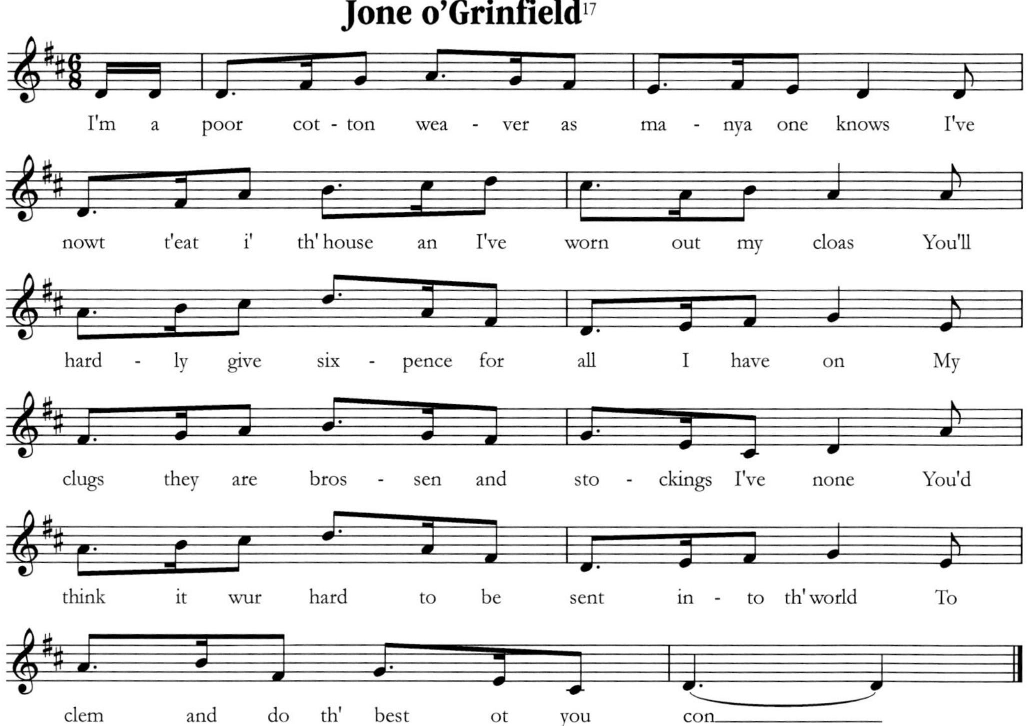

I'm a poor cotton weaver as many one knows,
I've nowt to eat i'th house an I've worn out my cloas,
You'd hardly give sixpence for all I have on,
My clugs they are brossen and stockings I've none,
You'd think it wur hard to be sent into th' world,
To clem [starve] and do th' best ot you con.

Our church parson kept telling us long,
We should have better times if we'd hold our tongues,
I've houden my tongue till I can hardly draw breath,
I think i' my heart he means to clem me to death;
I know he lives weel by backbiting the de'il,
But he never picked o'er [wove] in his life.

I tarried six week an thought each day wur t'last,
I tarried and shifted [made do] till now I'm quite fast;

I lived on nettles while nettles were good,
An Waterloo porridge were best of my food;
I'm telling you true I can find folks enew [enough],
That are living no better than me.

Old Bill o' Dan's sent bailiffs one day,
For a shop score I owed him that I could not pay,
But he wur too late for old Bill o' Bent,
Had sent tit [horse] and cart and taen goods for rent,
We had nou [nowt] bur a stoo [stool], that wur a seat for two,
And on it cowered Margit and me.

The bailiffs looked round as sly as a mouse,
When they saw aw things were taen out ot house,
Says one to the other all's gone thou may see,
Aw sad lads never fret you're welcome to me;
They made no more ado, but nipp'd up th'owd stoo,
And we both went wack upoth flags.

I geet howd of Margit for hoo [her] wur stricken sick,
Hoo sed hoo ne'er had such a bang sin hoo wur wick [alive]
The bailiffs scoured off with owd stoo on their backs,
They would not have cared had they brook our necks,
They're mad at owd Bent cos he's taen goods for rent,
And wuur ready to flee [skin] us alive.

I sed to our Margit as we lay upoth floor,
We shall never be lower in this world I'm sure,
But if we alter I'm sure we mun mend,
For I think in my heart we are both at far end,
For meat we have none nor looms to weave on,
Egad they're as weel lost as found.

Then I geet up my piece and I took it em back
I scarcely dare speak mester looked so black,
He said you wur o'erpaid last time you coom,
I said if I wur 'twas for weaving 'bout loom;
In a mind as I'm in I'll ne'er pick o'er again,
For I've woven myself toth' fur end.

Then aw coom out and left him to chew that,
When aw thought again aw wur vext till aw sweat,

To think that we mun work to keep them and awth set,
All the day o' my life and still be in their debt;
So I'll give o'er trade an work with a spade,
Or go and break stones upoth road.

Our Margit declared if hoo'd clos to put on,
Hoo'd go up to Lundun an see the big mon
An if things didn't alter when hoo had been,
Hoo swears hoo'll feight blood up toth e'en,
Hoo's nought again th'Queen, but likes a fair thing,
An hoo says hoo can tell when hoo's hurt.

This probably dates from soon after 1815, but Harland, who published a version under the title of 'Jone o' Grinfilt Junior', 'taken down from the singing of an old hand-loom weaver at Droylsden', described it fifty years later as 'still a favourite in many parts of Lancashire'.[18] A sheet issued by Bebbington of Manchester, with 'queen' replacing 'king' of earlier versions in the penultimate line, dates from between 1856 and 1861. Also known as 'The Oldham Weaver', the ballad features in truncated and attenuated form in chapter 4 of Elizabeth Gaskell's novel of working class life in Manchester, *Mary Barton* (1848). The footprint of 'Jone o' Grinfield' does not seem to have extended beyond Lancashire and possibly Cheshire. (I take 'The Four Loom Weaver'[19] to be Ewan MacColl's reworking of 'Jone o' Greenfield', though he claimed it was 'taken down from Becket Whitehead of Delph, near Oldham, Lancashire. Attributed to John o' Greenfield, jnr., weaver and balladmonger'.[20] However, when Seamus Ennis recorded Whitehead's repertoire in 1952[21] it did not include 'The Four Loom Weaver'; and no other version, either oral or printed, has turned up elsewhere).

A view of life within the factory was voiced by Samuel Laycock (1826–1893) when conditions were worsened by the necessity of using cotton from Shurat in India, as, during the American Civil War, the Northern states blockaded Southern ports, preventing the customary import of American cotton. The Indian cotton was inferior, and for generations afterwards the word Shurat was used in Lancashire as a synonym for rubbish. At the same time the employers took advantage of the shortage of work to force down wages to as little as 4 or 5s. a week. Despite their difficulties, cotton spinners and weavers, with Manchester in the forefront, supported the North (whereas Liverpool favoured the South).

Laycock, the son of a handloom weaver, was born at Marsden on the Yorkshire side of the Pennines. He started work in a woollen mill at the age

of nine, earning two shillings a week for six days' work, from six in the morning until eight at night. In 1837 the family moved to Stalybridge in Lancashire, where Laycock worked as a power-loom cotton weaver for seventeen years, then became a cloth-looker. Thanks to an education almost entirely acquired in Sunday schools he began writing poems, and achieved considerable success when he was out of work in 1862 with his *Lyrics of the Cotton Famine*. He later published a large number of poems, many of them worthy but dull. However, they also include homely,

Jack o' t' Bog Eggs, one of the few remaining handloom weavers at the end of the century, working a pair of looms at Wadsworth in 1896. Courtesy of the Hebden Bridge Local History Society Archive.

affectionate and tender pieces such as 'Bowton's Yard' and 'Welcome, Bonny Brid'.

These poems circulated orally well into the first half of the twentieth century, and were revived in the second half by folksingers such as Harry Boardman who specialised in Lancashire folk songs.[22] Boardman also took up Laycock's 'Shurat Weaver's Song',[23] which in contrast is both work- and world-weary:

Shurat Weaver's Song[23]

Confound it! Aw ne'er wur so woven before,
Mi back's welly brocken, mi fingers are sore;
Aw've bin starin' an' rootin' among this Shurat,
Till aw'm vert near getten as bloint as a bat.

Every toime aw go in wi' mi cuts [lengths of cloth] to owd Joe,
He gies mi a cursin', an' bates me [reduces price] an' o;
Aw've a warp i' one loom wi' booath selvedges marr'd, [spoiled]
An' th' other's as bad for he's dress'd it to' hard.

Aw wish aw wur fur enuff off, eawt o' th' road,
For o' weavin' this rubbitch aw'm getting' reet stow'd; [fed up]
Aw've nowt i' this world to lie deawn on but straw,
For aw've only eight shillin' this fortni't to draw.

The themes of prolonged poverty, shortage of food, furniture lost and fault found with work exhibit marked similarities (and not merely because of the dialect) with 'Jone o' Greenfield' – to the extent that one wonders whether Laycock knew the earlier ballad. On the other hand, the Shurat weaver has the luxury of holiday clothes, even if they have been pawned ('An' mi halliday clooas are o on 'em "up th' speawt"'). In addition, he rather weakly hopes that the American Civil War will end:

Oh, dear! Iv yon Yankees could only just see
Heaw they're clemmin' an' starvin' poor weavers loike me,
Aw think they'd soon settle their bother, an' strive
To send us some cotton to keep us alive.

The most striking difference between the two songs, however, is that instead of the raw anger of Jone o' Greenfield's (or rather his wife's) conclusion, Laycock piously extols the virtues of charity, a vein which continued in some of the songs of the unemployed until the twentieth century:

Come give us a lift, yo' 'at han owt to give,
An' help yo're poor brothers an' sisters to live;
Be kind, an' be tender to th' needy an' poor,
An' we'll promise when th' times mend we'll ax yo' no moor.

It is possible that Laycock's tone derived from an anxiety to raise money; if so, it is similar to that employed in many ballads dealing with industrial disasters and also with unemployment.

On the other hand, 'Jone o' Greenfield', like other ballads which did not conceal their anger, spoke directly to those suffering from low pay and poor conditions, such as the jute mill workers of Dundee. The shifters of Dundee (equivalent to the doffers of cotton mills) worked with spinners and piecers on the 'flett', the platform on which spinning machinery stood. Their wage of 10s. 9d. a week was traditionally paid, just before the First World War, in the form of a gold half-sovereign and nine pennies.

Union banner of the Dundee Jute and Flax Workers Union established in 1906. In this new union half of the Executive Committee had to be women.

One of the workers, the redoubtable Mary Brooksbank (1897–1980), who recalled first going on strike in 1912, wrote this song, based on a fragment heard in the mill:

The Jute Mill Song[24]

Oh dear me, the mill's gaen fest,
The puir wee shifters cannae get their rest.
Shiftin' bobbins, coorse and fine,
They fairly mak you work for your ten and nine.

Oh dear me, I wish the day was done,
A-rinnin' up and doon the pass is no nae fun;
Shiftin', piecin', spinnin', warp, weft and twine,
To feed and clothe my bairnie affen ten and nine.

Oh dear me, the world's ill divided:
Them that work the hardest are the least provided,
But I'll just bide contented, dark days or fine,
But there's no much pleasure living affen ten and nine.

Another song like Mary's, probably filled out from fragments, was 'Poverty Knock'. According to the singer, Tom Daniel (1890–1970), it dated from the time of the early power-looms, when 'Owing to the low wages and the slow dreary "knockity knock" sound of the looms, weavers were called "Poverty knockers".'[25] William Woodruff, who when he was six or seven (which would have been in 1921 or 1922) first took his father's hot-pot dinner to him in a Blackburn weaving shed, represented the sound differently:

> Inside, I was overwhelmed by the steam, the heat, the clatter, the smell of gas and the shattering din of the machines. Too frightened to move, I froze where I was. Hundreds of looms stretched as far as I could see – all of them crashing frantically. Most of the workers were women and young girls. I was mesmerised by the army of picking sticks jerking backward and forward, ready to give me a crack on the head. The sticks hit the shuttles across the loom faster than I could watch: lat ti tat. Lat ti tat. Lat ti tat.[26]

Tom Daniel, born in Pudsey, claimed to have first heard the song 'Poverty Knock' soon after starting work in a Batley woollen mill in 1905. It was first recorded from him in 1964 by the folklorist A.E. Green, who later inclined to the opinion that Daniel could have written much of it himself. The complete absence of a sighting from any other traditional singer[27] could well support the point; and when Daniel published it, in late 1965 or early 1966, the sub-title of his eight-page *Yorkshire Broadsheet* was *Folk songs collected, revised or rewritten, by Tommy Daniel*. Even so, he was indubitably a West Riding working-class singer and songwriter who dealt with local conditions. He demonstrated, according to Green, 'the kind of ironic, inward-looking humour which seems to be a special property of industrial song'.[28]

Poverty Knock[29]

(Chorus)
Poverty, poverty knock, my loom is a-sayin' all day,
Poverty, poverty knock, gaffer's too skinny to pay.
Poverty, poverty knock, keepin' one eye on the clock.
I know I can guttle [eat] when I hear my shuttle go
Poverty, poverty knock.

Up every mornin' at five, I wonder that we keep alive;
Tired and yawnin' on the cold mornin',
It's back to the dreary old drive.

Oh dear, we're goin' to be late; gaffer is stood at the gate.
We're out o' pocket, our wages they're dockit,
We'll 'a' to buy grub on the slate.

And when our wages they'll bring we're often short of a string
[length of cloth];
And while we are fratchin' [quarrelling] wi' gaffer for snatchin',
We know to his brass he will cling.

We've got to wet our own yarn by dippin' it into the tarn;
It's wet and soggy and makes us feel groggy,
And there's mice in that dirty old barn.

Oh dear, my poor 'ead it sings; I should have woven three strings,
But threads are breakin' and my back is achin',
Oh dear, I wish I had wings.

Sometimes a shuttle flies out and gives some poor woman a clout.
There she lies bleedin' but nobody's 'eedin;
Who's goin' to carry her out?

Tuner [maintenance man] should tackle my loom: 'e'd rather sit on his bum.
'E's far too busy a-courtin' our Lizzie,
And I cannot get 'im to come.

Lizzie's so easy led, I think that 'e takes her to bed.
She always was skinny, now look at her pinny,
I think it's high time they was wed.

The song displays the resilient humour of workers, while also reflecting their struggles with employers over hours, pay and conditions. It also raises the matter of factory accidents. On occasion, such incidents were very serious.

Waiting for news

In June 1848 a boiler explosion at the Royal Sovereign Mill at Preston, one of the oldest cotton mills in the town, killed seven workers, including Elizabeth Lower, a cop-skewerer, aged 13, and James Ashton, an engine-tenter, aged 17. The local newspaper, the *Preston Guardian*, reported that the factory had 'been the scene of many mishaps'.[30] The local printer, John Harkness, issued a ballad on the subject:

A Copy of Verses composed on the Accident at Preston, on the Boiler Explosion at the Royal Sovereign[31]

You tender hearted Christians, I pray you will attend,
To this sad lamentation that lately has been penn'd;
At the Royal Sovereign Factory, at Preston town we hear,
Where seven work people lost their lives, and others wounded severe.
It was one Saturday morning, just at breakfast time,

The boiler burst asunder all in a moment's time,
And spread awful destruction to all who were standing nigh,
And sent them to Eternity, to meet their Maker's eye.

The lugubrious tone continues throughout, relieved only by the consoling thought that the victims 'have left this wicked world, and have done with earthly care', and the news that 'the worthy Mayor of Preston has given contributions, and hopes you will do the same'. No indignation is expressed, and no question is raised as to the cause of the accident. It is significant that, rather than exhorting people to strive to improve their working conditions, he exhorts them to prepare to meet their God in case an accident happens.

A similar cast of mind is often found in reactions to mining disasters. Ballads reflected on the sudden end to miners' lives and the potential plight of their dependents, and by doing so sought to stimulate charity, as well as he sale of copies of the sheets. By a tacit convention, anger and indignation did not feature, one presumes in order not to offend potential donors. Miners' protests were vehement enough on other occasions (see below).

The hazards and routines of work underground are explored in 'Five in the Morning', a ballad published in about 1870 by T. Pearson of Manchester.[32] As well as the steady yearly attrition of accidents, characterised in a telling phrase quoted by John Benson as 'a colliery disaster in instalments',[33] which caused individual injuries and deaths, there were recurrent disasters which left large numbers of victims.

Joseph Skipsey wrote in 1862 a moving and dignified poem which he read at meetings to raise funds for the relatives of the 204 workers, ranging in age from 10 to 71, who were killed by choke damp at the Hester Pit, New Hartley, Northumberland, when half the beam of the massive steam engine broke off and sealed the only shaft. Skipsey avoids neither cliché ('old homestead', 'daily bread') nor bathos ('Each bosom thuds, as each his duds, He snatches . . .'), and he veers at times into sentimentality and religiosity. Yet the piece has genuine strength of diction ('streams of sweat still glue, The stour into their skins'), as well as telling reiteration, which echoes the incremental repetition of traditional balladry. In 'The Hartley Calamity'.[34] Skipsey announces disaster at the outset, but cleverly draws back to evoke a normal day's work:

The Hartley Calamity[34]

The Hartley men are noble, and
Ye'll hear a tale of woe;
I'll tell the doom of the Hartley men
– The year of sixty-two.

'Twas on a Thursday morning, on
The first month of the year,
When there befell the thing that well
May rend the heart to hear.

Ere chanticleer with music rare
Awakes the old homestead,
The Hartley men are up and off
To earn their daily bread.

On, on they toil; with heat they broil,
And streams of sweat still glue
The stour into their skins, till they
Are black as the coal they hew.

Now to and fro the putters go
The wagons to and fro,
And clang on clang of wheel and hoof
Ring in the mine below.

Then, 'the din and strife of human life' are dramatically interrupted by 'a shock', which causes miners to rush towards the shaft. They find it blocked, and set about clearing it. Twice they pause, thinking they hear sounds of rescuers above; twice they are disappointed. Sleep, from which they will not awake, gradually takes a son, a father and a brother. On the surface:

> ...fathers and mothers, and sisters and brothers –
> The lover and the new-made bride –
> A vigil kept for those who slept,
> From eve to morning tide.
>
> But they slept – still sleep – in silence dread,
> Two hundred old and young,
> To awake when heaven and earth have sped
> And the last dread trumpet sung!

The disaster at New Hartley was one of the twenty-four mine accidents of various kinds between 1835 and 1913 in which over a hundred lives were lost.[35] (During the same period the number of miners rose to 1,130,000). In addition, according to Benson, 'by the end of the [nineteenth] century, if not before, more working days were lost from injuries than as a result of the far better-known strikes and lockouts'. He adds: 'Between 1868 and 1919 a miner was killed every six hours, seriously injured every two hours, and injured badly enough to need a day off work every two or three minutes'. In addition, according to Benson, 'by the end of the [nineteenth] century, if not before, more working days were lost from injuries than as a result of the far better-known strikes and lockouts.'[36] (During the same period the number of miners rose to 1,130,000.)

'The families of miners lived always in the shadow of calamity,' wrote J.F.C. Harrison. '"Waiting for news" was a common theme of photographs and drawings depicting crowds of wives and relatives wandering around the pithead.'[37] Nor did these losses end with the nineteenth century.

They were frequently accompanied throughout the coalfields of England, Scotland and Wales by ballads. These, mostly anonymous, date mainly from the mid-nineteenth century onwards, though the earliest I have seen is 'The Submissive Petition of the Distressed Hugh Boyd, late Collier in Darnel, near Sheffield, in the West-riding of Yorkshire. Who was confined Six Days and fourteen Hours under ground, with six more, by reason of the roof falling upon them, by which Accident he lost two of his Fingers, which renders him incapable of gaining his Family Bread, which consists of four Mother-less Orphans, she dying soon after he was delivered from the Pit, which happened the second of September, 1777'.[38]

Much earlier than this, some church registers record individual deaths with laconic entries such as 'killed in a coal pit'. More details are provided in these cases from the Black Country, where the earliest record of a collier's death was that of Humphrey Mattocks at Bilston in 1382:

> Andrew Nicklin, collier, and Edward Robbinson, collier, were killed by the damp [firedamp] in a Colepit (Sedgley, 1685).
>
> Thomas Teese, a collier, killed by a fall of coals in Wolverhampton cole pit (Bilston, 1735).
>
> Jane Rowley. She was landing coals at ye pitt-eye [mouth], and ye board on which she stood broke. N.B. Ye landing board stands over ye pitt-eye, so that on breaking of this board she fell to the bottom of ye pitt, and was so much bruised that she died soon after (Bilston, 1756).
>
> John Blewer. He was going down into a colepitt in ye work belonging to Mr. Gibbons, of Ettinghall, and ye rope broke, by which accident he fell to ye bottom of ye pitt and was killed (Bilston, 1758).
>
> Henry, son of John and Mary Edmands ...was killed in a coal pit ... His cloathes were caught in a hook or something of that kind, of the skep, which took him up a considerable way, at length his clothes tore, and he held by his hands till being unable to hang any longer, he fell and spoke no more (Rowley Regis, 1803).[39]

'Get Up!', oil painting (1884) by Alfred Dixon (1842-1919), which was accompanied by four lines from Joseph Skipsey's poem of the same title. By permission of the Laing Art Gallery, Newcastle upon Tyne

Such records could and should be traced in mining areas throughout the country. I happened to be at Zennor, Cornwall, in June 2009, where a memorial is preserved to: 'Matthew Thomas of this Parish who was killed in Wheal Chance Tin Mine in Trewey Downs near this Church Town by a fall of ground ye 16 of August 1806 aged 44 years.' Extended epitaphs inscribed on gravestones may have provided the germ which later led to the growth of printed ballads sold to raise funds for bereaved families. This came from the churchyard at Brierley Hill, again in the Black Country:

Cornelius Plant, aged 27 years;
Daniel Plant Turner, aged 22 years;
John Thompson, aged 21 years;
Thomas Dimmock, aged 18 years;
Colliers, who died August 23rd, 1815.

The coal pit rope asunder broke; we fell, and dead we lay;
Our sudden ends warn you, my friends, to work while yet 'tis day.
When blooming youth is snatched away by death's resistless hand,
Our hearts the mournful tribute pay which pity must demand;
Let this vain world delude no more; behold the gaping tomb,
It bids us seize the present hour; to-morrow death may come.[40]

The language and tone of hymns also contributed to disaster ballads. One of these, 'The Collier's Hymn', was used with the change of a single word for different occasions. The version in eleven verses issued by the London printer, H.P. Such, begins:

Colliers Hymn[41]

Each feeling heart pray lend an ear, unto this mournful tale,
To draw a tear of sympathy, I'm sure it cannot fail;
The fate of these poor colliers, I'm sorry for to say,
By fire-damp near Wigan, was lately swept away.

Reduced to six verses, and with Wigan replaced by Oswestry, this was apparently reprinted in the latter town by Thomas Thomas, with a prose appendix relating to the deaths in an accident at Luna Main Colliery of eighteen men and five boys.[42] However, enquiries in Oswestry have failed to trace any pit or for that matter any printer with those names, and it is likely that the sheet was spurious – intended to be hawked by fraudulent collectors.

Thomas Derby, who wrote in 1913 of street ballad singing in Manchester when he was 'a lad', recalled that after a bad colliery accident in a nearby town there were:

> three or four poor victims – who have lost an arm or a leg or been disfigured in some other way – trying to arouse the pity of their fellows and to pick up a few coppers; they carry several implements of their trade, a spade, a pick and a Davy-lamp. One of them, lying on his side on the pavement, pick in hand, proceeds, as it were, to hew coal out of the hard paving stones, his companions in misfortune meanwhile busying themselves with their collecting boxes among the sympathetic crowd, whilst they all drone out a dolorous ditty, of which I only remember the chorus; indeed, I almost think it was their whole song repeated at intervals. It ran:
>
> All standing round,
> Pity poor Collier,
> That works underground.

Derby went on to remark: 'Some of these fellows were imposters no doubt – at one time doing the "poor collier", and at another the "ship-wrecked sailor"... indeed, I have heard it said that their injuries were often faked and that they were well known in the neighbourhood of Charter Street, Manchester, where there lived at that time an artist in deformity who could transform the physically perfect into the maimed, the halt or the blind on the shortest notice.'[43]

Ballads of mining disasters, like those of shipwrecks with which they share many features, followed well-worn conventions. Two of many examples are: 'The late Colliery Explosion, *Wherein 89 Men and Boys were burnt to Death, and 11 others severely injured,* at Patricroft, Wigan' (1854) and 'Copy of Verses on the Explosions at Pentre Ystrad and Ebbe [Ebbw] Vale Collieries, February 24th & March 3rd, 1871'.[44] Though tunes are not indicated, both ballads were clearly intended to be sung. The latter has a chorus and the former a typical opening invocation: 'You feeling Christians one and all, of high and low degree, I pray you give attention and listen unto me.'

The melody suggested at the head of a sheet was likely to be well known to potential purchasers of the text, or there would have been no point in nominating it. Somewhat sentimental tunes were favoured. 'Teddy O' Neale' was prescribed for 'Truly Descriptive Lines on the Colliery Explosion near Pontypridd',[45] which probably refers to the disaster at Ferndale Colliery of November 1867 in which 178 miners died. A typical verse runs:

Truly Descriptive Lines on the Colliery Explosion near Pontypridd[45]

On Saturday two hundred and sixty-seven workmen,
Went to their labour so far underground,
Death with its terrors was there setting for them,
Too many victims alas he has found.
Strong boys and men in the prime of their lives,
God help them all we say it in pity,
Heaven look down on their mothers and wives.

[Chorus]
Near Pontypridd among the Welsh mountains,
Two hundred and fifty dear lives we deplore,
Sad bitter tears from Nature's pure fountain,
Are falling for those who will come back no more.

The writer's perceived need to situate Pontypridd might well indicate that the sheet was intended for sale over a wide area. The same is true of another disaster ballad which seeks 'the help of christains [sic], In England, Scotland and South Wales'. 'Terrible Explosion At Pontypridd'[46] stems from the accident of April 1893 in which 63 died in an underground fire. The tune this time was 'Just Before the Battle, Mother' (see p. 240)

Terrible Explosion at Pontypridd[46]

We now record a sad disaster,
That has happened in South Wales,
Where flames have proved a fearful master
To describe the truth words almost fail,
Such a shocking death for miners,
Burnt alive while earning bread,
The Rhonda Valley now reminds us,
'Tis the valley of the dead.

[Chorus]
Flames of fire did there surround them,
And suffocating smoke as well,
Poor Colliers died just as they found them
The Church bells sound their funeral knell.

It was upon the tenth of April,
Eight hundred men were underground,
Working as hard as they were able
Until the pit on fire they found.
A lamp had caught the dry worn timber,
And the fire around the coal soon spread,
All chance of life was gone for ever,
For those who were found lying dead.

A wall of burning coal behind them,
A stifling smoke in front we're told,
Though rescuers were trying to find them,
Their faces they could not behold,
One poor collier led his comrades,
Through the smoke to find his way,
He stepped into a shaft and falling,
At the bottom dead he lay.

Explorers were soon in the working,
Risking life dear life to save,
Danger on every hand was lurking,
But men were there, but strong & brave,
From Pontypridd and all around them,
Willing hearts and hands was there,
Friends and neighbours as they found them
Were brought above with tender care.

Most of those that's gone for ever,
Were men just entered in life's prime,
Many of them with a poor old mother,
In quiet content had passed their time
There's many a widow and little orphans,
Whose grief each feeling heart bewails,
We hope they have the help of christains [sic]
In England, Scotland and South Wales.

A man by the name of Thomas Rosser,
Was in the pit when it took fire,
He knew the workings from his boyhood,
To save his comrades did desire,
One hundred and fifty dying colliers,
By bravery he did preserve
From death to life Tom Rosser led them
The Victoria Cross he does deserve.

TERRIBLE

MINE EXPLOSION

Near Pontypridd.

Loss of 250 Lives.

'Terrible Mine Explosion near Pontypridd'. Ballad sheet from 'Ballads and Fugitive Pieces'. Courtesy of Cardiff Council Library Service

Pontypridd had a particularly bad record of pit accidents, at least two more of which were commemorated in ballads: 'A Copy of Verses On the melancholy and dreadful Colliery Explosion, at the Cummer [Cymmer] Colliery, neart Pont-y-Pridd, Glamorganshire, on July 15, 1856, when 110 Colliers were killed by Fire-damp' and the bilingual 'Tanchwa yn Cilfynydd/Explosion at Cilfynydd' (1894, at the Albion Pit, less than a year after the disaster at Great Western).[47] The latter is unusual, in that it is a small four-page booklet rather than a single sheet, and that it understates the number of casualties: 279 against 290 in reality.

The only known image of Tommy Armstrong, the 'pitman poet'.

Seventy-four men and boys died in an underground explosion at Trimdon Grange in County Durham, on 16 February 1882. Within a few days, Tommy Armstrong, known as 'the pitman poet', was singing his response in the local Mechanics' Hall. He would no doubt have run through a range of possible tunes before deciding on that of 'Go and leave me if you wish it', a song with the necessary sorrowing atmosphere, since it tells of a slighted and grieving woman who is separating from her lover. This tune would therefore also provide the metrical dimensions, which Armstrong's words would follow.

Armstrong's song is still widely known, albeit to a tune which he did not originally specify. Now, his words and chosen tune appear together for the first time.

Trimdon Grange Explosion[48]

Let us not think of tomorrow,
Lest we disappointed be;
All our joys may turn to sorrow,
As we all may daily see.
Today we may be strong and healthy,
But how soon there comes a change,
As we may learn from the explosion,
That has been at Trimdon Grange.

Men and boys left home that morning,
For to earn their daily bread,
Little thought before that evening
That they'd be numbered with the dead;
Let us think of Mrs Burnett,
Once had sons but now has none,
By the Trimdon Grange explosion,
Joseph, George, and James are gone.

February left behind it
What will never be forgot;
Weeping widows, helpless children,
May be found in many a cot,
Homes that once were blest with comfort,
Guided by a father's care,
Now are solemn, sad and gloomy,
Since the father is not there.

Little children, kind and loving,
From their homes each day would run
For to meet their father's coming,
As each hard day's work was done.
Now they ask if father's left them,
Then the mother hangs her head;
With a weeping widow's feelings,
Tells the child that 'father's dead'.

God protect the lonely widow,
Help to raise each dropping head;
Be a Father to the orphans,
Never let them cry for bread.
Death will pay us all a visit,
They have only gone before;
We may meet the Trimdon victims
Where explosives are no more.

Ballad sheets were ephemeral, serving their purpose, being sung and perhaps kept as mementos for some time, but then disappearing, except that one sometimes served as a model for use on another occasion. For example, save for adjustment of name and date, 'Lines on the Dreadful Explosion at Bunkers Hill Mine' at Kidsgrove, Staffordshire in August 1875, is identical, down to its engraving of gaunt church, funeral procession and flag at half mast, with 'Lines on the Terrible Colliery Explosion near Barnsley' at Swaithe Main Colliery, four months later.[49] Rarely, such a ballad continued to circulate orally, long after the events it evoked.

Scotland's worst underground disaster occurred in October 1877 at Dixon's Pits, High Blantyre, near Hamilton, when 207 men and boys were killed, out of a workforce of 223. There was intense local resentment at perceived failings of the management, and Alexander McDonald, the local miners' leader, only with the utmost difficulty dissuaded the men from

THE SORROWFUL

LAMENTATION

OF

JANE SNEDDON,

For the Loss of her Lover, JOHN MURRAY, who lost his life at the late disaster at High Blantyre.

On the Clyde's bonny banks as I lately did wander,
Near the village of Blantyre I chanced for to rove;
I saw a young female dressed in deep mourning,
She sadly lamented the fate of her lover.
I stepped up to her, and my poor woman
Pray tell me the cause of your sorrow and woe;
I hear you lamentns the fate of some young man,
His name, and what happened, I'd like for to know.

While sobbing and sighiug, at length she made answer,
John Murphy, kind sir, is my true lover's name
Twenty-one years of age, and of a mild, good behaviour,
For to work in the mines of High B antyre he came.
The twenty second of October I long will remember,
In health and in strength to his labour go;
On that fatal morning, without one momen's warning,
Twa hundred and ten there in death did lie low.

Now widows and orphans, for husbands and fathers,
In Stonefield and Blantyre in hundreds do mourn,
And old aged parents for the sons they loved dearly,
By the dreadful explosion they will never return.
I knew that 'tis right for the dead to be grieving,
But comfort to me none on earth can ror
He has gone from this world but a short time before me,
And I hope I'll rejoin him where parting's no more.

Oh never again will I walk with my lover
With hand locked in hand on the banks of hhe Clyde
Where we told our love tales in a green shady bower
'Twas here I consented for to be his bride.
The day it was fixed and the guests were invited,
And had he but lived my dear husband he'd be,
But by the disaster that occured at High Blantyre
He was killed and in life I no more him will see.

But spring will return, and the flowers of the summmer
Will bloom in their wildness, so lovely and fair,
And I'll gather snowdrops, primroses and daisies—
On my true lover's grave I ll transplant them there
With my tears I will water those wild little flowers,
And fervently pray to the Ru'er on high,
For I know that my days on this earth are numbered
And soon in the cold grave beside him I'll lie.

By John Wilson, B. S., G.

'The Sorrowful Lamentation of Jane Sneddon….' Broadside ballad reproduced by permission of the National Library of Scotland

violence against owners and officials. Even so, the two extant contemporary sheets dealing with the disaster follow the conventional pattern. 'Fearful Colliery Explosion in Scotland'[50] concludes with the thought of 'kind angels … waiting' to carry the victims' souls to a better clime. 'Appalling Colliery Accident in Scotland'[51] expresses this wish:

> May heaven receive them in their prayer
> And angels with their loving hands
> The colliers heavenly home prepare
> In that bright and glorious land.

Like other disaster broadsides, these disappeared, apparently leaving no trace in oral tradition. By contrast, another sheet of the time, 'The Sorrowful Lamentation of Jane Sneddon, For the Loss of her Lover, John Murray, who lost his life at the late disaster at High Blantyre',[52] lingered for the best part of a century in Scotland, albeit in attenuated form. The elegiac element no doubt had a strong appeal, and the idiom was akin to that of a wide body of traditional song. John Maguire, an Irishman from Roslea in County Fermanagh, working as a miner in the Glasgow area in the 1920s, learned the song from an old Highlander who said he had 'wrought in that pit the shift before the explosion happened'. His version preserves 28 of the 40 lines of the printed text of 1877:

The Blantyre Explosion[53]

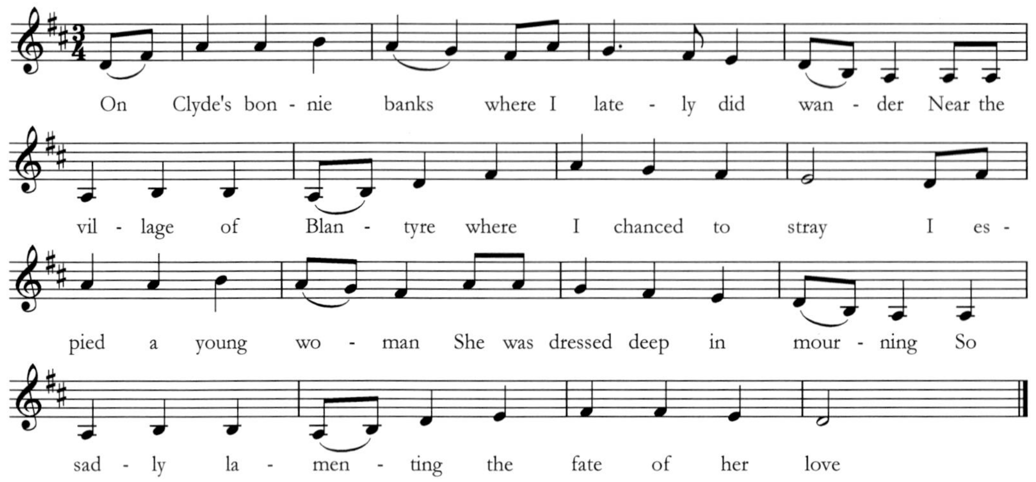

On Clyde's bonnie banks where I lately did wander,
Near the village of Blantyre where I chanced to stray,
I espied a young woman, she was dressed in deep mourning,
So sadly lamenting the fate of her love.

I boldly stepped to her, said I, 'My poor woman,
Come tell me the cause of your trouble and woe.
I do hear you lamenting the fate of some young man,
His fate and what happened him I'd like for to know'.

With sighing and sobbing she at length then made answer,
'John Murphy, kind sir, was my true lover's name.
Twenty-one years of age and a mild good behaviour,
To work in the mines of High Blantyre he came.

'And the day was appointed, her friends were invited,
Oh had he lived, my true love, husband he'd be,
But woe to that disaster, occurred in High Blantyre,
He's gone and alas I will never more him see.

'On the eleventh of December I long will remember,
In health and in strength to his labour did go,
But on that fatal morning without one moment's warning,
Two hundred and ten in cold death did lie low.

'There were fathers and mothers, there were widows and orphans,
In Stonefield High Blantyre where hundreds do mourn.

Ah there were old aged parents, for their sons they loved dearly,
By that sad explosion will never return.

'But the spring it will come with the flowers of summer,
That bloom through its wildness so lovely and fair.
I will gather the snowdrops, primroses and daisies,
Round my true lover's grave I will transplant them there.

'For they say it's not right for the dead to be grieved,
There's nothing but trouble bestowed on me,
He is gone from this world but a short time before me,
In hopes to rejoin him in sweet purity.'

The expression of grief here is poignant, but again the attitude is passive, fatalistic: the bereaved woman looks forward to fulfilment in the next life.

The spirit of resignation persisted for another century, to reappear in many of the poems and songs inspired locally, right through to the deaths of seven miners at Lofthouse Colliery in Yorkshire in 1973. While resentment was expressed at the Coal Board's refusal to call the accident a disaster, since it held that the latter required a minimum of ten casualties, the heroic if unavailing efforts of rescue workers received warm praise, and there were reflections on the price of coal.[54] The anger was voiced in 'The Lofthouse Colliery Disaster', a song written by the folksinger Sam Richards:

The Lofthouse Colliery Disaster[55]

Wednesday morning, Lofthouse Colliery,
Water flooded into the mine.
No one knew of the disused workings.
Seven men died for that crime.
Keep on working, get the coal out,
Safety takes up too much time.
There's seven of those greedy miners
Lying in a sea of grime.

Yet Richards later repudiated his own song, on the grounds that it sought to make political capital out of tragedy, and that he had come to feel uncomfortable at having intervened as an outsider.[56]

The disaster of September 1934 at Gresford Colliery, near Wrexham, caused the deaths of 265 miners, including three would-be rescuers. The manager was later fined £15 on charges of negligence. A moving contemporary song expressed fierce resentment:

The Gresford Disaster[57]

You've heard of the Gresford disaster,
Of the terrible price that was paid;
Two hundred and forty-two colliers were lost,
And three men of a rescue brigade.

It occurred in the month of September:
At three in the morning the pit
Was racked by a violent explosion
In the Dennis where gas lay so thick.

Now the gas in the Dennis deep section
Was heaped there like snow in a drift,
And many a man had to leave the coalface
Before he had worked out his shift.

A fortnight before the explosion,
To the shotfirer, Tomlinson cried:
'If you fire that shot we'll be all blown to hell!'
And no one can say that he lied.

Now the fireman's reports they are missing,
The records of forty-two days;
The colliery manager had them destroyed
To cover his criminal ways.

Down there in the dark they are lying,
They died for nine shillings a day.
They have worked out their shift and now they must lie
In the darkness until Judgement Day.

Now the Lord Mayor of London's collecting
To help out our children and wives;
The owners have sent some white lilies
To pay for the poor colliers' lives.

Farewell, our dear wives and our children,
Farewell, our old comrades as well.
Don't send your sons down the dark dreary pit;
They'll be damned like the sinners in hell.

Without questioning the song's validity or effectiveness, one must point out that there is uncertainty over its provenance. The text and tune given here first appeared in print in 1952 in A.L. Lloyd's *Come All Ye Bold Miners*, with the note: 'Text and tune communicated by Ewan MacColl, "from the singing of a young miner named Ford in Sheffield Miners' Training Centre".'[58] It is slightly curious that when MacColl published it himself, two years later, he cited the song's source as being Lloyd's book.[59] There is no record from oral tradition: the version recorded by Alan Lomax from Mrs A. Cosgrove of Newtongrange, Midlothian,[60] was in fact, with several others, learned from Lloyd's book by the singer. A letter of mine to the *Wrexham Gazette* in May 1972 enquiring about both the disaster and the song drew a wealth of information on the former and a complete blank on the latter.[61] Lloyd later wrote to me: 'I suspect the song is Ewan [MacColl]'s creation anyway.'[62] Internal evidence in terms of the nature of the tune and the verbal idiom seems to me to support the contention. The sharp anger of 'The Gresford Disaster' may differ from the approach of the standard ballad but it certainly accords with the deep feelings of miners and their families on pit accidents.

In the early years of the twentieth century, few collieries paid any compensation for a fatal accident. A whip-round for a workmate's widow seldom amounted to more than ten or twelve pounds, at a time when on average a miner earned £1 8s. a week. The Denaby and Cadeby Main Collieries in South Yorkshire would match such an amount, provided that miners were willing to forgo the cessation of work which customarily marked a fatal accident in the pit. By so doing the firm could save thousands of pounds which loss of production would have occasioned. It then evicted the dead miner's family from his tied house within a few weeks.[63]

Walter Haydn Davies (born at Bedlinog, Glamorgan, in 1903) remembered this from his childhood and youth:

'Carrying someone home on a stretcher was a common sight…' from a watercolour by John Jones

> Carrying someone home on a stretcher was a common sight in those days, yet the tenseness of the atmosphere surrounding such a procession never abated in such a closely-knit community. Every calamity was felt in common because everyone was concerned. … How grim and determined the miners looked in these processions on such tragic occasions! With worm-like, visible sweat marks on their faces – effects of the daily toil of their job – they looked like black warriors marching relentlessly forward to battle with an unseen foe who always lurked around, ready to pounce at any time, to do them injury or rob them of their lives.[64]

Conflict with the 'unseen foe' was inevitable, but many miners bitterly resented the secondary war which they had to wage against coal-owners. As a result they sought trade union solidarity and beyond that social advance, and indeed, socialism. One family which exemplified such an outlook was the Elliotts of Birtley in County Durham.

Jack Elliott started work underground in 1920 at the age of thirteen, just in time to be involved in the great strikes of 1921 and 1926. He died in 1966 at the age of 59 after a lifetime as a miner, mainly working in twenty-inch seams. His fund of stories and songs included the cautionary 'Jowl, Jowl an' Listen', which, together with 'Rap 'er te Bank', entered his repertoire only in 1962.[65] According to Pete Wood in his study of the Elliott family, the songs' original source was 'a pitman from Hetton-le-Hole in East Durham. His nephew, a schoolteacher called Henry Nattress of Low fell, obtained them and passed them to the Birtley headmaster, Walter Toyn.'[66] The songs were first published in 1965 in the magazine *English Dance and Song*[67] before becoming widely known thanks to the singing of the Elliott family.

Jowl, Jowl an' Listen[68]

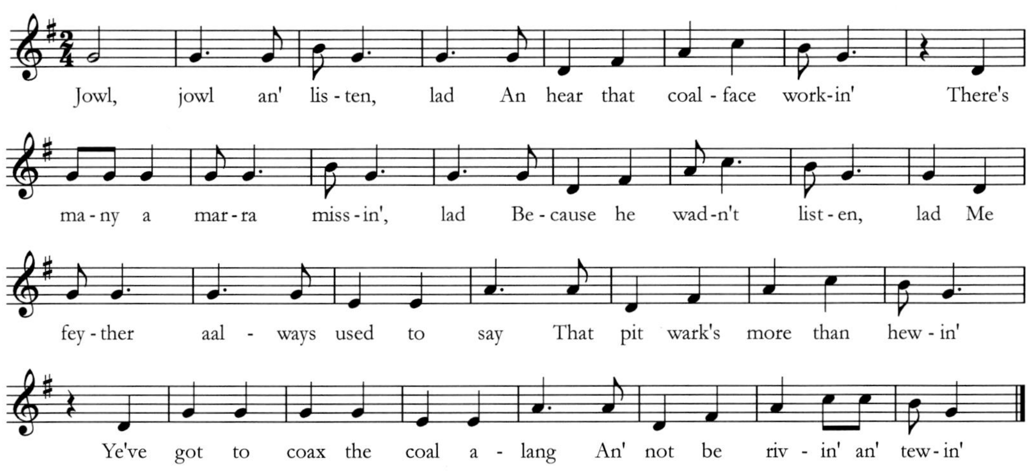

[Chorus]
Jowl, jowl an' listen, lad, an' hear that coalface workin'.
There's many a marra missin', lad, because he wadn't listen, lad.

Me feyther aalways used to say That pit wark's more than hewin'.
Ye've got to coax the coal alang, an' not be rivin' an' tewin'.
Noo, the depitty craals fre flat te flat, while the putter rams the tyum uns,
But the man at the face hes te knaa his place like a mother knaas her young uns.

(*Jowl*: test roof by tapping with pick handle or the like; *marra*: workmate; *rivin' an' tewin'*: hacking and tearing; *depitty* (deputy): chargehand; *flat*: area being worked; *putter*: person moving tubs; *tyum uns*: empty ones.)

Seven years before her death, Jack Elliott's wife Em reflected in this anecdote (one of many) the fierce anger of miners at their earlier treatment by the coal-owners:

> I remember there was two men killed at the Birtley New Pit. And I'll never forget the indignity of those men being brought home. They picked them up, put them in a sack and trundled them to their home in an open hand-cart. . . . I knew this man, they called him Fawcett, and he'd left seven or eight bairns. And I was only tiny but I remembered them, this hand-drawn cart coming up, and these two bundles, you know, and coarse sacking on the thing. And it struck me, . . . no respect for them alive and less for them when they were dead.[69]

COUNTY of LEICESTER.

The Magistrates for the said County residing in the Hundred of West Goscote,

CAUTION

ALL PERSONS AGAINST THE CRIME OF

FRAME BREAKING.

EVERY Person forcibly entering a House in the Night time, WITH INTENT TO BREAK A FRAME, and every Person IN ANY MANNER aiding or assisting others in so doing, is guilty of BURGLARY, which is punishable by DEATH.

Persons being entrusted with the Frames of their Employers, who in any way connive at their destruction, are ACCOMPLICES IN FELONY. CONCEALING THE NAMES OF FRAME BREAKERS, in order to screen them from Justice, is punishable by FINE AND IMPRISONMENT.

Every Person EXTORTING MONEY for the support of Frame Breakers, IS A FELON, and punishable with DEATH.

Every Person USING THREATENING LANGUAGE respecting the Persons or Property of others, is liable to be imprisoned, untill he shall find SUFFICIENT SURETIES for his future good behaviour.

And the Magistrates hereby call upon all good and loyal Subjects TO BE VIGILANT, and to give the Constables of their respective Parishes THE EARLIEST NOTICE of all such Felonius ACTS or THREATS that the Offenders may be apprehended and dealt with, according to Law.

By order of the Magistrates,

CHARLES LACEY, their Clerk.

Loughborough, December 10, 1811.

W. RISTE, PRINTER, LOUGHBOROUGH.

The caution against frame breaking carried the threat of being 'punishable by death'. Reproduced by permission of the Record Office for Leicestershire, Leicester & Rutland.

4 Hunger breaks fences

Food rioters and machine breakers

On Thursday [21st October 1782] a Party of Colliers ... arrived here about four o'clock in the afternoon, and were met in the [Birmingham] Bull-Ring by one of the Officers of the Town, who desired to speak with their Leader, who immediately appeared. He demanded of him, what he and his Party meant, in coming into the Town in that hostile manner? And was answered, They did not come with the intention of committing any Depredations, but to Regulate the Prices of Malt, Flour, Butter, Cheese etc. ... The Gentleman promised them, if they would immediately go out of the Town peaceably, and commit no Outrage, that he would do everything in his power to have the Prices of the different articles they complained of properly regulated. ... In the meantime ... the Military were drawn up in the Square ... and ... they paraded in different Streets, with Drums beating, etc.[1]

These events, described in the local newspaper, Aris's *Birmingham Gazette,* inspired a ballad by John Freeth (1731–1808). Freeth, who would have been characterised in our day as a left-wing singer-songwriter, is shown in portraits as a bold figure, stocky and pugnacious, invariably crowned with a capacious tricorne hat. One image, on a trade token, is accompanied by these words:

BRITONS BEHOLD
THE BARD OF FREEDOM
PLAIN & BOLD
WHO SINGS AS DRUIDS
SUNG OF OLD

After earning a living for a time as an itinerant ballad singer, he took over in 1786 as landlord of a Birmingham inn and coffee house, where he proceeded for forty years to entertain customers with some 400 ballads of his own composition, many of these published in slim volumes with titles such as *The Political Songster* and *A Touch on the Times*. He wrote not only on current events – wars, taxation, elections – but also on 'more trivial matters: on pugilism and the manufacture of shoe buckles, on the Duke of Rutland's birthday and the jocular boiling of a vintner's wig, on ale-tasting, bull-baiting, and the cock-fight, and on all types of sport from quoits and fishing to fives and hunting'.[2] In addition, he celebrated his home town, and commented on local events.

John Freeth's ballad on the colliers' appearance in Birmingham was meant to be sung to the tune of 'The Staffordshire Fox Chace', which, unfortunately, does not seem to have survived. A possible substitute, requiring a division of the text into four-line stanzas, was written by Pam Bishop of Birmingham.

The Colliers March[3]

Britons for news upon tip-toe were got,
Longing to hear from OLD GIB – or what not;
The summer was over, the season unkind,
In *harvest a snow* how uncommon to find;

The times were oppressive, – and well be it known,
Hunger will strongest of fences break down;
'Twas then from their cells the *black gentry* stept out,
With bludgeons, determin'd to stir up a rout.

The Prince of the party, who revel'd from home,
Was a terrible fellow, and call'd IRISH TOM;
He brandish'd his bludgeon, with dexterous skill,
And close to his elbow was plac'd BARLEY WILL;

Instantly follow'd a numerous train,
Chearful as bold *Robin Hood*'s merry men;

Sworn to remedy a capital fault,
And bring down th'exorbitant price of the MALT.

From *Dudley* to *Walsall* they trip it along,
And '*Hampton* was truly alarm'd at the throng;
Women and children, wherever they go
Shouting out, *O the brave Dudley Boys O!'*

Nailors and spinners, the cavalcade join,
The markets to lower their flatt'ring design;
Regulation of Consciences holding in view, –
But MALTSTERS with *Conscience* have nothing to do.

Six days out of seven poor nailing boys get,
Little else at their meals but potatoes to eat;
For bread hard they labour, good things never carve,
And swore, 'twere as well to be hang'd as to starve:

Such are the feelings in every land,
Nothing Necessity's call can withstand;
And RIOTS are certain to sadden the year,
When *Six-penny Loaves* but *Three-pounders* appear.

Freeth's reference to 'Old Gib' was no doubt occasioned by the siege of Gibraltar which Spanish and French forces conducted between 1779 and 1783. His good-humoured attitude to the 'black gentry' and their allies clearly shows where his sympathies lay at home.

Colliers above ground at a pithead. Author's own collection

E.P. Thompson, whom I quote here, observed that 'Not wages, but the cost of bread, was the most sensitive indicator of popular discontent', and added that 'a consumer-consciousness preceded other forms of industrial antagonism'.[4] Menacing crowds seeking 'the markets to lower' to force down prices and appealing to 'Regulation of Consciences' for honorable dealing were 'legitimised by the assumptions of an older moral economy' where customary fair practice was considered to take priority over the vagaries of the free market.

'The Colliers' March', with its support from women and children, its dismay at the price of bread (sixpence buying only a three-pound loaf) and its measured threat, exemplifies the kind of action on which, after studying many examples from the eighteenth and early nineteenth centuries, Thompson commented: 'It is the restraint, rather than the disorder, which is remarkable; and there can be no doubt that the actions were approved by an overwhelming popular consensus. There is a deeply-felt conviction that prices *ought*, in times of dearth, to be regulated, and that the profiteer put himself outside of society.'[5] Those involved were not always as responsible.

Halfpenny trade token from Dublin. Author's collection

The couplet in 'The Colliers' March', 'Women and children, wherever they go, Shouting out "O the brave Dudley Boys O!"', may allude to another song, of which only two versions exist, one sung by an unnamed man breaking stones on the road between Tipton, Staffordshire, and Dudley, Worcestershire, in about 1850, the other recited a century later by a Birmingham alderman, W. Byng Kenrick. Only texts were noted, but the structure in each case closely resembled that of a late seventeenth- century ballad, 'The Benjamins' Lamentation for their Sad Loss at Sea'.[6]

The Dudley Boys[7]

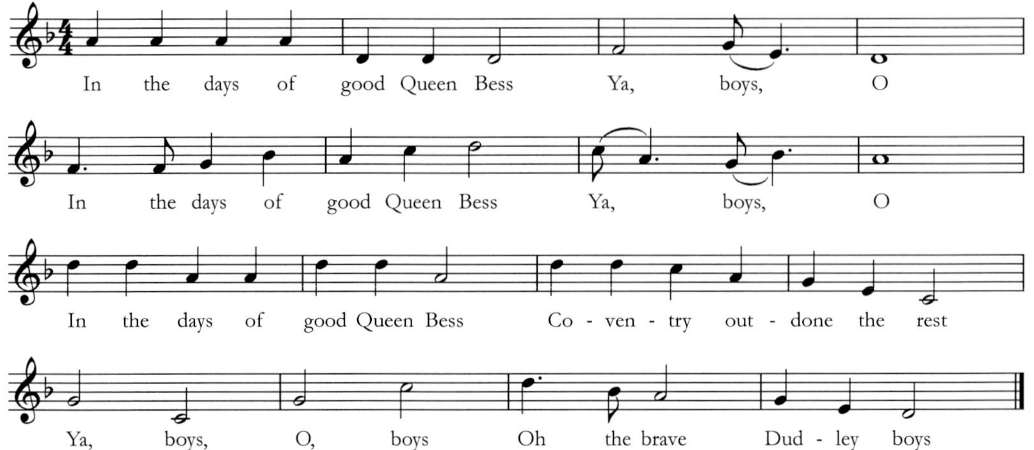

In the days of good Queen Bess,
Ya, boys, O.
In the days of good Queen Bess,
Ya, boys, O.
In the days of good Queen Bess
Coventry outdone the rest.
Ya, boys, oh, boys,
Oh the brave Dudley boys.

[Following the same pattern:]
But in the times as be,
We'm outdone Coventry.

Tip'on [Tipton] lads they did us join,
And we formed a strong comboin.

We marchen into town,
Resolved to pull the housen down.

Toimes they were mighty queer,
And vittle it was very dear.

So fur to mek corn cheap
We burned un all of a yeap.

But the work was scarce begun
When sodgers come and spoiled the fun.

We all ran down our pits,
Frightened a'most out of our wits.

God bless Lord Dudley Ward;
He knowed as times bin hard.

He called back the sodger men,
And we'll never riot again,
Na, boys, no, boys,
No, the brave Dudley boys.

If the Freeth reference indeed indicates 'The Dudley Boys', the song must have been current by 1782, and the Lord Dudley Ward mentioned would have been John, who held the title from 1763 to 1788. Thompson remarks on 'the swiftness of the crowd's changes of mood, from passivity to mutiny to cowed obedience',[8] yet one wonders whether the song's concluding vow 'never to riot again' was not uttered through firmly clenched teeth. Certainly, the Dudley colliers retained a reputation for turbulence well into the nineteenth century,[9] and food riots remained a sporadic feature of the national scene until the 1840s.

'Hunger will strongest of fences break down,' wrote Freeth, and the hungry viewed millers and others concerned with the supply and processing of grain as potential profiteers. Chaucer's stereotype of the miller ('Wel cowde he stele corn, and tollen thries [thrice]') would have been unhesitatingly endorsed by the London poor, who were deeply suspicious of the steam-powered Albion Mills, established in the 1780s on the Surrey side of Blackfriars Bridge – ironically enough, 'by a quasi-philanthropic syndicate formed for the avowed purpose of running in opposition to the general millers of the city', and looking to 'reduce the cost of grinding in the metropolis'.[10] The prime mover was Matthew Boulton, the Birmingham manufacturer and engineer who financed the production of James Watts's steam engine. By 1790 the two fifty-horsepower engines of the Albion Mills each drove twenty pairs of millstones, which between them ground 360 bushels of flour every hour. As a result the Albion Mills Company more or less monopolised the flour trade in London, and although prices went down there was resentment among millers and mealmen who had gone out of business. Perhaps it was they who spread the rumour that flour from the Albion Mills was adulterated. Nevertheless, the building became a tourist attraction, and artists climbed to the roof to paint panoramic views of the city.

£150 REWARD, AND THE King's Pardon.

WHEREAS,

Some evil-disposed Person or Persons did, on the Night of *April* the *12th*, wilfully and maliciously *SET FIRE* to the Drying-house, Out-houses and Mills, GREAT MARLOW, *Bucks*, occupied *by* Mr. JOSEPH WRIGHT, *Paper-Maker*, with a View to *DESTROY* the same; and did on the SAME NIGHT place Fire-Brands with Pitched or Tarred Cloth *round them*, in the *PAPER-MILLS* of Mr. WM. WRIGHT (*adjoining* those of his Brother), *with intent to* Destroy *them also.*

The above Reward of £150 will be paid to any Person who will give such Information as shall bring the Perpetrators to Conviction, by applying to Mr. JAMES ILBERY, 1, Great Titchfield Street, *London*, or to the *West-of-England Assurance Office*, *Exeter*, or *Bridge Street*, *Blackfriars*, *London*.

And beyond the Reward offered above, His Majesty's Free Pardon will be extended to any Accomplice or Accomplices, who shall give Information as will lead to Conviction.

Signed — JOSEPH WRIGHT,
WILLIAM WRIGHT.

J. INNES, Printer, 61, Wells Street, Oxford Street, London. — *APRIL* 22, 1826.

The offer of rewards show how seriously the authorities responded to the arson attacks on mills and factories

When the mills caught fire on 2 March 1791 Boulton strongly suspected foul play, and called for a government investigation. However, his manager, Wyatt, believed that lack of grease in part of the machinery was to blame. The burnt-out shell of a building, which for Londoners symbolised the industrial revolution, is said to have provided William Blake with his image of dark satanic mills. After the fire, according to Robert Southey, 'ballads of rejoicing were printed and sung on the spot'.[11] Were these genuine expressions of popular opinion, or did they demonstrate special pleading by small millers put out of business?

Two such ballads have survived. 'The Baker's Glory, Or, the Conflagration', a slip song (so called because of its size, 3 ½ inches wide by 12 ½ down) certainly relished the disaster:

'Where is the fire, now? Says one,
At the A——- Mills, the people say,
Why d—-n it let it burn away!
For its destruction who does care,
For it has been wished many a year;
For the bread at such price did keep,
Now let's hope it will be more cheap.

£200.Reward

WHEREAS

The WAREHOUSE of Mr. William Radcliffe,
COTTON MANUFACTURER,
ADJOINING TO HIS DWELLING-HOUSE IN THE HIGHER HILLGATE,
STOCKPORT, IN THE COUNTY OF CHESTER,

Was, between the Hours of 2 and 3 in the Morning of FRIDAY the 20th of March, instant,

Wilfully, maliciously, & feloniously

Set on Fire,

By some wicked and desperate Incendiaries, who broke the Windows thereof, and threw in five Flambeaux or Torches, composed of Pitch, Tar, Oakum, and Spirits of Turpentine; and some Waste Cops of Cotton-weft, which had been dipped in similar Spirits.

The Villains left on the Outside of the said Warehouse, three Clubs or large Sticks of a peculiar Sort, which may be the future Means of a Discovery.

A Reward of £200. will be paid to the Person who may give such Information as may lead to the Discovery and Conviction of the Principals concerned in this diabolical Crime, upon Application to

J. LLOYD, *Solicitor.*

Stockport, March 21st, 1812.

LOMAX, PRINTER.

Bakers and millers, says the writer, 'came afar the Mills to view, And laughing then they went away, Said, twas the best sight seen that day'. He then repeats the allegations of adulteration: 'They say, they Indian wheat [maize?] did grind, Which they did mix with our corn'. After expressing the hope that 'these lines that I have penn'd, None will affront', the writer concludes:

The price of bread so dear you see,
Let's hope it will much cheaper be,
That people all may have their fills,
It will make more work for other Mills.[12]

The same pious hope is expressed in another ballad, this time printed from an engraved plate with the text in cursive script, accompanied by a graphic engraving of fire pumps in action:

The Albion Mills on Fire[13]

Wednesday March the second day,
At six in the Morning (people say)
In Seventeen Hundred, Ninety One,
The fire at the Albion Mills began.
Ri toll, loll de roll.

The Albion Mills on Fire

Wednesday, March the second day,
At six in the morning (people say)
In Seventeen Hundred Ninety One,
The Fire at the Albion Mills began.

This noble building burnt so fast,
Black Friars Bridge could not be past,
Nor could they get the engines nigh,
Those mills did burn so furiously.
And now the folks begin to chat,
How the owners they did this and that,
But very few did sorrow show
That the Albion Mills were burnt so low.

Says one, they had it in their power
For to reduce the price of flour,
Instead of letting the bread raise,
But now the Mills are all on blaze.

Now pray God bless us one and all,
And send the price of bread may fall,
That the poor with plenty may abound,
Tho' the Albion Mill's burnt to the ground.

This noble building burnt so fast,
Black Friars Bridge could not be past,
Nor could they get the Engines nigh,
Those Mills did burn so furiously.

At length the roof did all fall in,
And then the Engines did begin,
But tho' with vigour they did play,
The Albion Mills were burnt that day.

Says one, they had it in their power,
For to reduce the price of flour,
Instead of letting the bread raise,
But now the Mills are all on blaze.

In lighters there was saved wheat,
But scorched and scarcely fit to eat.
Some Hundred Hogs saved difrent ways,
While the Albion Mills were in a blaze.

Now pray God bless us one and all,
And send the price of bread may fall,
That the poor with plenty may abound,
Tho' the Albion Mills burnt to the ground.

In Snow Hill, Birmingham, another steam-powered flour mill was destroyed in 1795.

Steam-powered looms also attracted popular opprobrium. They were developed by Edmund Cartwright (1743–1823), an eccentric and philanthropic clergyman apparently sharing the radical views of his brother, Major John Cartwright, who agitated for 'direct and pure democracy, . . . for forty-four years, without discretion and without fear, living on a diet chiefly of raisins and weak gin and water'.[14] It seems paradoxical that the democratically-orientated seeker of progress should come into conflict with workers, but they were fully aware, like the Luddite croppers, that technical advance would come at their expense, in terms of redundancy of skills and loss of employment.

After promoting an unsuccessful power-loom venture at Doncaster, Edmund Cartwright looked further afield, and in 1790 accepted a contract to supply several hundred looms to a Mr Robert Grimshaw of Gorton, Manchester, for a factory at Knott Mill. 'Two dozen were deployed at a 50 per cent saving on hand weavers' wages, when the premises were mysteriously destroyed by fire.'[15] A gleeful ballad greeted the event.

Grimshaw's Factory Fire[16]

Come all ye country gentlemen, come listen to my story;
It's of a country gallant who was cropp'd in his glory,
All by a new invention, as all things come by natur',
Concerning looms from Doncaster and weyvin' done by wayter.

Chorus:
Then, eh, the looms from Doncaster that lately have come down –
That they never had been carried into Manchester town.

For coal to work his factory he sent unto the Duke [Bridgewater], sir;
He thought that all the town should be stifled with the smoke, sir;
But the Duke sent him an answer, which came so speedily,
That the poor should have the coal, if the Devil took th' machinery.

He got all kinds of people to work at his invention,
Both English, Scotch, and Irish, and more that I could mention.
He kept such order over them, much more than they did choose, sir,
They left him land for liberty; please God to spare their shoes, sir.

The floor was over shavings, took fire in the night, sir;
But now he's sick in bed some say it's with affright, sir.

The ballad, which breaks off at this point, was the work of a Gorton man 'named Lucas, a handloom weaver and crofter or bleacher. Though very illiterate, – not able to write, and scarcely to read, – he enjoyed considerable local fame as a rhymester.' According to Harland and Wilkinson, the piece 'was regularly set to music, printed, and sold by the ballad-dealers of Manchester'. No copy has come to light; and the fragment was 'orally gleaned from five old men, each of whom well recollects singing it at the time of its currency'.[17]

Action of this kind helped to delay the inevitable by a number of years: 'notwithstanding the fears of the hand-loom weavers, fewer than 2500 power-looms were operating as late as 1813. The wider introduction of the new technology was deferred until the investment booms of the early 1820s and 1830s, but by 1833 more than 100,000 were in operation.'[18] If from the outset, power-looms had the potential to displace half the weavers, it is easy to understand opposition to their introduction in Lancashire.

In Derby, Nottingham, Leicester and elsewhere the stocking weavers (otherwise called stockingers or framework-knitters) also resisted innovation. At Leicester in 1773 they broke up a frame capable of weaving twelve pairs of hose at once, and fourteen years later they wrecked Joseph Brookhouse's worsted-spinning frame. During a period of prosperity, stockingers could earn 14s. or 15s. a week for some twelve or thirteen hours' work a day. However, from about 1810 conditions worsened, partly through changes in fashion, partly through over-production. It was perhaps then that the saying, 'As poor as a stockinger', was coined. Instead of continuing to produce stockings on the normal narrow frames, some employers turned to the wide frames previously used only for such items as pantaloons. The material produced was cut up for gloves, socks or stockings, and then sewn up; but in the absence of proper selvedges the items were of poor quality, which further depressed the trade, infuriating some hosiers and also the stockingers.

The word 'Luddite' was first recorded about this time, but long before that, people in Leicestershire had told stories of 'an ignorant youth, ... of the name of Ludlam, who, when ordered by his father, a framework-knitter, to square his needles, took a hammer and beat them into a heap'. Alternatively, in about 1779, Edward Ludlam, 'a person of weak intellect, in a fit of insane rage rushed into a stockinger's house and destroyed two frames so completely that the saying "Lud must have been here" came to be used throughout the hosiery districts when a stocking-frame had undergone extraordinary damage'.[19] Again, after the death of his mother in 1763 Ned Lud is said to have been apprenticed to a stocking-weaver who thrashed him for laziness. Lud responded by hammering a frame to pieces; alternatively, his action was in response to having been mercilessly taunted with being stupid. A saying, once current, was: 'as daft as Ned Lud, who ran ten miles to see a dead donkey.' Oral tradition identifies Ned's village as Anstey, a few miles from Leicester. My mother (1906–1999), who spent the whole of her life in the county, told me that the people of Anstey were formerly known as 'Neddoes'.[20] According to a local historian:

> As early as 1757 a mob destroyed bolting-mills at Loughborough, as also at Sileby and Mountsorrel; but the Luddite movement began in March, 1811, when the framework-knitters, in consequence of the depressed state of trade and the poverty of the workmen, began to hold secret midnight meetings, and resolved to organise themselves for the purpose of advancing wages, and to destroy such improved machinery as they supposed injurious to manual labour.

> Accordingly, throughout the country [district], bands of men prowled about at night to destroy the obnoxious frames and machines; and they were so disguised and organised that but very few were brought to justice, compared with their great numbers and the vast amount of property which they destroyed.[21]

A curious ballad, presumably dating from that period, purports (with tongue firmly in cheek) to express the views of factory owners, and it faithfully reflects their 'horrid fright' which Luddite action caused:

A Dialogue between Bill and Joe[22]

J. – Good morning, brother (said Joe to Bill),
I hope you've had a happy night;
But I have dreamed about the mill,
Which puts me in a horrid fright.

B. – What have you dream'd, my dearest brother,
Do not from me your horrors hide;
Our rebel slaves we soon shall smother,
And make them by our laws abide.

J. – Oh, I have dream'd the mill was burning,
And all the stocking-frames laid down
The warehouse shut, and we were mourning,
Slaves triumphant all around.

B. – 'Tis but a dream, and I can ne'er suppose
That dreams are omens of great evils;
Take care, to-night, to slumber with old Rose,
And never fear the slaves, or dreams, or devils.

J. – Dreams may torment, but devils there are none,
Nor hell, of which I ever felt a fear;
I'll grind my slaves, together flesh and bone,
And while I grind them, scorn to shed a tear.

B. – Yes, and I will fleece and spin the hosiers too,
Masters we are, and masters we'll remain;
And if they raise the slaves we'll make them rue,
One farthing profit they shall never gain.

J. – Cursed be they who with such men unite,
And cursed by their children, trade, and wives;
Go sleep with Rose, then every night,
Until the slaves are free, and gain their price.

A clear testimony to the extreme fear of at least one manufacturer, John Heathcote of Loughborough, came to light only in 2006, when a network of tunnels, accessible by removable floorboards and a sandstone trap door, was discovered beneath his house. These were independent of the normal cellars and one of them, an obvious escape route, led to a place in the garden where a coach house used to stand.[23] Heathcote and Boden's Mill (illustrated on p.76) was attacked in June 1816 by armed Luddites from Beeston and Lenton in Nottinghamshire, who destroyed the 55 lacemaking frames there, cut or burned the stocks of lace, and broke all the windows. Heathcote moved from Loughborough to Tiverton in Devon immediately after this attack, so the tunnels must have been constructed earlier. At Leicester Assizes in April 1817 six men were sentenced to death for the attack, and two to transportation for life. Before a crowd of 10,000 people, the six sang a hymn and were then 'launched into eternity' on the drop at the New Bridewell, near the Infirmary at Leicester.

The climate of fear and repression had led in 1812 to frame-breaking being made a capital crime, in spite of Lord Byron's passionate opposition. Byron not only spoke in the House of Lords but also published the following verses in the *Morning Chronicle* in May 1812:

An Ode to the Framers of the Frame Bill[24]

Oh well done Lord E[ldo]n! and better done R[yde]r!
Britannia must prosper with councils like yours;
Hawkesbury, Harrowby, help you to guide her,
Whose remedy only must *kill* ere it cures:
Those villains, the Weavers, are all grown refractory,
Asking some succour for Charity's sake –
So hang them in clusters round each Manufactory,
That will at once put an end to *mistake.*
The rascals, perhaps, may betake them to robbing,
The dogs to be sure have got nothing to eat –
So if we can hang them for breaking a bobbin,
'Twill save all the Government's money and meat:
Men are more easily made than machinery –
Stockings fetch better prices than lives –
Gibbets on Sherwood will heighten the scenery,
Shewing how Commerce, how Liberty thrives!

Just two months earlier, when the Prime Minister, Spencer Perceval, was assassinated, 'Popular elation was undisguised. ... The news that Bellingham [the assassin] was probably deranged, and had acted from motives of private grievance, was received almost with disappointment...'.[25] A less than sympathetic reference to the event comes in a ballad of the time from which the printer prudently (but illegally) left off his name. We know, thanks only to a manuscript note on a surviving copy, that it was George Coates of Alfreton.[26] The main themes of the piece, though, are popular distress and the Luddite campaign of machine breaking:

Hunting a Loaf [27]

Good people I pray give ear unto what I say,
And pray do not call it sedition,
For these great men of late they have crack'd my pate,
I'm wounded in a woeful condition.
[Chorus] Fal lal de ral, &c.

For Derby it's true, and Nottingham too,
Poor men to the jail they've been taking,
They say that Ned Lud as I understood,
A thousand wide frames has been breaking.

Now is it not bad there's no work to be had,
The poor to be starv'd in their station;
And if they do steal they're strait sent to jail,
And they're hang'd by the laws of the nation.

Since this time last year I've been very queer,
And I've had a sad national cross;
I've been up and down, from town unto town,
With a shilling to buy a big loaf.

The first that I met was Sir Francis Burdett,
He told me he'd been in the Tower;
I told him my mind a big loaf was to find,
He said you must ask them in power.

Then I thought it was time to speak to the prime
Master Perceval would take my part,
But a Liverpool man soon ended the plan,
With a pistol he shot through his heart.

Then I thought he'd a chance on a rope for to dance,
Some people would think very pretty;
But he lost all his fun thro' the country he'd run,
And he found it in fair London city.

Now ending my journey I'll sit down with my friends,
And I'll drink a good health to the poor;
With a glass of good ale I have told you my tale,
And I'll look for a big loaf no more. [27]

The radical reformer Sir Francis Burdett was imprisoned in 1810 for breaching the parliamentary privilege of the day by publishing a speech he had given in the House of Commons. According to John Burnett, the standard, quartern loaf, weighing four pounds and five and a quarter ounces, cost 6d. or 7d. in the latter half of the eighteenth century but in 1812 increased to 17d., though it fell to 9d. or 10d. in the 1820s and 1830s.[28] The particular importance of the price of bread has already been mentioned.

The writer of 'Hunting a Loaf' may well have given a favourable mention to frame-breaking, but he stopped short of advocating it. Those who wished to do so, especially after the introduction of the death penalty, passed on their ballads, orally or in writing, in clandestine fashion. Inevitably, some of these ballads will have disappeared; those which have come to light provide precious examples of Luddites speaking for themselves, and hence are revealing and rare historical sources.

In the wrong hands, such material was dangerous. A manuscript ballad formed part of the case against Charles Milnes, who appeared in court in York in January 1813, together with William Blakeborough, on a charge of stealing lead from a roof. The lead apparently was to be cast into bullets for the Luddites. The song had been written out by Milnes for Joseph Taylor, a special constable who had infiltrated Luddite circles around Halifax:

You Heroes of England who wish to have a trade
Be true to each other and be not afraid
Tho' the Bayonet is fixed they can do no good
As long as we keep up the Rules of General Ludd.
As we have begun we are like to proceed
Till from all those Tyrants we do get freed
For this heavy yoke no longer can we bear
And those who have not felt it ought to have a share.[29]

The ‘General Ludd’ of this song is the central figure in one of the finest Luddite ballads, ‘General Ludd’s Triumph’. It is deeply ironic that this survived thanks to a copy, made in a clear, round hand, probably by the Town Clerk of Nottingham, and sent by him to the Home Office as potentially incriminating evidence in January 1812.[30] Following the practice of John Freeth, who wrote songs ‘Adapted to Common Tunes’, an anonymous Luddite took as a model ‘Poor Jack’, from a song of 1788 by the popular composer, Charles Dibdin (1745–1814).

General Ludd’s Triumph[31] *Tune “Poor Jack”*

Chant no more your old rhymes a - bout bold Ro - bin Hood His
feats I but lit - tle ad - mire I will sing the At - chieve - ments of
Ge - ne - ral Ludd now the He - ro of Not - ting - ham - shire Brave
Ludd was to meas - ures of vio - lence un - used Till his suff' - rings be - came so se -
vere That at last to de - fend his own Int' - rest he rous'd And
for the great work did pre - pare That at last to de - fend his own
Int' - rest he rous'd And for the great work did pre - pare

Chant no more your old rhymes about bold Robin Hood,
His feats I but little admire
I will sing the Atchievements of General Ludd
Now the Hero of Nottinghamshire
Brave Ludd was to measures of violence unused
Till his sufferings became so severe
That at last to defend his own Interest he rous’d
And for the great work did prepare.

Now by force unsubdued, and by threats undismay'd
Death itself can't his ardour repress
The presence of Armies can't make him afraid
Nor impede his career of success
Whilst the news of his conquests is spread far and near
How his Enemies take the alarm
His courage, his fortitude, strikes them with fear
For they dread his Omnipotent Arm!

The guilty may fear, but no vengeance he aims
At the honest man's life or Estate
His wrath is entirely confined to wide frames
And to those that old prices abate
Those Engines of mischief were sentenced to die
By unanimous vote of the Trade
And Ludd who can all opposition defy
Was the great Executioner made.

And when in the work of destruction employed
He himself to no method confines
By fire, and by water he gets them destroyed
For the Elements aid his designs
Whether guarded by Soldiers along the Highway
Or closely secured in the room
He shivers them up both by night and by day
And nothing can soften their doom.

He may censure great Ludd's disrespect for the Laws
Who ne'er for a moment reflects
That foul Imposition alone was the cause
Which produced these unhappy effects
Let the haughty no longer the humble oppress
Then shall Ludd sheathe his conquering Sword
His grievances instantly meet with redress
Then peace shall be quickly restored.

Let the wise and the great lend their aid and advice
Nor e'er their assistance withdraw
Till full-fashioned work at the old fashion'd price
Is established by Custom and Law
Then the Trade when this ardorus [sic] contest is o'er
Shall raise in full splendor its head

> And colting, and cutting, and squaring no more
> Shall deprive honest workmen of bread.

The unforgettable opening line, 'Chant no more your old rhymes about bold Robin Hood', audaciously rejects the deeds of a philanthropic hero of the past in favour of a contemporary leader, albeit equally mythical. The song expresses longstanding objections to 'colting' (the employment of excessive numbers of apprentices, which deprived journeymen of work) and 'cutting', and calls for 'full fashioned work at the old fashion'd price', supported by 'Custom and Law'. J.L. and B. Hammond, who first discovered the song in the Home Office papers, commented:

> The promise that Ludd's wrath should be 'confined to wide frames, and to those that old prices abate' was strictly kept, except in one or two instances where mistakes were made ... The cut-up goods made on wide frames were destroyed, and on at least one occasion the rioters searched the bags of a carrier as he was coming into Nottingham, and burnt all the cut-up hosiery, leaving the goods with proper selvedges.

The Hammonds go on to make this point: 'The distinguishing mark of the frame-breaking in 1811–12 was that it was not a wild outburst of popular anger, but a well-planned and organised policy.'[32]

As we have seen, Charles Milnes's manuscript song was used as evidence against him; and the Town Clerk of Nottingham did not take the trouble to copy 'General Ludd's Triumph' out of academic interest. Luddite singers were best advised to confine their songs to oral transmission. Even then, care was needed, as John Hogg of Birkby near Huddersfield found out in September 1812 when, after being reported by several complainants, he was charged with singing this seditious version of the national anthem: 'The devil take the King, Rid England of the King, God save us all, God damn his soul in hell, And throw him down to hell, The devil will serve him well, God save us all.'[33]

Other singers were more careful. Particularly after 1812, no-one was going to advertise his presence on a machine-breaking expedition by publicly singing songs on the subject, and so courting a possible death sentence. Such songs were indeed sung, and in some cases over sixty years passed before they were divulged. The Luddites' ability to keep a secret is illustrated by the story of the nineteen-year-old John Booth, shot and mortally wounded during the attack on Cartwright's Mill (see below). As Booth lay dying, a clergyman, depicted under the name of Mr Helston in

Charlotte Brontë's novel *Shirley*, hovered nearby in the hope of receiving information. On the point of death, Booth signalled, and gasped: 'Can you keep a secret?' 'I can,' was the eager reply. 'So can I,' said Booth – and died.[34]

William Cartwright's mill at Rawfolds in Liversedge, near Huddersfield, was attacked on the evening of 11 April 1812 by some 150 men from Halifax, Huddersfield, Liversedge, Heckmondwike and elsewhere, armed with weapons, axes and hammers. The unpopular Cartwright, expecting trouble, had arranged for a small group of soldiers to be on guard. These repelled the onslaught and the Luddites fled, leaving behind two mortally wounded men, one of them the unfortunate John Booth. Eight men, all croppers of good character, in the prime of life, were brought to trial in January 1813.

Croppers, wielding great shears, trimmed the nap on cloth to an even length, and were highly respected for their strength and skill. 'The new machinery, by which one man could do the work of four, was in the form of a frame in which two or more pairs of shears were fixed and worked by power at the same time.'[35] As a result, instead of earning a good wage of 36s. or 40s. a week (at a time when a labourer earned 8s.) the croppers were reduced to penury. Desperation drove them to break the machines which had taken away their livelihood. Five of the Rawfolds eight were tried at York, found guilty, and hanged a few days later.

One of their number, John Walker of Longroyd Bridge, in an attempt to avoid arrest had fled to Woolwich and enlisted in the Royal Artillery. For many years afterwards he was remembered for his singing at the Shears Inn, not far from Rawfolds, of 'The Croppers' Song': 'Taking a hearty swig at his mug of ale, Walker cleared his voice and then struck up in true ballad patterer's style ... the rollicking chorus was eagerly caught up by his delighted audience, and when the end was reached the refrain was twice

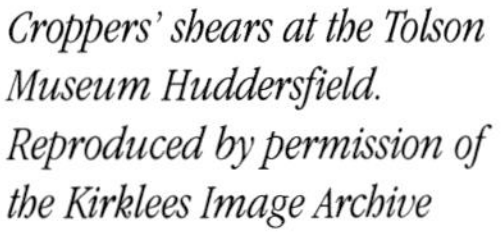

Croppers' shears at the Tolson Museum Huddersfield. Reproduced by permission of the Kirklees Image Archive

repeated with extraordinary vigour, many of the men beating time on the long table with their sticks and pewter mugs.'[36] As it happens, we can form a good idea of what Walker's song sounded like, since it seems to have given rise to a piece dealing with conflict between gamekeepers and poachers, beginning 'Come all you lads of high renown, That loves to drink good ale that's brown, And pull the lofty pheasant down, With powder, shot and gun', which was printed on broadsides in the nineteenth century, and survived in oral tradition until the late twentieth.[37]

The language used by the croppers is simple, strong and direct, with some highly evocative passages such as 'night by night when all is still, And the moon is hid behind the hill'. The affectionately-named 'Great Enoch' was the hammer 'used in the work of destruction, after the firm of Enoch and James Taylor [of Marsden], who made not only the shearing frames but the hammers that destroyed them'.[38] The implement also featured in a Luddite saying: 'Enoch has made them and Enoch shall break them.'

Come, cropper lads of high renown,
Who love to drink good ale that's brown,
And strike each haughty tyrant down,
With hatchet, pike, and gun!

[Chorus]
Oh, the cropper lads for me,
The gallant lads for me,

Who with lusty stroke, the shear frames broke,
The cropper lads for me!

What though the specials still advance,
And soldiers nightly round us prance;
The cropper lads still lead the dance,
With hatchet, pike, and gun!

And night by night when all is still
And the moon is hid behind the hill,
We forward march to do our will
With hatchet, pike, and gun!

Great Enoch still shall lead the van,
Stop him who dare! Stop him who can!
Press forward every gallant man
With hatchet, pike, and gun!

To return to the trial at York, another singer, John Hirst of Liversedge, was among the three acquitted, thanks, in his case, 'to the unwillingness of William Hall to bring to the gallows his old shopmate who had often concealed his own irregularities'.[40] Frank Peel writes of him:

> Knowing that he had escaped the hangman by the skin of his teeth and conscious that he was more blameworthy than some of the men who had been hanged, he would never discuss Luddism nor give any information respecting it; but years after when he came to be an old man and fell into dotage he seemed to live over again that period of his eventful life, and was constantly muttering mysterious pass words, administering secret oaths, or going through imaginary drills. During the last few years of his life he lived with a married daughter, and when engaged in rocking his grandchildren to sleep, he invariably crooned out some Luddite ditty, generally the following:

Come all you croppers, stout and bold,
Let your faith grow stronger still,
These cropping lads in the County of York,
Broke the shears at Horsfall's Mill.
They broke the shears and the windows too,
Set fire to the tazzling mill;

They formed themselves all in a line,
Like soldiers at the drill.

The wind it blew, and the sparks they flew,
And awoke the town full soon.
People got up in the middle of the night,
And they ran by the light of the moon;
When these lads around the mill did stand,
And they all did vow and swear,
Neither blanket nor can nor any such thing,
Should be of service there.[41]

The song, 'Horsfall's Mill', may date from 1803, when dressing machines, both 'tazzling' or 'teaseling' mills (used for raising the nap on cloth, and otherwise known as gig mills) and shear frames, were destroyed at William Horsfall's Ottiwells Mill at Marsden. It was certainly sung during 1811–12, and applied with a simple change of title to the attack on Joseph Foster's mill at Horbury, where at midnight on 9 April men with blackened faces broke in and smashed the machines in the cropping shop.[42]

Foster's Mill[43]

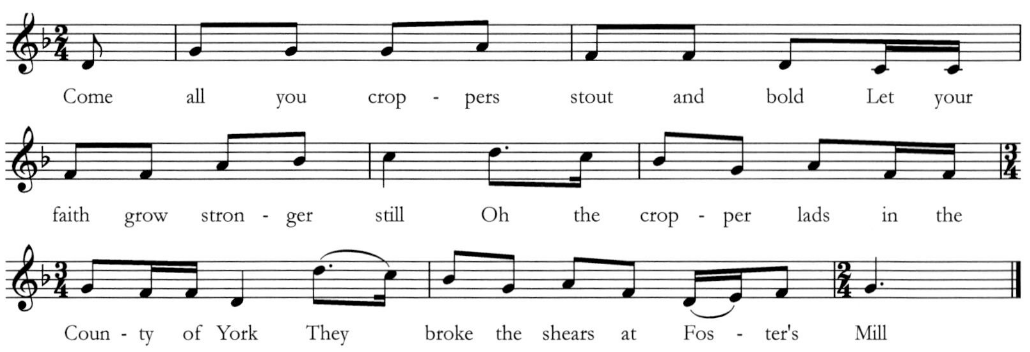

The singer of 'Foster's Mill' was, wrote Peel, 'an intelligent, bright-eyed old lady, who, though she was nearly four score, retained all her faculties unimpaired. She was just one of those garrulous, sharp witted people, full of old world tales and folk-lore, which it delights the hearts of antiquaries to converse with. She knew a great deal about the Luddites, and gave us snatches of ballads which were universally sung amongst them in those troubled times.'[44]

The 'old lady', identified elsewhere as a Mrs Langley, the daughter of a mill foreman called Fearnsides, also sang a fragment of a song composed after the failure of the attack on Cartwright's Mill:

How gloomy and dark is the day
When men have to fight for their bread;
Some judgement will sure clear the way,
And the poor shall in triumph be led.[45]

'More than any other Luddite text from Yorkshire,' wrote Kevin Binfield, 'this song reflects the increasingly millenarian disposition of suffering workers whose efforts at self-help were coming to nothing and who waited for some external force to effect change.'[46]

While some former Luddites turned to religion, others chose politics in the shape of parliamentary reform, and later of Chartism. Others preferred to devote their organisational skills and strong convictions to the cause of trade unionism. However, Ammon Wrigley, writing in 1912, clearly felt the Chartists to be the natural heirs of the Luddites.

Wrigley (1862–1946), largely self-educated, was working in a mill as a half-timer by the age of nine, yet went on to build a considerable reputation as a poet and antiquarian in his native Saddleworth, a salient of Yorkshire projecting westwards into Lancashire, not far from Oldham. 'One cannot think of Blackstone Edge moors,' he wrote, 'without hearing, in fancy, the old fighting songs of the Chartists, the rude rhymes of lean, wolf-eyed singers, who used to assemble there on every first Sunday in May. One can still hear the wild, furious song of the Luddites which, a hundred years ago, shook the Colne Valley like the roaring of wild beasts, making people tremble in their houses at night; a song which ... hung men in chains at York Castle.

The bold men of the County of York
Who fought at Cartwright's mill.'[47]

A generation after the Luddites came another desperate and doomed attempt by working men, this time farm labourers, to protect their livelihood by smashing machinery. They, too, had a mythical leader, Captain Swing, in whose name, over a period stretching from February 1830 until September 1832, agricultural labourers, with allies among craftsmen and small farmers, rioted, destroyed machinery, including threshing machines, demanded money and demonstrated, sometimes rowdily, for higher wages and against enclosures and workhouses. These actions, affecting thirty-four English counties, were sporadic and small scale. Injuries to people were minimal.

The authorities' response was ruthless repression. Of almost 2,000 men brought to court, 644 were jailed, 252 sentenced to death and 505 to transportation. In the end nineteen were hanged, and 481 transported to New South Wales or Van Diemen's Land (Tasmania). In Hampshire, second only to Wiltshire for its number of cases, 68 were jailed, 101 sentenced to death and 117 to transportation. In fact, three were hanged and 107 transported.[48]

John Boys, a small farmer from the village of Owslebury (pronounced Ullsbry), near Winchester, was one of those transported. In November 1830 he had been among a crowd demanding money from Lord Northesk's steward. In addition, he had canvassed signatures from other small farmers to a paper which ran: 'we the undersigned are willing to give 2s. per day for able-bodied married men, and 9s. per week for single men, on consideration of our rents and tithes being abated in proportion.' Boys was tried for felony, but acquitted by the jury, whereupon he was brought before another court, and with James Fussell, 'a genteel young man of about twenty, living with his mother', was 'found guilty of heading a riotous mob for reducing rents and tithes and sentenced to seven years' transportation'.[49] The sentence on Boys was not commuted. As one of the judges, Mr Justice Alderson, thoughtfully explained to those convicted in another case:

> You will leave this country, you will see your friends and relations no more; for though you will be transported for seven years only, it is not likely that at the expiration of that term you will find yourselves in a situation to return. You will be in a distant land at the expiration of your sentence. The friends with whom you are connected will be parted from you forever in this world.[50]

Given the crushing weight and ruthless trajectory of the justice machine, it is barely believable that one of its victims could respond with a song. Yet this was indeed the case, though over sixty years elapsed before it was published, and even then the source wished to remain anonymous. Rev. T. Roach wrote in 1896:

> The following song I took down from the lips of an old man, now bedridden, who, as a lad of 17, was present on the occasion referred to in the first lines. My informant, M.H., who is anxious that his name should not be divulged at present, tells me that the men marched to the house of a bailiff to the then Earl of Northesk, and demanded some of 'my lord's money' which they eventually obtained. M.H. received 2s. as his share. . . . Next day it was put about that those who gave back their 2s. to the vicar of Owslebury

would not be proceeded against, and a number of them accordingly did so, M.H. apparently amongst them. M.H.'s brother got off at this time, but they 'put him away', a euphemism apparently for Van Diemen's Land. This brother wrote the song which I enclose, and as M.H. 'has had many a pot of beer for singing it', he probably has given it me pretty correctly...

The Owslebury Lads[51]

On the thirtieth of November last, Eighteen hundred and thirty,
Our Owslebury lads they did prepare,all for the machinery,
And when they did get there, My eye! How they let fly;
The machinery fell to pieces in the twinkling of an eye.

[Chorus:]
Oh! Mob, such a mob never was seen before,
And if we live this hundred years we never shall no more.

Then to Winchester we was sent our trial for to take,
And if we do have nothing to say, our counsel we shall keep;
And when the judge he did begin I'm sorry for to say,
Some they transported for life and some they cast to die.

At six o' clock in the morning our turnkeys they comes in,
With a bunch of keys all in their hands tied up all in a ring;
And we can't get no farther than backward and forward the yard
And only a pound and a half of bread and don't you think it hard?

At six o' clock in the evening our turnkeys they does come,
The locks and bolts they rattle like the sounding of a drum;
We are shut all in the cells, all in the cells so high,
There we must be till morning whether we live or die.

Sometimes our friends comes in, all for to see us all,
Sometimes they brings tobacco or a loaf that is so small;
We goes out in the kitchen, and sits all round about,
There is so many of us it's very soon all smoked out.

Now to conclude and to finish my new song,
You gentlemen all around me you think that I'm not wrong,
If all the poor of Owslebury for rising of their wages,
I hope that all their enemies may live for want of places'.

The tune has been added here thanks to another version of the song noted in 1906 from James Stagg of Winchester.[52] It seems likely that this was James Stagg, farm labourer, born at Upham and living at Normansland, Morestead, according to the 1891 census, at which time he was 55. Morestead is only about a mile and a half from Owslebury, where 'M.H.' can be identified as Michael Hoare, an agricultural labourer born in the village in 1813, and still living there in 1896 at the age of 83.[53] The song, though defiant, depicts those punished, 'Not criminals but good, brave men', according to W.H. Hudson[54] – as rather making the best of their predicament.

His brother, John (aged 19), was indeed acquitted in November 1830 but later, according to Michael, 'put away' – a euphemism for transported. Of the 345 prisoners at Winchester in 1830 after the Swing Riots, 2 were hanged, 131 transported and 65 imprisoned with hard labour.

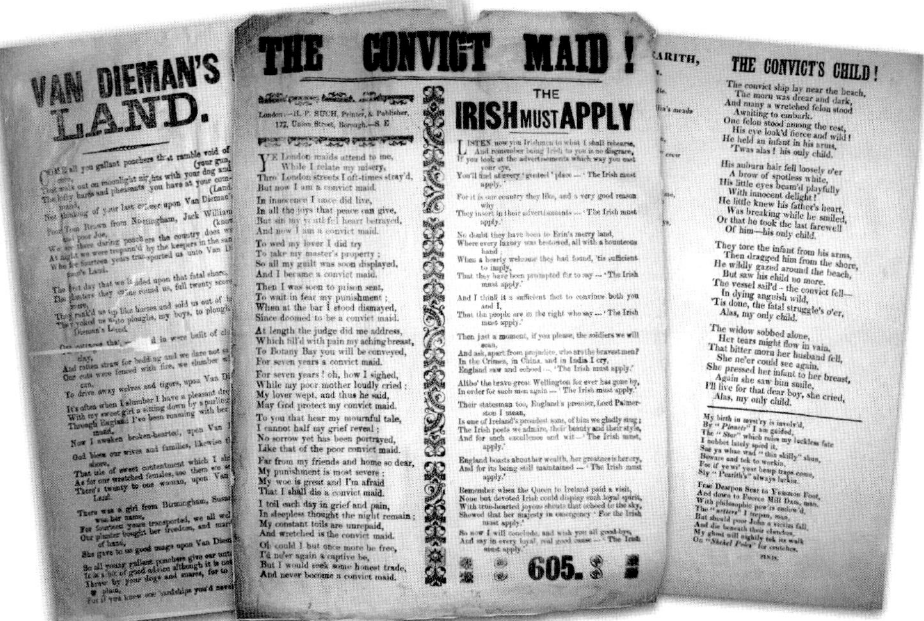

The authorities' response to the 'Swing' riots was ruthless repression. Of almost 2,000 men brought to court, 644 were jailed, 252 sentenced to death and 505 to transportation to New South Wales or Van Diemen's Land (Tasmania).

The searing pain of separation is expressed in this account by Sturge Gretton, who lived in Burford, Oxfordshire. It tells of a vigil which followed what has been called the Last Labourers' Revolt:

> For sixty-five years … one woman not far from my home, through her young womanhood, and middle, and old, age slept wakefully at nights and moved softly by day listening always for footsteps. In 1831 her husband and her brother had both been transported – one for fourteen and the other for seven years – for their part in one of these village riots. Till the fourteen years had passed she would not let herself expect them. 'The one must wait for the other', she said. But from the end of that time for almost fifty years she hoped through each hour; and she died in her chair turned towards the east because she had heard that it was out of the sunrise travellers from Australia must come.[55]

THE WORKMEN'S APPEAL,

Who are out of employment owing to the present Strike.

"So early in the morning."

Fellow workmen and tradesmen all,
Pray listen to your comrades' call,
O help us in the time of need,
And stand we will till our hearts will bleed.

With open hearts together,
Be true to one another,
And help us all as brothers,
To draw the tyrants down.

We have been by them too long kept down,
In countries and in every town;
But now we'll raise our voices high,
And down with tyrants is the cry.

With open hearts together, &c.

Our wives and children are in distress
Is the reason why we on you press,
And tears flowing down their cheek,
Enough to make your hearts to break:—

With open hearts together, &c.

Our children's crying night and day,
Pray listen to their painful cry,—
And tears down their cheeks do shed,—
O! father, mother, give us bread.

With open hearts together,
Be true to one another,
And help us all as brothers,
To draw the tyrants down.

Price ONE PENNY, or what you please to give.

No one will be allowed to Print this Song without the permission of the author.

5 Striking Work

Walk-outs and lockouts

In 1768 a group of sailors marched to the cross in Sunderland, read a document setting forth their grievances and then 'went on board the several ships in that harbour, and struck (lowered down) their yards, in order to prevent their proceeding to sea'.[1] Thus the word 'striking' came into the vocabulary of trade disputes? Not so, unfortunately. 'This is an attractive theory,' writes C.R. Dobson, 'but four years earlier the London tailors had "struck (as they term it)", and in 1763 a hiring bond made at Newcastle required miners to "continue at work, without striking, combining or absenting themselves".'[2] Dorothy George confirms: 'From about 1760 onwards we hear progressively more of strikes and combinations for higher wages.'[3] The *Oxford English Dictionary* records early instances of the use of 'to strike' in 1768, 1793 and 1801, and of 'striking work' in 1803.The nouns 'strike' and 'strike of work' quickly followed.[4]

A century before that, strikes, by whatever name, were already familiar, thanks, as Dobson remarks, to 'the beginnings of a trade union movement in the west of England, based on journeymen's clubs in the wool-manufacturing towns'.[5] One thinks of the combers, weavers, spinners, fullers and shearmen of 'The Clothiers Delight' (see Chapter 3 p. 73). In his book *Masters and Journeymen: a Prehistory of Industrial Relations, 1717–1800,* Dobson gives details of over 450 trade disputes in Britain and Ireland, the huge majority of which, as one might expect, concerned matters of pay, hours and conditions.

The diversity of workers involved was tremendous. There were tailors (particularly militant in London), builders (carpenters and joiners, bricklayers and masons, house painters), miners, canal navvies and bankers, gardeners, haymakers and farm labourers, potters from Liverpool and Stoke-on-Trent, nailers from Dublin, Dudley, Halesowen and Walsall, keelmen (see below) and merchant seamen. One third of the disputes concerned textile workers, including stocking-knitters and weavers of woollen, linen, silk, velvet and baize. Of these, a significant number between the 1770s and the 1790s involved resistance to the introduction of

'Who are out of employment owing to the present Strike.' The Workmen's Appeal, Courtesy of Cardiff Council Library Service

machinery. The introduction of labour-saving devices such as spinning jennies, carding machines, gig (nap-raising) mills and stocking frames were opposed by workers in Wiltshire, Gloucestershire, Leicestershire and Nottinghamshire, because they feared that reduced employment would follow.

So many struggles, but were they reflected in song? During the eighteenth century there was no lack of street ballads which complained of the condition of the poor. Workers suffered at times from too little work, and on occasion from too much. 'General Distress' (to the tune of 'Gee ho Dobbin') begins:

> You surely have heard of great General Distress,
> Who has march'd through this land which once plenty did bless,
> If this beggarly gentleman means long to step [stop],
> I fear every tradesman must shut up his shop.
>
> [Chorus]
> O Old England, wonderful England, plentiful England,
> What is this world come too [sic]?

The final verse makes a sardonic allusion to the roast beef which Englishmen once considered their birthright:

> The face of the hungry looks hagged [haggard] and thin,
> And their bones are just ready to start through their skin,
> And trade is so slack that unless some relief,
> We shall eat one another instead [sic] of roast beef.[6]

The call here is for 'relief' rather than for some form of concerted action, but then immiseration does not produce revolution. Relief is also sought in 'The Complaints of the Poor':

The Complaints of the Poor[7]

> Poor people of England, with tears in their eyes,
> Stand and look at a six-penny loaf with surprise,
> Their hearts they are full, and are always in dread,
> When they hear their poor children a crying for bread.
>
> 'Tis the bakers and millers that causes our grief,
> I think it is time that they give us relief,
> If they make their loaves bigger, as they do of their heads,
> I'm sure I shall always have plenty of bread.

The ballad's conclusion (despite the power of the language) is simply that the poor should be pitied:

> The poor working men are to be pitied good lack,
> They are loaded with work till their bones they do crack,
> They may work till they drop, and be taken up dead,
> They can hardly get cheese to eat with their bread.

It was inevitable that more militant songs should emerge.

Like John Freeth (see Chapter 3, p. 113) of Birmingham, Joseph Mather (1737–1804) of Sheffield was a singer-songwriter, and the two were almost exact contemporaries. After serving an eight-year apprenticeship (1751–1759) as a file cutter (otherwise known as a file hewer), Mather became a journeyman and at one stage a 'small mester'.[8] His efforts (unsuccessful, as it turned out) to make a living for himself, 'Our Nell' and five children are described with some acerbity in 'The File Hewer's Lamentation'. Mather selected the tune (and therefore metre) of 'A Pilgrim Blithe and Jolly', a begging song, in order to make a very different kind of statement. It began:

> In penance for past folly, A pilgrim blithe and jolly,
> Sworn foe to melancholy, Went out strange lands to see:
> With scallop lace his hat brim'd, A scrip and staff and band trim'd,
> As well might suit a Pilgrim, Begging for Charity.

While a number of texts for Mather's 'Lamentation' existed, the tune seemed to be lost, but then a correspondent of mine produced it, from *The Compleat Tutor for the Common Flute* of 1770:

The File Hewer's Lamentation[9]

Ordained I was a beggar,
And have no cause to swagger;
It pierces like a dagger –
To think I'm thus forlorn.
My trade or occupation
Was ground for lamentation,
Which makes me curse my station,
And wish I'd ne'er been born.

Of slaving I am weary,
From June to January!
To nature it's contrary –
This, I presume, is fact.
Although, without a stammer,
Our Nell exclaims I clam [starve] her,
I wield my six-pound hammer
Till I am grown round-back'd.

I'm debtor to a many,
But cannot pay one penny;
Sure I've worse luck than any;
My traps are marked for sale.
My creditors may sue me,
[And curse the day they knew me,]
The bailiffs may pursue me,
And lock me up in jail.

As Negroes in Virginia,
In Maryland or Guinea,
Like them I must continue –
To be both bought and sold.
While Negro ships are filling
I ne'er can save one shilling,
And must, which is more killing,
A pauper die when old.

My troubles never ceased,
While Nell's bairn time increased;
While hundreds I've rehearsed,
Ten thousand more remain;
My income for me, Nelly,
Bob, Tom, Poll, Bet, and Sally,
Could hardly fill each belly,
Should we eat salt and grains?

At every week's conclusion
New wants bring fresh confusion,
It is but mere delusion
To hope for better days.
While knaves with power invested,
Until by death arrested,
Oppress us unmolested
By their infernal ways.

A hanging day is wanted;
Was it by justice granted,
Poor men distress'd and daunted
Would then have cause to sing –
To see in active motion
Rich knaves in full proportion,
For their unjust extortion
And vile offences swing.

Elsewhere, Mather wrote high-spirited celebrations of the pleasures of artisan life, but he also turned out fierce invective, often drawing on vocabulary and imagery from the Old Testament. Mather could read, but his inability to write meant that the process was oral, with some pieces taken down from his dictation and printed as broadsides.

One of these was 'Watkinson and his Thirteens', his attack in 1787 on the master cutler of the day, Jonathan Watkinson, during an industrial dispute. On a memorable occasion Watkinson was forced to leave the theatre when the audience 'in the gods' struck up the vitriolic chorus:

> And may the odd knife his great carcase dissect,
> Lay open his vitals for men to inspect,
> A heart full as black as the infernal gulph,
> In that greedy blood-sucking bone-scraping wolf.

The broadside, 'W————-'s THIRTEENS. Indicted By FIVE PENKNIFE CUTLERS'[10], bizarrely headed by a quotation in Latin from Virgil's *Eclogues*, does not bear Mather's name. However, John Wilson, who edited a collection of Mather's songs described it as 'perhaps the most popular' of them all, adding:

> I can never forget the impression made on my mind when a boy on hearing it sung by an old cutler. This event happened on a 'good saint Monday' [see chapter 9, pp. 340 ff.], during a 'foot ale' which was drunk in the workshop. After the singer had 'wet his whistle', he requested his shopmates to assist in chorus, and then struck off in a manly voice, laying strong emphasis on the last two lines of each stanza, at the conclusion of which he struck his stithy [anvil] with a hammer for a signal, when all present joined in chorus with such a hearty good will that would have convinced any person that *they felt* the 'odd knife' would have been well employed in dissecting Watkinson's 'vile carcase'.[11]

The ballad deals with broad strokes rather than fine brushwork. Wilson relates this account of the origin of the dispute:

> During Watkinson's year of office some of the manufacturers complained of workmen keeping the *odd* materials as perquisites (a grinder's dozen being fourteen, while horn, wood and bone scales were thirteen). To stop this system of *appropriation* the respectable masters desired the workmen to make thirteen and *be paid for them*; but the others, more unscrupulous, only paid for twelve. But the manufacture being a monopoly Watkinson only acted in his capacity as the head of the corporation. The resolutions of that body would be officially signed by the master cutler upon whom fell the popular displeasure.[12]

The ballad's widespread popularity made it a landmark intervention in an industrial dispute. It discredited the policy of a body of employers and caused personal discomfiture to their spokesman.

Five years later, in 1792, John Wolcot (1738–1819), who wrote under the pseudonym Peter Pindar, wrote – surely with tongue in cheek – 'Resignation: an Ode to the Journeymen Shoemakers Who lately refused to work, except their Wages were raised'.[13] He offered this advice:

> Sons of Saint Crispin, 'tis in vain!
> Indeed 'tis fruitless to complain.
> I know ye wish good beef or veal to carve:
> But first the hungry Great must all be fed;
> Meantime, ye all must chew hard, musty bread,
> Or, what is commonly unpleasant, starve.
>
> Closed be your mouths, or dread the jail or thong;
> Ye must not for your money have a song,
> Cease, cease, your riots, pray, my friends;
> It answereth (believe me) no good ends –
> And yet the time will come, I hope to God,
> When black-faced, damned Oppression to his den
> Shall howling fly before the curse of men,
> And feel of angered Justice the sharp rod.

Walcot's verse illustrates the huge odds which workers faced when they made efforts to improve their lot, and it was logical that they should seek strength in numbers. Faced with the law, the justice system and at times the intervention of the armed forces, groups of workers resorted at times to subterfuge, covert action and violence.

1800s: steeks, strikes and turnouts

The naval mutinies and the rising of the United Irishmen in 1797 were followed by repressive legislation which inhibited political agitation and effectively made trade union activity illegal. The passing of the Combination Act of 1799 was thanks to the efforts of William Wilberforce, whose work for the emancipation of slaves has diverted attention from his enthusiasm for the repression of workers.

The Act, as amended in 1800, 'made liable (for the first offence) to three months in gaol, or two months' hard labour, any working man who combined with another to gain an increase in wages or a decrease in hours, or solicited anyone else to leave work, or objected to working with any other workman. … A further provision was that the defendants were forced to give evidence against one another.'[14] The sentence was to be determined by two magistrates, with appeals permitted subject only to the provision of two sureties of £20, which were out of reach of working men.

Such summary justice meant that strikes could be quickly broken. 'The acts also nominally forbade employers' combinations, without the provision about evidence and without a penalty of imprisonment. But this prohibition was never enforced, though employers' combinations were open and frequent in the next quarter of a century.'[15]

Trade unions were forced into clandestinity, though workers might succeed in taking action with a degree of impunity in the case of walk-outs or what we now call 'wildcat strikes', which had no detectable organising body. In the early 1800s, according to Thomas Wilson (1773–1858), the author of *The Pitman's Pay*, who went down the pit at an early age and left at nineteen to become a schoolteacher:

> Whenever they [miners] considered themselves aggrieved, they 'struck'; or, in the language of that day, a 'steek' took place. These 'steeks' generally originated on the Wear; and, by way of enforcing their demands, the malcontents immediately 'laid in' all the pits in the district. The mode of proceeding in such cases was this: – the men with whom the strike commenced visited all the neighbouring collieries; and, on their arrival at each pit, they hung on a corf, filled with stones, at the same time hanging on the clog [log]. The weight of the corf moved the gin; and as the former descended the latter gained velocity, until the clog, flying out in the air, knocked away the supports of the gin and laid it on its side, thus rendering it totally unfit for use and thereby putting a stop to all work for some time to come.[16]

If on this occasion miners escaped sanctions, their Durham colleagues were less fortunate when they came out on strike in the winter of 1809 in an attempt to prevent the employers from altering to their disadvantage the terms of their 'binding' or contract. 'So many "leaders" were arrested that once Durham gaol and the House of Correction were filled people were imprisoned in the bishop's stables. The strike momentarily ended in a truce, negotiated by the rector of Brauncepath and the captain of the militia, whom the miners trusted when they would not their employers, but ultimately the use of the law broke the strike.'[17]

Despite the Combination Acts, strikes continued to take place. As the Napoleonic Wars came to an end, over a two-year period (1814–1816) some 120,000 men were discharged and abandoned to their fate. Ship-owners took advantage of the surplus of labour to drive down wages. Sailors resisted and, as a result: 'During the summer of 1815 strikes broke out in several ports including Hull, Yarmouth and the Tyne and Wear, spreading later to Leith, Aberdeen and Clydeside.'[18]

The dispute dragged on in the north-east of England, where the owners of collier vessels wished drastically to lower the wartime rate of £8 or £9 for a voyage to London. Sailors were willing to accept £5 in winter and £4 10s. in summer, but held out for the wartime manning ratio of three men per hundred tons to be raised to six men and a boy. An agreement was reached on the Wear but not on the Tyne, where:

> Magistrates proved unable to prevent seamen from stopping ships and striking sails, and even from creating a barrier of boats across the estuary of the Tyne at Shields. In effect the seamen ran the Tyne for the duration of the strike, with committees determining local strategies, organising relief funds and applications and hiring lawyers to negotiate with the ship-owners.[19]

The description has a surprisingly familiar feeling.

To the charge that Nelson would have disapproved of their actions, the seamen of Sunderland replied that 'many of us have fought under his victorious banners', adding that: 'if a shipowner's property has been preserved during the time we have been fighting for King and Country, a British sailor cannot but expect to be employed on his return home as a reward for his services.'[20] Precisely the same point was made in:

The Seamen['s] Complaint[21]

A new Song written by a Sailor who was present at the Battle of the Nile

I sing the British Seamen's woe,
There pain an' grief an' a' that;
Whose hearts wi' anguish overflow,
Denied relief for a' that.
For a' that, an' a' that,
We still may mourn for a' that,
We've shed wur blood, for England's guid,
An' what return for a' that.

When gallant Nelson at the Nile,
Defeat the French and a' that;
We Sailors there did share the toil,
And scorn'd to flinch for a' that,
For a' that, an' a' that,
Our Country's claim an' a' that,
To what a height, of honour bright,
We rais'd her fame for a' that.

We nobly did wur Country serve,
Bore toils severe an' a' that;
But now we're basely left to starve,
In deep despair for a' that,
For a' that, an' a' that,
We may complain for a' that;
Our Children cries for fresh supplies
They can't obtain for a' that.

They make us to London hie
For three Pounds ten and a' that;

Will that support a Family,
Or life sustain for a' that.
For a' that, an' a' that,
An' hundreds here for a' that,
Deprived of Joy, without employ,
Must famine bear for a' that.

Wi' mind indignant I survey
This gloomy scene an' a' that
But ev'ry Dog must have his day
And we'el have ours for a' that
For a' that, an' a' that,
The time will come for a' that;
When fortunes smile shall pain beguile
And break the gloom for a' that.

Again should wars dread trumpet sound,
And Gallia threat an' a' that;
Where will the Seamen then be found,
To Man your Fleet for a' that.
For a' that, an' a' that,
We ne'er were slack for a' that
When sounds of war, are heard afar,
Ye'll wish us back for a' that.

The use of Burns's song as a model, as well as the adoption of his tune, probably implied sympathy with his views. Although the strike is not mentioned (perhaps because of wariness as to possible consequences) it is highly likely that 'The Seamen's Complaint' was intended, or at least used, to support it.

1820s: keelmen's stick and weavers' turnout

Equally uncompromising songs emerged from the keelmen, who waged an admirable and prolonged, if ultimately unsuccessful, struggle to maintain their standards of living and to protect their livelihood from what appeared to them as deleterious innovation. On the River Tyne they proudly traced their history back to the fourteenth century. They were tough men, many of who originated in Redesdale and Tynedale or over the border in Scotland.

By the early eighteenth century there were 1,600 of them, living mainly in the Sandgate district of Newcastle, and working some 400 keels, open craft forty feet long and 15 feet six inches wide, which transported coal from the riverside staiths or spouts to ships lying in the river. The keels were propelled mainly by a single oar forward worked by two keel 'bullies' (crewmen) and a boy, paid by the crew, and known as a 'P.D.'. The latter seems to have been held in great affection locally: a song entitled 'Little P.D.' was reprinted six times over a sixty-year period.[22] The craft's skipper steered at the stern with an oar called a 'swape' (sweep). There was a single mast, which could be lowered, with a square-rigged lug sail (replaced after about 1800 with fore and aft rig).

The men, employed by the collieries, were on an annual 'binding' (contract) from Christmas to Christmas, until 1872, when they changed to fortnightly engagements. Their flourishing friendly society provided mutual support and also funded a hospital. Their holiday dress in the eighteenth century consisted of short blue jacket, yellow waistcoat and slate-coloured trousers, with a black neckerchief and black, flat-brimmed hats decked with black ribbon. Their pride is reflected in songs still well known in the north-east of England, and indeed further afield, such as 'Weel may the Keel row' and 'Bonny Keel Laddie'.[23]

It is no surprise that such men had a record of militancy going back to a recorded 'stick' as early as 1671. Strikes in 1708 and 1719 were broken when the pressgang seized men for service in the navy. In 1738 and 1740, the strikers were suspected of having Jacobite sympathies. In 1749, 1769, 1771 and 1794 considerable damage was caused to the staiths.

The issue of the staiths surfaced again in 1822, when the main cause of a strike lasting from October until December was that ships were loading direct from staiths built below the Tyne bridge, thus cutting out the keelmen.

Government unhesitatingly intervened. Marines were drafted in, and at one stage seven intimidatory men-of-war were moored in Shields harbour. At local level, militiamen were mobilised, and large numbers of special constables sworn in. The strikers retaliated by damaging spouts and sinking keels. There were riots in Scotswood and North Shields. A locomotive from the Wylam Collieries line was mounted on a keel, guarded by marines, and this, acting as a sort of paddle tug, towed keels full of coal up and down the river, and so broke the blockade which strikers were trying to enforce. The keelmen returned to work in December, their main aim unachieved.[24]

A ballad to the tune of 'Lancashire Dick' (alias 'Gee Ho Dobbin') provided a clear exposition of the circumstances which led to the strike:

The Keelman's Lamentation[25]

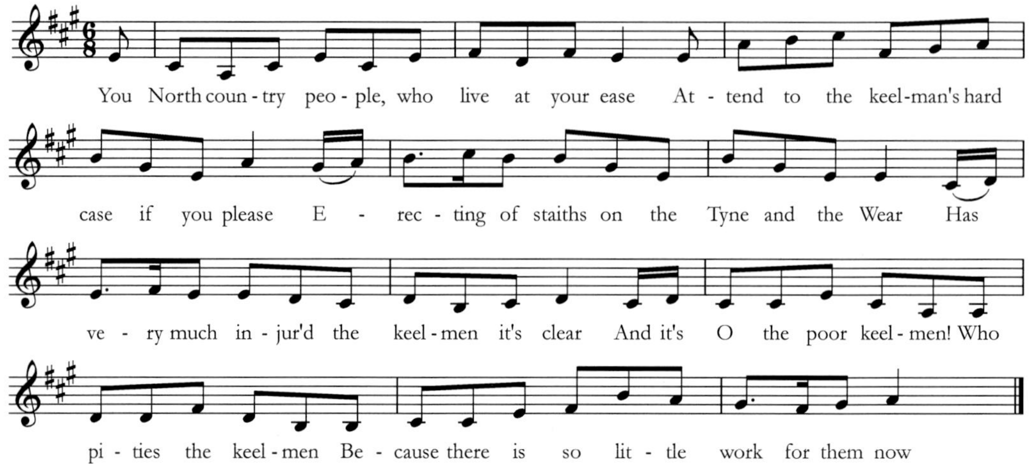

You North Country people, who live at your ease,
Attend to the keelmen's hard case, if you please:
Erecting of staiths on the Tyne and the Wear,
Has very much injur'd the keelmen, it's clear.

[Chorus]
And it's O the poor keelmen! – who pities the keelmen?
Because there is so little work for them now.

Although the coal trade has increased so much,
The effects of the staiths on the keelmen is such,
Great numbers of them are from work thrown quite out,
Since so many shipping now load at the spout.

A keelman he told me, when he was a boy
Then six hundred keels they had all full employ;
Tho' there are no more than three hundred keels now,
Yet many of them have but little to do.

They would be content, and no more they would seek,
If they could get three or four tides in a week;
But many of them can get but one or two,
And a great many more can get nothing to do.

The poor keelmen's wives they now cry fish and fruit,
While keelmen nurse children – but that does not suit,
The husband can't quiet the child when it cries,
And that causes great many quarrels to rise.

Against the poor keelmen we hear many cry,
And say they are idle; but that I deny:
They often work harder and longer each day,
Than convicts transported to Botany Bay.

One time bucklemakers apply'd to the king,
To stop folks from tying their shoes with a string:
I never heard whether they lost or they won,
But their trade has fail'd, as the keelmen's has done.

It would make better times if the rich and the high
Would do unto all as they would be done by;
When coal owners oppress, let the keelmen combine,
And defend the just rights of the sons of the Tyne.

While Mather's file cutter compared his lot with that of 'negroes in Virginia', the keelmen here profess themselves worse off than 'convicts transported to Botany Bay'.

The printer of the keelmen's ballad was John Marshall of Newcastle, who either for commercial or political reasons (or both) printed a good deal of material supportive of radical causes, including strikes by miners. Another of his publications illustrates the point that, as well as in standard English, strike ballads appeared in the local vernacular. 'The Keelmen's Stick', after the arresting opening of 'Smash! Jamie, aw's glad for to see that thou's well. Some rare news aw've getten, mun, now for to tell', relates various events during the strike of 1822:

The Keelmen's Stick (John Marshall, printer)[26]

Then efter a while, for to keep a' things well,
They gat a gun-ship like a good cockle shell;
To frighten the keelmen it was their design,
But they fan that the keelmen had *pluck* on the Tyne.

Then they gat some *moreens* [marines] and some landsmen an' a',
To bring a' the laden keels doon, ye mun knaw;
But they myed sic a bummell wi' sail and wi' line,
That they varry near cowpt theirsels intiv the Tyne.

Another printer, the ardent reformer and republican William Stephenson of Gateshead, issued a further ballad under the title of 'The Keelmen's Stick', to the tune 'Chapter of Donkies' [sic], better known as 'Chapter of Kings'. (Did the republican Stephenson deliberately choose the former title?) The text again provides a sardonic commentary on the strike-breaking efforts of police, special constables and soldiers, and uses military imagery to mocking effect:

The Keelmen's Stick (William Stevenson, printer)[27]

Wor varge an' the noodles a' cut a grand shine,
They went to protect baith sides o' the Tyne,
They put one i' mind, they luikt so complete,
Of Nelson blockading an enemy's fleet.

But a king's cutter com an' laid a' their pride,
Mareens they say fights best on the tide,
The noise o' their guns set wor bairns into fits,
And a canny awd barber they've shak'd a' to bits.

Wor keelmen they own put them a' in a maze,
At the mouth o' their cannon so bold they did gaze;
Their captain said, 'Turks wiv a' their lang knives,
Was nowt tiv an army of Sandgate awd wives.'

There was a mareen, the deel clag up his eye,
That shot a poor fellow, aye, clean throw the thigh,
He luikt like a monkey in his coat an' cockt hat,
And they say he expects a promotion for that.

If they'd come a-shore wi' just their bare fist,
My sang we wad gean their necks sic a twist,
They wad fund a' wor foes iv baith sides o' the line,
Were just nowt at a' to wor brave sons of Tyne.

In contrast with Mather's personal vituperation, and also with his bitter rage, these ballads, though not without vehemence, perhaps for the first time provide a review of the issues and incidents of a strike from a collective viewpoint.

Despite their defeat, the keelmen, who maintained that the spouts amounted to a public nuisance, lodged an 'information' which obliged representatives of the owners of Wallsend Colliery to appear at the York Assizes in August 1824. Henry Brougham, reformer, Whig politician and future Lord Chancellor, appearing for the keelmen, argued that the spouts were a danger to navigation and had caused the river to silt up. Mr (later Sir) James Scarlett, barrister and future Lord Chief Baron of the Exchequer,

THE Civil Authorities regret to find the deluded Keelmen still continue to insult His Majesty's Boats, by throwing Stones when protecting those that are willing to work; and finding Forbearance any longer will endanger the Lives of those so employed,—This is to caution the peaceable Inhabitants, and Women, and Children, to keep within their Houses during the Time the Keels are passing from the Staiths to Shields, as the Marines have Orders *to fire on the first Man that shall dare to throw a Stone at them.*

November 23rd, 1822. G. Angus, Printer, Newcastle.

acting for the coal-owner, persuaded the jury to bring in a verdict favourable to the defence. The proceedings were chronicled in another ballad, again printed by William Stephenson, 'The Keelmen's Trial. A New Song'.[28]

Still defiant, the keelmen applied for the verdict to be set aside on grounds of misdirection by the judge, but after considerable delay it was upheld in 1826. Further proceedings two years later were equally fruitless. 'With the advent of railways in the 1830s, many of the above-bridge collieries stopped using keels and had their coal transported to Shields by rail; while the removal of Newcastle bridge in 1876 and the subsequent deepening of the river channel to accommodate colliers meant the end of the keelmen's trade.'[29] Once again, the poor paid for progress. The keelmen's strike of 1822 took place despite the Combination Acts, which were not strictly enforced everywhere, and trade unions sometimes successfully operated in the disguise of friendly societies. Others worked in secrecy.

Repeal in 1824 'marked a significant changing point in labour protest. Its immediate result, coupled with a major trade boom, was a rapid increase in aggressive strike action.'[30] The government quickly responded with an amending act intended to limit the scope of workers' action, yet combination remained lawful provided that the unions 'confined themselves to peaceful bargaining about wages and hours, took care not to lay themselves open to charges of inducing breach of contract, and did not in any way "molest" or "obstruct" either employers or blacklegs.'[31] Conducting a serious strike therefore remained a ticklish operation, but at least trade unions, no longer effectively outlawed, could set about building their strength.

In April 1825 the Stroud Valley Weavers' Union called a strike for an advance in wages and against the longstanding practice of truck, under which a workman was paid in tokens exchangeable only at his employer's shop, often at inflated prices. Within a few days membership went up from 400 to 5,000. The strike went on for three months, with increasing anger shown to those who broke it: shuttles were taken away, parts of looms removed, men ducked in ponds, canals and brooks. A solitary ballad has survived on this 'turn-out' (another term for 'strike', first recorded in 1806):

The Weavers' Turn-out[32]

O. hark! My lads, and give an ear, to listen unto me,
A story unto you I'll relate which happen'd the other day,
It's concerning of weavers, who for their rights maintain,
We have been labouring many a year, but still it was all in vain.

[Chorus]
So let us all, while in our bloom,
Drink success to the weavers' loom.

In Dursley town in Gloucestershire, for wages we stood out,
It was for one 3 pence per yard on a chain of broad cloth,
Our clubs we have to support our wives and children dear,
We live in hopes of better times while we drink a jug of beer.

Look all around the neighbourhood and you will quickly hear,
We are in hopes our employers our wages will ensure
For provisions they are plentiful, they are so rich and good,
And so my boys we'll never fear our clubs they will stand good.

Behold the town of Bratford and Wotton-under-hedge too,
They weavers they are all combin'd to their colors will stand true,
The town of Trowbridge as yo hear, and not leave Milsom out,
And all around the neighbourhood for wages will stand out.

All round the neighbourhood the trade it has been good,
For all mechanics in the trade to support themselves with food,
But the weavers they are valiant men as you will understand,
Then for our wages we stand out and no more be at command.

So to conclude my ditty and to finish up my song,
We'll drink success to the weavers, may the trade be carried on,
Likewise to our employers wherever they may dwell,
May the trade be in a flourishing state, and never for to fail.

'Bratford' (Bradford-on-Avon), like a number of the other towns mentioned, is in Wiltshire. It has been crossed out by hand in this copy of the sheet, and 'Stroudwater' inserted. 'Wotton-under-hedge' should be Wotton-under-Edge.

The writer is unlikely to have seen the keelmen's strike ballads, which were printed in Newcastle and Gateshead. He (or she) nevertheless adopts the same traditional opening, with its call for attention, and then launches into 'a story'. After a brief mention of the main issue, the wages, he turns to a series of pious hopes and exhortations.

In contrast to this single sheet, another strike of hand weavers – this time in the carpet trade – at Kidderminster, three years after the events at Stroud, produced a blizzard of ballads and handbills, pamphlets and poems, many of them expressing passionate views. (This phenomenon would be repeated in other disputes, such as the (machine) weavers' strike at Preston, for which see Chapter 6. p. 188) One Kidderminster poem, by Rev. Humphrey Price, a clergyman sympathetic to the strikers, caused his being jailed for a year for libelling some of the employers.

The strike, which involved 2,000 weavers and several thousand dependent workers, lasted from March until August 1828, and attracted widespread attention in the press, both local and national. The matter in contention was simple: the manufacturers' decision to reduce payments to workers by one sixth (17%), on the grounds of competition from Yorkshire and Scotland.

A dozen ballads putting the workers' case have survived, many dating from the earlier stages of the strike. They were produced, probably at the behest of the well-organised weavers' committee, by local printers James Bromley and Thomas Pennell. The latter also printed material for the employers, so his motivation is likely to have been simply commercial. It is possible that the former was sympathetic towards the weavers, and one wonders whether he was the 'J.B.' who wrote 'The Carpet Weavers' True Tale'.[33]

Ballads enjoyed the advantage of selling at a penny a time since, unlike news-sheets, they did not pay the stamp duty imposed in 1819 to hamper the radical press. They not only generated income but also stated the strikers' case and raised their morale. In addition, they provided a form of entertainment, especially when they were sung. Just as ballads chronicled successive battles in the Napoleonic Wars, so they commented on successive clashes between employers and workers.

No tunes were prescribed on the Kidderminster sheets, but many had choruses, and also followed the traditional 'Come all ye' pattern, with openings such as 'Good people all I pray attend' and 'Come townsmen all and women too'. A favoured theme was the contrast between the masters' affluence and the workers' penury:

Were you to go around our town, their country seats to see,
You then would be convinc'd, what they have gain'd by we,
To see their livery servants, their carriages also,
You then would be quite satisfied whether we are right or no.

The manufacturers of this town, their fortunes they have made,
And in the space of twenty years, all by the carpet trade
To see how they do ride about, their pleasure for to take,
Leaving their poor journeymen, with scarce a meal to eat.[34]

The workers appeal both to scripture and to the rights of freeborn men:

> Now let us turn to God and pray that victory we may have,
> For Israel prayed to God, and he victory to them gave,
> Let love and union still preserve each member of the trade,
> And by that rule of faith I'm sure, weavers will ne'er be slaves.[35]

In a similar vein, 'The Carpet Weaver's New Song', looking back to a strike of 1789 in which a wage reduction was resisted, promises:

> Therefore in union we will join, our rights and prices to maintain;
> And never to oppression yield, while yet Britannia rules the main.[36]

'The Carpet Weaver's Determination' employs the military imagery of battle and flight, colours and guns, and claims:

> The enemy begins to fall, their ranks we will break through,
> And England does expect this day, our duty we should do.[37]

Despite moral and financial support (some £2,000 in total, almost half of this from other carpet weavers) from as far afield as Manchester, London, Dewsbury and Coventry, the strike crumbled, then collapsed. The Kidderminster weavers had suffered severely, and they resumed work at reduced rates, facing a burden of debt. The manufacturers succeeded, but at great cost: 'they had antagonised a reasonably well-disposed workforce; industrial relations were irreparably poisoned for the foreseeable future.'[38]

1830s: 'aflame with agitations'

E.P. Thompson very clearly summarised the concerns of working people at the beginning of the decade. 'The early years of the 1830s,' he wrote, 'are aflame with agitations which turned on issues in which wages were of secondary importance; by the potters, against the Truck System; by the textile workers, for the 10-Hour Bill; by the building workers, for the right to join trade unions. The great strike in the north-east coalfield in 1831 turned on security of employment, "tommy shops", child labour.'[39] All these issues led to strikes, which in many cases gave rise to ballads.

The words 'tommy' or 'truck' indicated payment in kind rather than cash. A law passed in 1831 provided that specified 'artificers' be paid only in coin, but this was not extended to all manual workers until 1887, and even then some exceptions were made for agricultural labourers. 'Tommy shops', where workers were obliged to buy goods provided for the purpose by their employers, took their name from the slang word for bread, which in turn may have derived from the loaves once traditionally handed out to the poor on St Thomas's Day (21 December).

The widespread abuse of the system inspired ballads such as 'The Tommy Note', printed in Birmingham in the 1820s by Theophilus Bloomer, in which colliers and canal boatmen complain that they are obliged to go to the tommy shop 'To fetch our week's provision, Their oatmeal, sugar, salt and soap, Short weight and little measure'.[40]

A rather wider range of commodities features in a ballad probably printed in the Potteries, which ironically sets out the beneficence of an employer who runs a tommy shop. It incidentally provides a fascinating list of what might be found in a working class household at the time.

The Truck Master. A New Song[41]

The times are bad, I can't command, a ready-money bill;
And I've so large a stock on hand, my works must soon stand still.
I really know not what to do, so wayward is my luck,
Unless that each and all of you your wages take in truck.

CHORUS
I've this, I've that, I've what you will, with prices on them stuck,
The same as on the invoice bill, for you to take in Truck.

I've tongues, pigs' tails, and catsup [ketchup] rare, for those who dainties choose;
I've feathers, soft as down, I'll swear, for all who feathers use.
Fine barcelonas [type of nut] too I've got, your teeth to exercise,
Each cabbage here would fill a pot, here's apples of all size.

I've rhubarb stalks here sound and hard, when you may c—stive [costive] be,
Or want a pie – how I regard your welfare you may see;
I know besides you must have bread your children's cries to stop;
And I have provided on this head a ready Tommy shop.

Welch flannels in abundance here, to screen you from the cold;
I've got, at prices rather dear, but then they must be sold.
West England clothes, and Yorkshire too of broad and narrow kind;
An invoice price I offer you so don't the flannel mind.

For painter girls I've cotton prints of every sort to sell;
The pattern's striking, and the tints will stand the washing well.
I've Irish cloth for chemises, and shirts to grace the men;
With things upon my premises, would take me months to pen.

So let the times run how they will, I've taken special care
Though I'm without a money bill, you've things to eat and wear;
You scarcely men can fail to see the great regard I shew -
So take the *Truck* and grateful be, and home contented go.

That this is very much tongue-in-cheek is confirmed by a companion sheet from the same printer (judging by the typography), to the same tune, 'Washing Day' (a variant title for 'Nae luck about the house'):

(This tune was used for both ballads by this printer)

The TRUCK Man's Wife on a Saturday Night [42]

Well, husband, what's the prize tonight? I guess some horrid thing
Enough to drive me crazy quite, you for your wages bring;
A two-month's rent last week was due, the Landlord will not stay,
Besides I want some money too to go another way.

[Chorus]
The Woman now a Poor Man's wife,may curse her ill-starr'd luck,
For I am weary of my life, the D—-l take the TRUCK!!!!!!

Put down your load and let me see what lumber you have got,
The first thing here's no use to me, of Pigs' Tails what a lot;
I see you've brought another tongue,you stupid silly elf,
I'll let you know before 'tis long I've tongue enough myself.

Why, bless me! Man, I vow by heaven I sha'nt for rhubarb stir,
What have you for these bundles given? What are they fitting for?
The stalks are wither'd, old, and dry, and troubled with the rot,
I would not give, indeed not I, a farthing for the lot.

Is this the Beef? 'tis but a bone for where's the lean or fat,
This Flour at three and five per stone is black as a cravat,
Why sure you must be mad indeed such rubbish home to bring,
And think that people in their need must stoop to any thing.

Here's Flannel, Lord! What horse-rug stuff, is this you flannel call,
I never saw a bag so rough hung drying on a wall,
More cotton rags – more catsup, how, with these you always swarm
But where's my tea, I'm fainting now for want of something warm.

How many Tommies [loaves] have you got, what butter for the week?
Is there no sugar in the lot? Where for it must I seek?
I've found it in the paper here, my life what wretched stuff,
And *twopence* in the pound too dear, they always charge enough.

Of ear-rings too you've got a pair have wives then nought to do,
But bore their ears and hang them there for every fool to view;
And why more stockings have you brought of such a texture sleek,
It seems as if the master thought we spoil'd two pair a week.

Dear husband shall we never see old times again to come?
When we once more shall happy be and bring you home,
I have no patience with the thing so take the stuff away,
I'll curse the plaguy TRUCK you bring unto my dying day.

Thanks to campaigning against truck, the Potters' Union, launched in 1830, had 8,000 members three years later. However, the vulnerability revealed when the union collapsed in 1837 after its defeat in a strike was one of the factors which convinced some potters of the need for the nationwide political support which would be provided by the Chartist movement.

In the north-east of England, tommy shops were among the grievances which led to the strike in March 1831 of some 10,000 miners. A long tradition of militant action there went back at least to 1765, when 4,000 men struck after an attempt by employers to impose a system of leaving certificates ('Binding'), which would have made it difficult for them to change pits. Twenty years later the 'magistrates and principal

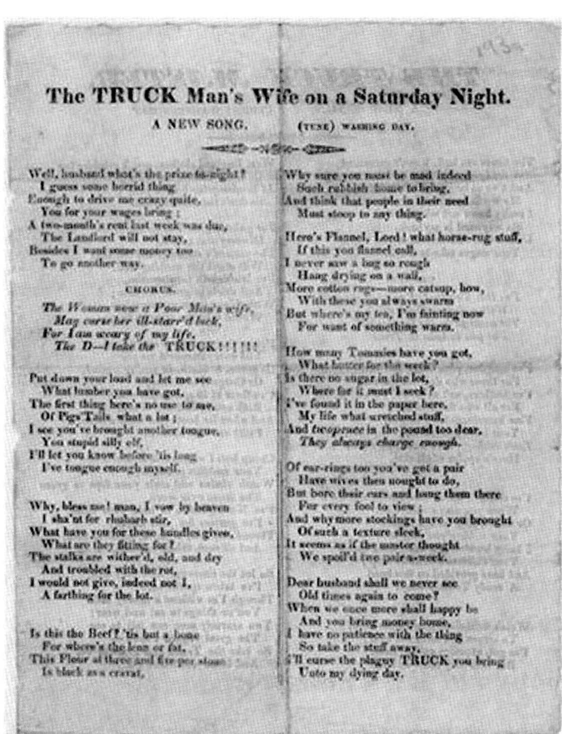

The TRUCK Man's Wife on a Saturday Night.

A NEW SONG. (TUNE) WASHING DAY.

Well, husband what's the prize to-night?
I guess some horrid thing
Enough to drive me crazy quite,
You for your wages bring;
A two-month's rent last week was due,
The Landlord will not stay,
Besides I want some money too
To go another way.

CHORUS.

The Woman now a Poor Man's wife,
May curse her ill-starr'd luck,
For I am weary of my life.
The D—l take the TRUCK!!!!!!

Put down your load and let me see
What lumber you have got,
The first thing here's no use to me,
Of Pigs'Tails what a lot;
I see you've brought another tongue,
You stupid silly elf,
I'll let you know before 'tis long
I've tongue enough myself.

Why, bless me! man, I vow by heaven
I sha'nt for rhubarb stir,
What have you for these bundles given,
What are they fitting for?
The stalks are wither'd, old, and dry
And troubled with the rot,
I would not give, indeed not I,
A farthing for the lot.

Is this the Beef? 'tis but a bone
For where's the lean or fat,
This Flour at three and five per stone
Is black as a cravat.

Why sure you must be mad indeed
Such rubbish home to bring,
And think that people in their need
Must stoop to any thing.

Here's Flannel, Lord! what horse-rug stuff,
If this you flannel call,
I never saw a bag so rough
Hang drying on a wall,
More cotton rags—more catsup, bow,
With these you always swarm
But where's my tea, I'm fainting now
For want of something warm.

How many Tommies have you got,
What butter for the week?
Is there no sugar in the lot,
Where for it must I seek?
I've found it in the paper here,
My life what wretched stuff,
And *twopence* in the pound too dear,
They always charge enough.

Of ear-rings too you've got a pair
Have wives then nought to do,
But bore their ears and hang them there
For every fool to view;
And why more stockings have you brought
Of such a texture sleek,
It seems as if the master thought
We spoil'd two pair a-week.

Dear husband shall we never see
Old times again to come?
When we once more shall happy be
And you bring money home,
I have no patience with the thing
So take the stuff away,
I'll curse the plaguy TRUCK you bring
Unto my dying day.

'The Truck Man's Wife on a Saturday Night' Reproduced courtesy of The Potteries Museum & Art Gallery, Stoke-on-Trent.

inhabitants' of Sunderland petitioned the government for a permanent military force to protect them from the disobedience of the seamen and keelmen and the unruly behaviour of 'another description of Men called Pitmen'.[43]

Binding was again an issue in the strike of 1810, involving men from thirty-one collieries, and in 1826 it brought some 4,000 men into the newly established Pitmen's Union. In the 1831 strike the employers conceded the demand that boys' hours of work be reduced from fourteen a day to twelve, but resisted miners' claims for a minimum guaranteed wage of 33 shillings per fortnight and for the ending of an oppressive and fraudulent system of fines.

By the middle of June the pits were back to work; the men had secured an improvement in wages of 1s. a week and protection against fraud. The victory was partly due to the efforts of Thomas Hepburn, a pitman from Hetton Colliery, who later became a paid organiser for the union. Hepburn preached moderation and the avoidance of violence, telling miners that: 'On their orderly behaviour public sympathy depended, and public sympathy was an important factor, especially when it took the form of credit allowed by tradespeople to pitmen earning no wages.'[44]

Several ballads reflect aspects of the 1831 strike. 'First Drest Man of Seghill, Or the Pitman's Reward for Betraying his Brethren. – A New Song'[45] deals at some length with the humiliation of a would-be strike-breaker, who was publicly stripped. The same incident is mentioned in 'The Oppressions of the Pitmen'[46] and 'The Grievances of the Pitmen',[47] though these are principally concerned with the issues of the strike and with working conditions. These are some verses from the latter, written ostensibly by a putter boy from Newbottle Colliery:

The Grievances of the Pitmen[47]

Our hewers work like horses, 'twixt eight and eleven hours,
And breathing clouds of noxious dust, sweat down their body pours,
And all this hardship undergone to get a scanty living,
Their wages fortnightly for this, scarce more than twenty shilling.

The Corves we have are far too large, the fines also imposing,
And Corves set out from time to time, unreasonably oppressing;
But 'tis eleven days we want, each day we want three shillings,
Perhaps by this we may begin to get an honest living. . . .

The Putter Lads work very hard for sixteen hours a day,
With head and shoulders at the Corf, compell'd to thrust away,
With bodies nearly naked, along the way they go,
'Midst thick and pitchy darkness in the dreary vaults below.

The boys that drive the horses, have fourteen pence per day,
And working sixteen hours, as I before did say;
The little Trappers also, they seem to be unwilling,
To work so long for ten pence, when they ought to have a shilling.

Of all the trades in England there's none to be compar'd
To Colliers for danger, beside their labouring hard;
By leaving the Sun and suspended by a rope,
Descend many fathoms towards the centre of the Globe.

What a numerous train of ills do Pitmen undergo!
Destructive damps and noxious dust, infect the air below;
An instance I beheld myself, of death in awful form,
For he was crush'd beneath the weight of an enormous stone.

The unknown author of 'The Pitman's Complaint' concludes a dark piece with references to bondage, slavery and Israelites, and the exhortation:

Arise my brethren from the dust,
And in the Lord lets put our trust,
Then all our foes he will confound,
And in the sea proud Pharaoh dround.[48]

Another sheet with the same title is by Jeremiah Knox, a Winlaton man who also wrote a song on the keelmen's strike of the previous decade. He congratulates the men on their peaceable behaviour – which was true in general, though corves and winding machinery were thrown down shafts at Blyth, Bedlington, Hebburn and Jesmond, and yeomanry as well as marines were deployed to intimidate the strikers. Knox concludes:

Concerning now the pitmen's stick, a little more I'll say;
But I wish freely from my heart that they may win the day.
I hope their masters will consent to grant them their desire;
That those brave lads may hew once more, and we may all get fire.

[Chorus]
Stand true to each other, and never give way:
This is the method you must take if you'd wish to win the day.[49]

Knox returned to the subject in that rare phenomenon in the annals of strikes, a ballad celebrating victory, 'The Pitmen's Stick':

The Pitmen's Stick[50]

Ye collier lads I pray attend, to what I'm going to say,
For I am glad to hear that you have won the day.
Great many people did believe, that you would get the worse,
Because they thought your masters were too strong in the purse.

Another sheet, 'The Pitmen's Union; or, the Lads of the Wear and the Tyne', pays tribute to Hepburn and the pit delegates, calls for the protection of the Almighty, and proposes a toast to the king and queen:

Now let the colliers' hearts be glad, while plenty round them shines,
And blest contentment flows along the banks of Wear and Tyne.

[Chorus]
Still round our banners we will stand, in love and truth combine,
And children yet unborn shall sing, the lads of Wear and Tyne.

Brave Hepburn and our delegates, like rays of virtue shine,
Their fame shall long be echoed round the banks of Wear and Tyne.[51]

The triumph was short-lived. As early as 1832 the coal-owners manoeuvred the men into another strike lasting four months, which effectively broke the union. Hepburn, reduced to hawking tea for sale, was given work at Felling Colliery once he undertook to have no more to do with unions. He kept his word, and lived until 1873.

The north-eastern pitmen lost in 1832 but the Operative Builders' Union was winning various local battles and becoming the leading trade union in the country. In October 1833 it became part of the 'One Big Union' which a few months later took the title of Grand National Consolidated Trade Union. Heavily influenced by Robert Owen, 'its immediate object was nothing less than the entire supersession of capitalism and of the system of competition by a co-operative system of workers' control'.[52] In a great spurt of activity, branches covering farm workers, miners, tailors, gas workers, sweeps, bonnet-makers and bakers

were founded as far apart as Belfast and Aberdeen, Pembroke and Exeter. However, builders were already faced with lockouts in two of their strongholds, Manchester and Birmingham, and the employers hit on the expedient of requiring workers to sign 'the document', a pledge to renounce the union and to refrain from supporting any of its members.
Another ballad, 'The Operative Builders',[53] urged resistance to the signing of a similar 'declaration':

The Operative Builders[53]

Attend you Britons all, And listen to my ditty,
That a piece of work there is, In country, town, and city,
Because the masters have, Throughout the British nation,
Strove to compel their men, To sign a Declaration.

[Chorus]
If they can overcome, The tailors, sweeps, and gilders,
They conquer never will, The Operative Builders.

In Derby a lockout of 15,000 workers in 1834 inspired 'The Derby Strike, Being a development of the low cunning of the Masters against the Workmen, and encouragement to the men to be steady in their purpose, to frustrate the inhuman, unmanly, and tyrannic designs of their employers':[54]

The men of Derby long oppress'd,
Said they would have their wrongs redress'd,
Themselves and family's distress'd
They went and join'd the Union. . . .

The tyrants fear'd the pending blow,
And soon hostilities did shew,
They met that they might overthrow
The efforts of the Union.

It was particularly galling that the employers, who 'at oppression loud did storm' during the campaign for the Reform Act of 1832, afterwards united to oppose the union. The lockout broke the union, and in April 1834 the 'Derby brothers' went back to work.

Another assault on trade unionism soon took place in Scotland. The historian of Chartism, Dorothy Thompson, believes that the consequences were highly significant:

A Lancashire cotton mill in the 1830s. Cheap raw material from the colonies and low paid labour in factories at home contributed to the enormous wealth of the factory owners.

> The Glasgow Spinners' case was probably more influential in the working class movement than that of the Dorchester labourers, in that it was tied up with an attack on trade unions, and really led straight into Chartism.[55]

The Glasgow Cotton Spinners' Union, founded in about 1806, became one of the leading unions in Scotland, with a membership of a thousand. When it called a strike, in April 1837, some of the employers brought in non-union spinners to try to break it. One of these, an Irishman with the very un-Irish name of John Smith, was shot in the back in July, and alleged before he died that he had been murdered by strikers.

Five officials of the union, Thomas Hunter, president, Peter Hacket, treasurer (both of whom were Irish themselves), Richard McNeil, secretary, James Gibb, assistant secretary, and William McLean, guard, were brought to trial in Edinburgh, after a series of postponements, in January 1838. They were found not guilty on charges of murder and conspiracy to murder, but were sentenced to seven years' transportation for being members of an association engaged in illegal activities (mainly picketing). They received strong support from Dublin working men, despite Daniel O'Connell's bitter opposition to trade unions. However, Feargus O'Connor and the Chartist newspaper, *The Northern Star*, strongly opposed the sentences, and were supported by A.H. Beaumont of the *Northern Liberator*. Lawrence Pitkethly, the Huddersfield Chartist, organised a national campaign, as a result of which the spinners were not sent overseas, but kept in the hulks at Woolwich, and pardoned in 1840.

The Cotton Spinners' Farewell[56]

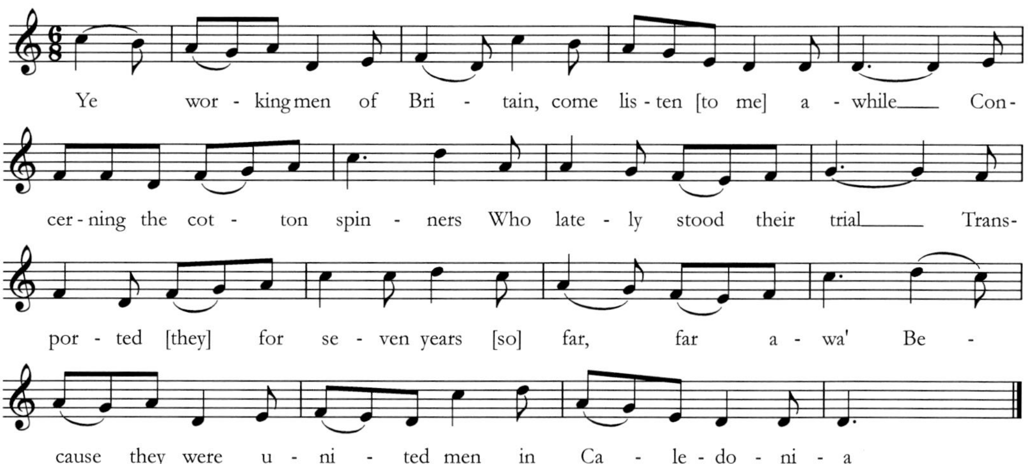

Ye working men of Britain, come listen awhile,
Concerning the cotton spinners who lately stood their trial,
Transported for seven years, far, far awa',
Because they were united men in Caledonia.

When first we were arrested, and lodged in Glasgow gaol,
They stripp'd us of our clothing, left us naked in our cell;
No sympathy they shewed to us, no not the least ava',
Because we were united men in Caledonia.

Our trial they postponed for time after time,
Indictment on indictment, and crime upon crime,
Which turned out all a humbug, for this was their claw,
To prevent our combination in Caledonia.

Success to our friends in Ireland, who boldly stood our cause,
In spite of O'Connell and his support for whiggish laws,
Away with his politics, they are not worth a straw,
He's no friend to the poor of Ireland, or Caledonia.

Success to O'Connor, who did nobly plead our cause,
Likewise to Mr Beaumont, who abhors oppressive laws,
But after all their efforts, justice, and law,
We are banished from our country, sweet Caledonia.

Ye brave men of Northumbria we bid you all farewell,
Were our voices like trumpets, to our enemies we'd tell,
Your actions to us was noble, although your band was sma'.
To crush the monster Tyranny from Caledonia.

Whigs and Tories are united, we see it very plain,
To crush the poor labourer it is their daily aim,
The proverb now is verified, and that you all knaw,
In the case of those poor spinners in Caledonia.

Adieu to those that are near us, our wives and children dear,
Put your trust in the Lord, your enemies need not fear,
Although we are banished far far awa',
You will find friends in old England and Caledonia.

The idiom employed is strongly traditional in feeling, which is not surprising, since the ballad uses the haunting tune, and necessarily follows the verbal pattern, of 'Jamie Raeburn's Farewell', dating possibly from the early 1830s, and telling of a convict faced with transportation.[57]

The dispute may also have occasioned a revival of the street song, based on the Jacobite 'Whaur wad nae fecht for Cherlie, whaur wad nae draw the sword', which became:

Saw ye the Cotton Spinners[58]

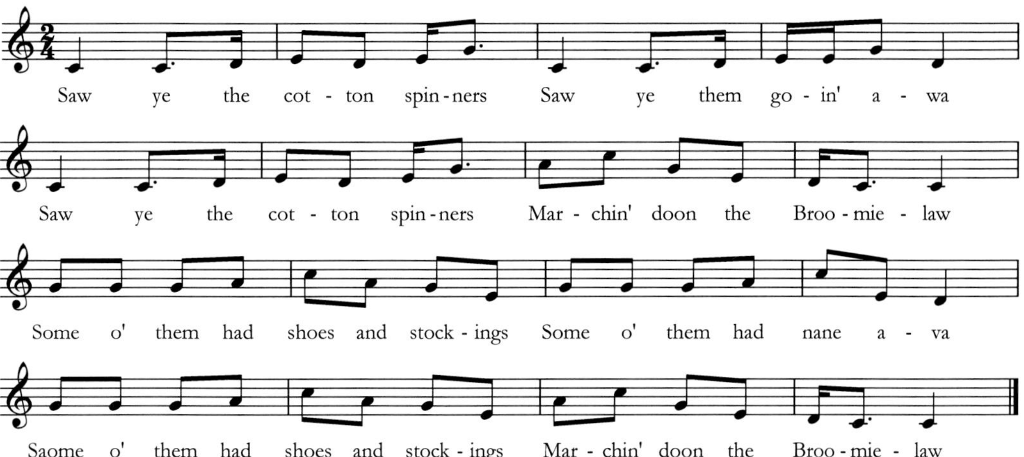

Saw ye the cotton spinners, saw ye them goin' awa?
Saw ye the cotton spinners marchin' doon the Broomielaw?
Some o' them had shoes and stockin's, some o' them had nane ava,
Some o' them had shoes and stockin's, marchin' doon the Broomielaw.

Something like this must still have been circulating at the time of the Boer War, and again in 1914, when the words became:

Wha saw the 42nd, wha saw them go'n awa?
Wha saw the 42nd sailin' doon the Broomielaw?
Some o' them had tartan troosers, some o' then had none ava.
Some o' them had tartan troosers, sailin' doon the Broomielaw.[58]

A somewhat sceptical view of strikes was expressed by John Morgan, a professional London writer. Several scores of his ballads, such as 'Blow the candle in', 'John Bull and the Taxes', 'The Life of an Honest Ploughman'. 'My Grandfather's Days' and 'The Pleasing Wife and Satisfied Husband', became very widely known.[59]

Morgan's political stance was 'three groans for the Tories and two groans for the Whigs'. When in 1837 the London police force, which had been in existence for only eight years, threatened to strike for an increase on its daily pay of 5s. 6d., Morgan wrote a mocking commentary:

The Reported Strike of the Policemen [60]

Although we've got new fashion'd hats,
We do not care a fig for that,
With our truncheons we will lay them flat,
The strike says the Policemen.
The serjeant prowls about by night,
To see we do our duty right,
But soon we get right out of sight,
Snug warm in bed with our hearts delight,
But soon if girls should go astray,
And have a child – no one must pay
Towards the same, good lack a day!
Then strike says the Policemen.

1840s: the hungry forties

Between 1838 and 1842 widespread unemployment coincided with rising food prices and falling wages. The widespread poverty which resulted may not have greatly differed from conditions in other periods, but the decade (retrospectively, since the term dates only from 1904) became known as the 'Hungry Forties'. Perhaps it should have been called the 'Militant Forties' because it saw an attempt at a general strike, with strong support from the Chartist movement.

The National Charter Association, with an individual membership of subscribers, was particularly strong among factory workers in the north and Midlands. A severe trade depression in 1841 led to wage reductions, which in turn provoked a series of strikes and also a wave of political agitation. Dorothy Thompson writes:

> 1842 was the year in which more energy was hurled against the authorities than in any other of the nineteenth century. More people were arrested and sentenced for offences concerned with speaking, agitating, rioting and demonstrating than in any other year, and more people were out on the streets during August 1842 than at any other time. It was the nearest thing to a general strike that the century saw. Whole districts stopped work. [61]

In Lancashire the power-loom weavers and cotton spinners were in the forefront of the strike movement, which spread to Yorkshire and Staffordshire and also involved other trades. 'A New Song on the Great Lock-Out and Strike of the Lancashire Factory Operatives'[62] probably appeared in August 1842. The imposing coat of arms at its head shows both a male and a female figure, accompanied by slogans – stand firm, fortitude, sobriety, domestic comfort, fidelity, be thou faithful unto death – which would surely have been equally acceptable to the employers. Even so, the writer permits himself what would now be called a sexist joke:

And all you men that beat your wives,
Just take them by the wizen [throat],
You can't afford to kick them now,
Since clogs and boots have risen.

There are other sallies, and it is unusual for a serious strike song produced by or for the workers themselves to include levity.

In contrast, 'The Factory Worker's Song' from precisely the same time, is sharp and bitter:

The Factory Worker's Song[63]

Come carders an' spinners an' wayvers as weel,
Stop yo'r frames an' yo'r jennies, strip roller an' creel;
Let yo'r lathes cease to swing, an' yo'r shuttles to fly,
For there's gone through owd England a leaud battle-cry, –

[Chorus] Derry deawn!
They'm turned eaut at Ratchda' [Rochdale] an' Owdham an' Shay [Shaw]
An' th' Stalybridge lads are at Ash'n to-day;
'*Fair wage for fair wark*' is the motto they'n chose,
An' what'll be th' upshot no mortal man knows.

Eaur mesthers are screwin' eaur noses to th' dust,
An' if we don't strike we'n no' maybe seen th' wust;
They've cheeant up eaur bodies to slavery's wheel,
And they'd sell, if we'd let 'em, eaur souls to th' deil.

The full text of this piece has not survived, but the source provides further extracts. The singer complains about the use of the truck system by his employer, 'Twitcher', of Shoddy Croft Mill:

He's mesther, an' londlort, an' baker likewise,
N' he finds me i' clooas – though ne'er th' reet size;
He praiches o'th' Sunday at th' Factory Fowt Skoo,
So chus what else I'm short on I've sarmons enoo.

He says that his rent is 'stop't ov a Saturday eaut o' my wage', and:

When I send deawn to th' shop for my butter an' bread,
He looks into th' wage-book to see 'ut he's paid;
I never know the price on't – it's nothing to me,
For he tells me to' ne'er fret, I'se be straight when I dee.

Finally, the singer resolves somehow to win his freedom, for:

What's a mon if he conno' stond up in his shoon,
An' say, 'I'm as free as owt else under th' moon.'

The strikers of 1842, confronted by the justice system, sentences of transportation and the presence of military force, were starved back to work by September. Their resolve remained, and within a further year there was another strike at Ashton-under-Lyne.

Meanwhile, the miners, recovering from earlier setbacks such as the defeat of the pitmen in 1832, launched a new union covering Yorkshire, the north-east of England, and also Scotland, Wales and Ireland. James Wardaugh of Wakefield celebrated the occasion in November 1842 with a song entitled 'The Miners' Philanthropic Society'.[64] As the National Miners' Association, the union soon grew to 60,000 members, about half of them from Northumberland and Durham. In 1844, against the advice of the union nationally, the north-east pitmen came out on strike. They wished to be paid not by measure but by weight, to be determined by scales open to public inspectors. They also sought half-yearly instead of annual contracts; abolition of the system of fines; and a guaranteed working week of at least four days, or wages in lieu.

Through their 'attorney-general', W.P. Roberts, a Chartist solicitor originating from Bristol, the miners put these terms to the coal-owners, whose leading light was Lord Londonderry (1778–1854), half brother of Castlereagh. Londonderry, a virulent opponent of the Reform Bill, had surprised and infuriated his colleagues by meeting Thomas Hepburn in an attempt to settle the 1831 strike. To the disappointment of many, he played no such part in 1844.

'This agreement was submitted to the "coal kings",' wrote Frederick Engels, 'and a deputation appointed to negotiate with them; they answered, however, that for them the Union did not exist, that they had to deal with single workmen only, and should never recognise the Union.'[65]
Thomas Burt, born near South Shields, was a child of seven living at Seghill at the time of the strike. He later wrote:

> In the April of 1844 began the great pitman's strike, one of the severest and most prolonged industrial battles that ever occurred in England or elsewhere. The strike extended over the whole of the counties of Northumberland and Durham. It affected more than 22,000 men and boys, and continued for seventeen weeks … The first intimation to me of anything unusual was the crowds of women, youths, and children, who, armed with tin pans, 'blazers', and other improvised cymbals, rushed down to the wagon-way every evening to greet the blacklegs in transit between their homes by the side of the Tyne and the Cramlington pits.[66]

Burt glosses 'blazers, or "bleezers", as they are commonly called', as 'thin sheets of iron, which, placed in front of the upper portion of the kitchen fireplace, exclude the cold air from direct access to the chimney, and thus assist the draught'. He adds that:

> 'The term, "blackleg", as applied to men who continued at work during a strike, or who took the places of strikers, is said to have originated in the colliery districts, owing to these men appearing with their legs blackened with coal-dust, while the strikers' legs were clean. Until very recently [1924] all pitmen in Northumberland wore short breeches and always travelled to and from work with their legs partly exposed. In this connection the term would gain pungency through being a commonly accepted title for racecourse swindlers and card-sharpers.

Burt also comments on:

> The candy-men [who] at that time made a living by collecting rags, bones, etc., in exchange for which they gave candy. They were a dirty, blackguardly lot, and were looked down upon by the miners. The denizens of the slums who were engaged as evictors, being of the same type as the candy-men, and, indeed, numbering many candy-men in their ranks, were all so designated by the pitmen and their families.[67]

Blacklegs – the word, oddly, not recorded by the *OED* until 1865 – attract the intense scorn of William Roxby in his 'Song to the Blacklegs and All that's not in the Union'.[68] In 'A New Song on The Pitmen's Grievances', Jane Knight, possibly a miner's wife and certainly one of only two women who wrote on the strike, used biblical language to make a direct denunciation:

Ye Black-legs of Wingate, I would have ye mind your ways.
You follow Christ for fishes, and then for gold betray,
You have sold us all for silver, and what can ye do more;
Which causes us to wander, and charity implore.[69]

The reference to wandering probably indicates homelessness, a consequence of the eviction of striking miners and their families from colliery-owned houses. The evictors, who were known as 'candymen', were enrolled for the purpose 'from the slums of Newcastle and other towns on Tyneside', and accompanied 'by a strong force of police armed with cutlasses and stout, formidable-looking staves'. The proceedings were quiet and peaceful, though the women jeered at the candymen.

Burt tells the story of a man who drew a keg of gunpowder from under his bed, then seized a red-hot poker from the fire and shouted to his wife: 'Tyek the bairns alang the road: aw'm gannin' to hell wi the bums', who 'not being inclined to embark on such a voyage, promptly took to their heels'. Burt added:

> Apart from these lighter interludes, such evictions are always touchingly pathetic, sometime almost tragic. Hundreds of helpless children cast upon the bare, shelterless roads; the mothers standing disconsolately beside their household goods, their whole earthly possessions, in which they took such pride, and which represented the toil, struggles, and savings of many thrifty years – this represented a picture at once sombre and pitiful.[70]

Eviction inevitably featured in some of the thirty-odd ballads produced during the strike. 'Munkwaremouth [Monkwearmouth] Turn-out'[71] treats the operation in mock-heroic fashion, with the man in charge, 'Great George ... ridin' in his gig... Wiv fayce se white a' flaid wi fear', accompanied by a 'guard o' royal blue' (the police) as the 'Viewer-bums' set about their work:

Munkwaremouth [Monkwearmouth] Turn-out[71]

So George, the Bum, and Ha'-penny Jack,
Bill Redford and Tom Shields,
Pulled down, and carried clocks and drawers,
Beds, mugs, and traps, and creels;
Chalk pussey-cats, and chairs, and stuils;
Claise-horse, and brush, and pan,

And out wiv pokers, skeels, and rakes,
These nobil viewers ran.

The strikers are unbowed:

A fair day's wage for fair day's wark,
The Miners want te see.
Toil in the deep and dreary mines,
Rewarded ought to be.
We hev ne house aboon our heeds –
The sky's wor coverin',
Yet tho' we starve, we'll keep the peace,
Wor rights we so shall win!

The ballad's chorus dinned in the message:

So keep up your hearts, ye Miners brave,
Tho' ye're turned te the door
Wiv all yer sticks, and wives, and bairns,
Yet heaven will help the poor.

Several miners set forth their complaints and objectives in stirring style. John Atkinson wrote, with one excursion into irony:

Come All You Colliers in This Place [72]

The monthly bonds they offered us,
Have forced us now to strike;
Six weeks now idle we have been,
Which Owners do not like.
And if we go to work again,
We vow to have our rights,
The Six cwt [hundredweight] Tub we will regain,
And no more Sevens or Eights.

Our price they lowered from time to time,
Which to our grief we know:
We'll ne'er forget their bounteous deeds
Wherever we may go. –
They're bet this time they all confess
Our Union's spread so far:
Against us they've combined for long,
Now, Sirs, we're on a par.
The Blackleg-men, have proved untrue

And sought for rest & ease:
They've undermined their fellow men,
Their Masters for to please.
They hope for favors after this,
And how they hew away!
But the time is coming fast, my lads,
When they will rue the day!

In 'The Colliers' Appeal',[73] a pitman, R. Holder, deals with child labour ('boys at six years old – early in the morning rise, In winter trudge through frost and snow with bitter moans and cries'), the dangers of fire damp and flood, accidents in shafts and with falls of stone, long hours, low pay and the employers' chicanery with weights and measures. He, too, turns to biblical precedent:

When the Israelites in Egypt were by Pharoah 'prest severe,
With heavy burdens day by day too much for them to bear,
Then God a Moses did prepare to set his people free,
And drowned Pharoah and his host when crossing the Red Sea.

Lord, let a Moses rise again the colliers to release,
And free them from the tyrant's hand and bid them go in peace;
'Tis not the colliers thus alone, but view the country o'er,
Look at the starving multitude how masters press them sore.[73]

In contrast with such earnest appeals, William Hornsby of Shotton Moor, a veteran of the strikes of 1831 and 1832, adopted a lighter touch:

The Old Woman and the Coal Owner[74]

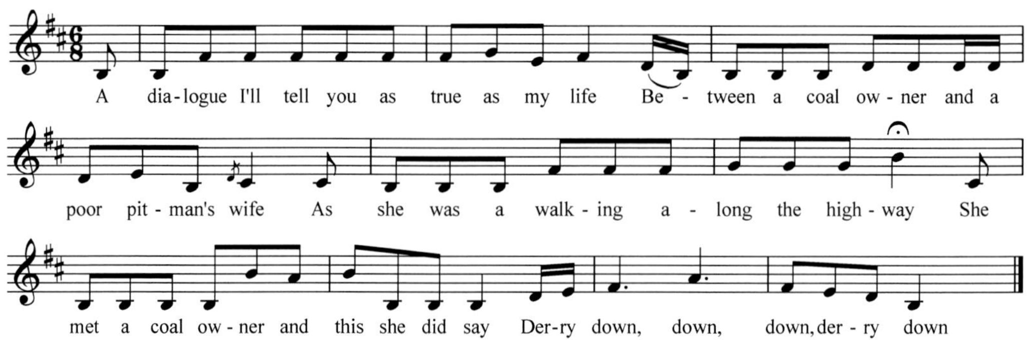

A dialogue I'll tell you as true as my life,
Between a Coal Owner and a poor Pitman's wife:
As she was travelling all on the highway
She met with a Coal Owner and to him she said –
Sir, to beg on you I'm not afraid.

[Chorus: Down hey derry down]

Then where do you come from the owner he cries?
I come from h—l the old woman replies,
If you come from h—l, come tell me right plain,
How you contrived to get out again:

Aye the way aw gat out the truth aw will tell,
They are turning all the poor folk out of h—l;
This is to make room for the rich, wicked race;
For there is a great number of them in that place;

And the number is not known Sir, that is in that place,
And they chiefly consist of the rich, wicked race;
And the Coal Owners are the next on command,
To arrive into h—l as I understand.

How know you the owners is the next in command?
How div ah naw ye shall understand!
Aw hard the awd devil say when aw cam out
The Coal Owners all had received their rout.

Then how does the awd devil behave in that place?
O, Sir, he's cruel to the rich, wicked race.
He's far fiercer than you can suppose,
Aye even a mad bull with a ring through his nose.

Good woman, says he, I must bid you farewell,
You give me a dismal account about h—l;
If this be all true that you say unto me
I'll go home and with my poor men I'll agree.

If you be a Coal Owner, Sir, take my advice,
Agree with your men and give them their full price,
For if you do not aw naw very well
You'll be in great danger of going to h—l.

For all ye Coal Owners great fortunes have made,
By these jovial fellows that works in the Coal trade,
Now how can ye think to prosper or thrive,
For wanting to starve your workmen alive.

Now all ye gay gentlemen that's got riches in store
Take my advice and be good to the poor,
And if ye do this all things will go well,
Perhaps it will save ye for ganin to h—l.

So now the poor Pitmen may join heart and hand,
For when they're off work all trades are at a stand;
Yon town of Newcastle all cry out a main,
O since the pits were at work once again.

It's now to conclude, little more I've to say,
I was turned out of my house on the 13th of May,
But it's now to conclude and finish my song,
I hope you'll relieve me and let me carry on.

When in 1951 A.L. Lloyd appealed for mining songs in the magazine *Coal*, among the many he received, and later published in an anthology, were both a full text and a fragment of this ballad. The latter had a tune, which may indicate that it had been sung long after the strike of 1844. Lloyd streamlined the words, renamed the song 'The Coalowner and the Pitman's Wife', and launched it on another half century of active life.[75]

The broadside text of 'The Old Woman and the Coal Owner' is one of only a handful of the 1844 songs which makes some attempt to hint at vernacular pronunciation. Others, with a much stronger flavour, are

'Munkwaremouth Turn-out' (previously quoted), 'Fish Betty's Account of Herself' and 'A New Song' (beginning 'Now, Jobson, has the heard the news').[76] As it happens, tunes are prescribed for all three, respectively 'Nae luck about th' house', 'Billy Oliver' and 'Auld Lang Syne'.

Only about a third of the songs have tunes indicated, but many of the rest were clearly intended to be sung, judging from openings like:

> 'Come all kind-hearted Christians,
> And listen to my song' ('A New Song on the Pitmen's Grievances');
> 'Come all you bold miners wherever you be' ('A New Song');
> 'A song I'll sing if you attend and pay attention to my ditty' (also entitled 'A New Song').[77]

Other tunes may have been obvious at the time. For example, 'The Collier Boy', beginning 'Yon starry light that rules the night', which was issued a month or so before the strike, has no tune specified, but is clearly a remake of 'The Chartist Mother's Song', and would therefore have shared its tune, 'The Rose of Allandale'.[78] The coincidence also illustrates the point that Chartism had influence with the miners.

The Collier Boy[78]

Yon starry light that rules the night in yonder distant sky,
It sheds its bright and bonny light, on thee my Collier Boy!
In silent flight o'er hills at night, for rights with alloy;
It ne'er ask'd who wander'd past, but lit my Collier Boy!

For all yon viewer scourges the hewer, and robs him of his joy;
It shines as free and bright on thee, my honest Collier Boy!
Away, away from light of day to your toilsome labour hie,
And take the view of freemen now, my gallant Collier Boy!

Away, away, no longer stay, for freedom live or die;
The heart that's true shall have its due, my brave young Collier Boy!
Away my brave forsake thy grave, forget each slavish tie;
And raise a light an English night, be free my Collier Boy!

Be free, be free, and let them see, that Heaven's laws defy,
Their Baal shrine shall ne'er be mine, my own young Collier Boy!
Thy father's gone, then on my son, my heart shall beat with joy,
To see the foe in death laid low, my own dear Collier Boy!

For all the rousing songs, the bright hopes and the fierce struggles, the strike eventually collapsed. By September the men were back at work on the previous terms, save that a monthly bond was imposed. Robert Colls has drawn the conclusion, which the evidence of ballads underlines, that: 'An 1844 north east summer of hunger, provocation and organised blacklegging destroyed the strongest trade union of its era just as the summer of 1832 had destroyed Hepburn's "United Colliers".'[79]

A number of strong union men were victimised and denied work, Thomas Burt's father among them. The Burts moved to the Durham coalfield, and it was there that Thomas started work as a trapper at the age of ten. He later moved back to Northumberland and was in turn victimised for his union activities: ironic, because he believed in industrial co-operation and class harmony. Starting in 1874, he sat as Liberal MP for Morpeth for 44 years.

The defeated pitmen did manage to exact some measure of revenge:

> the blackleg miners, who during the strike had protection from the police, found themselves alone in hostile communities. A colliery gallery offers ample opportunity for ambush and victimisation. There the blacklegs' children suffered indignities at the hands of vengeful colliers; they were tipped from trucks by ropes stretched

> between pit props and left in the dark. The blacklegs themselves suffered worse, for they not only lost self-respect; they also lost money. At that time wage payment was based on output and it was the practice to hang an individual's tally disc on full corves before they went to the pitbank. When the strike was over it became common usage for the local men to remove these markings from blackleg corves so that when the interlopers surfaced, having put up with abuse and violence below ground, they sometimes found there was little or no financial compensation.[80]

Writing in 1913, Thomas Derby recalled 'the itinerant street ballad-singer, who, as far as Manchester is concerned, has practically ceased to be, but who, when I was a lad, was still a popular institution'. 'In those days,' he continued, 'a fierce election fight would have yielded a rich harvest to the ballad singer; he would have been howling discordantly to audiences of reds or blues about the "'ungry forties".' Derby also remembered seeing 'a group of ill-clad, hungry-looking turnouts', who sang:

> It was in 'forty-eight when work was scant,
> Our wages was reduced full ten per sent.
> But truth is on our side, with cheering ray,
> Help us then fellow-men to win the day.[81]

The Ballad Singer by William Henry Hunt (1790-1864). Courtesy of Aberdeen Art Gallery & Museums Collections.

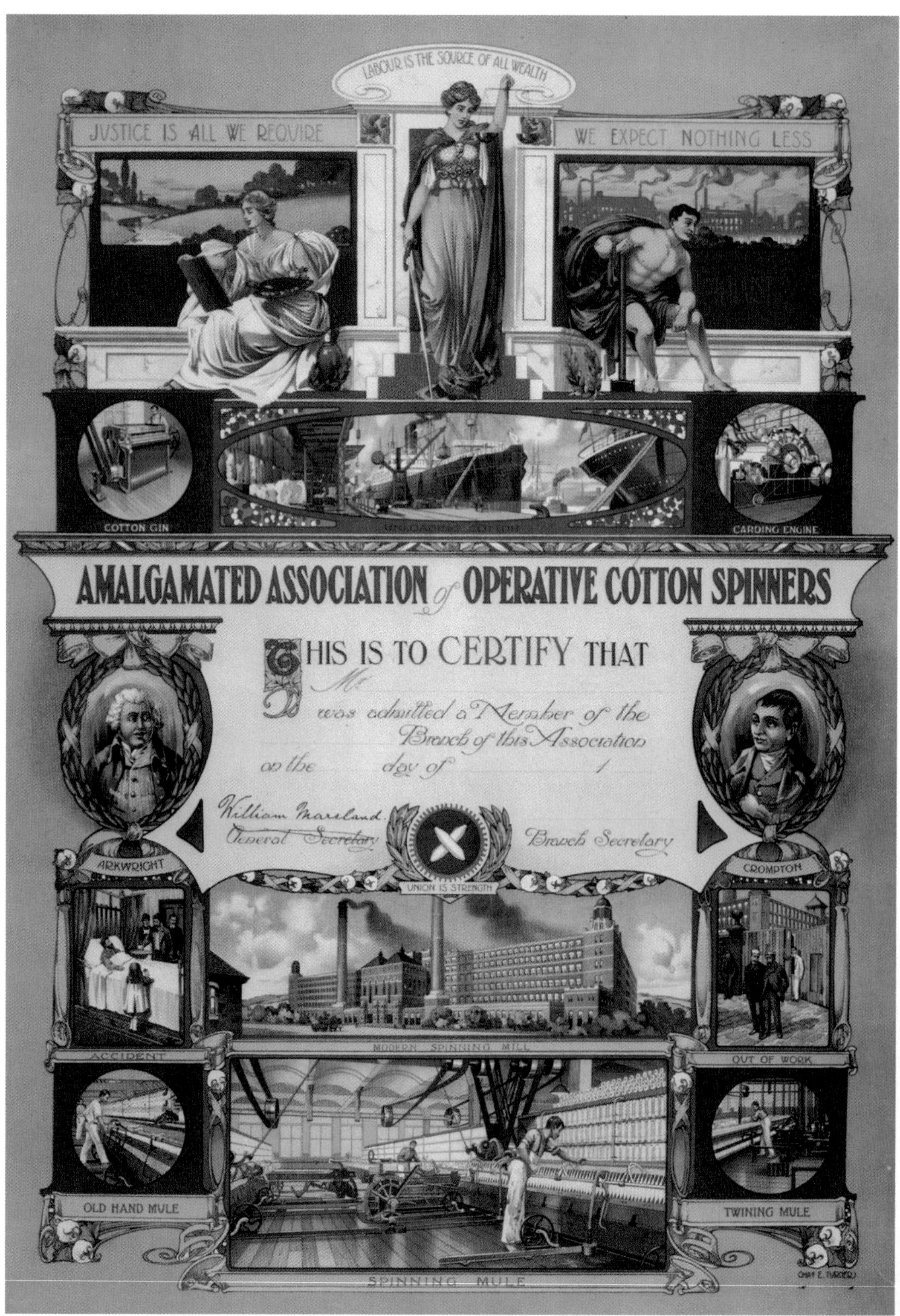
LABOUR IS THE SOURCE OF ALL WEALTH
JUSTICE IS ALL WE REQUIRE
WE EXPECT NOTHING LESS
COTTON GIN
CARDING ENGINE
AMALGAMATED ASSOCIATION of OPERATIVE COTTON SPINNERS
THIS IS TO CERTIFY THAT
Mr
was admitted a Member of the
Branch of this Association
on the day of 1
William Marsland.
General Secretary
Branch Secretary
ARKWRIGHT
CROMPTON
UNION IS STRENGTH
ACCIDENT
MODERN SPINNING MILL
OUT OF WORK
OLD HAND MULE
TWINING MULE
SPINNING MULE

6 Striking Times (1850-1900)

On strike in the workshop of the world

The Great Exhibition opened on 1 May 1851, which happened to be the eighty-second birthday of the Duke of Wellington, who was still commander-in-chief of the army. Fearing that working class radicals would seize the occasion for some form of militant action, Wellington had moved 10,000 additional troops into or near London. However, although some 500,000 people turned up in Hyde Park to see Victoria and Albert's opening ceremony, there was no uprising. In the six months it ran, the exhibition was a huge success, with six million tickets sold, many of them from Mondays to Thursdays, when admission cost one shilling. Mondays were particularly popular, a reflection, perhaps, of the Saint Monday tradition favoured by working people.

Ballad printers rushed to cash in. In London alone, Birt, Disley, Fortey, Hodges, Ryle and Such issued sheets, as did their colleagues in Birmingham, Bradford, Carlisle, Glasgow, Newcastle, Northampton, Preston and York. The exotic and outlandish exhibits featured strongly in many cases, albeit combined with homely themes drawn from familiar pieces on the fun of the fair, including predictions as to the resultant crop of babies. John Harkness of Preston combined on one sheet 'Kendal Fair' and 'Exhibition of All Nations', in the latter of which is this verse:

Exhibition of All Nations[1]

There's Ned and Poll with Joe and Bet will drink a butt of heavy wet,
And in nine months time perhaps will get another exhibition.
And then it will be plainly seen, that they together must have been,
A-rolling in the park so green, to view the exhibition.

Membership certificate for the Amalgamated Association of Operative Cotton Spinners, a trade union for male mule spinners, which existed for just over a century from 1870. Courtesy of Bolton Museum and Archive Service.

A few sheets, such as 'Chrystal [sic] Palace', attempt a more sober approach:

Chrystal Palace[2]

Britannia's sons an attentive ear one moment lend to me,
Whether tillers of our fruitful soil or lords of high degree
Mechanic too and artisan Old England's pride and boast
Whose wondrous skill has spread around far far from Britain's coast.

[Chorus]
For the world's Exhibition, let's shout with loud huzza,
All nations never can forget the glorious First of May.

'The era that lies between 1850 and 1875 – or let us say between the Great Exhibition of 1851 and the proclamation of Queen Victoria as the Empress of India in 1876 – has been called, not inaptly, the "Golden Age" of British capitalism.'[3] The writer here, G.D.H. Cole, goes on to remark that '[T]hough every effort was put forth to make the grand show at the new Crystal Palace in Hyde Park a demonstration of the wonders of the world's foremost industrial country, the effect, to a modern reader, is rather one of petty craftsmanship than of mass production in the sense in which the phrase was later to be understood.'[4] A similar conclusion was reached by Raphael Samuel in a paper published in 1977: '[L]abour power was much more important than capital equipment in making Britain, at mid-century, "the workshop of the world".'[5] Curiously, the writer of 'Chrystal Palace' made the same point: 'Oh surely England's greatest wealth, Is an honest working man.'[6]

Workers naturally sought a share in increased prosperity. Trade unions, where they existed, were locally rather than nationally based. Yet as Chartism faded in the 1840s, '[O]ther roads were opening out, above all in the trade union field. The small, local craft clubs and large, militant but unstable industrial unions of the earlier period were giving place to solid craft unions often on a national basis, bodies that were highly exclusive, financially solid and strongly centralised, with a permanent staff of full time officials and a quite new political and social outlook.'[7]

The Amalgamated Society of Engineers, founded in 1851, was the first of what came to be called the 'New Model' unions. It soon had 11,000 members, mainly in Lancashire and London, who paid a subscription of 1s. a week. In January 1852 a dispute over excessive overtime led to a national lockout by the employers, who revived the old tactic of 'the document' (see p.164). The men signed, under duress, and went back to work, but the union, contrary to the employers' hopes, was not broken, and within a few years had some 12,500 members.

However, the New Model unions replaced their predecessors' determination to change society with a desire to secure the best possible deal from capitalism for skilled workers. They did not seek strikes, but if they were forced into them, fought with great determination.

1850s: 'the crucible of struggle'

Not all strikes inspired ballads. Determining factors must have included the length of time a dispute continued, the existence or otherwise of a tradition in the trade involved, the presence or absence of a striker or sympathiser willing to devise or initiate a ballad, and sheer chance. Ballads that were produced may have disappeared, but those which survive may well yield records of disputes long lost not only from popular memory but from the knowledge of most historians. In a parallel way, Raphael Samuel has observed: 'Strikes throw up a great deal of information about working arrangements, and show how custom and practice was shaped in the crucible of struggle.'[8]

Striking sailors in 1851, just like the Lancashire weavers at a time of rising prosperity a few years later, were seeking improvements in pay and conditions. The printed ballad entitled 'The Sailors' Strike'[9] is undated, but it presumably refers to 1851. It claims that men were taking action 'In every part of London town, And in every port through England round':

The Sailors' Strike[9]

Every sailor for his right,
And for his pay does boldly strike,
If to the Baltic or America we sail to,
Five pounds a month it is our due,

And may every sailor gain the day,
And show the skipper pretty play,
Stick up like bricks, and shout huzza!
For the jolly tars of England.

Low freights in every seaport town,
Long has the sailor been kept down,
Now freedom, cries Britannia round,
The jolly tars of England.

From Clyde and Leith, North and South Shields,
From Liverpool they'll never yield.

Then sailors all speak up like men.
And tell the gaffers what you mean,

Four pounds a month for New Orleans,
Or go to sea we never mean,
But stop on shore and try all scenes,
Cries the jolly tars of England.

In fact the seamen claimed £3 a month, plus 'small stores' of tea and sugar, which would have been worth 5s. The shipowners offered the bare £3, which was one reason for the strike. A second grievance concerned some of the twenty-two regulations, backed by fines, listed in the Mercantile Marine Act of 1850. These included:

> [No.] 17. Interrupting divine service by indecorous conduct, one day's pay.
> 18. Not being cleaned, shaved, and washed on Sundays, one day's pay.
> 19. Washing clothes on a Sunday, one day's pay.

Another contentious issue was the manner of signing on and off at the beginning and end of voyages.

The strike lasted for about a month and ended on 22 February 1851 after the regulations were declared to be permissive, not compulsory. During it, seventy policemen were sent at one stage from Newcastle to Shields to occupy the quay, with cutlasses drawn, and a warship, the *Hecate*, sailed into the Tyne. The government was ready, as with the keelmen of a generation earlier, to demonstrate its willingness to resort to military action. In response, strikers boarded ships and ordered them ashore; blacklegs were tarred and feathered, and run out of town. Women, presumably sailors' wives, gathering in crowds of as many as 200, strongly supported the strike, and they, too, attacked blacklegs. Up to 1,000 men met to hear the progress of a deputation sent to the Board of Trade in London. One 'watcher' (picket) was drowned in a boat accident. A number of collier vessels, an emigrant ship, and some Greenland whalers from Hull, were unable to sail.[10] All this is in marked contrast to the paean to progress which was about to emanate from the Great Exhibition.

The ballad 'The Seaman's Strike' emphasised the patriotism of the seamen, while calling for them to be treated fairly:

We are loyal, true and right,
Willing for our Queen to fight,
In war they struggle with all their might,

Does the jolly tars of England.
Just and honest is our cause,
We neither break not abuse the laws,
We have done our duty all like men.
And we can do the like again!
But we will not be trampled down,
And trod like worms upon the ground,
More useful men cannot be found
Than the jolly tars of England.

The pretty girls of the Highway,
Old and young, they all do say,
They'll go to work both night and day,
For the jolly tars of England.
One and all they'll prove so true,
And always stick to the jacket blue,
In battle without them we could not do,
In the wooden walls of England.
Then when we have gained our rights,
We'll do what is just and never strike,
But if called to war will boldly strike,
Will the jolly tars of England.

'Strikes and lockouts were constant features of London life,' writes Jerry White. 'Even when the Combination Acts had punished strikes by transportation, London labour was restless and tough-minded.' [11]

As well as celebrating the Great Exhibition, commercial ballad printers were quick to see the potential of strikes. As well as printing 'Chrystal Palace' (see p. 182), Elizabeth Ann Hodges printed a series of sheets on strikes. (She was the former housekeeper of John Pitts, who after his death in 1844 took over his Toy and Marble Warehouse at 31 Monmouth Street in Seven Dials. This was renamed Dudley Street in 1845, and it is possible that ten years later W.S. Fortey bought up Hodges's stock, together with any remaining from Pitts.) 'Strike of the London Cabmen',[12] which, incidentally, has precisely the same metric pattern as 'The Sailors' Strike', is as unfavourable towards the strikers as it is to the customers who paid 'a tanner a mile'. 'The General Strike'[13] is chiefly concerned to look for knockabout humour, though it expresses the hope: 'May the poor men gain their rights, And be happy and contented They'll have no occasion then to strike, When Masters have consented.' A third sheet, while still containing jokes, shows much greater commitment:

Striking Times[14]

Cheer up! Cheer up! You sons of toil and list - en to my song While
I try to a - muse you and I will not keep you long The
work - ing men of Eng - land, at length be - gin to see They've
made a bold strike for their rights in eigh - teen fif - ty three I It is
high time that wor - king men should have it their own way And
for a fair days la - bour re - ceive a fair days pay

Cheer up! Cheer up! You sons of toil & listen to my song,
While I try to amuse you and I will not keep you long,
The working men of England, at length begin to see
They've made a bold strike for their rights in eighteen fifty-three.

[Chorus]
It is high time that Working men, should have it their own way,
And for a fair day's labour receive a fair day's pay.

This is the time for striking at least it strikes me so,
Monopoly has had some knocks, but this must be the blow,
For Working men by thousands complains their fate is hard,
May order be their conduct, and success be their reward.

Some of our London Printers, this glorious work began,
And surely they done something, for they've upset the sun,
Employers must be made to see they can't do what they like,
It is the masters' greediness, causes the men to strike.

The labouring men of London on both sides of the Thames,
They made a strike last Monday which adds much to their fame.
Their masters did not relish it, but they made them understand,
Before the next day's sun had set, they gave them their demand.

The unflinching men of Stockport, with Kidderminster in their train,
Three hundred honest weavers have struck their ends to gain,
Tho' the masters find they are losing deal, the tide must soon be turning,
They find that men won't quietly be robbed of half their earnings.

Our London Weavers mean to show their masters and the trade,
That they'll either cease to work, or else be better paid,
'Twas in Spitalfields the weavers workd with joy in former ages,
But they're tired out of asking for a better scale of wages.

The monied men have had their way, large fortunes they have made,
For things could not be otherwise, with labour badly paid,
They roll along with splendour, and with a saucey tone,
As Cobbett says, they eat the meat, while the workmen gnaws the bone.

Woodcut illustration from a handbill. Reproduced by permission of the Record Office for Leicestershire, Leicester & Rutland.

The slop [cheap clothes] sellers & tailors had an ugly dream
The needle-women swear they'll strike before they sew a seam,
But as they make all our trousers before the evil comes,
We had better give them what they ask, or we shall show our bums.

In Liverpool, the Postmen struck and sent word to their betters,
Begging them to recollect that they were men of letters;
They asked for three bob more a week, and got it in a crack
And though each man has got his bag, they have not got the sack.

The cabmen and their masters made up their minds last week,
To stop the Cabs from running, now was that not a treat:
The Hackney Carriage Act has proved a very bitter pill,
It was no use to call out Cab, Cab, drive fast and show your skill.

The Coopers and the Dock-yard men are all a going to strike
And soon there will be the devil to pay without a little mike
The farming men of Suffolk have lately call'd a go
And swear they'll have their wages rose before they reap or mow.

Despite its lower-case initial, 'the sun' (verse 3) was a newspaper even then.

The Kidderminster strike mentioned came to an unsuccessful end on 22 August. The quotation (verse 7) from Cobbett attests to his continued influence, almost twenty years after his death. The Hackney Carriage Act (verse 11) of 1853 transferred the supervision of cabs to the Metropolitan Police, who proceeded to institute a much stricter regime, greatly to the chagrin of 'the cabmen and their masters'. The final verse alludes to a jocular ballad, 'The Devil and Little Mike'.[15]

The 'unflinching men of Stockport' (verse 5) were the spinners and weavers who went on strike in 1853 for the restoration of a ten per cent. cut in pay, which they had accepted five years earlier. As 'A New Song on the Stockport Strike' put it:

A New Song on the Stockport Strike[16]

It was in Forty Eight, when work was scant,
Our wages were reduced full Ten Per Cent.

Our masters pledged to pay, thould [sic] trade revive,
The Ten Cent. they took, the Panic to survive.

But now trade is good again, our wants we have made known,
But our employers tell us, we must "let well alone".

On 6 August the employers conceded, but the gains at Stockport were short-lived. The employers rescinded the increase, and a retaliatory strike collapsed within a few weeks.

This was bad news for the Preston workforce, which had been hoping to emulate their Stockport colleagues' earlier success, and had been locked out by their employers since October 1853. Some 18,000 Prestonians were involved, 11,800 of them women and teenage girls, the remainder men and youths. They were supported by donations from textile workers in other Lancashire towns, principally Blackburn, and they enjoyed 'the sympathy and support, if not the approval, of the middle-class public'.[17]

The Preston magistrates, who did not share these attitudes, prohibited evening meetings, and when workers met in the daytime, banned those gatherings, too, so they were obliged to hold meetings outside the borough limits. The strike leaders, for peacefully dissuading blacklegs – 'knobsticks', as they were known – from taking work in the town, were charged with conspiracy.

After seven months, including an exceptionally severe winter, the workers went back in May 1854, defeated. Mrs Gaskell, transferring their struggle to Manchester, used it in her novel, *North and* South (1855). Unlike her, Charles Dickens visited Preston, spending 48 hours there during the strike before featuring it in *Hard Times* (1854). According to Jenny Uglow, 'although both attacked the dehumanisation of working relations, her [Gaskell's] intimate fiction was very different from Dickens's brilliantly schematic drama of heartless Gradgrinds, scheming agitators and victims'.[18] Dickens also published in the magazine he edited, *Household Words*, an article of his own on the dispute and another by J. Lowe.[19] In December 1853 Lowe wrote:

> We ... reach a locked-up and smokeless factory, at the gates of which a knot of young girls are singing and offering for sale some of the Ten Per Cent. Songs, taking their name from the origin of the strike. ... The songs are not remarkable for much elegance and polish, but they possess some earnestness and fire, and are undoubtedly composed by the operatives themselves. We step forward, tender a penny to one of the singers, and received the following song, composed by an operative [William Abbott] at Bamber Bridge:

> **Ten Per Cent!** *A New Song, on the Preston Strike*[20]
>
> Come all you men of freedom, wherever you may be,
> I pray you give attention, and listen unto me.
> It's of this strike in Preston town, their courage being good,
> I do believe they will stand firm whilst they have life and blood.
>
> *Chorus*
> So now, my boys, don't daunted be, but stand out to the fray;
> We ne'er shall yield, nor quit the field, until we've won the day.

Lowe quotes the item in full, adds that 'These ballads vary constantly to meet the exigencies of passing events', and patronisingly remarks: 'Tyrtaeus [Spartan poet] wakened not more enthusiasm in the breast of his auditors, than these simple doggrels [sic] do among the rude but earnest crowds which throng to hearken to them.'

Of these 'simple doggrels', over forty have survived on the Preston strike and lock-out, with a further three from Stockport. Copies of all of them are in the Madden Collection[21] at Cambridge University Library, though some are duplicated elsewhere, in the Harris Library at Preston and in the Lancashire Record Office. They are all without imprint but it is most likely they were produced by John Harkness, the prolific Preston printer, who certainly sent them to Sir Frederic Madden. Harkness was favourably disposed towards the textile workers, as is seen from a sheet which did appear over his imprint early in 1852, judging by its reference to the engineers' strike, which began in January. 'The Preston Steam-Loom Weavers'[22] seems to imply the tune known as 'The Nutting Girl' or 'A-nutting we will go'.

The Preston Steam-Loom Weavers[22]

You power loom weavers far and near, come listen to my song,
I will sing to you a verse or two and not detain you long,
In Preston town there is a mill, if work you chance to get,
I'd have you mind each day or else at night you'll be in debt.

[Chorus]
Then weavers all in Preston town, unite all in a band
And let us banish tyranny, then we'll have a happy land.

In the morning just at six o'clock the engine does begin,
You must set off a running for a prize you have to win,
For should it happen that you be ten minutes there too late,
You must give in your number and twopence they'll surely bate [dock].

And while the engine's running O, I'm sure it is very hard,
There's threepence more if you should chance to go out in the yard,
If any thing about your looms should chance to break that day,
There's no excuse they'll tell you plain you will get off for pay.

Four shillings for a temple box and eight pence for a stud,
Sixpence or eightpence for a fork, they'll suck your very blood,
Two shillings for a driving wheel, and twopence for one day's waste
Threepence for a gold bobbing if it does not run its race.

Should sickness overtake you and you stay away one day,
They'll fine you two shillings, or else they'll stop your pay,
And should you never mend again it's true what I have said,
You must go and serve your notice there, after you are dead.

It is his daily study friends, and all that he can plan,
Which way to rob his brothers and his fellow workingman.
For should you make a good week's work, this cunning old fox
Is sure to take a cut or two and hide them in a box.

The engineers of England are doing all they can,
And standing up in every town to better their fellowman,
Then Preston weavers do the same and stand firm every one,
Then other towns will back you and assist you all they can.

Now to conclude and make an end, let's all unite and quick,
And never cease to labour till we drive him to Old Nick,
For these have always been his plans, both town and country knows
The devil his right will never have till he has got him in his claws.

This is an admirably sharp piece of writing, straight from the factory floor. Technical terms are effortlessly manipulated and there is complete familiarity with the issues involved. Deductions from wages, a perennial grievance, feature strongly, including fines for lavatory breaks ('out in the yard'), and charges for various replacement parts for machinery, presumably when workers were deemed to have been negligent in some way. The abrupt introduction of 'the cunning old fox' (could a verse have been omitted here for the sake of fitting the text to the sheet?) brings the revelation of wages kept down by a detested overlooker's hiding lengths of finished cloth ('a cut or two').

A verse detailing various stoppages from wages is followed by this priceless flight of fancy:

Should sickness overtake you and you stay away one day,
They'll fine you two shillings or else they'll stop your pay,
And should you never mend again it's true what I have said,
You must go and serve your notice there, after you are dead.

Preston weavers are exhorted to follow the engineers' example:

The engineers of England are doing all they can,
And standing up in every town to better their fellowman,
Then Preston weavers do the same and stand firm every one,
Then other towns will back you and assist you all they can.

The harsh factory regime evoked here explains why, when the strike began, some felt the keen sense of liberation which is expressed in a ballad using the sprightly tune of 'Old Uncle Ned', written in 1848 by the popular American lyricist Stephen Foster:

Uncle Ned; *or*, The Preston Strike[23]

You may see of a truth that the people are not dead,
Though 'tis said that they died long ago
But we've risen from our sleep a holiday to keep
Determined to work under price no more.

[Chorus]
So we've put by the roving on the kreel
And hung up the wire on the wall
And we'll never be content till we get the ten per cent
In spite of their 'let well alone'.

Old Ned [the steam engine] wants a rest for we're sure that he is tired,
And as he cannot speak for himself,
We'll put in a word that's certain to be heard,
And place his crank grinding music on the shelf.

The fields they are green & fragrant are the flowers,
And the birds sweetly warble their tunes,
These things we'll enjoy while we hold our holiday,
'Twill be pleasanter than piecing up our ends.

We have spirit tho we're poor, we've pride altho' a mob,
We wish for the honour of our town,
Yet we'll wander far and wide whatever may betide,
Aye cadge too before we'll knuckle down.

Operatives in the weaving shed at Waterside Mill in the West Riding of Yorkshire. Photo: Roger Birch

In an alternative version, 'The Haslingden Strike', the words 'Aye! *egad* too' are preferred at the beginning of the last line, together with this opening couplet for the chorus: 'So we've put by the reed-hook and the comb, And hung up the shuttle on the loom.'[24]

A significant part of the strikers' fundraising (or 'cadging'), as well as their publicity, was done through the sale of ballads. A. Hewitson, the Preston historian, disparagingly remarks: 'Ballad-like verses, depicting the grievances of the operatives, and soliciting charity on their behalf, were dolefully sung, from town to town, by squalid-looking bands of men, women, and children.'[25] The workers themselves, not surprisingly, took a different view, in a ballad to the tune of 'The King of the Cannibal Islands':

The Cotton Lords of Preston[26]

Have you not heard the news of late?
About some mighty men so great,
I mean the swells of Fishergate,
The Cotton Lords of Preston.
They are a set of stingy Blades,
They've lock'd up all their Mills and
Shades [sheds],
So now we've nothing else to do,
But come a singing songs to you,
So with our ballads we've come out,
To tramp the country round about,
And try if we cannot live without
The Cotton Lords of Preston.

[Chorus]
Everybody's crying shame,
On these Gentlemen by name;
Don't you think them much to blame?
The Cotton Lords of Preston.

The working people such as we,
Pass their time in misery,
While they live in luxury,
The Cotton Lords of Preston.
They're making money every way,
And building Factories every day,
Yet when we ask them for more pay,
They had the impudence to say,
To your demands we'll not consent,
You get enough to be content,
But we will have the Ten per Cent,
From the Cotton Lords of Preston.

Our Masters say they're very sure,
That a strike we can't endure,
They all assert we're very poor,
The Cotton Lords of Preston,
But we've determined every one,
With them we'll not be done,
For we'll not be content,
Until we get the Ten per cent,
The Cotton Lords are sure to fall,
Both ugly, handsome, short and tall,
For we intend to conquer all,
The Cotton Lords of Preston.

So men and women all of you,
Come and buy a song or two,
And assist us to subdue,
The Cotton Lords of Preston,
We'll conquer them and no mistake,
Whatever Laws they seem to make,
And when we get the Ten per Cent,
Then we'll live happy and content,
O then we'll dance and sing with glee,
And thank them all right heartily,
When we gain the victory,
And beat the Lords of Preston.

The manufacturers are similarly belaboured in other sheets ('The Cotton Lord's Last Shift', 'The Down Fall of the Cotton Lords' and 'Punch's Lamentation for the Cotton Lords'), and also categorised as tyrants ('A New Song on the Preston Tyranny', 'Song of the Preston Tyrants').[27]

Irritated, not to say incensed, by such effrontery, in October 1853 the Preston magistrates prohibited the singing of 'ten per cent' ballads in the streets of the town. Judging by the comments of the journalist from *Household Words* in December 1853 (see p.189), the ban seems rapidly to have fallen into abeyance, possibly because the sheer quantity of singing made it unenforceable. The texts of the ballads are full of 'Come all you' openings, of choruses, and of references to singing. Many prescribe or clearly imply popular tunes such as 'Cheer, Boys, Cheer' (by Henry Russell, written in 1852), 'Fine old English Gentleman', 'Oh Susannah' and 'Old Uncle Ned' (both written in 1848 by Stephen Foster), 'King of the Cannibal Islands' and 'Mistletoe Bough'.

There are rather fewer traditional tunes ('Bonny Bunch of Roses, O', 'A-Nutting we will go'), though an appreciable number of these (such as 'The Boys of Kilkenny', 'The Minstrel Boy') have an Irish origin, which may reflect the significant Irish presence in Preston. 'The Shan Van Vocht' ('An Sean-Bhean Bhocht', meaning 'the poor old woman', a phrase often taken as personifying Ireland) is not cited but it seems clearly indicated by the unusual structure of the ballad involved:

Betty Martin, or The Steam Loom Lass[28]

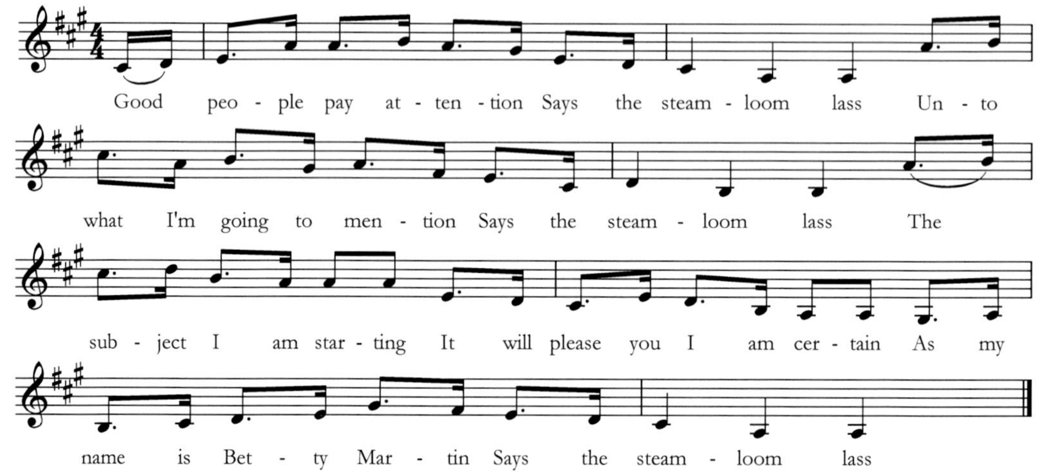

Good people give attention,
Says the steam-loom lass,
Unto what I'm going to mention,
Says the steam-loom lass,
The subject I am starting,
It will please you I am certain,
As my name is Betty Martin,
Says the steam-loom lass.

You are all well aware no doubt, says etc.,
That there's been a great turn-out, says etc.,
And the lads and lasses say,
That they never will give way,
Not until we gain the day, says etc.

We will never be content, says etc.,
Until we get the Ten Per Cent, says etc.
Around the country we will go,
With our fiddle and banjo,
And rattle up Jim Crow, etc.

Too long we've felt the stroke, says etc.,
Of the tyrants heavy yoke, says etc.,
But we've risen from the dead,
Not like poor uncle Ned,
We have hair upon our head, says, etc.

We will stand the grand attack, says etc.
We've the public at our back, says etc.,
Until we get the Ten Per Cent.
We will never be content,
For no less will pay the rent, says etc.

The nobsticks [sic] and the vipers, says etc.
They are nothing more than pipers, says etc.
They are not fit to gather rags,
May some unlucky wags,
Stick a needle in their bags, says etc.

Cheer up your hearts my boys, says etc.
Keep the peace and make no noise, says etc.
And the masters not a doubt,
We will shove them up the spout,
I'm afraid they'll get the gout, says etc.

I know a factory master, says etc.
He got a warming plaster, says etc.
His wife got on the table,
For to stand she was not able,
And she clapt it on his ———, says etc.

He began to tell his Sister, says etc.
For it gave him such a twister, says, etc.
He began to swear and jangle,
For he kick'd up such a wrangle,
Did your Mother sell the mangle, says etc.

Like many of the Preston ballads, 'Betty Martin' avoids solemnity and is full of zest. It appeals to both sexes, throwing in somewhat scurrilous humour.

The Preston lockout was probably the last industrial dispute in which printed ballads played so prominent a part, and a similar observation could be made about the Crimean War, which was partly contemporaneous with the strike. In both cases the ballad corpus would merit further study. The Crimean campaign, for all its disasters, ended in a victory celebrated in parlour and popular songs as well as in street ballads, some of which went on to flourish in oral tradition for another century. On the other hand, the Preston songs would rapidly, perhaps immediately, have fallen from favour: after six months on strike pay of a few shillings a week, workers would have been highly unlikely to have sung the jaunty and optimistic ballads of a few months earlier. As they returned to work they had to accept the conditions appertaining before their defeat, when 'In Preston, 52 per cent of all working-class families with children below working age, working full-time in a year of memorably good trade (1851), could be expected to live below the poverty line'.[29]

1860s: 'Strike, Boys, Strike'

Strike songs were inevitably concerned with local and even parochial issues, until the national coverage achieved by wider industrial disputes in the late nineteenth or twentieth centuries. By contrast the Crimean songs could appeal to the country as a whole, and the same is true of the phenomenon of sheet music, reinforced by the early music halls, which 'provided a vehicle for bourgeois morality and values in the songs of "respectable" entertainers like Harry Clifton'[30] (see p.200). In complete contrast, the writers of street ballads, even though they were working for printers just as commercially inclined as those of sheet music, treated with great familiarity and scant respect not only politicians but members of the royal family. This ballad appeared in 1863:

New Song on the Strikes[31]

Come all you gallant Britons bold,
And listen unto me,
We'll be better paid, have better trade,
And better times we'll see;
Let every man throughout the land
Just do the thing that right.
See, one and all both great and small
Through England's on the strike.

[Chorus]
Here, there, and everywhere,
Things scarcely can be right,
For every grade and every trade,
Through Britains on the strike.

Earl Russel said the other day,
I'll tell you of a lark
That did occur the other night
When all was still and dark,
The Prince of Wales jumped up in bed,
And began to thump his wife,
He said my dear its very clear
That I am on the strike.

Jemmy Mace got in disgrace
When he went down with Goss,
Who in the ring did swiftly spring
And won the fancy toss.
Like dunghill cocks on wooden blocks
Neither of them could fight,
So with Goss and Mace no fight took place,
For they were on the STRIKE.

The Sailors they are out on the Strike
And will not go to Sea,
Mechanics, Painters, and Joiners too
Are striking for better pay.
The jolly snobs so help my Bob
Both old and young alike,
Swear they'll have leather cheaper
Or go upon the Strike.

When the little children cry for bread
Their darling mothers shout,
And with a stick begin to lick
And knock the kids about,
There is no bread the mothers said
And bawled with all their might,
You'll get none to day, go out and play
Your father's on the strike.

The Tailors they are striking too
And say it is no use
They'll have more pay and cabbage they say
Or else they'll eat their goose.
Labouring men are out again
And every one do say,
They're not content but full bent
To have four shillings a day.

The women now are going to Strike
Against the price of meat,
All pretty girls with flowing curls
That nightly walk the streets,
They're all alike, and say they'll Strike
And will not walk the town,
Or do a job, so help my bob
For less than half a crown.

The times are queer, and meat so dear
We find it hard to live,
Each master man throughout the land
Must better wages give,
Or they'll be done, to destruction run
And that they will not like,
They'll curse the day, my lads huzza,
The men went on the strike.

The printer of this sheet, W.S. Fortey, of 2 Monmouth Court, Seven Dials, 'the Oldest and Cheapest House in the World for Ballads (4,000 sorts), Children's Books, Song Books, &c,' was a sharp operator with an unashamedly commercial approach. He – or the writer he commissioned – sought to bring in as much humour as possible, with references to the Prince of Wales (married in 1863), to tailors, a traditional target for mockery ('cabbage' was left-over cloth, a perquisite, and a 'goose' was a smoothing iron), and he includes the apparently obligatory verse about prostitutes. Jemmy Mace (verse 3) met and decisively defeated Goss in a prize fight at Long Reach, Wiltshire, on 1 September 1863 after earlier delays caused by the intervention of the police, which may explain why the sportsmen were deemed to be 'on the STRIKE'.[32]

In complete contrast is the militant language of 'A New Song on the Turn-Out',[33] which recalls the passion of the Preston strikers, even though it was produced by another fully commercial printer, William M'Call or McCall (1822–1890) of Liverpool. The background was the formation in 1866 of the Liverpool Master Builders' Association 'for mutual protection against the aggressive and unreasonable demands of the building trade', and its subsequent decision to impose a form of contract, which recalls the 'declaration' of 1834 (Chapter 5 p. 164) and the 'document' of 1853 (see p.182):

New Song on the Turn-Out[33]

Hurra for every sporting blade, of Liverpool and Birkenhead,
That will support the strike in trade, against the Master Builders;
Let every man now well agree, united in society,
The banners of sweet liberty, will crown your cause most glorious.

The master men are not content, unless that you will give consent,
To sign a binding document, against the law of nature.
Why should you rob your family? and drive yourselves to misery,
To yield unto their tyranny, of silly Master Builders.

A ballad like this would have circulated in a small area over a short period of time. The use of employers' initials – 'S. H——s' (for Mr S. Holmes) and 'Mr T—-' (for Mr W. Tomkinson) – would have left their identities crystal clear to those involved in the dispute. The practice, which would have been familiar to Joseph Mather a century earlier, may have represented a certain timidity on the part of the printer, which sits uneasily with the firmness of the sentiments expressed:

So to conclude and make an end, success attend each loyal friend,
That will a hand to freedom lend, to crush Monopoly;
Be firm, undaunted, loyal and true, the Master Builders you'll subdue,
They are beginning to look blue, the tyrannizing creatures.

In the year of this strike, 1866, Harry Clifton (1832–1872) wrote 'Paddle Your Own Canoe', one of his trademark 'motto' songs of great banality. He also produced a string of pieces, first printed as sheet music, then taken up by the broadside printers, and finally embedded in oral tradition: 'The Calico Printer's Clerk', 'Jemima Brown', 'Polly Perkins of Paddington Green' and 'The Watercress Girl'. In 1867, to the tune of G.F. Root's song of the American Civil War, 'Tramp, Tramp, Tramp', he wrote:

Work, Boys, Work[34]

I'm not a wealthy man, but I've hit upon a plan,
That will render me happy as a king;
And if you will allow me, I'll tell it to you now,
For time you know is always on the wing.

Work, boys, work, and be contented,
As long as you've enough to buy a meal.
The man you may rely, will be wealthy by and bye,
If he'll only put his shoulder to the wheel.

Will fretting make you fat; no there's nothing gain'd by that,
Assist yourselves and fortune will help you;
Tears are only vain, if defeated try again,
You'll find it all the better if you do.
So work, boys, work and be contented, etc.

Discontented people say, all work and little play,
Will make a boy a blockhead as a rule;
You can answer them and say, *'Never work'* and *'always play'*,
Will make him both a blockhead and a fool.
So work, etc.

You'll enjoy a *'quiet crust'*, more by 'rubbing off the rust',
It's a maxim that should never be forgot,
Whilst labour leads to wealth, and will keep you in good health,
So it's best to be contented with your lot.

The music not only had an accompaniment which would have required a competent pianist, but it cost 3s., thirty-six times the price of a street ballad. Nevertheless, the ballad printers also appropriated the text and the song became current among working men. It infuriated Robert Noonan (1870–1911), who, writing as Robert Tressell, described its being sung during a 'beano' of painters and decorators at 'Mugsborough' (Hastings) in his classic novel, *The Ragged Trousered Philanthropists*: 'As this song is the Marseillaise of the Tariff Reform party, voicing as it does the highest ideals of the Tory workmen of this country, it was an unqualified success, for most of them were Conservatives.' [35] It is deeply and satisfyingly ironic that in due course 'Work, Boys, Work' was parodied as 'Strike, Boys, Strike':

So strike, boys, strike, don't be contented,
The landlords to you will have to kneel,
Good wages they will pay, for a fair working day,
If you all put your shoulders to the wheel.

1870s: Nine Hours' Movement

By the 1870s industrialisation had advanced enormously in the two decades since the Great Exhibition. Between 1871 and 1874 the fledgling Trade Union Congress (founded in 1868) reported a tripling in membership from 375,000 to 1,191,000. Workers achieved advances in wages and reductions in hours, but in 1874 a slide began into what came to be called the Great Depression. By the end of the decade, Joseph Arch's agricultural workers' union was largely destroyed, and miners' wages were back to the levels of ten years earlier.

Starting at the age of nine, Alexander McDonald (1821–1881) worked in Lanarkshire coal and ironstone mines for sixteen years. Despite acting at times as overman, the lowest echelon of management, he actively promoted trade union membership.Then, after studying Greek and Latin at evening classes, he went to Glasgow University for three years, paying his way by working in the pit during the summer months. Next, he became a teacher and private tutor, during which time he made money out of speculative investment in mining, while continuing his labour activism. In October 1855 he helped to set up a united coal and ironstone miners' union in Scotland, and then in 1863 a National Miners' Association in England. He was a controversial figure, criticised for his friendship with Lord Elcho, a wealthy mine owner, and for his notion of working within capitalism rather than against it. Nevertheless, conferences which he organised led to the repeal in 1867 of the Master and Servant Act, which had been used against strikers, and the passing in 1872 of a Mines Act, which regulated working underground. Back in Scotland, he campaigned throughout the industrial areas in 1870 for the Eight Hours Movement; and in June of that year, after a stay-down strike, the Fife pitmen secured an eight-hour day, the first miners in Europe to do so. A collier called John Wilson celebrated the progress made:

Alexander McDonald

The Collier's Eight Hours a Day[36]

Now all you jolly collier lads, come listen unto me,
You know how we are sore oppressed by masters' tyranny,
For the improvement of our minds, no leasure time is found,
And our children are neglected too, by working under ground.

[Chorus]
M'Donald is the colliers friend, by us he true is found,
He thinks eight hours is plenty, for to work beneath the ground.
Coal masters are tyrannical, and that they must confess,
They over tax their workmen, and does them sore oppress,

No other occupation so dangerous can be found,
We cannot say our lives our own, while working under ground.

The sailor he does plough the main, and perils does go through,
But he sees his danger coming, which a collier cannot do,
With falling roofs and fire damp, the records can be found,
How hundreds yearly lost their lives, while working under ground

Down in the bowels of the earth, our lively hood we gain,
Our wives and little familys we toil for to maintain,
With five shillings a day some people think, like kings we might be found,
But colliers cannot work full time, you know beneath the ground.

The most of trades and callings, wherever that we go,
Have gained the short time movement, wherever that we go,
And why should we brave colliers, behind the rest be found,
We think eight hours is quite enough, to work beneath the ground.

Johnston, Kilbirnie and Daley, Irvine, Kilmarnock and Ayr,
Glasgow, Coatbridge and Airdrie, with the whole of Lanarkshire,
Falkirk, Alloa and Fife, and the Loathen [Lothian] men all say,
That the colliers should like other men, but work eight hours a day.

Some useful books we will procure, for to improve our mind,
Or healthful recreation among the fields we'll find,
The leasure hours we have to spare, will not be thrown away,
And we'll pray for brave M'Donald, who has gained 8 hours a day.

In 1874 McDonald became MP for Stafford, coinciding in the House of Commons, as it happened, with Michael T. Bass (1799–1884), a native of Burton-on-Trent, and a brewer turned politician. Bass served as Liberal MP for Derby from 1847 until 1883, and during that time endowed the town with a new library, art gallery, recreation ground and swimming baths, actions construed by the cynical as 'some feathers being given back by the man who had taken the goose'.[37] Bass favoured free trade and low taxation but he also supported improved living standards for the working class. In 1872, concerned by the long hours worked by railwaymen, he helped to found the Amalgamated Society of Railway Servants. He receives a favourable mention in 'A New Song on the Carters' and Railway Servants' Strike', [38] which went to the tune of 'Red, White and Blue' (otherwise known as 'Britannia, the Pride of the Ocean'):

A New Song on the Carters' and Railway Servants' Strike [38]

Through England the news is just spreading,
Of the Carters in Manchester on strike,
The masters the future are dreading,
The men will now have what is right:
The masters may boast of their number,
And with gold they may think they are strong,
But our Union will make England wonder,
We strike against tyranny and wrong.

[Chorus]
Here's to the Amalgamated Union for ever,
The Railway and Lurrymen [sic] as one,
May the ties of love and brotherhood ne'er sever,
Until injustices and tyranny are gone.

The writer, a William Herdman, very reasonably offers to submit to arbitration, and concludes:

> May success attend the Union men of England,
> And Mr. BASS, the Union men's best friend,
> May the strike have a peaceful termination,
> And may blessings our labour attend;
> Our children will learn in the future,
> That their fathers together did stand,
> Against tyranny and injustice united,
> They drove it away from the land.

The Amalgamated Society existed until 1912, when it became part of the newly-established National Union of Railwaymen.

On 1 April 1871 engineers in Sunderland struck for a long-cherished objective, a reduction of the working week from 59 to 54 hours. Within a few weeks their employers conceded, but by then Tyneside engineers were out, after forming a Nine Hours' League. This time a hard struggle ensued, lasting over five months, but in early October the men were able to return to work with the nine-hour day secured, albeit only from 1 January 1872. Their cause had attracted tremendous support, including that of *The Times*. As a result: 'The dispute in the North-East had become, in effect, a national dispute by proxy and its outcome led to capitulation by employers in many other districts. ... In most cases, no strike occurred: the employers agreed to a request from their workers, or even volunteered a reduction in hours.'[39]

When the Sunderland men achieved success a Newcastle engineer, Matthew Dryden, wrote, to the tune of 'Nelly Ray':

Perseveer; or, The Nine Oors Movemint[40]

Yen Munday neet aw went oot just te hev a walk,
When aw met a chep frae Sunderland, an' we got on te tawk;
He says, 'Wor working clivvor noo, an' likely for te thrive,
We've got the Nine Oors Movemint noo, an' we drop wor work at five'.

[Chorus]
Perseveer! Perseveer! awl ye that's sittin' here!
Perseveer! Perseveer! they've gettin't on the Wear!
Ye men upon the banks o' Tyne, aw think thor's little fear,
But ye'll get the Nine Oors Movemint if ye only perseveer!

Says aw, 'Me man, aw think yor reet biv aw that aw can reed;
But mind ye myed a gallant fite before ye did succeed.
Se tell yor mates at Sunderland, when ye gan ower hyem,
That wor lads aboot Newcassel thor gawn te de the syem!' …

Noo, strikes are what aw divvent like, but if they'll not agree,
We'll heh te be like Sunderland, an' close wor factories, tee;
The maistors then'll start te fret, and own 'it they were rang;
It's then they'll see they cannot de without the workin man.

Aw myek nee doot wor maistors think think they'll just de what they like,
For they knaw it hurts a working man when he hes te cum te strike;
But if we prove as true as steel wor maistors will be fast,
Thor contracts mun be finished, as they will give in at the last.

The writer worked for Sir William Armstrong, a bitter opponent of the Nine Hours, whose factory at Elswick made him the biggest single employer. Dryden came out on strike with the rest, returned to Armstrong's afterwards, and was still working there in 1890 at the time of his death, aged 45. In concerts to raise funds for the cause, Dryden sang 'Perseveer' to a tune which the better known and more prolific Joe Wilson (1841–1875), had employed in about 1870 for 'Keep Your Feet Still, Geordie Hinney', which turned out to be a perennial favourite in the North-east. Wilson, who often, like Dryden, adapted orthography to represent local speech, offered his support during the dispute with 'The Strike!':

The Strike![41]

Cum, me canny Tynesiders, an lissen
Tiv a sang that aw's sartin ye'll like,
An' aw'll whisper a word kind an' cheeron'
Te mony poor fellows on strike.
Let them keep up thor hearts as they hev deun,
Thor's a day for the true an' the brave,
An' the time'll yit cum when greet Maisters
'Ill find oot a Mechanic's ne slave!

Is Nine Oors an unreasonable movement?
Is't not plenty for labour te men?
Let them that condemn'd hev a try on't,
An' see if they'll alter such plan;
An' if lang oors industry increases,
Heh they fund it wi' them that they've tried?
Wi' thor capital heh they got labour
Like *that* frae the men they've defied?

At the end of the strike, the anonymous writer of 'A New Song on the Nine Hour' [sic] Movement',[42] despite giving a welcome to the victory, concludes with a very conciliatory, not to say defeatist, message:

A New Song on the Nine Hour' [sic] Movement[42]

Strikes we know ne'er do much good, lock outs, they are worse;
To the British Workman's Interests, they always prove a curse:
They import foreign labour, as lately has been shown;
And cause our own skilled artisans, to leave their native home.

Let's hope that each employer throughout this Nation great,
May follow the example, that has been so nobly set;
May every British Workman try, to raise his masters store,
Let amity his motto be, of strikes let's hear no more.

A more spirited and also more humorous approach is adopted in 'Stick up for the Women, and Nine Hours a Day',[43] which provides an intriguing insight into the struggle to balance work outside the home with family responsibilities. The tune adopted, 'Act on the Square', was written by Alfred Lee in 1866:

All through this good old land of ours Com - mo - tion there has
been And in the poor man's wor - king hours Great chan - ges we have
seen But whilst they strug - gled for their rights And to im - prove their
lot Our poor white slaves are left at home ne - glec - ted and for - got
Act on the square, boys, act on the square
Stick up for the wo - men, for that's on - ly fair For a
wo - man is pride of the land we all say The
why should she work more than nine hours a day

All thro' this good old land of ours,
Commotion there has been,
And in the poor man's working hours,
Great changes we have seen;
But whilst they struggled for their rights
And to improve their lot,
Our poor white slaves are left at home,
Neglected and forgot.

Act on the square, boys, act on the square,
Stick up for the women, for that's only fair,
For a woman's the pride of the land we all say,
Why should she work more than nine hours a day.

What can a woman have to do?
The men will often say,
They only have to cook and stew;
And pleasant pass the day;
But let a man just take her place,
When baby begins to roar,
He'll find himself in such a mess,
He'd never try no more.

You would first the children have to dress,
And breakfast get, you know,
There's Tommy standing on his head,
While Jack upsets the Po;
There's Sally at the water,
With firewood setting sail,
While Bobby makes an awful noise,
By twisting pussy's tail.

At one o'clock the 'Hooter' goes,
The men come home to dine,
And if it is not ready done,
Look out then for a shine.
At five o'clock he's done his work,
And then can do the grand,
While you are slaving like a Turk,
He's singing 'Happy Land'.

You factory girls of England now,
Who get such little pay,
The roses from your blooming cheeks,
Hard work has driven away;
Oft-times to please your masters,
You are working past your time,
But if your [sic] are late they'll shut the gate,
And make you pay a fine.

Young women then take my advice
When courting your young man,
Tell him when the knot is tied,
That this will be your plan –
Eight hours for work, eight hours for sleep,
And then eight hours for play,
Sundays must be all your own,
And 'night work' double pay.

The final verse neatly adopts the slogan, famously inscribed on twelve watch cases in 1860, of the International Association of Working Men (known as the first International): 'We require 8 hours for work, 8 hours for our own instruction and 8 hours for repose.' The song clearly indicates that within a decade this had secured widespread acceptance.

If in the end the employers' opposition to the Nine Hours' Movement collapsed dramatically, 1872 was nevertheless a year of strikes, part of what Theodore Hoppen has described as the 'great wave of industrial unrest in 1871–3 involving colliers, plumbers, carpenters and joiners, shoe and bootmakers, ironworkers, engineers and fitters, masons, and many more'.[44] Workers were clearly determined to take advantage of boom years, and in turn, a London ballad printer, Henry Disley, who normally specialised in sordid crime and was the leading publisher of murder broadsides in Seven Dials, seized the opportunity to issue several light-hearted sheets:

A watch celebrating International Association of Working Men: 'We require 8 hours for work, 8 hours for our own instruction, and 8 hours for repose.'

The Strike of 1872[45]

The railway servants are on the strike,
It is the truth now, you will own,
All married men say they'll strike,
Their wives when they get home.
The builders too they're on the strike,
They want to have their way,
And the washerwomen they've all struck,
It's true now what I say.

The Strike of the Laundresses[46]

There are English, Irish, Scotch & Welch
Goes washing every day,
There's blooming girls from Erin's isle,
Who have but little pay,
They rub and scrub, & wring and sweat,
For which they have bad pay,
But they won't give in till they have their beer,
And three shillings every day.

'The Strike Alphabet' [47] combines a jocular tone with sharp class consciousness:

The Strike Alphabet[47]

C stands for Carpenters, they all want better pay,
They want ninepence an hour, and work nine hours a-day.
E stands for Engineers, who acted like noble fellows,
For they freely sent two hundred pounds, to help the Warwickshire labourers.
J stands for John Bull, who brags of his noted fame
The working men create the wealth, and the masters pocket the same.
L stands for Labouring men
And when they are old and feeble to the workhouse they can go.
M stands for Masters, they are not all alike,
Some gave way to the men, before they would have a strike.
N stands for Newcastle, where the strikes they first began,

They showed an example to every working man.
P stands for Parliament, where Whigs and Tories shout
But the interest of the working man they always do leave out.
S stands for strikes, the men want shorter time,
Instead of working ten hours, they are determined to work nine.
X stands for Ten, the hours men used to toil,
But nine they think is quite enough throughout the English soil.

Joseph Arch

The Warwickshire farm labourers, to whom the engineers had in fact donated not two hundred but three hundred pounds, had formed a union after the historic occasion in the village of Wellesbourne where a meeting in February 1872 was addressed by Joseph Arch, freelance farm worker who later became an M.P. A strike quickly followed. The union went national, and became for a time the biggest in the country. The farmers then organised in opposition, and after a lockout in 1874 the union collapsed. Even so, the National Agricultural Labourers' Union was 'a significant forerunner of the "new unions" of the 1880s and 1890s'.[48] The NALU can be seen a sort of a bridge: it was partly inspired by the struggles of skilled workers such as the engineers, and it pointed the way for the achievements of the so-called unskilled such as gas workers and dockers.

Continuing a Chartist tradition, the farm workers regularly sang at union meetings, with the help of a book circulated by the union with song texts set to the tunes of the day.[49] Two of these, 'The Fine Old English Labourer' and 'My Master and I',[50] found their way on to broadsides issued by the London printer, H.P. Such. Using the same illustration of a labourer sharpening his scythe in a harvest field, Such also printed, to the tune of 'Work, Boys, Work' (see p.200):

Success to the Farm Labourers, And the Agricultural Strike[51]

Come all you farming men and list to what I pen,
And throw aside the rake and the plough,
If you wish to free yourselves, from a lot of greedy elves
You'll find it is the time to do it now.

[Chorus]
Strike, boys, strike, for better wages,
Stand out as long as you can get a meal,
For farming men I say, will surely win the day,
If they only keep their shoulders to the wheel.

On the farms of Warwickshire the labourers we hear,
Have risen up, determined to be free,
With the gallant Mr. Arch, they nobly did march,
And rallied round the Willsbourne [Wellesbourne] chestnut tree.

Can anyone say why you shouldn't have a try,
To make the farmers treat you more like men,
For I'm sure you'll say 'tis true, they think no more of you
Than the sheep or the cattle in the pen.

Then don't give away to grief, for you soon will have relief
From your brother working men of every trade,
Every honest working man will lend a helping hand,
When he sees the hearty courage you've displayed.

Many hours you did work, and starving like a Turk
And a holiday to you was something strange,
It was only twice a year, when you went to —— fair,
That you ever got a little bit of change.

The farmer's sons so fine, can live on goose and wine,
And expect to be treated like a lord,
The ploughman gets no beef to stick between his teeth,
And a glass of beer he seldom can afford.

Now upon the farmer's land, agriculture's at a stand,
A famous crop of weeds it will yield,
The cattle in the sheds, are eating off their heads
And the ploughs are getting rusty in the fields.

They are in a precious rage, there's no one will engage
To work like a nigger all the day,
Their trouble will increase, when the ducks have eat the geese,
And all the little pigs have run away.

Altho' the year round, you cultivate the ground
You musn't take a turnip from the land,
For a farthing's worth of sticks, you would soon be in a fix,
And you musn't go a poaching, understand.

So strike, boys, strike, don't be contented,
The landlords to you will have to kneel,
Good wages they will pay, for a fair working day
If you all put your shoulders to the wheel.

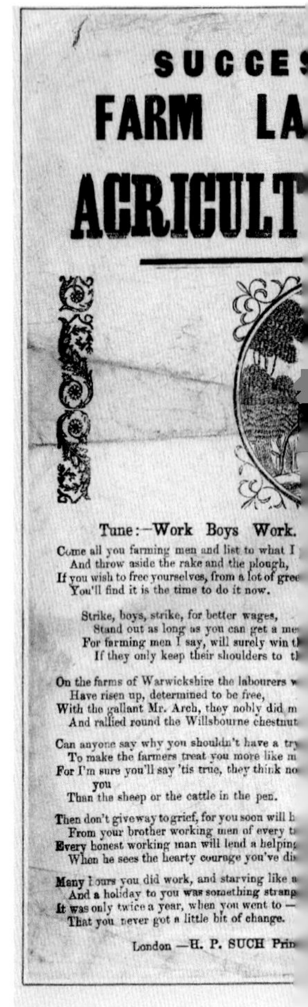

SUCCES
FARM LA
AGRICULT

Tune:—Work Boys Work.

Come all you farming men and list to what I
And throw aside the rake and the plough,
If you wish to free yourselves, from a lot of gree
You'll find it is the time to do it now.

Strike, boys, strike, for better wages,
Stand out as long as you can get a me
For farming men I say, will surely win t
If they only keep their shoulders to t

On the farms of Warwickshire the labourers
Have risen up, determined to be free,
With the gallant Mr. Arch, they nobly did m
And rallied round the Willsbourne chestnut

Can anyone say why you shouldn't have a try
To make the farmers treat you more like m
For I'm sure you'll say 'tis true, they think no
you
Than the sheep or the cattle in the pen.

Then don't giveway to grief, for you soon will h
From your brother working men of every t
Every honest working man will lend a helping
When he sees the hearty courage you've di

Many hours you did work, and starving like a
And a holiday to you was something strang
It was only twice a year, when you went to —
That you never got a little bit of change.

London —H. P. SUCH Prin

'Success to the Farm Labourers,....' A broadside printed by H.P. Such supporting The Farm Labourers and Agricultural Strike. (Harding Collection B13). Reproduced courtesy of the Bodleian Library, University of Oxford.

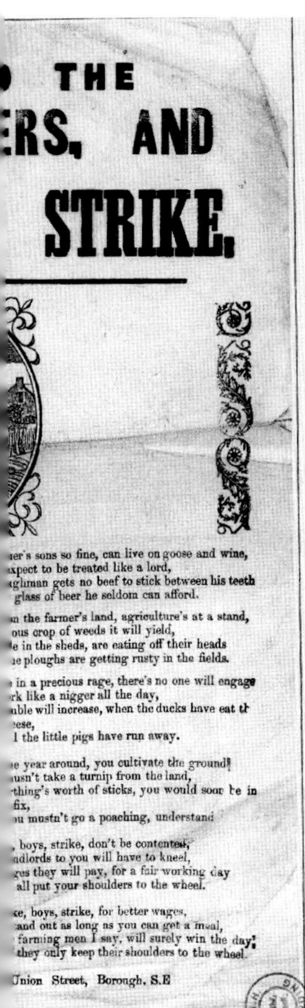

THE
RS, AND
STRIKE.

ner's sons so fine, can live on goose and wine,
xpect to be treated like a lord,
ghman gets no beef to stick between his teeth
glass of beer he seldom can afford.

n the farmer's land, agriculture's at a stand,
ous crop of weeds it will yield,
e in the sheds, are eating off their heads
e ploughs are getting rusty in the fields.

in a precious rage, there's no one will engage
rk like a nigger all the day,
uble will increase, when the ducks have eat th
ese,
l the little pigs have run away.

e year around, you cultivate the ground!
usn't take a turnip from the land,
thing's worth of sticks, you would soon be in
fix,
u mustn't go a poaching, understand

, boys, strike, don't be contented,
ndlords to you will have to kneel,
ges they will pay, for a fair working day
all put your shoulders to the wheel.

ke, boys, strike, for better wages,
and out as long as you can get a meal,
farming men I say, will surely win the day;
they only keep their shoulders to the wheel.

Union Street, Borough, S.E

Strike, boys, strike, for better wages,
Stand out as long as you can get a meal,
For farming men I say, will surely win the day,
If they only keep their shoulders to the wheel.

Another lively ballad, to the tune of 'Oh, dear what can the matter be', stems from the lockout of 1874:

Oh, dear what'll become of us?[52]

What's a labourer's prospect in this land of freedom?
Six young uns to keep and twelve shillings to feed 'em,
A jail and a workhouse for all those who need 'em,
Pray, what does a poor labourer lack?

[Chorus]
Oh, dear, what will become of us?
Oh, dear, what will become of us?
Oh, dear, what will become of us?
If he should give us the sack?

Twelve shillings a week, it'll just fill one belly,
But Bill, Tom and Hal, Polly, Susan and Nelly,
They eat all day long, my old woman'll tell ye,
I only can just get a snack.

There came an old chap whom the union engages
To show the poor man how to go for more wages;
Says he: Ask for more, and if Farmer Grumps rages
The union will stand at your back.

Says Grumps: If you join it will end in disaster.
How dare you offend such an excellent master?
Says I: if you say so, we'll join all the faster.
Oh, he looked awfully black.

He says in the harvest we're putting him quite about,
Yet if he'd be just there'd be nothing to fight about,
But he swears he'll send us all to the rightabout,
When he begins to get slack.

There's plenty of work to be had by the willing,
With wages at double the paltry twelve shilling,
And land o'er the sea to be had for the tilling,
If he should tell us to pack.

A further piece, entitled 'A New Song on the General Trades' Strike' [53], begins confidently:

A New Song on the General Trades' Strike[53]

Since striking has become now, the order of the day,
I'll strike you up a song, if you'll list to what I say;
All trades they are now striking, in country and in town,
And the rich they are determined for to keep the poor man down.

[Chorus]
So I hope they will get what they want, the working classes all o'er,
For there never was such striking, in this country before.

It offers support for miners striking at Cannock Chase, and nailmakers at Dudley, but in conclusion remarks: '. . . many women and children too, Have cause to dread the strike, For they miss the Sunday dinner, And their Father's Saturday night.' A similar reference to pay-day occurs in a ballad written by 'Mat the Rhymer', which with some considerable skill and affection shows through a child's eyes the life of a family struggling to manage during a dispute:

Father's on the Strike[54]

Oh! When will father go to work? Dear mother tell us true;
He never says good morning now as once he used to do.
We go to school, and leave papa so Sadly in his chair
And when we all come back again we find him sitting there.

[Chorus]
Let people say whate'er they please, and do whate'er they like,
Our home is not so happy now, since Father's on the strike.
Poor Mother's looking pale and thin, she goes out ever day,
To do a little washing now, to help her pay her way.
She tells us coals are very dear, and all provisions too,
And when the dreadful winter comes, what will poor people do?

The good old clock that sung cuckoo, we miss it now it's gone,
And the pretty pictures too are all away in pawn.
Poor Mother tried to take it off, and pledge her wedding ring,
But when Father goes to work, they'll all come back again.

We are too small to understand, if strikes are wrong or right,
But old enough to feel the want, of Father's Saturday night.
May men and masters all agree, to the best terms to work,
And end it soon, this sad dispute, for wives' and children's sake.

Father might well have rejoined, given the opportunity, that he was on strike precisely 'for wives' and children's sake'; and in the case of a lockout, that he had no choice other than capitulation.

Three handbills produced for sale by miners, 'South Yorkshire Lock-out. Barnsley Collieries', 'The Great Lock-out of Miners at Barnsley' and 'The Barnsley Miners' Lock-out',[55] can be dated from a reference in the last item ('Each firm must have a manager, Dwelling on the ground, With Government certificate') to the Coal Mines Act, 1872, which made it obligatory for colliery managers to have a state certificate of competence. Though these sheets were essentially intended for collecting money, they emphasised that the Barnsley men were standing up for their rights and seeking 'A fair day's wage for a fair day's work'.

In Wales the Amalgamated Association of Miners, pursuing the same objective, became involved in a series of strikes and lockouts, culminating in a five-month-long struggle in 1875, which inspired Ioan Eslyn to write in two languages, to the tune of 'Robert is shy', 'Robyn yn swill', 'A New Song on the Lock Out in South Wales', 'Cân ar y Lock-Out yn Neheudir Cymry',[56] beginning:

A New Song on the Lock Out in South Wales[56]

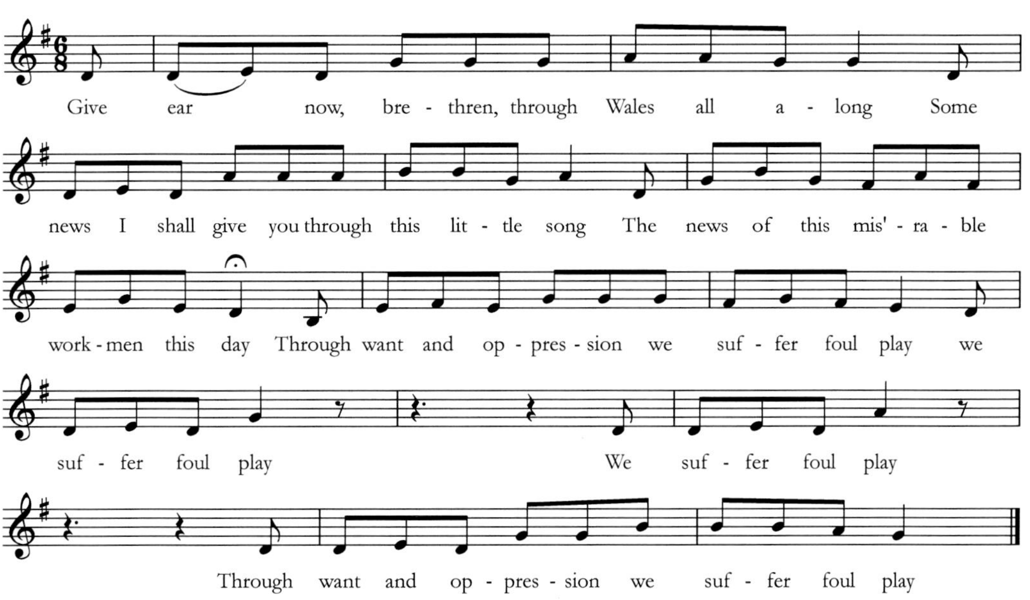

Give ear, now, brethren, through Wales all along,
Some news I shall give you through this little song;
The news of the miserable workmen this day –
Through want and oppression we suffer foul play.

[Chorus]
We suffer foul play, we suffer foul play,
Through want and oppression we suffer foul play.

Rhowch glust ymwrandawiad trwy Gymru o'r bron
Cewch genyf fyr hanes trwy'r ganig fach hon;
Sef hanes trueni y gweithwr yn awr,
Trwy orthrwm a gormes ein beisieu sydd fawr.

[Cydgan]
Ein beisieu sydd fawr, ein beisieu sydd fawr,
Trwy orthrwm a gormes ein beisieu sydd fawr.

The 60,000 men locked out were forced to return to work, defeated, when their union's funds were exhausted, and the organisation broke up.Wages fell by 12%, and were linked to the price of coal in a sliding scale which put dividends for shareholders before wages for miners. Undismayed in defeat, miners in Wales (and elsewhere) looked to improve conditions by extending the concession won in part of Scotland by Alexander McDonald at the beginning of the decade:

Wyth awr i weithio, with awr o rhyddid;
Wyth awr i gysgu, a with swllt y dydd.
(Eight hours work, eight hours play;
Eight hours sleep, and eight bob a day). [57]

There were other problems, too: miners' average earnings were lower in 1880 than in 1870.

1880s: New Unions

Now begins the era of the 'New Unions' mentioned earlier, covering workers previously regarded as unskilled. Leaders emerged who were willing to organise mass action and to look beyond Liberalism to socialist ideas. In so doing they returned to earlier hopes of transforming society.

When Tommy Armstrong, born at Shotley Bridge, County Durham, started work as a trapper boy at the age of nine, his legs were so bowed by rickets that his older brother had to carry him to the pit. Armstrong (1848–1920) never exceeded five feet in height, but he fathered fourteen children and was a prodigious beer drinker. As a boy of fifteen he heard Joe Wilson sing, and while working as a pitman he developed a reputation of his own as an entertainer, delivering readings and recitations

TRADES' UNION.

E all you good people, come listen awhile,
're in hopes very soon that our country will smile,
the noble mechanics of every town
resolved to have their rights very soon.

CHORUS.

uzza, for the Union, stand firm in union,
'ou noble mechanics of every town.

masters have join'd hand in hand, as we hear,
oull down the Unions they vow and declare;
y say the Trades' Union will very soon
them of their rights, so they will have them down.

masters are plotting, their roguery to hide,
y want Billy and Parliament both on their side;
our tight little Union will smile at the fun,
what they propose it will never be done.

us stand as firm as the King to his crown,
nderhand dealings shall e'er put us down,
we are all join'd by the Powers above
true reformation and brotherly love.

hands they are join'd, and our hearts are the same;
ongues shall repeat the brave Union's fame;
have suffered like martyrs, you all know it well,
for the sake of our country we ne'er will rebel.

, the Union for ever, my boys do not fret,
our firmly-built Union will never be beat:
Union 's our laurel, and take it who can,
re we resign it we'll die to a man.

w to conclude, and to finish my song,
in a body, and keep yourselves strong;
are a match for Tom Pepper, and what's my delight,
rue Union lads will put all things to right.

Broadside ballad on Trades' Union. Reproduced by permission of the City Library, Derby

interlarded with extempore witticisms. Though he was no singer, he excelled in chronicling local events by devising songs prescribed to be sung to well-known tunes. The texts were printed and sold on penny sheets. None of these has survived, but after Armstrong's death one of his sons put together a slim volume of texts.[58]

Like other north-eastern writers, including Joe Wilson, whose work influenced him a good deal, Armstrong used both standard English and a sort of phonetic rendering of the vernacular, which can be irksome to read but convincing when sung. He became known as 'the pitman's poet' in Durham and Northumberland, thanks to writing songs such as 'The Row between the Cages'[59] and, after a disaster in 1882, 'Trimdon Grange Explosion' (see Chapter 3, p. 103). In addition, Armstrong strongly supported the miners' cause during strikes and lockouts in the 1880s, and indeed in 1892.

During the stoppage of November 1885 in the Stanley–Consett–Chopwell area of County Durham the time-dishonoured eviction of striking miners from their company-owned houses was conducted with particular roughness by the 'candymen' (rag and bone men and general riffraff), supported by the bellman (bailiff) and police. Armstrong wrote two songs on the subject, their titles giving the names of pits: 'Sooth Medomsley Strike' (tune, 'Castles in the Air') and 'Oakey's Strike' (tune, 'The Pride of Petticoat Lane').[60] The latter's scornful ridicule is memorable:

Oakey's Strike[60]

It wis in November en aw nivor will forget
Th' polises en th' candymen it Oakey's hooses met;
Johny, th' bellmin, he wis thare, squinten roon eboot;
En he plaic'd three men it ivory hoose te torn th' pitmen oot.

CORUS [sic]
Oh wat was aw dee if add th' power me sel,
Aw wid hang th' twenty candymen en Johny thit carry's th' bell.

Thare th' went freh hoose te hoose te put thing on th' road,
But mind th' didn't hort thorsels we liften hevy loads;
Sum wid carry th' poker oot, th' fendor, or th' rake,
If th' lifted two it once it wis e greet mistake.

Sum e these dandy-candy men wis drest up like a clown;
Sum ad hats wivoot e flipe, en sum wivoot e croon;
Sum ad nee laps ipon thor cotes but thare wis one chep warse:
Ivory time he ad te stoop it was e laffible farse.

Thare wis one chep as nee sleves nor buttins ipon hees cote;
Enuthor ad e bairns hippin lapt eroond his throte.
One chep wore e pair e breeks thit belang tiv e boi,
One leg wis e sort iv e tweed, th' tuthor wis cordyroi.

Next thare cums th' maistors, aw think thae shud think shem,
Depriven wives en familys of a comfortable yem.
But wen thae shift freh ware thae liv, aw hope thail gan te th' well,
Elang we th' twenty candy men, en Johny thit carrys th' bell.

Armstrong's son, William, interviewed by A.L. Lloyd in 1953, 'recalled a lyrical duel fought between his father and a newcomer to the district, William McGuire, who put himself up as a song-maker'. This was in the Red Row Public House at Beamish Burn. The evictions at Oakey Colliery, a few miles away, were chosen as the theme for the contest. 'McGuire's effusion is long since forgotten, but Armstrong's lives on, in the form subsequently polished up a bit by its maker.' [61]

As well as writers already well known, at least within a particular area, others felt moved to express themselves during strikes – a phenomenon still notable during the miners' action of 1984–85. In some cases individual authorship failed to be recorded, perhaps to avoid intimidation by employers once a strike was over. Other songs may have evolved bit by bit in a collective fashion.

A dispute in 1886 involving 400 ironworkers in Shropshire, no doubt insignificant against a national background, was a severe trial for the men concerned and their families, who had to depend on credit to survive for twenty-two weeks. One of their number, signing himself 'Nil Desperandum', wished, once arbitration brought the strike to an end, to emphasise a principle ('As this is the greatest struggle, Mill or forgeman ever knew; Let it teach us all the lesson, Unity has brought us through.') and to remind fellow workers:

All who work in mills and forges,
Foundry, fitting shop or mine;
Look through our subscription papers,
You'll know where to spend your coin.

Patronise the open hearted,
Those who once our children fed;
Show contempt to those who slighted
Us, when we were wanting bread. [62]

Two years later, a report on the year 1888 lists 509 strikes, of which 320 were for increased wages.[63] One of them was at Bryant and May's match factories at Bow in London, where 1,200 women struck in July. Hours at the factory were long, from 6.30 am until 6 pm in summer, and from 8 am to 6 pm in winter. Adults could earn on piecework between eleven and thirteen shillings a week, girls between five and nine shillings. In fact, though, the highest paid women averaged only 6s. 3d. a week. Outworkers were even worse off. Thanks to the materials they were handling, most suffered from 'phossy jaw' – phosphorous necrosis of the jaw – which among other things caused teeth to drop out.

Annie Besant

Three women briefed the radical campaigner Annie Besant for an article which she published on their conditions of work, under the title of 'White Slavery in London', in her weekly paper, *The Link*. The workers were identified by the management and dismissed. The rest of the workforce, required to sign a declaration of satisfaction with working conditions, walked out. Besant helped to organise a strike fund and a strike committee, the London Trades Council mediated, and within three weeks shorter hours, better pay and improvements in conditions were conceded by the employers. The strike committee went on to organise the Union of Women Matchworkers, which by early September had 600 members.

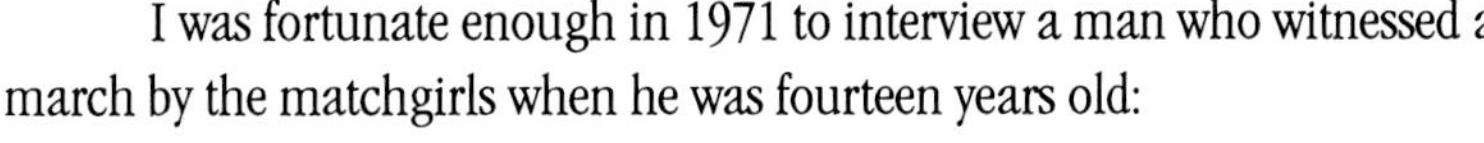

I was fortunate enough in 1971 to interview a man who witnessed a march by the matchgirls when he was fourteen years old:

> When they went on strike they walked through Bow, all the way up Mile End Road, Whitechapel Road and Leadenhall Street, and straight through to Trafalgar Square. And on the way through Leadenhall Street particularly they used to sing:
>
> > We'll hang old Bryant on a sour apple tree,
> > We'll hang old Bryant on a sour apple tree,
> > We'll hang old Bryant on a sour apple tree,
> > As we go marchin' in.
> > Glory, glory, hallelujah, glory, glory, hallelujah,
> > Glory, glory, hallelujah,
> > As we go marchin' in.
>
> And while they were walking along, the people in the offices overhead would throw some coppers down; and then there'd be a scramble among the girls to get these coppers up. That caused a bit of an interlude from the singing; and when they'd picked up all the coppers, on they'd go again, singing and marching.[64]

Bryant and May match girls on strike in Bow in 1888.

The successful action at Bryant and May's was followed by the organisation of a union for gas workers by Will Thorne (1857–1946), helped by Tom Mann (1856–1941), John Burns (1858–1943), Edward Aveling (1849–98) and Eleanor Marx (1855–98), daughter of Karl. In August 1889 the Gas-workers' and General Labourers' Union demanded and (surprisingly) obtained from their employers a reduction in hours from twelve to eight daily, with at the same time an increase of 6d. in pay. Shortly afterwards, on 12 August, a few casual labourers went on strike over a trivial dispute at the South-west India Dock. Within days, for the first time since 1797, the entire Port of London was at a standstill, with 75,000 men idle.

Will Thorne

The strikers were led by Ben Tillett (1860–1943), an English-born Irishman, an itinerant labourer with a gift for impassioned oratory, who subsequently became secretary of a new and powerful Dock, Wharf, Riverside and General Labourers' Union. He was supported by Thorne, Mann and Burns, the last of whom, a striking figure, straw-hatted, black-bearded and charismatic, organised mass meetings on Tower Hill and led spectacular processions through the City of London, with stevedores,

Ben Tillett

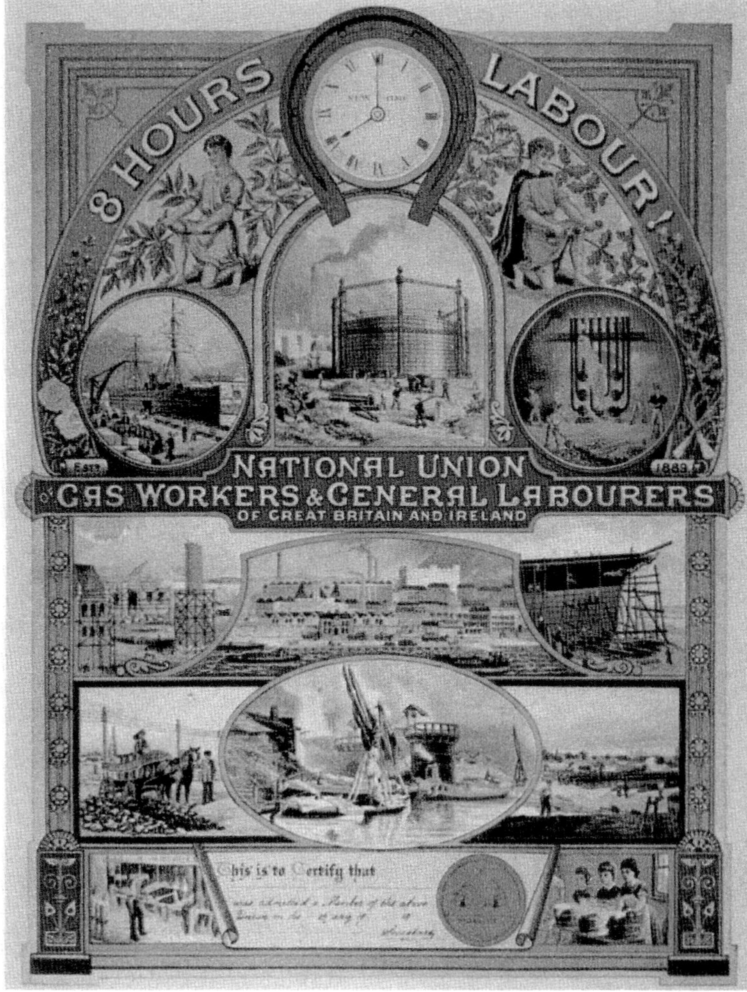

Emblem of the gas workers commemorating the winning of the eight-hour day, 1889.

lightermen, ship painters, sailors, firemen, riggers, scrapers, engineers, shipwrights, labourers and watermen, joined by Father Neptune and Britannia. Banners flew and poles were crowned with such things as stinking fish-heads and rotting onions to exemplify the dockers' diet.

There was no walkover. Blacklegs were brought into the docks. Relief funds for the strikers and their families poured in from other unions, from workers in Australia (the sum of £30,000) and in donations from middle-class people. These were soon exhausted, but after five weeks, thanks to mediation by Cardinal Manning (who was thereafter rewarded by being depicted on union banners), the employers conceded the minimum wage of sixpence an hour demanded by the strikers, or 'the full round orb of the dockers' tanner', as they put it.

This was a massive victory. Frederick Engels wrote: 'It's the greatest event to have taken place in England since the last Reform Bills [some

twenty years earlier], and marks the beginning of a complete revolution in the East End.'[65] As well as the material advance, he was impressed by the priceless change in working class consciousness: 'Hitherto the East End had been in a state of poverty-stricken stagnation, its hallmark being the apathy of men whose spirit had been broken by hunger, and who had abandoned all hope ... Then, last year, there came the victorious strike of the match-girls. And now, this gigantic strike of the most demoralised elements of the lot, the dock labourers.'[66]

A song celebrating the triumph of the dockers' tanner continued to be affectionately remembered and sung for many years after the event:

Strike for Better Wages[67]

At the docks there is a strike that the company don't like:
A tanner on the hour they'll have to pay.
Like slaves they'd have us work far more than any Turk,
And make us sweat our lives out every day.

[Chorus]
Strike, boys, strike for better wages!
Strike, boys, strike for better pay!
Go on fighting at the docks,
Stick it out like fighting cocks,
Go on fighting till the bosses they give way.

Every morning there are flocks for employment at the docks,
Hard-working men who scarce can get a meal;
With wives and children dear it would make you shed a tear

DOCK LABOURERS'

STRIKE!

RELIEF FUND.

Fellow-workmen—An earnest appeal is made to you to help your fellow-workmen, the half-starved, under-paid Dockers, in their great struggle. The men MUST win, or so much the worse for all of us. It will be our fault if they do not. Their cause is the most righteous and reasonable in modern times.

GIVE LIBERALLY & SECURE THE VICTORY!

Public Relief Fund Sheets supplied to duly authorised Collectors. All Clubs and Institutions are asked to co-operate. Shops and Factories should appoint their own Collectors.

SUBSCRIPTIONS RECEIVED at the OFFICE OF COMMITTEE, 23, RUTLAND STREET, every Evening at 7.30; 4 on Saturday.

COMMITTEE–

John Potter, (Leicester School Board), Harry Woolley, (New Co-op. Shoe Works), Hipwell, (Vine St Radical Club), C. O'Sullivan, (Irish Nationl Club). Messrs. L. Brown, Staughton, Warner, Gorrie, Barclay, Richards, &c.

If you only knew the hardships that they feel.
If it's slavery that you seek, for about a quid a week,
They'll take you on as soon as you come near.
Sweat your guts out with a will or they'll try your job to fill,
But that won't wash with working men, that's clear.

We'll stand up for our rights and the company we will fight,
Supported by our brothers everywhere,
For we have friends galore – the good old stevedores,
And the seamen and the firemen they are there.

Starvation, 'tis they bids to a man with seven kids,
When he brings home only fifteen pence a day;
For what can you get to eat on seven-and-six a week,
When it often takes it all the rent to pay?

Heare's a health to Mr Burns, he's done us all a turn,
Ben Tillett, Mann, and Mr Toomey, too.
We won't give in a bit, for we've got 'em in a fit,
And we've put the old dock company in a stew.

1890s: 'Billy Fair Play'

According to one estimate, between the 1890s and the 1970s there were 100,000 strikes, of which 40,000 were in the mines.[68] In February 1892, at a time of depression, the Durham coal-owners called for a reduction in wages. The miners responded by going on strike, but then offered to take a 10% reduction. This was deemed insufficient, and the owners declared a lockout. The Durham Miners' Union, which had withdrawn from the Miners' Federation of Great Britain (launched in 1889 and attaining a membership of 200,000 by 1893), could afford only minimal strike pay. 'The pitmen's poet', Tommy Armstrong, reacted with a ballad, to the tune of 'Castles in the Air'. The raw anger of its chorus recalls that of Sheffield's Joseph Mather, a century earlier:

Durham Strike[69]

In our Durham County, I am sorry for to say
That hunger and starvation is increasing every day;
For want of food and coals we know not what to do,
But with your kind assistance, we will stand the struggle through.
I need not state the reason why we have been brought so low,
The masters have behaved unkind, which everyone will know;
Because we won't lie down and let them treat us as they like,
To punish us they've stopt their pits and caused the present strike.

[Chorus]
May every Durham colliery owner that is in the fault,
Receive nine lashes with the rod, then be rubbed with salt;
May his back end be thick with boils, so that he cannot sit,
And never burst until the wheels go round at every pit.

The pulley wheels have ceased to move, which went so swift around,
The horses and the ponies too are brought from underground;
Our work is taken from us now, they care not if we die,
For they can eat the best of food, and drink the best when dry.
The miner, and his partner too, each morning have to roam
To seek for bread to feed the little hungry ones at home;
The flour barrel is empty now, their true and faithful friend,
Which makes the thousands wish today the strike was at an end.

We have done our best as honest working men,
To let the pits commence again we've offered to them 'ten'.
The offer they will not accept, they firmly do demand
Thirteen and a half per cent., or let their collieries stand.
Let them stand, or let them lie, to do with them as they choose,
To give them thirteen and a half, we ever shall refuse,
They're always willing to receive, but not inclined to give,
Very soon they won't allow a working man to live.

With tyranny and capital they never seem content,
Unless they are endeavouring to take from us per cent.;
If it was due what they request, we willingly would grant;
We know it's not, therefore we cannot give them what they want.
The miners of Northumberland we shall for ever praise,
For being so kind in helping us these tyrannising days;
We thank the other counties, too, that have been doing the same,
For every man who reads will know that we are not to blame.

In our Dur ham coun - ty I am sor - ry for to say That
hun - ger and star - va - tion is in - crea - sing e' - vry day For the
want of food and coals we know not what to do But
with your kind as - sis - tance we will stand the strug - gle through I
need not state the rea - son why we have been brought so low The
mas - ters have be - haved un - kind, which e - v'ry one will know Be -
cause we won't lie down and let them treat us how they like To
pu - nish us they've stopt their pits and caused the pre - sent strike May
e - v'ry Dur - ham col - lie - ry ow - ner that is in the fault Re -
ceive nine la - shes with the rod, then be rubbed with salt May
his back end be thick with boils so that he can - not sit And
ne - ver burst un - til the wheels go round at e - v'ry pit

Men and boy colliers at New Hawne Pit, Halesowen, Worcestershire, c. 1900. Author's own collection

Armstrong's apologetic opening seems to portend the begging ballad conventionally used after a pit disaster or in times of unemployment, but the piece rapidly turns to strong criticism of the coal-owners. The pit's inactivity ('The pulley wheels have ceased to move') itself becomes a novel and memorable reproach to the employers.

Dating from the following year, 'The Miners' Lock-Out',[70] also set to the tune of 'Castles in the Air', lacks Armstrong's assurance. Nevertheless, it has a jaunty chorus ('Then let us be united, We never must give way. Uphold the Federation, lads, And we will win the day.') and includes praise for 'our trusty leaders ... well worthy of their steel'. The writer, a Wigan miner called Burnett O'Brien, looks forward optimistically: 'The day is fast approaching, when the victory we will shout, And we'll remember those who helped us when we were all locked out.' Unusually, his hope was realised.

In 1892, though, the Durham men were defeated. Then in the following year the Miners' Federation faced a lockout in most of the areas it covered in Scotland, Wales and England. Some 300,000 of its members were involved. During the dispute over the employers' wish to reduce wages by 25%, which ran from the last week of July until 17 November, well over two million working days were lost. W.E. Gladstone, the Prime Minister, intervened when it became clear in mid-November that other attempts at conciliation had failed. The dispute was threatening to cause major disruption to other industries, was jeopardising fuel supplies for the winter and was becoming increasingly bitter in many places (most notably on 7 September at Featherstone, where the military shot two men after the Riot Act was read).[71]

The deaths at Featherstone were remembered with great bitterness by generations of miners. The ballad written at the time by a local miner, E. Allen, is unfortunately lacklustre ('In the fray two men were slain, And their blood has left a stain, This is why miners complain'), but it goes on to claim victory in the dispute:

The Miners' Great Struggle[72]

Want and hunger reigned supreme, (Fruits of an oppressive scheme),
Mind this is not fancy dream; such things we can't disguise.
Thousands without food or fire, and those things nature require,
But of fighting didn't tire, and thus we won the prize.

The prize was that immediate wage cuts were halted. The arbitration to which the union agreed resulted in a ten per cent reduction of wages in August 1894. As a result the MFGB lost members which it only regained

after 1900, when pay levels were restored.

It was not only in Yorkshire that troops were called out. In South Wales a state of siege was declared in 1893 during a strike, and soldiers sent in. Six years later the military again intervened when some 120,000 Welsh miners, many of them earning under £1 a week, went on strike for an increase of 2s. a week. The men were locked out, and the dispute lasted for five months. A handbill headed 'A Bitter Cry for Help' appealed for funds and made a case:

A Bitter Cry for Help[73]

Imprisoned in darkness and danger, we toil for the well-being of all,
And should we get a fair living, the wages we get are too small;
All that we now ask for is justice, that we for our homes may provide,
And willing for fair arbitration that justice alone may decide.

The sheet bears at its foot a supporting bible text ('The labourer is worthy of his hire'). Old Testament imagery also featured in this hymn-like printed ballad:

A Song On the present Lock-Out, 1898, in the South Wales and Monmouthshire Mines[74]

All fellowmen our Colliers, and workmen everywhere;
Come listen to our story, a tale full of despair:
It tells you of depression, we've suffered many years;
Thro' Monmouth and Glamorgan, which fills our eyes with tears.

Cast down in pits of slavery, amidst dangers manifold,
Beneath the lash of tyranny, too shameful to be told:
We are working for low wages, but food and rent being high;
Our children and all ages from pangs of hunger cry.

Some Garw Valley Grocers, and others it is said;
They have put up their shutters, that no collier may have bread,
And many a poor family, are now in sore distress;
May God look down in pity, provide and also bless.

They say that Military might, to coal owners is sent;
To terrify by fear and fright, Glamorganshire and Gwent;
By firearms and gun-powder, they innocent they'll smite;
While many a praying mother prays God defend the right.

The reference to 'dangers manifold' is placed into context by the figures of miners' deaths in South Wales. Between 1890 and 1896, 783 miners died in major incidents. The figures do not include the attrition which John Benson called a 'colliery disaster in instalments', nor the non-fatal accidents which meant that in Britain as a whole, 'by the end of the century, if not before, more working days were lost from injuries than as a result of the better-known strikes and lockouts'.[75]

Walter Haydn Davies (1903–1984), born at Bedlinog, Glamorgan, remembered his Bopa (Aunt) Sarah's song about the issues of the 1898 strike, to the tune of the Welsh national anthem:

Mae'r glowyr Morgannwg, Sir Fynwy a'r Fro,
Yn ymladd yn brysur a'm bris ar y glo.
Ond gyrthod mae'r meistri wneud sylw o'm Bil
Gwell ganddynt ywcynllun Syr Wil.
Syr Wil sy'n gwrthod cymorth i'm Bil.
O Gymru Wen, cwyd fyny'th ben i helpu y glowr. Amen.
(The miners of Glamorgan, Monmouthshire and elsewhere,
Are seriously fighting for the price of coal,
But the masters take no notice of our Bill
They prefer some scheme of Sir Will's'
It is Sir Will who ignores our appeal.
O beloved Wales, raise your head to help the miners. Amen.) [76]

'Our Bill' was William Brace (1865–1947), miners' leader, powerful orator, and fierce opponent of the sliding scale system, which meant that a drop in the market price of coal led automatically to a reduction in miners' wages. He was born in Risca, and started work in the pit at the age of 12. Sir William T. Lewis (1837–1914), the first Lord Merthyr, chairman of the Colliery Owners' Association of South Wales and Monmouthshire, was, according to Beatrice and Sydney Webb, 'the most hated man in the Principality'. He presided over the sliding scale joint committee from 1880 until 1899, and styled himself 'Billy Fair Play'.

Miners repeated this sarcastically, but also coined 'Billy Foul Play'.[77] Walter Haydn Davies also remembered what he called 'a doleful lay', entitled 'Working Today':[78]

Working Today[78]

Working today, sir, working today, sir,
Filling small coal, sir, for Billy Foul Play;
But utter a grumble and gaffer would say:
'Pack up your tools and finish today.'

A variant, possibly dating from 1910, runs:

> Billy Fairplay, boys, Billy Fairplay,
> I'm digging small coal for a penny a day,
> And if you'll grumble, Dai Goose he will say:
> 'Go to the office and get your pay.'[79]

Oddly enough, Billy Fair Play was also the miners' nickname, both in Wales and in England, for the machine introduced in about 1860, which separated small coal from large. This was important, because miners were paid only for the latter. They not only had to pay twopence per man per ton towards the running of the machine, but they suspected that it over-estimated the amount of small (and therefore unpaid) coal. A Welsh ballad commented:

> Mae'r glowyr yn tori glo'n galed o hyd,
> Heb entll fawr arian, a'i gael ef i gyd;
> Ac wrth gael ei bwyso mae'n myned yn llai,
> Os holir p'am hyny, ar Billy mae'r bai.
> (The collier is hard at it cutting the coal
> Without earning much and getting his due
> When it's weighed the coal gets much smaller
> If you ask me it's all Billy's fault.)

And in conclusion:

> Os holir pwy roddes y geirau'n un swn,
> Atebwch ei enw, 'Hen Colier o'r Cwm',
> Yr hwn sydd yn tori glo mawr a glo mân.
> Dewch, prynwch a thelwch i gyd am y gân.
> (If it is asked who expressed these words
> Tell them his name was Old Collier from the Valley,
> Who cuts both large and small coal.
> Come, buy and pay for this song.)[80]

'British Industries. Coal'. Poster (1924) for London, Midland and Scottish Railway by George Clausen (1852-1955). Reproduced courtesy of the National Railway Museum, York

7 The enemy within

Rather be a picket than a scab

During their strike of 1984–85 the Prime Minister, Margaret Thatcher, characterised miners as 'the enemy within'. Her remark was in a way entirely predictable. When capitalism brought into existence the working class as a disciplined, organised body, it brought into existence the body which would ultimately overthrow it. (Marx predicted that this would be the case). Any occasion when a substantial body of workers downed tools potentially raised fears of a world turned upside down. Hence, anger and abuse. Strikers, to cite examples from the twentieth century alone, allegedly posed a revolutionary threat (railwaymen in 1919), raised the spectre of civil war (miners in 1926, resisting wage cuts), plotted against the state (seamen in 1966): they held the country to ransom, they were led by agitators, they acted as wreckers.[1]

And if they were the enemy it was right to use against them the whole power of the state if necessary: army, police, the justice system, and the dirty tricks department; in short, to wage what Seumas Milne has termed a 'secret war'.[2]

White Slaves of England

An unusual exhibition held in 1909 at London's Earl Court sought to publicise bad working conditions. In an imaginative demonstration an eighteen-year-old woman made chain at a hearth specially brought down from Cradley Heath in the Black Country. A placard informed visitors that she could make two hundredweight of chain a week, for which she would be paid 6s. 6d., less 2s. for fuel. Thanks to the exhibition, organised by the Chainmakers' Union and the Anti-Sweating League, and to the campaigning of such people as Robert Sherard, whose articles on alkali workers, nailmakers, slipper makers and tailors, woolcombers, white-lead workers and chainmakers came out in book form in 1897 under the title of *The White Slaves of England*, Parliament passed the Trade Boards Act which set a timetable for the introduction of minimum rates of pay for the 'sweated' trades, beginning with the chainmakers. During the six months' grace allowed by the Act before minimum rates came into force the employers set about stockpiling chains produced at the old rates. In 1910 the women chainmakers, led by Mary Reid Macarthur (1880–1921) of the Women's Trade Union League, went on strike to secure the new levels of pay. They sang campaign songs:

The Chainmakers came along

(Tune, 'Yankee Doodle')
The chain masters came along with their fine agreement,
They asked us all to sign our names for taking power payment.
Then the union came along, said, 'Do you want your price, O?'
We said, 'We do!' – they didn't have to ask the question twice, O.

Strike, strike (Tune 'John Brown's Body').

Strike, strike, strike a blow for freedom every time,
Cast your chains away from you upon the ground;
Strike, strike, strike a blow for freedom every time,
As you go marching round.

Rouse, ye Women (Tune 'Men of Harlech')

Rouse, ye women, long enduring, beat no iron, blow no bellows
Till ye win the fight, ensuring pay that is your due.
Through years uncomplaining, hope and strength are waning,
Your industry a beggar's fee, and meagre fare was gaining.

Women chainmakers on strike at Cradley Heath in 1910. Author's own collection.

Now a Trade Board is created, see you dearth and pain abated,
And the Sweater's wiles checkmated Parliament's decree!
Rouse, ye women, rouse, around you, Towns and Cities cry, 'God speed you'.
Rouse, shake off the fears that bound you, Women, rouse. Be true.

At length the light is breaking, the Sweater's throne is shaking,
Oh, do your part, with all your heart, a sweeter world in making!

Stand together, strong and splendid, in you Union till you've ended
Tyranny, and with toil blended, Beauty, Joy and Art.[3]

Like most strike songs, these faded from memory after the event which inspired them. However, until the 1970s, on pay-day in Black Country chainshops someone would strike up the jocular portmanteau song 'Holly Ho', the rest 'bostin' out' with the chorus. Soloists in turn contributed a favourite verse, one of which went:

Holly Ho[4]

The lady chainmakers they'm all gone on strike,
The bosses they think they can pay what they like.
They work 'em so hard by night and by day,
And for it they get such rotten pay.

[Chorus] Holly ho, holly ho,
Fol the whack dol the doodle da day.

Again in 1910, other women, led by the Federation of Women Workers, showed their militancy by resisting wage cuts and by insisting on better conditions at the Idris soft drinks factory in London. During the following year the management decided to make the workforce pay for improvements which had been introduced; and when the women objected their leader, Mrs Lewin, a widow with two children and thirteen years' service with the company, was sacked for being three minutes late on a single occasion. Some of her fellow workers came out on strike and picketed the factory. To the tune of the hit song of the previous year, 'All the nice girls love a sailor', they sang:

Idris Strike[5]

Have you been to work at Idris?
No, we won't go in today,
For we're standing by a comrade,
And we'll never run away;
She stood bravely by the union,
And she spoke up for us true,
And if she gets the sack,
No we never shall go back,
Whate'er they do, whate'er they do.

Now you girls who do the labelling
And you girls in ginger beer,
When you see us stick together
Don't you feel a little queer?
Don't you think it would be braver
To join nobly in the fray,
So that we all may stand right firmly
hand in hand
For our rights and our pay?

Now, you boys who're washing bottles,
It really is a shame
To take the place of women.
Don't you think you are to blame?
Come with us and join the union,
Never heed what Idris say,
We are out to right the wrong,
and now we shan't be long.
Hip hurray! Hip hurray!

Master Willie, Master Willie,
You must give in once again:
It was wrong to sack a woman
With two children to maintain.
Thirteen years she's faithful served you,
Though she was three minutes late;
But our little sister Anne,
why she never checked the man
At the gate, at the gate.

Oh you great king in the palace
And you statesmen at the top,
When you're drinking soda water
Or imbibing ginger pop,
Think of some who work at Idris
For very little pay,
And who only get nine bob
for a most unpleasant job,
Alack a day, alack a day!

Now then, girls, all join the union,
Whatever you may be,
In pickles, jam or chocolate,
Or packing pounds of tea,
For we all want better wages,
And this is what we say:
We're out to right the wrong,
and now we shan't be long,
Hip hurray, hip hurray![5]

Thanks to the boys mentioned in the song, and to men also brought in as blacklegs, the strike was eventually broken.

Widespread militancy among women workers reached as far as the jute mills of Dundee. Mary Brooksbank (for whom see also Chapter 3, p. 90) first went on strike there in 1912, when, to the tune of 'Tramp, tramp, tramp, the boys are marching', she sang:

We are out for higher wages, as we have a right to do,
An' we'll never be content till we get oor ten per cent,
For we have a right tae live as well as you.[6]

Strikers cordially detested blacklegs, whom they condemned as class traitors responsible for sabotaging what should have been the united struggle. The opprobrium in which they were held is reflected in the adoption, from the 1880s, of the term 'scabs', which became ubiquitous. (Although 'scab', with the meaning of rascal or scoundrel, was widely known in this country from the late sixteenth century onwards, the industrial usage came over from America.) It featured in this vehement denunciation of 1911, from Ireland:

Description of a Scab[7]

Who steals along the silent street?
Who dreads a shopmate's eye to meet?
Who skulks in some obscure retreat?
The Scab.

Who shuns the face of open day?
Who wanders out in gloomy grey?
Who gets his price and sneaks away?
The Scab.

Whose spirit shrinks within its cell,
Like to a snail within its shell?
Whose bosom is a living hell?
The Scab.

Who never yet did give his mite
For to uphold the thing that's right,
So is always found in needy plight?
The Scab.

Feeling was just as strong in Wales. Walter Haydn Davies (for whom see also Chapter 3, p. 103 and Chapter 6, p. 228) remembered a strike at Bedlinog, Glamorgan, soon after the end of the First World War. This, he wrote, 'was largely concerned with trade union membership, an issue which often results in much industrial and social bitterness, as it did in my home village. So incensed did the miners there become during the struggle that angry words were spoken at meetings which the police considered were not conducive to public order, proscribing them thereafter as unlawful assemblies.' On lurid press headlines such as 'scenes similar to the French Revolution in a Welsh mining village', Davies comments:

> Although this put Bedlinog on the map at the time, I remember no Madame Defarge and heard no suggestions of bloodbaths. Indeed, if any assembly had suggested such an event and the marchers had been prepared to attack blacklegs and cause damage to colliery property they would have been prevented for there were at the time nearly as many policemen in the village as violently minded strikers.

He nevertheless was well aware of the feeling towards 'the blackleg or scab, who was considered to be a traitor to his kind', and he remembered 'the singing of significant words to a well known folk tune, entitled "Ffarwel i blwy Llangywer" [Farewell to old Llangower]':

O Claddych y Blaclegwr/ O Bury now the Blackleg[8]

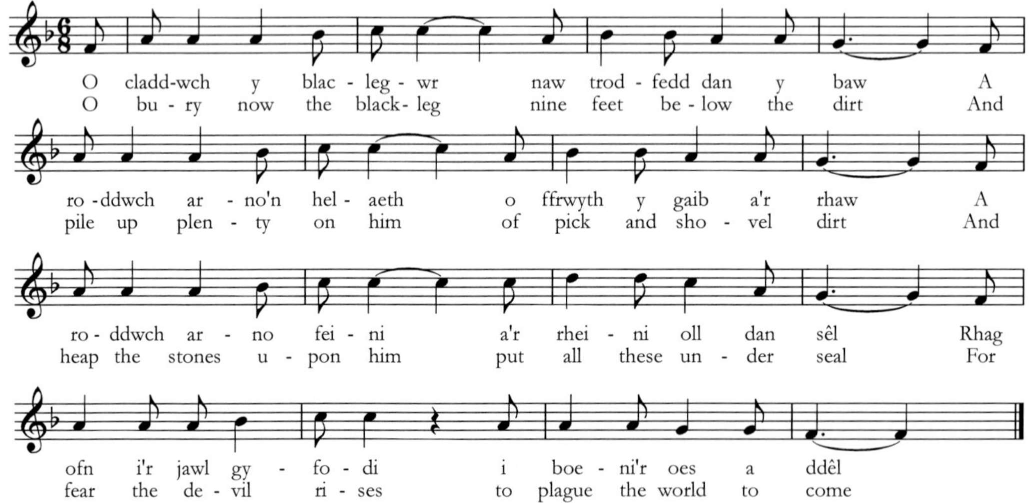

O claddwch y blaclegwr naw troddfedd dan y baw,
A roddwch arno'n helaeth o ffrwyth y gaib a'r rhaw;
A roddwch arno feini a'r rheini oll dan sêl,
Rhag ogn i'r jawl gyfodi i boeni'r oes a ddêl.

(O bury now the blackleg nine feet below the dirt,
And pile up plenty on him of pick and shovel dirt;
And heap the stones upon him, put all these under seal,
For fear the devil rises to plague the world to come.)

Wigan pit brow women road clearing. Courtesy of Wigan Heritage Service

The General Strike

When the coal-owners announced a lockout from 30 April 1926 the Trade Union Congress responded with a national strike, which began at midnight on 3 May. The call was answered in overwhelming numbers not only by miners but by transport workers, printers, the iron and steel trades, chemical workers, builders (except those of hospitals and houses), electrical and gas workers. These were joined on 11 May by a second wave, shipyard workers and engineers. In total, two and a half million workers were involved. There were many confrontations between strikers on one side and police and strike-breakers (often middle-class volunteers and students from the older universities) on the other. Hundreds of strikers were detained under the Emergency Powers Act of 1920.

Salvation Army Soup Kitchen serving 300 to 500 meals daily, during the 1921 Barnsley miner's strike.

The government, which had long been preparing for confrontation, used the army and navy, not to intervene directly but to intimidate with a show of force. 'The largest concentration of troops was in the Docklands of East London, where armoured cars were used to escort supply convoys, and machine guns were mounted at the dock gates, while battleships were moored in the lower Thames.'[9] Warships (including a submarine sent to Cardiff) and soldiers were deployed in South Wales and on Clydeside.

On the other hand, the general council of the TUC was ill-organised and irresolute, fearful of the action it had launched. As a result, after only nine days, the leaders called off the strike, which 'had just got into its stride'. The news was received by trade unionists 'with universal anger, as from an army which felt itself to be victorious'.[10] G.D.H. Cole's conclusion is supported by a recent academic study: 'There is little evidence that the support for the strike was waning, especially in its heartlands. It was not worry that the strike was disintegrating which caused the TUC to call it off as much as fear that it would escape their control.'[11] The miners fought on alone, for what turned out to be six months.

Their deep sense of grievance went back to the spring of 1921 when, after a fall in coal prices, the pit owners looked for cuts of up to 50% in miners' wages and for an end to national agreements with their union, the

Miners' Federation of Great Britain. In April the miners issued a strike call and appealed for railwaymen and transport workers (including dockers) to come out in sympathy. The government responded by sending troops to the main industrial areas. Two of the principal union leaders, Ernest Bevin of the transport workers and J.H. Thomas of the railwaymen drew back, and on what became known as 'Black Friday' (15 April), declared that their members would not take supporting action. On the following day this poem by Siegfried Sassoon (1886–1967) appeared in *The Nation*:

The Case for the Miners[12]

Something goes wrong with my synthetic brain
When I defend the Strikers and explain
My reasons for not blackguarding the Miners.
'What do you know?' exclaim my fellow-diners
(Peeling their plovers' eggs or lifting glasses
Of mellowed *Château Rentier* from the table),
'What do you know about the working classes?'

I strive to hold my own; but I'm unable
To state the case succinctly. Indistinctly
I mumble about World-Emancipation,
Standards of Living, Nationalization
Of Industry; until they get me tangled
In superficial details; goad me on
To unconvincing vagueness. When we've wrangled
From soup to savoury, my temper's gone.

'Why should a miner earn six pounds a week?
Leisure! They'd only spend it in a bar!
Standard of life! You'll never teach them Greek,
Or make them more contented than they are!'
That's how my port-flushed friends discuss the Strike.
And that's the reason why I shout and splutter.
And that's the reason why I'd almost like
To see them hawking matches in the gutter.

The miners, left isolated, had to return to work on the owners' terms – 1s. per hour (and therefore £2 8s. for a 48-hour week). Even so, there were further local strikes and lockouts, including at Clydach Vale, near Swansea (starting in August 1921). The Clydach men, following a practice which would have been instantly familiar to their nineteenth-century counterparts, had songs printed to sing and sell. One of these, 'Song On behalf of the victimised men of Clydach Vale',[13] was written by a Moses Blake. Another, 'Composed by one of the Unemployed at Clydach Vale', was, according to internal evidence, issued in 1924. It went to the tune of 'Just before the Battle, Mother', written over sixty years earlier by G.F. Root (1820–1895), the American composer of 'Tramp. Tramp, Tramp':

Locked out at Clydach Vale[14]

We are colliers from the Rhondda,
Locked out of work at Clydach Vale,
And it will surely make you wonder
When you've listened to our tale;
Since we had the new agreement
Old customs they have tried to steal,
And though they had us at their mercy,
They never made us squeal.

When they introduced Conveyors
Half our wages then they stole,
Now they say the Pits aren't paying,
And they have thrown us on the dole;
Let the story of this outrage
Ring out over land and seas,
And may the kind South Wales Coalowner
Know the want of bread and cheese.

Our kids are practically naked
Since the Strike three years ago,
And with slack time and slump in wages
We have never had a show;
What care they with all their millions
In Guest, Keen and Nettlefold,
While we starve with unemployment
They are saving up their gold.

Assistance is the thing we need,
Cast out of work to starve with hunger
Through the owners' selfish greed;
Can't you hear the children crying
In that dark and gloomy dell?
And may the Cambrian Directors
Find the warmest place in ——.

Pit brow lasses; coal pickers at Chanters Pit, Atherton in Lancashire in 1905. Courtesy of Wigan Heritage Service.

The Clydach Vale Collieries, dating from the 1870s, were sold in 1885 to the Cambrian Colliery Co. Ltd, which sank two more shafts, making a total of four. In 1918 these employed just over 4,000 men. An explosion killed 31 miners in 1905 and the disaster was repeated in 1965. The colliery closed in 1966.

In 1925, as in 1921, the coal-owners decided to impose a cut in miners' wages, this time of between 10 and 25%. The Miners' Federation of Great Britain planned to strike and appealed for support to the general council of the TUC, which with the agreement of the transport and rail unions declared an embargo on the movement of coal from the proposed date of the employers' action (Friday, 31 July). At the last minute the Conservative Prime Minister, Stanley Baldwin, offered the coal-owners a subsidy for a period of nine months, during which time a commission would enquire into the state of the industry. The unions celebrated 'Red Friday' (in contrast with the 'Black Friday' of four years earlier), ignoring 'more cynical warnings that the time would merely be spent in organising to smash both the miners and the General Council'.[15]

As the date for the end of the subsidy drew near the coal-owners announced that miners were to suffer both a reduction in their pay (of 13%) and an increase in their day (from seven to eight hours). The Miners' Federation once more asked the TUC for support, this time successfully, and the General Strike began at midnight, only to be aborted nine days later. Its brevity may explain why few songs seem to have emerged. Nevertheless, the strike bulletin put out by workers in the St Pancras area of London found space for this, to a well-loved formula:

The Strikers' Alphabet[16]

A is for ALL, ALL OUT and ALL WIN,
And down with the blacklegs and scabs who stay in.
B is for Baldwin, the Bosses' Strong Man,
But he's welcome to dig all the coal that he can.
C is for Courage the workers have shown,
Class Conscious and Confident that they'll hold their own.
D is for DOPE that the Government spread –
Dishwash for Duncos and Dubbs – 'nuf sed'.
E is for Energy that will carry us through,
Every-one class-conscious, steadfast and true.
F is for fight, our fight to the end,
For we're solid together, not an inch will we bend.
G is for Grab-all, the bosses, you know,
Greedy and grasping, one day they must go.
H is for Hardship, we all must endure;
However, keep smiling, for Victory is sure.
I is for Interest, Profits and rent
Into the pockets of the Indolent.
J is for Jix, the stirrer of strife,
Just waiting the chance to have your life.
K is for Knife that is wielded by Jix,
Keep yourself orderly and frustrate his tricks.
L is for London, where the T.U.C. meet,
Leading the workers the bosses to beat.
M is for Miners, for whose rights we must fight,
Maintaining the cause, which we know to be right.

'Jix' is the nickname applied Sir William Joynson-Hicks (1865–1932) by friends and opponents alike. He was also known as 'Mussolini Minor', and noted for 'his stridently anti-union line during the general strike and his obsessive pursuit of communists thereafter'.[17] As Home Secretary he chaired the government's committee for emergency arrangements. At the beginning of the strike there were 109,000 special constables in the country as a whole, 11,000 of them in London. Thanks to Joynson-Hicks, these figures rose by 11 May to 100,000 in the provinces and 40,000 in the capital.

The Prime Minister's attempts to encourage strikebreaking inspired a scornful anonymous contribution to the TUC's official news bulletin, *The British Worker*, which was printed on the presses of the *Daily Herald*:

Meditations of a Trade Unionist on Reading Mr. Baldwin's Latest Guarantees to Strike-Breakers[18]

So you will 'guarantee' that all I'd lose
In Union benefits should be made up,
And you MIGHT keep your promise, though the woes
Of them that gave up everything to fight
And now are starving with their wives and kids
Make one a bit suspicious; Still, you MIGHT!

And you've promised you'd protect my skin
And save my bones and make it safe for me
To walk about and work and earn my keep,
I'm not afraid for that. I know my mates;
They're decent, quiet chaps, not hooligans.
They wouldn't try to murder me, Not they!

But could you make them treat me as a pal,
Or shield me from their cold, contemptuous eyes?
Could you call back my ruined self-respect,
Give me protection from my bitter shame,
From self-contempt that drives out happiness?
Such guarantees are not in mortal power.
I'm sticking to my mates: That's my reply.

THE
BRITISH WORKER
OFFICIAL STRIKE NEWS BULLETIN

IN LONDON AND THE SOUTH

WONDERFUL RESPONSE TO THE CALL

General Council's Message: Stand Firm and Keep Order

SOUTH WALES IS SOLID!

MESSAGE TO ALL WORKERS

Another poet, Eleanor Farjeon (1881–1965), better known as a children's writer, also in *The British Worker,* recalled the unfulfilled promises made by the government to those who served in the 1914–18 war, and suggested that assurances made to those who held back from striking in 1926 would be equally worthless:

Promises[19]

'Stand by me!' said the Government
Twelve years since, in 'Fourteen.
'The Country's in a fix, lads,
And needs you on the scene.
Stand by the Country's Standard
And see the trouble through –
And when the war is over
Count on US to stand by you!'

'Stand by us!' says the Government,
In Nineteen-Twenty-Six,
'There's trouble in the air, lads,
And the State is in a fix.'
'Stand by us!' says the Government
'And see the trouble through –
And when the Strike is over
Count on us to stand by you!'

Oh hark! The twelve-years' Echo:
'Count on Us to stand by You…'

During their long struggle the miners received welfare payments for their wives and families, but not for themselves. Strikers in South Wales dug for coal in the 'patches', small opencast workings. To raise funds for the soup kitchens, which provided one free meal a day, they formed touring minstrel troupes and what they called jazz bands. Tim Greeney from Rhymney, interviewed in 1970, described how he took part:

> We had a wonderful summer that year. No question about it, it was one of the finest summers I remember. Everybody was enjoying themselves. And I was a member of a minstrel troupe …, and we toured practically South Wales, to different places, you understand, giving concerts. A penny or twopence used to cover expenses, you know. The people of each town were running their soup kitchens – [the concerts raised] finance for the soup kitchens. … Every town or village had their concert parties put together, like. They were entertaining the people through the strike. We were singing, you know. We were blacked up, white shirt, white flannels, but practically most of them borrowed, to tell the truth like, at that time. It was all for the fun of the day and keeping our spirits up throughout the strike. [20]

At the age of nine, Arthur Clayton, who was working as a pony driver at Elsecar Colliery in the West Riding in 1926, even attributed his longevity to the General Strike: 'I should not be living now were it not for that strike. It lengthened men's lives. There was no holidays with pay. We were like young ponies let out to grass.'[21] Idris Davies (1905–1953), who spent seven years as a miner from the age of fourteen, lost a finger in a colliery accident early in 1926, and had barely returned to work when the strike began. Afterwards his pit closed, and he started a second career as a schoolteacher. He later wrote a sequence of poems on the strike of 1926, published under the title of *The Angry Summer*, in which he echoed the initial joy of release from the mines ('Now is the month of Maying, When collier lads are playing, And many mothers sighing, Tra la la la la la'), as well as the anger which lay behind the miners' action:

The Angry Summer[22]

These men went into the gloom and the danger day by day,
Went down with a curse and a joke and believed that
Britain should be greater for all the toil.

And when the profits were high and the bags of gold were full,
The men who created the gold were told that the time was come
To lower the standards of life and exist on fewer loaves,
Less meat and butter and cheese.

So out of the grime they came, insulted and angry and proud,
Together to march in the sun with a song and a curse and a vow,
Together to challenge the creed that blood is baser than gold,
Together to stand to the end, together to live or die.

Davies also expressed the miners' universal admiration for their leader:

Here is Arthur J. Cook, a red rose in his lapel,
Astride on a wall, arousing his people,
Now with a fist in the air, now a slap to the knee,
Almost burning his way to victory!
And tomorrow in all the hostile papers
There will be sneers at Cook and all his capers,
And cowardly scribblers will be busy tonight
Besmirching a warrior with the mud of their spite.[23]

A.J. Cook (1883–1931) began his working life as a Somerset farm labourer, aged 12. Six years later he moved to a pit in the Rhondda Valley, where on his first day a miner was killed near him by a roof fall. He became a Baptist preacher, then a convinced socialist, and in 1924 he was elected general secretary of the MFGB. When the TUC called off the general strike, 'Cook threw himself into the dispute, touring coalfields. He was a magnetic orator with an emotional style. He was revered by the miners for his unstinting commitment to their cause and for his public defence of "Not a Penny off the Pay, Not a Second on the Day".'[24] If he had lived a century earlier strikers, would have been composing ballads in his praise.

Between July and December 1926 the miners were driven back to work by hunger. Their ordeal remained etched on their memories for decades. 'Do you remember 1926?' asked Idris Davies:

Do you remember 1926?[25]

Do you remember 1926? That summer of soup and speeches,
The sunlight on the idle wheels and the deserted crossings,
And the laughter and the cursing in the moonlit streets?
Do you remember 1926? The slogans and the penny concerts,
The jazz bands and the moorland picnics,
And the slanderous tongues of famous cities?
Do you remember 1926? The great dreams and the swift disaster,
The fanatic and the traitor, and more than all,
The bravery of the simple, faithful folk?
'Ay, ay, we remember 1926,' said Dai and Shinkin,
As they stood on the kerb in Charing Cross Road,
'And we shall remember 1926 until our blood is dry.'

During the miners' strike of 1926 few songs seem to have emerged. The so-called jazz bands in South Wales and the 'Tommy Talkers' (kazoo-

'A penny or twopence used to cover expenses,' The Tredegar Jazz Band 1926. Courtesy of the South Wales Coalfield Collection, Swansea University

players) in the north of England who went round performing in order to raise funds may have taken the place of printed strike ballads hawked in earlier times. Copies of one sheet, a frail survivor of an old tradition, written in April 1926 by Fred Stott, of Barrow Colliery, near Barnsley, were sold at a penny a time to raise money to feed children.

Where the Trouble lies[26]

There is trouble in England on this very day.
Royalty owners say there will be while Cook wants his way,
But it's those people who above miners hold the hammer
We say out of every ton of coal you get we only want a tanner.

It is this class of people who have got the cheek
Never get out of bed before ten not one day in the week
While just four hours before they awake,
For the idle rich the collier's life is at stake.

They say they need these tanners to send their kids to college,
But it's hard luck for the miners to have to pay for their knowledge,
Their children must have tennis and other sorts of games
Whilst a collier can't afford a fireguard to keep his off the flames.

A collier's kid on a scooter generally scoots,
When he has had it just a week he needs a pair of boots,
But he cannot have any although he uses cheek
Because his father is a miner and gets thirty bob a week.

We miners don't want the earth to which the owners say we belong,
But we want a living wage, in that there's nothing wrong,
Nor we cannot help our forefathers who fought and lost the land,
So a fair day's work and a fair day's pay, then we shall be a happy band.

By contrast, women garment workers generated vigorous songs in profusion during disputes within a year or so of the miners' ordeal. In 1928, 600 women from the Rego Clothing Factory at Edmonton, in London, went on strike, initially over rates of piecework, then for union recognition. The national executive of the Tailors' and Garment Workers' Union, meeting in Leeds, not only failed to support the women's action but firmly opposed it. However, the union's London organiser, Sam Elsbury, enthusiastically backed the women, whose twelve-week strike ended in victory at Christmas, 1928, partly thanks to financial support from other workers. Yet Elsbury wrote:

> But, more important than funds, in such a strike was the maintenance of the morale of the strikers and it was the high standard of this, which enlisted the great support given to the strike and ensured its eventual success. Here it was that the Strike Songs played such an important part. The strikers marched frequently to all parts of London to obtain aid and became known as 'The Singing Strikers' by reason of their extensive use of the Strike Songs.[27]

'The girls caused a tremendous stir with their picketing and marching through London, singing their special songs,' commented another trade unionist, who particularly remembered this, to the tune of 'How long's this been going on':

Stick Together[28]

We've never had decent wages, and always done our work well.
How long must this keep going on?
Our work they've made it harder, we've had to travel farther.
How long must this keep going on?
More work, less pay, but every dog will have its day.
We'll stick, by gum, by golly, the bosses they'll be sorry.
We'll show them how they're in the wrong,
We'll never drift back one by one, we'll always stick together
In every kind of weather until the fight is won.

More songs emerged in an associated strike in 1929. The Tailors' and Garment Workers' Union, having received a complaint about the militancy of its London officials from the Clothing Employers' Federation, responded by sacking Sam Elsbury, on the pretext that he was associated with the Communist Party and the National Minority Movement. The Tailors' London branch then seceded, and set up the United Clothing Workers' Union, with Elsbury as general secretary.

Polikoff, one of the biggest London clothing employers, whose factory was in Mare Street, Hackney, declined to recognise the new union, and as a result 700 workers, mainly women, came out on strike in May 1929. The UCWU published a sixpenny booklet, *Rego and Polikoff Strike Songs*, complete with a picture of a very respectable-looking Sam Elsbury, a cartoon of the TGW executive members grovelling to a clothing boss, and an appeal for recruits to join 'the militant union' ('Entrance Fee: Males 1/- Females free. Contributions: Males from 8d., Females from 3d. per wk').

The texts of over thirty songs included went to the tunes of nursery rhymes ('London Bridge is falling down'), hymns ('Jesus loves me') and old and newer favourites ('John Brown's body', 'Poor Old Joe', 'Tramp,

Tramp, Tramp', and 'Tipperary'). Overwhelmingly, though, they are drawn from recent commercial sources: for example, 'Charmaine' and 'Bye, bye, blackbird' (both 1926), 'Ramona', 'Souvenirs', 'Chloe' and 'Misery Farm' (1929). Two-thirds of the texts consist of a single verse, such as 'The Rego Strikers',[29] which, 'sung with defiant determination, was always the one which "led off" the Rego Strike songs in the Strikers' Marches'. The passage irresistibly recalls the Match Girls' processions through London street in the previous century.

The Rego Strikers[29]

We are the Rego Strikers! We are no dirty shirkers!
We know our manners,
Behind our Union banners,
We want Justice wherever we go.
When we went to Edmonton,
They thought they had us whacked!
But we know we're in the right,
And we're sure to win the fight,
We are the Rego girls!

The tune prescribed is 'Donkey Row Lads', which I have been unable to trace. However, this may be an alternative title for 'Who were you with last night' (used here), which dates from 1912, and served for lyrics boasting the superiority of residents of particular areas or soldiers of particular regiments.[30] 'The Rego Girls'[31] shows a very similar spirit, even cockiness:

The Rego Girls[31]

The Rego girls are marching with spirits all aglow,
Shouting out the battle cry of freedom.
And everywhere that Elsbury went the girls were sure to go,
Shouting out the battle cry of freedom.
Hurrah for Elsbury! Never mind the 'Daves'!
Hurrah for the Rego girls who won't be slaves!
And everywhere that Elsbury went the girls were sure to go,
Shouting out the battle cry of freedom.
Hurrah, hurrah, hurrah-rah-rah!
Wizz-bang, wiz-bang, wizz-bang. Rah!
Who the hell d'ye think we are?
STRIKERS!

'The Busted-hearted Boss'[32] cleverly exploits the sorrowful question of the love-lorn Charmaine ('I wonder why you keep me waiting?') to ridicule the employer deprived of his workers:

Busted-Hearted Boss[32]

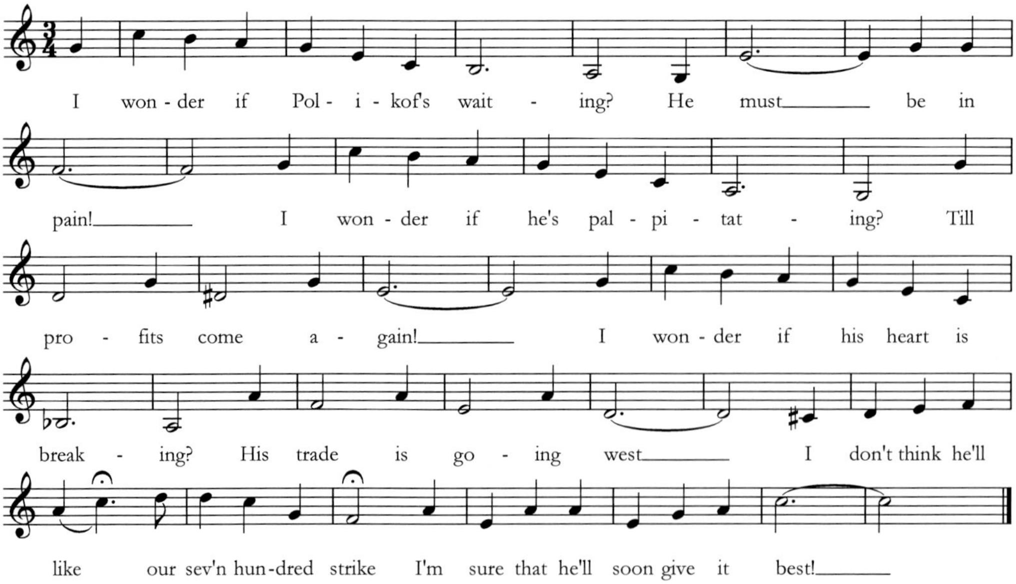

I won - der if Pol - i - kof's wait - ing? He must_______ be in
pain!_______ I won - der if he's pal - pi - tat - ing? Till
pro - fits come a - gain!_______ I won - der if his heart is
break - ing? His trade is go - ing west_______ I don't think he'll
like our sev'n hun-dred strike I'm sure that he'll soon give it best!_______

I wonder if Polikoff's waiting?
He must be in pain!
I wonder if he's palpitating?
Till profits come again!
I wonder if his heart is breaking?

His trade is going west.
I think he don't like our 700 strike;
I'm sure that he'll soon give it best!

Polikoff seems to have been particularly unpopular with the strikers, who taunted him in a number of songs, including 'The Koff Drop!' (tune, 'Constantinople'):[33]

The Koff Drop![33]

We are the strikers
Of a P and an O and an L and an I and a Koff!
And he don't like us!
At our militant Union he is pretending to scoff.
But we'll make him koff until his throat is very sore.
Until he cries 'Sufficient!' but we'll keep on giving him more!
We've got him running
With his P and his O and his L and his I and his Koff! (cough) Koff!

In time-honoured fashion, the strikers appealed for the support of their fellow workers in 'Solidarity for Ever' and 'The Union Banner'. The latter went to the rousing tune of the Italian revolutionary song 'Bandiera Rossa', of which the words originated in 1911 as 'Avanti! Sciopero!' ('Forward! Strike!').[34] The melody, which derived from Lombard folk tunes, provided the English women strikers with a very different sound:

The Union Banner[34]

We work at Polikoff's: All factory workers;
United under the Union Banner.
We raise our emblems to all the blacklegs,
The Union Banner triumphantly.

[Chorus]
Raise the Union Banner triumphantly!
Raise the Union Banner triumphantly!
Raise the Union Banner triumphantly!
For recognition and liberty!

For our employers we built up profits
From all our toiling, from all our labour.
It was our blunder; We now march under
Our Union Banner triumphantly.

When this strike's over we will remember
Our fighting Union; We'll ne'er surrender,
And to the last fight we'll still march under
Our Union Banner triumphantly.

The blacklegs mentioned in the first verse here also feature in 'The Picket Song' and 'Only Playing at Scabbing'.[35] 'Song for the Blacklegs',[36] to the tune of 'Ramona' (one of Gracie Fields' favourites), included this elaborate chorus:

Song for the Blackleg[36]

Oh, blacklegs! Your time is coming very soon.
We strikers will make you sing a diff'rent tune.
When this strike is over
You'll rue the day you scabbed on your class.
You'll always remember!
Till your mean body's under the grass!
Oh, blacklegs! Have you a soul to call your own?
To scab on the workers
Your heart it must be made of stone!
You'll rue the day the strike is won,
And we return!
You'll wander, outside, on your own!

More succinctly, 'Bye-bye Blacklegs'[37] had this to say, to the chorus of the popular song of 1926:

Bye-bye Blacklegs[37]

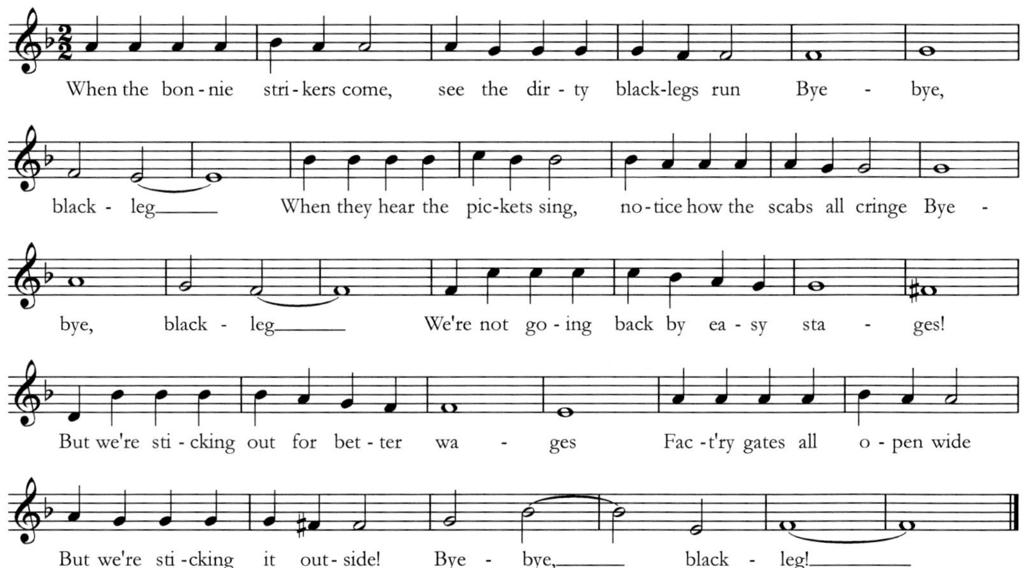

When the bonnie strikers come, see the dirty blacklegs run;
Bye-bye, blackleg!
Now they hear the pickets sing, notice how the scabs all cringe,
Bye-bye, blackleg!
We're not going back by easy stages!
But we're sticking out for better wages.
Factory gates all open wide, but we're sticking it outside!
Bye-bye, blackleg!

Miners, angels

One legacy of the strike of 1926 was a breakaway from the Nottinghamshire Miners' Association (NMA), an affiliate of the Miners' Federation of Great Britain. The new Nottinghamshire and District Miners' Industrial Union became known (and vilified) as the Spencer Union, after its prime mover, the right-wing Labour MP George Spencer. The coal-owners then refused to deal with the NMA. In November 1936 the NMA called a strike over working conditions at Harworth Colliery in Nottinghamshire, and this soon turned into a dispute over union recognition. More than 1,000 miners came out, with some five or six hundred women demonstrating in support. However, 900 men remained at work, escorted twice daily by police in what became known as 'the chain gang'. Miners and wives were arrested under the new Public Order Act of 1936 for offences such as the use of insulting language or threatening behaviour.

The strike, seen from the early twenty-first century, provides a remarkable foretaste of the features of 1984–85, not least in the important role played by women in support of the strikers. There is also a familiarity about the forces ranged against the striking miners: the creation of a bosses' union, the careful organisation of blacklegging, and the use of the justice system. In particular, the Public Order Act, wrote David Gilbert, 'gave the police great potential for control and intervention in local life, and there are direct continuities between the policing of Harworth in 1937 and the 1984–5 strike where public order offences under the 1936 act and related common law offences made up over half of the 10,000 charges brought against miners in England and Wales.'[38]

The strike leader, Mick Kane, a Communist Party activist, was sentenced to two years' imprisonment for 'besetting', and eleven others went to gaol. The dispute ended in April 1937 when the government intervened to impose a compromise, which amalgamated the rival bodies into a new Nottinghamshire and District Federated Union. The detested Spencer continued as president.

The Communist Party's support for strikes and its considerable influence on the trade union movement were reflected in a jocular song, featuring its secretary, Harry Pollitt (1890–1960). Pollitt, born at Droylsden in Lancashire, left school at 13 after a year as a half-timer in a cotton mill (see Chapter 2, pp. 52-54), and served an apprenticeship as a boilermaker at Gorton Tank works in Manchester. He was an effective, no-nonsense speaker: I first heard him myself in Leicester's Corn Exchange, where he drew a good crowd in the late 1940s. He was widely known for his anti-fascist commitment, and for a time, because of his opposition to the Nazi–Soviet Pact, relinquished his post as general secretary of the CP, resuming it when Germany's invasion brought the Soviet Union into the Second World War on the allied side. He was well known nationally, and viewed with certain affection by the general public as the bluff, plain-speaking Lancastrian he was. On the other hand, especially during the Cold War, he was viewed by the establishment as a potential enemy within.

Harry was a Bolshie[39]

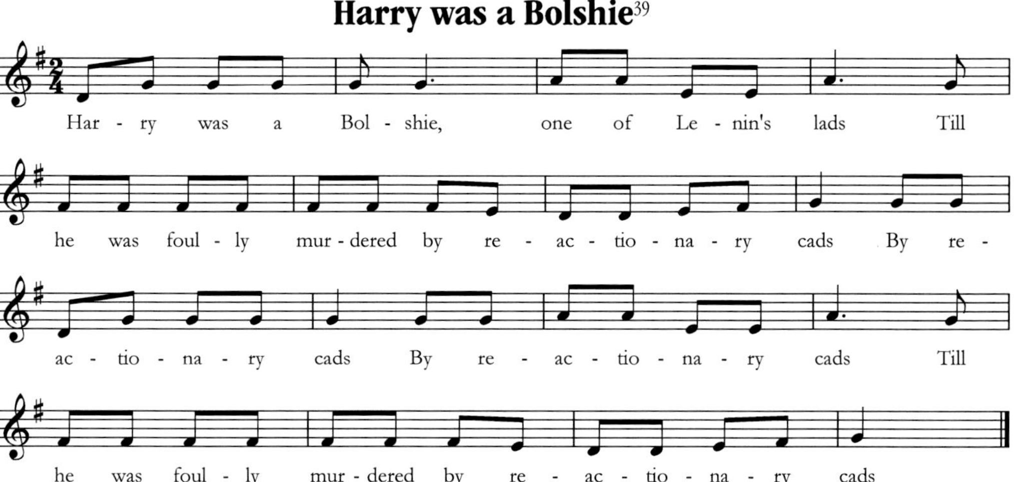

Harry was a bolshie, and one of Lenin's lads,
Till he was foully murdered by counter-revolutionary cads.
By counter-revolutionary cads, by counter-revolutionary cads,
Till he was foully murdered by counter-revolutionary cads.

Up spoke the soul of Harry: 'In death I will not lie,
I'll go up and do some party work in the kingdom up on high.'

He stood before the pearly gates all trembling at the knees:
'A message here for Comrade God from Harry Pollitt, please.'

Said God: 'Who is this person, all humble and contrite?
A friend of Neville Chamberlain's? Oh that will be all right.'

They put him in the choir, put a harp into his hand,
He taught the *Internationale* to the Hallelujah band.

They put him in the choir but the hymns he did not like,
So he organised the angels and brought them out on strike.

They put him up on trial before the Holy Ghost
For spreading disaffection among the heavenly host.

The verdict it was guilty but Harry he said 'Swell';
He tucked his nightie round his knees and floated down to hell.

Now seven long years have gone and passed, and Harry's doing well,
He's just been made people's commissar of the whole of Soviet hell.

The moral of this story, it's very plain to tell,
If you want to be a Communist you'll have to go to hell.

The song, written for a lark in 1935 by a student, Erin Williams, during a National Unemployed Workers' Movement camp (see Chapter 8, p 286), became very popular, and remained so until at least the 1950s. For some reason, possibly to avoid giving offence, when Pinto and Rodway printed it in 1957 (quoting an unspecified oral source) they relegated it to an appendix of 'Forces' Ballads' and gave the name throughout as H—y P—tt. The song developed a number of variants as it circulated. For example, the fourth verse appears in one version as: 'Said Peter unto Harry: "Are you humble and contrite?"."I'm a friend of Lady Astor's so I'm sure I'll be all right."'[40]

'Work-shy, strike-happy!'

In the 1960s a small group of companies produced almost all British cars, and their manual workforce, at a time of rising expectations of living standards, was strongly unionised: 100% at BMC, Rootes, Rover and Jaguar, 99% at Ford and 85% at Vauxhall.[41] During the same period (in fact, between 1960 and 1973) strikes in the industry averaged 273.7 per year and involved 43.9% of the workers.[42] These strikes generated controversy and impassioned speeches but not, so far as I know, ballads. Car workers were pilloried in much of the tabloid press as greedy, work-shy, strike-happy, manipulated by power-hungry and politically-motivated shop stewards. However, an independent study took the view that 'the frequency with which managements themselves lay men off, put them on "fall-back" rates, or vary their overtime, makes it seem nothing abnormal for workers to withhold their labour'.[43] An altogether more warm-hearted attitude, albeit concerned with a champion worker of the 1930s, was expressed in Alasdair Clayre's song 'The Tyre Fitter', to the tune of 'Patsy Fagan'. Clayre wrote this in 1966, basing it on anecdotes from car workers at Cowley, near Oxford, for a BBC radio programme, *Landmarks*, produced by Charles Parker:

The Tyre Fitter[44]

They called him Tiny Newman because he was so small,
No higher than a lamppost, not so broad as he was tall.
His job was fitting motor tyres, he did it with his hands,
And he took some home when his mother made jam to use for
elastic bands.

One day there was a power cut, the coal supply was low;
The presses all dropped idle and the line went creeping slow,
So Tiny turned it with his hands and he sent it whirling past,
Till a copper ran him in for driving two hundred cars too fast.[44]

Much closer, perhaps, to the feelings of car makers of the 1960s was the more acerbic song written by one of their number, Don Perrygrove of Birmingham, who had worked at Longbridge. In 1769 the balladeering publican John Freeth (see Chapter 4, p. 113), appropriated the tune of Charles Dibdin's 'Warwickshire Lads' for a jaunty song of his own, celebrating the opening of the first canal in Birmingham. When this piece, 'Birmingham Lads', was revived for the bicentenary, Perrygrove in turn took the tune for his own:

Motor Trade Workers[45]

Oh, we are two motor trade workers,
We're labelled as loafers and shirkers;
We're crippling the country, the newspapers say,
With too low an output and far too much pay.
Far too much pay, far too much pay,
With too low an output and far too much pay.

Each morning we leave around seven
And drive to our mechanised heaven;
We make cans of tea, have a laugh and a crack,
till the half-seven bell rings and off goes the track.
Off goes the track, off goes the track,
Till the half-seven bell rings and off goes the track.

Our track is a steel overseer;
We pray he'll break down but no fear,
For his vital organs are switches and knobs,
And he has us poor working lads sweating great cobs.
Sweating great cobs, sweating great cobs,
And he has us poor working lads sweating great cobs.

We're pressing and turning and milling,
We're finishing and trimming and drilling;
We paint and wet-flat and we rivet and bore
While the foreman walks round like a Varna Road whore.
Varna Road whore, Varna Road whore,
While the foreman walks round like a Varna Road whore.

The big banker who's running our nation
Claims we are the cause of stagnation;
He sits at his desk on his fat pin-striped arse:
While we do the donkey work he counts the brass.
He counts the brass, he counts the brass,
While we do the donkey work he counts the brass.

Our trade fluctuates with the season,
And that is the cause and the reason
We organise now and go in with both feet,
For tomorrow we may well be walking the street.
Walking the street, walking the street,
For tomorrow we may well be walking the street.

Investors and financial backers
Are greedily counting the ackers
That they have procured by a working man's sweat,
Then the bastards begrudge us the wages we get.
Wages we get, wages we get,
Then the bastards begrudge us the wages we get.

So a word to you wealthy fat Tories
Who dream up those newspaper stories:
If it's true what they say and we're all in the stew,
Then we're the red peppers, the dumplings are you.
Dumplings are you, dumplings are you,
Then we're the red peppers, the dumplings are you.

1970s: 'In Place of Strife?'

It was perhaps thanks to the folk song revival of the 1950s and 60s, and its stimulation of new writing, that songs commenting on or even calling for industrial action again began to emerge. Taking as a model 'Dark as a Dungeon', the mining song by Merle Travis, Brian Jacques (born 1939), once a Liverpool docker himself, and later a well-known author, wrote:

The Docker's Lament [46]

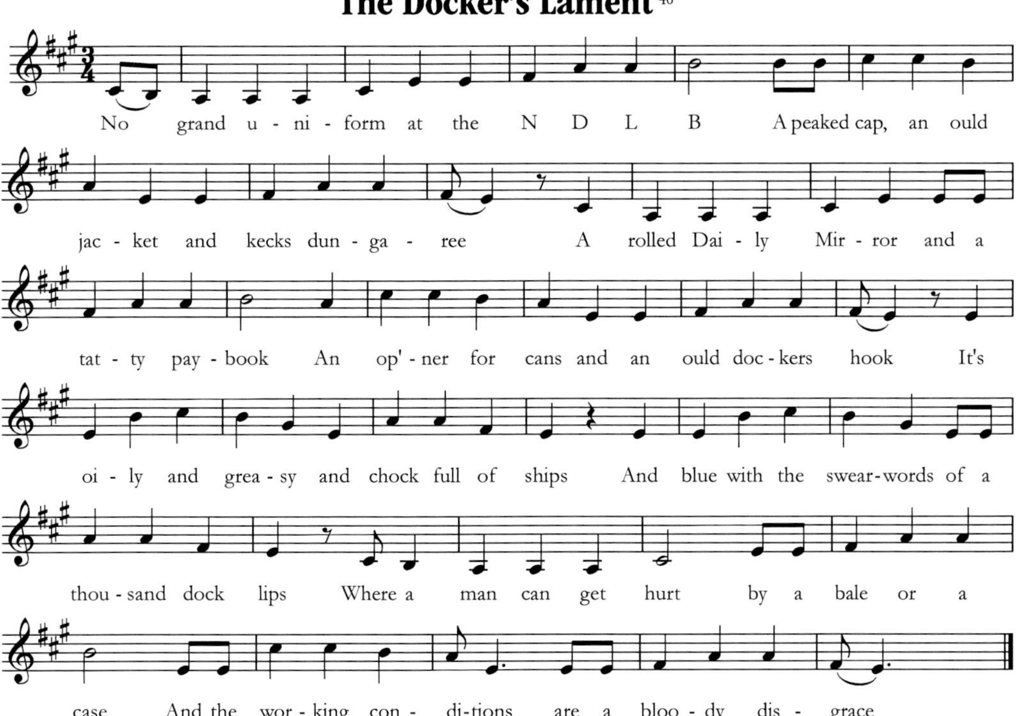

No grand uniform at the NDLB:
A peaked cap, an ould jacket and kecks dungaree,
A rolled *Daily Mirror* and a tatty paybook,
An opener for cans and an ould docker's hook.

[Chorus]
It's oily and greasy and chock-full of ships,
And blue with the swearwords of a thousand dock lips,
Where a man can get hurt by a bale or a case,
And the working conditions are a bloody disgrace.

We stand like dumb animals there in the pen,
To be hired out like beasts to the ship ownin' men.
They scramble for a nugget or clamour for nights;
All a-wavin' their pay books they shout for their rights.

At the Langston west side Dirty Mary's canteen
Was covered, not fit to be seen by the queen;
And the duke's silver hook gave us all a good laugh:
He thought it was fer pullin' the kids out the bath.

Don't leave the cranes idle, we're all makin' cash
On coffee bean, soya meal or the bag ash;
There'll be poke fer the long-'aired ones' HP account,
But the bastards in the Big 'Ouse make twice the amount.

I don't fancy this cargo, and nights are so hard.
That man on the winch hasn't got a blue card.
Go call in the union, we load no scab ship:
Let's all go on strike an' get home for some kip.

The NDLB (National Docks Labour Board) was a body set up by the Labour government in 1947 in an attempt to end the prevailing system of casual employment for dockers. The new code of working led in fact to unofficial strikes because dockers 'were forced to concede valued freedoms which they had enjoyed under casualisation'.[47]

Difficulties persisted, and over twenty years later the dockers' cause inspired the angry support of another folk revivalist, Rod Shearman, a singer with socialist views who had at one time been in the merchant navy:

Dock Strike 1970[48]

The ships are lying at the dock, but the cranes are standing idle.
The dockers they're in struggle, in a battle for survival.

[Chorus]
From Hull to the Mersey, from Glasgow down to Swansea,
From the Thames to Southampton, it's solid unity.

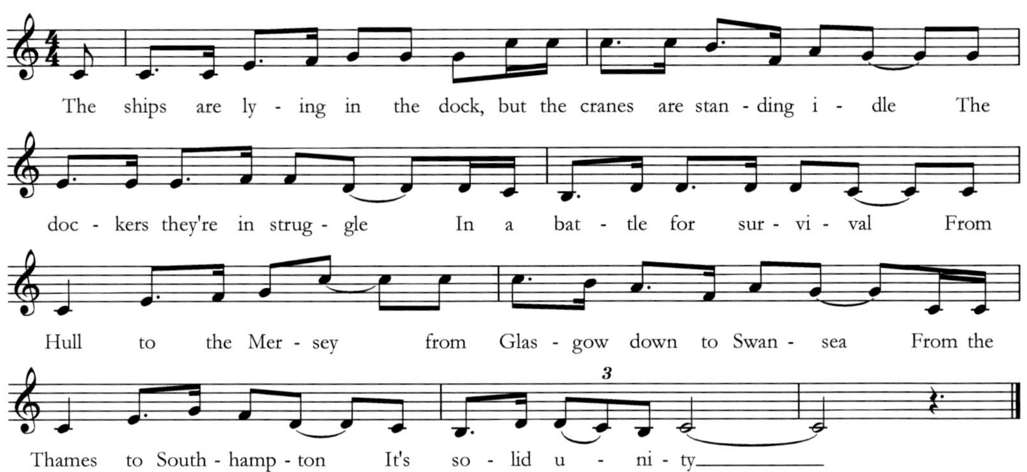

The boss's wife she has it fine with her caviar and her Rover;
When the docker's wife she goes to shop there's very little over.

It's twenty pounds a week, me lads, that's all that they are asking,
But the port employers they won't budge and precious time is passing.

Maudling to the palace went, on Lizzie he's attending,
For the royal permission must be sought, when the use of troops is pending.

Barbara Castle's on the ball, with the Tories she'll rub shoulders;
She remembers how in '52 when Labour used the soldiers.

But support is coming thick and fast, they'd better watch their manners,
For the dockers on the Continent hold high the workers' banner.

'We'll black the ships that come our way,' they said in France and Sweden;
The Germans and the Belgians too hold high trade union freedom.

The ships are lying at the dock but the cranes are standing idle.
The dockers they're in struggle, in a battle for survival.

The song coincides with a vital turning point in trade union history. In 1950, a Labour government used troops to unload ships when dockers went on strike, as indeed it had on other occasions. (The song has it in 1952 but in fact Labour had lost power the previous year.)

'Wombwell's last walk 1853 to 1969 R.I.P.' carried in front of the NUM banner Wombwell Main Branch.

Harold Wilson sought to curb the power of trade unions in what turned out to be the last year of his government, which lost power in 1970. His employment minister, Barbara Castle, produced a White Paper, *In Place of Strife,* which proved to be highly contentious. It remained a dead letter, and may have contributed to Labour's losing the general election of 1970.

The incoming Conservative government, led by Edward Heath, with Reginald Maudling as Home Secretary, was immediately faced with strikes by dockers and postal workers, and a go-slow by power station engineers. As a result Heath introduced an Industrial Relations Bill, which became law in 1972. This instituted an Industrial Relations Court with power to impose sanctions on trade unions and their members in certain circumstances of industrial disputes.

In January 1972, 280,000 miners came out in pursuance of an increase of £5 a week for face workers and £9 for badly paid underground labourers. This was their union's first such national action since 1926. Travelling or 'flying' pickets, the use of which had been pioneered during an unofficial strike by Yorkshire miners in 1966, quickly proved effective, and the movement of coal was halted after other trade unionists refused to cross picket lines. (A clause forbidding 'secondary picketing' in the Industrial Relations Act had not then come into force.) In February the death of a flying picket at a power station in Keadby, Lincolnshire, inspired a traditional-style song, reminiscent of elegies on victims of pit disasters, set to a version of the tune of 'The Famous Flower of Servingmen'. The writer Ron Elliott (1946–1989), printer, bookworm and sensitive player of the Northumbrian small pipes, put the narrative into the mouth of a bereaved and grieving lover:

Freddie Mathews[49]

Freddie Mathews was my true love's name,
A collier laddie of noted fame,
So fair of face and so straight and tall,
I knew him as the flower among them all.

He was not taken by fire or flood
Or by the dust that blackens a collier's blood.
It was not by gas or fall of stone
That he is dead and I lie here alone.

As a collier lad and a union man
On picket duty my love did stand.
On the picket line my love took his place,
Them cold and hungry February days.

Long days and nights while the frost lay hard
At the Keadby station there he took his guard

To stop the drivers who came that way,
To ask them: Turn around and not betray.
The miners' plea they could not ignore.
Most turned round and were seen no more,
But one man swore not to turn around:
My lad stepped up to him and stood his ground.

So firm and sure as he stood there
With his breath like smoke on the frosty air,
Then the crash of gears and the engine's roar,
And my sweet collier lad he breathed no more.

The snow may melt and the frost depart,
But the breath of winter is on my heart.
The flowers may rise with the soft spring sun,
But the fairest flower of all is dead and gone.

Pickets achieved a signal victory at Saltley in Birmingham, the last big fuel depot in the region to remain open, with a reputed stockpile of 100,000 tons. At the beginning of the dispute, some 700 lorries went in and out, though these numbers gradually fell to 43. On 10 February up to 10,000 workers from Dunlop, British Leyland, GEC and other Birmingham factories turned up to support the miners' pickets. Arthur Scargill, president of the Yorkshire area of the NUM, described what happened:

> Some of the lads were a bit dispirited, and then over the hill came a banner and I've never seen in my life as many people following a banner. As far as the eye could see, it was just a mass of people marching towards Saltley. Our lads were jumping in the air with emotion: fantastic situation. I started to chant: 'Close the gates! Close the gates!' And it was taken up, just like a football crowd. [50]

The Chief Constable of the West Midlands Police took the decision that there was a threat to life and safety, and ordered the gates indeed to be closed. Next day a triumphant picket of just twenty-four miners stood outside the locked entrance.

Within a few days of this turning point Ted Heath's Conservative government established an enquiry under Lord Wilberforce, which speedily declared the miners to be a special case and recommended a pay increase of 20%, between £4.50 and £6 per man per week, well beyond the norms of the time. Not only was the award backdated three and a half months but several minor claims in the union's shopping list were accepted.

The jubilant mood of the time was remembered by Dave Rogers in

1976 when for a documentary production by Birmingham's Banner Theatre he wrote:

Saltley Gate[51]

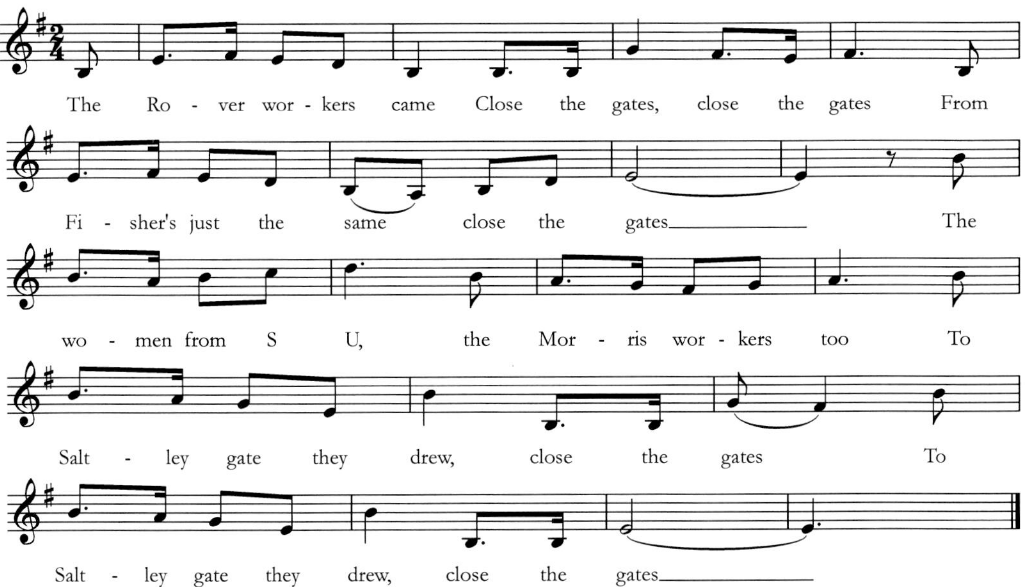

The Rover workers came, close the gates, close the gates,
From Fishers just the same, close the gates;
The women from SU, the Morris workers too,
To Saltley Gate they drew, close the gates, close the gates,
To Saltley Gate they drew, close the gates.

Down Bromford Lane we came …
We marched along Drews Lane …
Down the Tyburn Road, with heads held high we strode;
Our banners filled the road …

A solid wall are we …
Our strength is unity …
We marched across the years, through hunger, doubts and fears;
We are the engineers …

You men of high renown …
You servants of the Crown …
No power in the land can gain the upper hand
When we united stand ...

The flying pickets which had been so effective at Saltley ran into difficulties as a result of their part in another strike of 1972. In June of that year the Union of Construction, Allied Trades and Technicians (UCATT), began to call out workers on selected big sites, the first of them in Liverpool. The action gradually developed into an all-out national strike with the goal of securing wages of £30 a week for 35 hours' work. A substantial obstacle was 'the biggest force of scabs ever known in the history of trade unionism – the Lumpers'.[52] These were casual workers, paying no income tax or national insurance, who 'would ignore such considerations as hours of work, overtime payments or safety regulations. They worked in the rain, they worked in the dark and had no time to bother about toilet or canteen facilities.'[53] One picket's anger at finding a possible scab at work on a brand-new estate near Manchester led to this incident:

> We went on to the site and some of us went into one of the houses. There was this bloke kneeling down painting the skirting. One of the lads got hold of him and said 'You dirty scab bastard – you are still working.' The bloke pushed him off and said, 'I've only just moved in – it's my house.'[54]

On 6 September 1972, by which time the strike was eleven weeks old, some 200 pickets travelling by coach toured eight building sites in and around Shrewsbury. There were a number of incidents: confrontations,

Eric Tomlinson in the middle flanked by Ken O'Shea to his right and Des Warren to his left on trial in Shrewsbury 1973.

scuffles, some breaking of windows, a compressor overturned; yet the picketing was predominantly peaceful, and the police who were in attendance deemed that no arrests were warranted. The strike ended after a further week, with substantial pay increases conceded. Six months later arrests began. Some 800 people were interviewed by the police, and in October 1973, six building workers from North Wales, Des Warren, Ken O'Shea, John Carpenter, Eric Tomlinson, John McKinsie Jones and John Llywarch appeared in court at Shrewsbury on charges of affray, unlawful assembly and conspiracy (even though they had at no time met as a group before legal proceedings began). At one stage they were offered a deal by the prosecution: a fine of fifty pounds each if they would agree to plead guilty. They declined.

The trial lasted two and a half months, often with Liverpool dockers and engineering workers demonstrating in support outside. 195 witnesses, many of them Lumpers, were available to the prosecution. The evidence was far from damning, and the days dragged by with humdrum exchanges occasionally relieved by a funny incident, as when one of the defendants, Jones, was asked to repeat the remark he made at the end of his police interview. 'It was this: "I wish I had never been to fucking Shrewsbury." This was painstakingly written down by the judge who, as he wrote, repeated it thus: "I wish ... I had never been ... to ... fucking Shrewsbury." Jones said "So do I, m'lord."'[55]

On 19 December 1973 all six pickets were found guilty of unlawful assembly, with Warren, Tomlinson and Jones also guilty of affray and conspiracy.

Before being sentenced, Tomlinson (later to become very well known as an actor in such television series as *Brookside* and *The Royle Family*) made an impassioned speech, concluding:

> It is hoped the trade union movement and working classes of this country will act now to ensure that another charade like this trial will never take place again, and the right to picket or strike will be defended, even at the cost of great personal hardship or individual freedom.[56]

To the fury of the judge, Justice Mais, this was greeted by applause from the public gallery and cries of 'Hear! Hear!' Whereas Carpenter, Llywarch and O'Shea received sentences of nine months' imprisonment, suspended for two years, Tomlinson, Warren and Jones went to prison for two years, three years and nine months respectively. As the judge announced the custodial sentences the jury foreman stormed out of court, remarking 'It's disgraceful,' and was joined by another juror who slammed a door behind him.

Widespread indignation at the outcome was shared by Joe Kay, a builder from Salford, who wrote this song:

Some wor - king men from Shrews - bu - ry on a buil - ding site one
day They thought if they should stop work they would
try to get more pay They talked to all their wor - king mates just to
get the mat - ter clear Some pic - kets were put in the jail - house
and one of them got three years The Shrews - bury
three, the Shrews- bury three It could hap-pen to you and
it could hap-pen to me The Shrews - bury three, the Shrews-bury
three Let's make a stand for their li - ber - ty

Some working men in Shrewsbury on a building site one day
They thought if they should stop work they would try to get more pay.
They talked to all their working mates just to get the matter clear:
Some pickets were put in a jailhouse; yes, one of them got three years.

[Chorus]
The Shrewsbury three, the Shrewsbury three,
It could happen to you, it could happen to me.
The Shrewsbury three, the Shrewsbury three,
Let's make a stand for their liberty.

Some scuffles on the building sites, and I've seen such things before,
But according to the sentence you'd think there'd been world war:

The sentence didn't fit the crime – the punishment was the crime –
So let's try to get them out before they finish their time.
The clock it struck the hour of six as they took them down below;
You see, it was Christmas time, but no Christmas cheer to show.
The preacher in the church nearby was speaking for the needy,
But in court when the sentence was passed we saw who were the greedy.

Three years is a long time to serve when you think of the crimes that pay,
Just think of all the corruption that's knocking about today;
But there's certainly something we've got to learn, and that it is for sure,
There's a law that works for the rich and another one for the poor.

We live in this old land of ours. Is there nothing we could do?
To show we got something from our grandpas good and true?
They won for us a legacy that meant justice for us all,
And now it is the right time we should make the clarion call.

Kay's expression of hurt and anger, unsurprisingly, failed to make any impression on the judicial system. The sentences for affray were quashed on appeal but this made no practical difference to the terms of imprisonment, which were concurrent.

The Equal Pay Act of 1970 made pay differentials based purely on gender illegal. It came into force only on 29 December 1975, and even then employers were given a further five years' grace within which to comply. For some four hundred women workers at Trico, an American-owned windscreen wiper factory at Brentford in West London, this was too long to wait. In 1976 they came out on strike and mounted a round-the clock picket. This song, to the tune of 'John Brown's Body', helped to keep up their spirits:

Song for the Trico Women Workers[58]

The Trico women strikers are picketing the gate:
There's no pay for this shift though we're on from eight to eight.
We've been out for sixteen weeks now and we're well prepared to wait
Till we get equal pay.

[Chorus]
Equal pay for women workers, equal pay for women workers,
Equal pay for women workers, we want equal pay.

The management are not prepared to give us what we ask;
They are saying that they don't believe we're equal to the task.
But if men can do what we do, then their argument's a farce,
So we want equal pay.

Now the men they have more money and they get the shift work too,
Which is something that the management won't let the women do.
It's the scabs inside, their bloody pride, has made the talks fall through:
They don't want equal pay.

They called for a tribunal which is meeting with the bosses,
And it's Lord Sir This and Chief High That, with hoighty-toighty voices;
I'm sure they've had a lovely time complaining of the losses,
But we still want equal pay.

The tribunal's decision came out the other day,
And we were not at all surprised by what they had to say.
They didn't give us what we want, so out and out we'll stay
Till we get equal pay.[58]

The issue here was equal pay for women. Their basic right to belong to a trade union led to a prolonged struggle in another part of London, beginning in August 1976. At the Grunwick film-processing plant at Willesden in West London the workforce consisted predominantly of Asian ladies originating from East Africa. (They preferred the term 'ladies' because they would have been called 'women' during the colonial era.) About a third of the workers went on strike over pay and conditions, joined APEX (the Association for Professional, Executive, Clerical and Computer Staffs), and were sacked by the employer. Their picket lines received strong support from rank and file trade unionists and other sympathisers. Mrs Jayaben Desai, an immigrant of Gujarati origin from Tanzania, soon came to the forefront as a strike leader:

> The sight of her diminutive figure, with a yellow cloak thrown over her shoulders, remonstrating with hundreds of blue-uniformed policemen who, in helmets, stood half as tall again, was enough to capture the front page of even the most hostile newspaper.[59]

The struggle continued, with mass pickets, including miners led by Arthur Scargill, from Kent, Yorkshire and South Wales, joined from time to time by Labour MPs and even three ministers, Shirley Williams, Denis Howell and Fred Mulley. There were debates in Parliament, an enquiry by Lord Scarman, attempts at mediation by ACAS (the Advisory, Conciliation and Arbitration Service) and the intervention of extreme right-wing bodies such as the National Association for Freedom (NAFF).

After almost two years, the 'ladies' had to concede defeat. Their courageous and tenacious struggle received enthusiastic backing from rank and file trade unionists, but the TUC and the Labour Government failed to throw their weight behind what should have been a fundamental principle. A remarkable song by Peggy Seeger, based on interviews with Mrs Desai, and using in many cases her own words, serves as a memorial:

Union Woman II[60]

Management bleed, they bleach, they trample.
They hire neither man nor woman, just a worker.
A pair of hands for the wage.
The heart opens.
One, then twenty, then forty, a hundred and sixty,
Calling, 'Union!' Calling, 'Union!'

Back the English came,
English miners, English students – and English policemen.
More than a year, every day, all day,
Late in the night and in dark morning.
What matter the strike was lost,
The enemy showed his face.

Mrs Desai was seventy-three when Andy Beckett interviewed her in 2006. In response to a question as to whether her experiences in the 1970s had changed her, she said: 'No. Not Much. I am a capable person. I can handle home. I can handle work. I can explain things – always the words come to my mouth. I always put my foot first on the threshold. I was born like that. Determination is always there.'[61]

1980s: Work not Dole

Margaret Thatcher was Prime Minster from 1979 until 1990, a remarkable length of time during which she changed the political landscape – for the worse, as many thought, with her antipathy towards trade unions, her doctrinaire adherence to free-market philosophy, her stated belief that there was no such thing as society. She rejoiced in being known as 'the Iron Lady', was virulently antipathetic towards nationalised industries, and initiated a programme of privatisation. In 1980 steelworkers went on strike to seek a 20% increase in pay and to bring to an end the programme of plant closures, which Ian MacGregor (known as 'Mac the Knife') was implementing as a prelude to the sale of the industry. Some 8.8 million working days were lost in the dispute.

Of the many incidents during marches, meetings and pickets, one inspired a song by Dave Rogers. Early on 7 February 1980, steelworkers were on picket duty outside Pressed Steel Fisher's plant in Birmingham when they were attacked by members of the police Special Patrol Group (SPG), which was in fact a unit of Greater London's Metropolitan Police Service charged with combating serious public disorder and crime.

A Rotherham man, Kevin Casey, was dragged into the gatehouse and beaten up. 'They left him lying in the rain after they'd dragged him out, then they chucked him in a meat wagon like a carcase – just like a lump of meat out of the market.'[62] 'I wrote this song that morning,' said Rogers, 'and performed it at a strike social that Banner [Theatre] organised at the Star Social Club that evening. The social was memorable because two police spies masquerading as picket supporters were identified in the middle of the social. They were escorted off the premises for their own protection.'[63]

The Ballad of Kevin Casey[64]

Come all you steelworkers, wherever you be,
And I'll tell you the story of Kevin Casey.
They beat up our brother for all there to see,
To break our resolve and to smash unity.

Down to the Midlands the steel pickets came,
From Rotherham and Shotton, from Corby the same;
To stop steel moving it was their intent:

We want no more closures, and twenty per cent.
Kevin came down to help in the fight,
He came down to Fisher's that cold winter's night;
The pickets outnumbered by three coppers to one,
But we ain't gonna move till this battle is done.

They sent in the Specials to weaken our will;
With our backs to the wall, they moved in for the kill.
They grabbed Kevin Casey, got him down on the floor,
Dragged him into the gatehouse and locked up the door.

They beat him, they punched him, then punched him again.
One man on his own stood no chance against ten,
But you can't break a steel man with insult or pain,
So they left him unconscious to lie in the rain.

Come all you steelworkers wherever you be,
Stand up to those bastards they call SPG.
At Fisher's and Hadfield's they sent in the law;
One day very soon we must settle the score.

The song, graphically illustrated, was published in Rotherham by the South Yorkshire strike committee. Workers' wives, who joined the picket lines and demonstrations, bore placards with slogans such as 'THE IRON LADY SHOULD BE CAST IN STEEL. THEN SHE'LL KNOW HOW WORKERS FEEL'. They also had their own vehement song, based on Will Fyffe's well-known 'I belong to Glasgow', and addressed to workers who refused to support the strike:

I Belong to Sheffield [65]

I belong to Sheffield, dear old Sheffield town
And I've come here from Sheffield to shut you buggers down
I'm only a steel town working lass as anyone here can tell
But I'll put up a fight against your right
And see you scabs in hell.

Mrs Thatcher, whose government was deeply unpopular, returned to power after the election of 1983, saved by the Falklands victory of the previous year. As her biographer, Hugo Young, wrote:

> No name was scarred more deeply on the Conservative soul than that of the NUM. For Margaret Thatcher the miners were where she

> came in. If they hadn't humiliated the Heath government into fighting an election, which it lost, she would not now be party leader and prime minister. But this mattered less than the memory of that bloody defeat itself, and the apprehension that it might always be capable of happening again.[66]

The National Coal Board (NCB) systematically stockpiled coal and made arrangements to import more from as far away as Australia. After riots in London the police had been equipped with gear which ministers knew could be used effectively against miners' pickets. Immediately after the election the government appointed as head of NCB the American Ian MacGregor, the hard-nosed Reaganite Republican who had already taken on the steel unions.

On 1 March 1984 the NCB, in breach of agreed procedures, announced the closure of five collieries: Polmaise in Scotland, Snowdown in Kent, Herrington in Durham, Bullcliffe Wood and Cortonwood in Yorkshire. In the last case the NCB had lately invested a million pounds and forecast a working life of five years for the pit. The miners walked out there on 4 March, followed by fellow-workers elsewhere, and on 8 March the National Miners' Union executive declared the strike official. On 10 March MacGregor announced the closure of twenty more pits, with 20,000 job losses.

The miners were provoked into action at a very unfavourable time, the spring, when demand for coal falls. The walk-out was not confirmed by a ballot, contrary to legislation enacted in 1980. This in turn not only led to division in the miners' ranks but also left the NUM vulnerable to legal challenge and sanction. Within days of the start of the strike the NCB obtained an injunction in the High Court against 'secondary picketing', which was illegal under the industrial legislation of 1980. Even so, by the end of the month 123 out of 174 pits were either on strike or closed by pickets.

Miners at a number of Midland pits, mainly in Nottinghamshire, voted by three to one not to join the strike, their leaders pointing to the failure to ballot elsewhere. The continued working of these 50,000 miners throughout the strike was an important reason for its failure. The main factor, though, was the government's unprecedented determination to win, and in so doing to deploy the full power of the state. 'It was also shown in the apparently unlimited resources available during the strike, illustrations being the huge police presence over two months to get a solitary working miner in and out of a pit at Easington, the three thousand police mustered one day at Harworth Colliery to control 30 pickets and the NCB's expenditure of £4,566,000 on press advertising.'[67] The involvement of the intelligence services features in David Pearce's extraordinary novel, *GB84*, published in 2004.

On the other hand, there was widespread public sympathy for the strikers, and a notable contribution came from the Women Against Pit Closures organisation set up by Betty Heathfield (1927 –2006), wife of the NUM general secretary, Peter Heathfield. According to Geoffrey Goodman: 'Many observers believe the women's support movement was the most significant element of the miners' dispute; certainly, it was a powerful factor in sustaining the strike for 12 months . . . .'[68]

Women were also among the many who joined in a great upsurge of creativity in the shape of poems and songs. Jean Gittins in her 'Yorkshire Picket Song', reflecting on some of the smears she has heard, somewhat plaintively observes:

Yorkshire Picket Song[69]

Ah'm a picket, a Yorkshire picket,
'Appen some of you've seen me on TV.
Ah'm a picket, a Yorkshire picket,
Do you believe exactly what you see?

On Valentine's Day in 1985 the Rotherham Women's Support group devised this, to the tune of the song of 1942, 'You are my sunshine':

You Are Our Heroes[70]

You are our heroes, on picket lines,
You are our men, our Valentines.
Through all the weather, you stuck together,
Union men to end of time.

And when we win, as win we will,
And when the Yank has had his fill;
When Maggie knows that we won't be forced back
We will have our union still.

Rather more pugnacious, and sung by both men and women, to the tune of 'Coming round the Mountain', was the repetitious but effective: 'Oh I'd rather be a picket than a scab, I'd rather be a picket than a scab; Rather be a picket, rather be a picket, I'd rather be a picket than a scab.' This was heard again on the national television news when the twenty-fifth anniversary of the beginning of the strike came round in March 2009.

The devotion of pickets was celebrated in a song by John Young, a

Derbyshire teacher. This was recalled in 2009 by Georgina Boyes, who had heard Young sing it at the Red G'zunders Club. She ran this club, with Jim Boyes and Malcolm and Jenny Fox, at the Labour Club in Rotherham during the strike. Money raised went to Women's Support groups in local pits.

A Hundred Thousand Heroines[71]

Oh when this strike is ended and the victory lanterns shine
We'll sing in praise of everyone who held the picket line.
We'll sing in praise of every man in exile or in jail
But we'll not forget the women whose courage never failed.

[Chorus]
Oh here's to you Betty, and here's to you Anne
And a hundred thousand like you who took an honest stand
Endured every hardship, insults you bore
A hundred thousand heroines who fought in '84.

There were those that kept their distance, there were those that looked away
And leaders too that failed to lead and filled us with dismay
There were those whose courage weakened a sad misguided few
But the heroines of '84 were solid through and through

When they tried to starve the miners they made one more mistake
For money it means little when a principle's at stake
The Tory media surrogates are posing on page 3
But the heroines of '84 have won their victory.

Betty Heathfield is linked in the chorus with the NUM president's wife, Anne Scargill, who was also heavily involved in Women Against Pit Closures.

Well outside the mining areas, women also helped with collecting money. When in 1984 some members of the Elliott family from County Durham sang in the streets in Liverpool to raise money for the miners, one man wrote a cheque for £250. Then, 'at the concert that night, held in the Neptune Theatre, Doreen Elliott was able to announce both this, and that a newly-wed couple in the audience had donated their honeymoon money! Everybody who was there will remember the final number, led by the family: "Miner's Life", of course.'[72] Angela Tuckett (1906 –1994), who regularly turned up with others to collect on a Friday in the shopping centre at Swindon, sat down at times to play the concertina. On one of these occasions, in June 1984, 'a very old woman – she seemed to be about 80, a couple of years older than I – came up and said when she was a tiny child in North Staffs her miner father used to sing a song':

Blackbirds in a Cage[73]

For it's early in the morning,
Down, down, down to the pits.
Oh, oh, oh, for a very little wage,
And that's what puts us all into a rage.
We go down white and we come up at night
Like a lot of little blackbirds in a cage.[73]

The song, having been taken down in sol-fa, was sung the same evening at the local folk club as a token of support for the miners. Other items from earlier struggles were revived. 'Miner's Lifeguard' had the beginning of its chorus changed from 'Union miners, stand together, Do not heed the bosses' tale' to '. . .Do not heed MacGregor's tale', or 'Do not heed the Coal Board's tale'.[74] The Scots singer Dick Gaughan (born 1948), took an American miners' strike song of 1931, 'Which Side Are You On?', and wrote new verses, including these:

By bully boys in uniform and thugs with riot shields,
Our comrades' blood is being shed and still they will not yield.
Which side are you on? Which side are you on?

It's time for a decision and you really have to choose:
Support the miners' struggle or the next in line is you.
Which side are you on? Which side are you on?[75]

During a fund-raising concert in 1984 in a miners' welfare hall near Chryston, not far from Glasgow, the singing of 'The Auchengeich Disaster' provided a reminder, were it needed, of the dangers of pit work.[76] The song, by Norman Buchan, using the pseudonym of 'Tormaid', was written after the underground fire in 1959 at Auchengeich Colliery, which killed forty-seven men and caused the mine to be sealed:

The Auchengeich Disaster

Oh, coal is black an' coal is red,
An' coal is rich beyond a treasure;
It's black wi' work an' red wi' blood –
Its richness noo in lives we measure.[77]

Such reminders of dangers faced by miners, and of the long history of death and disaster underground, provided legitimate assistance in persuading people to contribute money in support. They provided a telling contrast to the view that miners were the enemy within.

Many professional or semi-professional songwriters hastened to align themselves with the miners. Billy Bragg, for example, wrote:

> For the previous 12 months I'd been travelling Britain trying to reinvent the political singer-songwriter. Now I had an opportunity to find out if my punk-edged songs had any relevance in a real political struggle. Soon I was travelling to the coalfields, doing gigs to raise money for the miners and their families. I was surprised to find that traditional folk singers were there ahead of me, singing songs more radical than mine.[78]

Dave Dale, Dave Rogers and Kevin Hayes performing at Lea Hall Miners' Welfare, 1985

Dave Rogers, Dave Dale, Kevin Hayes and others in the Birmingham Miners' Support group not only raised money by busking, but 'worked more or less full-time writing songs, singing at pit socials, demonstrations and on picket lines'.[79] The songs, all by Dave Rogers, included 'Maerdy, the Last Pit in the Rhondda', 'Busking for the Miners', 'Self-inflicted Injury' and 'Men of the Media'. The last of these, to the tune of 'McNamara's Band', begins:

Men of the Media[80]

Whenever the workers go on strike, we're down on the picket line
Ready to let the cameras roll, when the Super gives the sign
But if by chance a copper belts a picket in the gob
We tend to look the other way, 'We're only doing our job.'

[Chorus]
Oh we're the men of the media who control the nation's view
'Cos we're the ones who must decide what doesn't get in the news

> We'll tie you up in videotape, we'll put you down in ink
> 'Cos that's the way that we control what you're allowed to think.[80]

Miners' and their supporters' perception that the media were largely hostile received ample confirmation during the standoff between strikers and police at the British Steel coking plant at Orgreave, near Sheffield, in June 1984. Nationwide television news showed missile-throwing pickets persistently attacking police lines, after which police retaliated with arrests and mounted charges. Yet it emerged during a subsequent court case, when footage was shown uncut, that the reality had been precisely contrariwise, with police on the attack, and pickets retreating or attempting to defend themselves.

Ewan MacColl (1915 –1989), at once deeply immersed in traditional music and premier (and also political) songwriter on the English folk scene, responded with alacrity to the miners' cause:

> In March 1984 he hadn't written a song for two years [wrote his biographer]; in the first four months of the strike he wrote half a dozen. He wrote about the police – 'Remember the chap in the comical hat is one of humanity's crosses,' he sang. 'Whenever there's trouble, whenever there's struggle, he'll be on the side of the bosses.' He vilified blacklegs who'd been bought off by consumer goods and had 'forgotten the old-timers who made the union strong'. He took a line against the 'talking machine' that 'works overtime to prove that black is white'. 'Daddy, What Did You Do in the Strike?' provided an alternative account of events, and presented the strike as modern class-war in which miners had to stand and be counted . . . .[81]

A number of these songs were issued on a cassette[82] sold to raise funds for the NUM. They were sung during an extensive tour in support of the miners by Ewan MacColl, Peggy Seeger and their sons, Calum and Neil. I attended one of the performances in the cavernous and rather drab function room of a pub on the Stratford Road in Birmingham. A few local folkies arrived early, and then the room began to fill up with big, tough men, the miners. Early on, MacColl sang the traditional 'Collier Laddie', which received the audience's respectful attention, but this turned to increasing excitement, then exhilaration, as he embarked on his series of hard-hitting, deeply political songs directly about the strike, culminating in 'Daddy, What Did You Do in the Strike?':[83]

Daddy, What Did You Do in the Strike?[83]

It was in the year of eighty-four shit really hit the fan
When Mac-the-knife MacGregor (Maggie Thatcher's hatchet man)
Said, 'Another twenty pits will have to close to meet the plan
And we'll dump another thirty thousand miners.'
Daddy, were you with the first of the first?
Did you tell the NBC to do its worst?
Or did you save your lily-liver,
Sell the union down the river?
A scab, a blackleg, one forever cursed!

While the deeply-felt indignation of such songs was undoubtedly powerful and effective, other writers turned to humour. 'Mr Nesbit', to the tune of 'John Brown's Body', stems from an incident in February 1985 when the manager of a pit near Rotherham in a fit of pique tried to knock down with his car a snowman built by pickets, not realising that its core consisted of a substantial concrete post:

The pickets built a snowman around a concrete post (*x 3*),
And Nesbit knocked it down.

Silly bugger, Mr Nesbit (*x 3*),
And he needs a new Range Rover now.[84]

News of the manager's acute discomfiture, helped by the song, spread rapidly and became almost a folk tale, of which variants claimed different venues for the incident, including one in Nottinghamshire. After the strike the Rotherham Women's Support group produced an illustrated version to raise funds for victimised miners. The artist mistakenly showed a police Range Rover, thus further widening the story.[85]

'The Laughing Policeman' parodied the song popularised in the 1920s by Charles Penrose (1876 –1952). The new words were by the veteran singer and song-writer Ian Campbell (born 1931), who, with his son, David, sang it in Birmingham and elsewhere during the strike:

The Laughing Policeman[86]

I know a nice young policeman of disposition sweet
And all the little children greet him as he patrols his beat
He's kind to dear old ladies who want to cross the street
But he stamps on evil-doers with his great big plates of meat

He's always very helpful if you want to know the time
His every waking moment is spent in fighting crime

To out of work teenagers he lends a helping hand
He's never been known to tell a lie when on the witness stand

He'd never bend the evidence or take a bribe, of course
He's an upright heterosexual and a credit to the force
He is honest, kind and truthful, fearless, brave and keen
The finest human being that you have ever seen

He has no racial prejudice he is totally without sin
Protecting Pakistanis from the violence of the skins
Impartial on the picket lines to the striker he's a friend
He is stainless, faultless, peerless, conscientious to the end

[Chorus]
Ha ha ha ha ha ha ha tee hee tee hee hee
Ho ho ho ho ho ho ho oh goodness gracious me
Ha ha ha ha ha ha ha oh this is killing me
Ho ho ho ho ho ho ho ha ha ho ho hee hee!

Despite their spirited resistance, their courage and sacrifice, the miners were defeated. On 3 March 1985 a conference of union delegates voted by 98 to 91 votes for a return to work. Shortly afterwards, with banners flying and bands playing the miners marched, often through tearful crowds, back to pits, many of which were soon to close. So ended a strike which has been described as 'a watershed in post-war British history'.[87]

The moderate Roy Hattersley concluded: 'Arthur Scargill was almost certainly right to argue that Margaret Thatcher set out to break the NUM and then to destroy the coal industry. His claims – brushed aside at the time – that she had "hit-lists" of pits which she was planning to close, proved accurate in almost every particular.'[88] The pain of defeat was cutting and deep, though a winder from Hatfield Main probably spoke for many: 'I wouldn't swap that year for any other year in my life. I felt I stuck out for something really important. I was proud to have been part of it.'[89]

One Welsh miner, while proud of his efforts during the strike, eventually reached a disenchanted conclusion:

Picket Line[90]

I spent some time on the picket line, back in eighty-four,
Scargill was the union man and Thatcher was the foe.
We tried to stop pit closures, our one and only goal,
Our jobs were being threatened; we wanted Coal not Dole.

I spent some time on the picket line, trying to stop the scabs,
They drove them through in heavy trucks and guarded taxicabs.
Now Maggie said, 'These miners, we must not let them win.'
She called us 'Reds and Traitors' and 'The Enemy Within'.

I spent some time on the picket line; I did my duty there,
But Maggie used her bullyboys; they came from everywhere.
They were not your friendly Bobbies, to see that all was fair,
Those baton-beating maniacs, they hit and did not care.

I spent some time on the picket line, with no money coming in,
We survived on a weekly parcel and the help of friends and kin.
After twelve long months we'd had enough, nothing did we gain,
So one by one she closed the mines; our struggle was in vain.

I spent some time on the picket line, I sometimes wonder why.
Why fight to work in danger and dirt? It's stupid, I can't deny.
And the valleys are looking greener now the pits are no more.
Perhaps she did us a favour, back in nineteen eighty-four.

On the other hand, the minority of miners who had heeded the strike call in Leicestershire retained a strong sense afterwards that they had done the right thing. One of them, Dave Douglas, commented:

> They were never going to get the better of me, they were never going to break me even though they broke the strike. Because it was the scabs that broke the strike. They used to blame the national ballot – but even if we'd had one, they'd have still worked. At the end of the day there were 140,000 miners out on strike. What did you need a ballot for? They'd walked out, voted with their feet.[91]

Douglas, working on the surface, would use the tannoy to announce to the men working below, 'Come in, scabs,' and would then sing MacColl's 'Daddy, what did you do in the strike?'

> There were lots more verses to it, but it was the chorus that I liked to sing over the tannoy. It was a well-known song during the strike. I used to say, 'I'm going to come round when you're buried and write SCAB on your tombstone.' I got told off by this under-manager, Mr Fergusson. He said, 'Dave, you can't be calling them scabs over the tannoy system. You've got to think of something else.' I said that I couldn't think of anything else, and he suggested Henry. He said,

> 'Call them Henries.' And that was what they got for the rest of my time down the pit. . . . The thing was, the scabs hadn't got anything to argue with us. At the end of the day, they hadn't got an argument. Their jobs were in jeopardy because we'd lost the strike and that was down to them. They'd sold their own jobs down the river.[92]

During the strike, a Yorkshire miner, Dave Barker of Armthorpe Colliery, wrote to a tribute to the small band of thirty-nine men, known as the 'Dirty Thirty', who obstinately stayed out in non-striking Leicestershire and were seen in other coalfields as heroes:

The Dirty Thirty[93]

Of all the struggles that I've known
In all the history of the working class,
There are thirty men from
Leicestershire
Whose courage will never be surpassed.

They have faced up to the riot squads,
The scabs and the courts,
But no matter what the bribe will be
The Dirty Thirty can't be bought.

Day in, day out, they carry on
And heed the union call.
Their message to all miners
Is to fight for jobs for all.

They'll never bow to Thatcher,
McGregor and the rest,
For they know with Scargill's leadership
They are the very best.

Living up here in Yorkshire
Scabs are not often found,
But in Leicestershire where the thirty live
It's the opposite way round.

For it's easy to fight in Yorkshire
Where you've a thousand mates of more,
But if you're one of the Thirty
You've a scab at every door.

In 1984, Kay Sutcliffe, the wife of a miner at Aylesham in Kent, wrote 'the first, perhaps the only, poem' of her life.[94] Despite (or because of) its dreamlike quality, which was quite different from anything else which emerged from the strike, it was adopted up and down the coalfields, especially by women's support groups, and recited or sung to several different tunes. The silence of the mines during the strike prefigured the devastation which was to follow. The song later achieved considerable popularity on the folk scene, becoming not just a strike song but part of a wider cultural tradition.

Coal Not Dole[95]

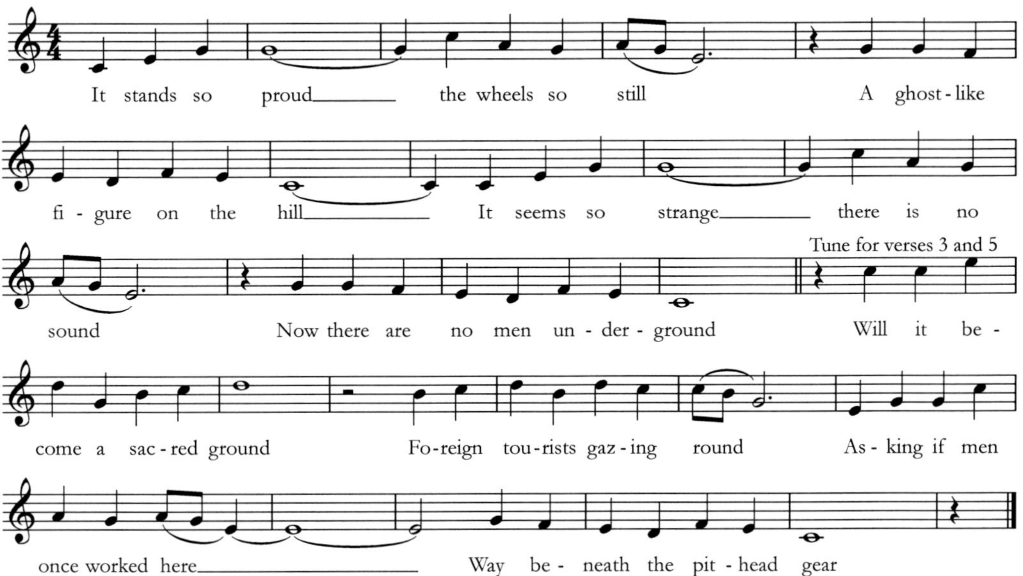

It stands so proud, the wheels so still,
A ghost-like figure on the hill.
It seems so strange, there is no sound
Now there are no men underground.

What will become of this pit-yard
Where men once trampled, faces hard,
So tired and weary, their shift done,
Never having seen the sun?

Will it become a sacred ground,
Foreign tourists gazing round,
Asking if men once worked here
Way beneath the pit-head gear?

Empty trucks once filled with coal,
Lined up like men on the dole,
Will they e'er be used again,
Or left for scrap just like the men?

There'll always be a happy hour
For those with money, jobs and power;
They'll never realise the hurt
They cause to men they treat like dirt.

What will become of this pit-yard
Where men once trampled, faced hard,
So tired and weary, their shift done,
Never having seen the sun?

There'll always be a happy hour
For those with money, jobs and power;
They'll never realise the hurt
They cause to men they treat like dirt.

The
National Unemployed
March to London

WHY ARE WE MARCHING?

Foreword by A. J. COOK

Determination

This pamphlet contains:

The MANIFESTO
The MARCHERS' CHARTER
The ROUTES & TIME TABLES

PRICE 1d.

Published by the National Unemployed Workers' Committee Movement, 105 Hatton Garden, London, E.C.1

8 Singing a pleading song

Want of employment

'When these people find no work and will not rebel against society, what remains for them but to beg?' Frederick Engels posed the question after coming to the conclusion that: 'English manufacture must have, at all times save the brief periods of highest prosperity, an unemployed reserve army of workers, in order to be able to produce the masses of good required by the market in the liveliest months.' He went on to remark: 'And surely no one can wonder at the great army of beggars, most of them able-bodied men, with whom the police carries on perpetual war. . . . Such a man usually goes about with his family singing a pleading song in the streets or appealing, in a speech, to the benevolence of passers-by. And it is a striking fact that these beggars are seen almost exclusively in the working-people's districts, that it is almost exclusively the gifts of the poor from which they live.'[1]

'Unemployment,' wrote John Burnett in his book *Idle Hands* (1994), 'has been an outstanding problem of modern Britain, and, at times, the overwhelming concern of domestic policies, overshadowing all other economic and social issues.'[2] According to the *OED,* the word 'unemployed', with the meaning of 'Not engaged in any work or occupation', was first used in print (by Milton) in 1667. The term 'unemployment' had to wait, so when '[i]n the second half of the eighteenth century, unemployment, poverty and rising prices became topics of everyday conversation',[3] other expressions were used, such as 'want of employment' or 'out of employ'; similarly in the nineteenth century, when unemployment was a continuing 'feature of metropolitan labour'.[4] Not until 1888 did *The Times* newspaper print the word 'unemployment', the reality of which it identified as 'the fundamental problem of modern society'.[5] Still then to come were the depressions of the 1930s and the 1980s, which have been likened to similar features of life in Tudor and Stuart times,[6] and which in turn saw sequels during the crisis beginning in 2007.

'Why Are We Marching?' The National Unemployed March to London, 1932. Reproduced with kind permission by Glasgow Caledonian University Research Collections:The Gallacher Memorial Library

The misery of unemployment (seasonal, cyclical and sometimes permanent) was compounded by underemployment and also irregular employment. Then there were problems resulting from the advent of old age and breakdowns in health. Old age amounted to a 'catastrophe' for

A march against unemployment past the Houses of Parliament, 1933.

working people, observed Eric Hobsbawm[7]. Short of independent charity, the only recourse was the workhouse. The same term, 'catastrophe', could also be applied both to the abrupt closure and the slow contraction of trades or industries, which threw people out of work.

Cries of the poor

Words like 'complaint' and 'lamentation' occur again and again in the titles of ballads dealing with hard times and 'distress'. 'The Poor Man's Complaint: Or, The Sorrowful Lamentation of Poor Plain-Dealing, at this Time of Distress and Trouble',[8] dating probably from as early as 1692, claims that heavy taxation, including excise duties, is causing workers to be laid off:

The Poor Man's Complaint[8]

The Times they are hard,
yet those that have Treasure,
and Wealth out of measure,
They little regard
poor Labouring Men,
Who are out of Employ,
Whose Children cry;
which troubles them sore:
I weep when I think of
I weep when I think of
The Cry of the Poor.

Somewhat lamely, the writer in conclusion merely calls on 'Kind Heavens [to] look down, and pity this Land'.

A decade later, assistance from a rather more accessible agency in the shape of Parliament was confidently expected by one group of workers. 'The Gentle Craft's Complaint; or, The Jolly Shoe-makers humble Petition to the Queen and Parliament; with their great hopes of the Advancement of each Leather Trade'[9] begins by stating a problem, then looking to immediate recourse:

The Gentle Craft's Complaint[9]

The jolly Shoemakers, it is said, ha[ve] found a great decay of Trade,
And lately have been sore dismay'd, and in a dismal taking,
Because the Leather was grown dear, and carried over sea, we hear;
But Gentle Craftsmen, never fear, you'll still be brisk Shoemak[ing].

This is the substance of their state, much unwrought leather was of late
Sent over, and the taxes great, made jolly hearts to ake, Sir.
To think their trade should so decay, for many out of business lay,
Each 'prentice had no heart to stay, that will be brisk Shoemakers.

The Parliament hath heard their grief, and quickly will extend relief,
For thousands of the very chief of them ha[ve] been undertake[rs]
In this great action to proceed, and there's no doubt but will succeed,
And by our Senate be decreed to make them brisk Shoemakers.

Towards the end of the eighteenth century another ballad looked to 'a new parliament ... which is all the hopes left our destrucion [sic] to save', and commented:

What numbers of tradesmen do hungry lye,
For the lack of employment their wants to supply,
Yet the wealthy are deaf when the hungry cry,
O the poor souls of old England,
We have lost our English roast beef.[10]

'The Weavers' Garland or the Downfal [sic] of Trade',[11] written in 1793, noting that 'A War breaking out, our Trade it grew low', expressed the fear that 'The Crofters, and Dyers, and Printers also, If weaving go down they a begging must go'. Printed, appropriately, on the same sheet as a ballad on a naval battle, 'A New Song, called The Tradesman's Lamentation',[12] explained that for lack of work artisans were having to join the navy:

A New Song, called The Tradesman's Lamentation[12]

Great numbers of our tradesmen have nothing now to do,
The weavers still lie idle, and daily wants renew,
Few can express our great distress, our comfort is but small;
Instead of having half a trade, we have no trade at all.

Another sheet couples 'The Sailor's Wedding' with 'Medley's Remarks on the Times'.[13] The latter, dated 1809, also reports on men driven by want into joining the army:

Poor tradesmen in Yorkshire, their case it is bad,
They're out of employment, no work to be had,
By the stoppage of trade, they're in poverty too,
Many hundreds and thousands for soldiers do go.

It also includes fierce denunciations of war profiteering and of enclosure:

They still keep continually to enclose the land,
So that the poor farmer cannot it withstand;
The wine drinking gentlemen have got all our right,
And the poor farmers is ruined quite.

There's many a poor man that did keep a cow,
Flock of geese, two or three pigs, and an old sow;
His rights are ta'en from him, he's nothing at all
So now on the parish his family must fall.

There were nevertheless hopes during the wars with France that life would improve once victory was achieved: 'Then we shall have a loaf for sixpence once again, And then the poor of England may cease for to complain; And every trading country will flourish here once more.'[14]

'For more than twenty years,' wrote G.D.H. Cole, 'all manner of hardships, grievances and abuses had been put down to the war, and redress had been promised on the coming of peace. … [A]bove all, manufacturers and workers looked to the reopened markets for the means of regular and profitable employment. These hopes were speedily disappointed.' There was agricultural depression; after a brief boom, foreign markets were quickly glutted; factories closed; banks failed. In short, peace brought 'the first great and general economic depression in the history of modern industrialism. …'. [15] This led to the saying that socialism was born in Britain 'on the morrow of the peace of 1815'.

Bitter recrimination found expression at the time in a number of ballads. 'Waterloo Times – A New Song',[16] published in Edinburgh, dwelt with malicious glee on the word, 'Waterloo'. 'But a few months ago we were taught to rejoice, And sing and give thanks with a loud cheerful voice, For a victory great …', commented the writer; and yet: 'The Waterloo peace has set us all fast':

Waterloo Times – A New Song[16]

Our Waterloo weavers are grown very thin,
And their Waterloo faces are all bone and skin,
And their Waterloo bellies, it runs in my mind,
Have not much in them but Waterloo wind. …

We have Waterloo tradesmen and Waterloo trade,
Waterloo workmen distrest and dismayed,
Whose Waterloo faces are clam'd [starved] till they grin,
And Waterloo noses grown down to their chin.

The final verse dismisses 'Waterloo meetings that talk of reform' as being 'just to amuse us while we weather the storm', and concludes 'we need not expect any regular trade, Until the demands of the nation are paid'.

Not for the first time, nor the last, returning servicemen felt both a deep sense of betrayal and a strong desire for change. John Marshall, at work in Newcastle from 1810 until 1829, was a radical printer responsible for issuing the powerful 'First Drest Man of Seghill' (see Chapter 5, p. 161). Soon after the victory of Waterloo he printed a ballad which expressed *après guerre* disillusion with great dignity:

The Tradesman's Complaint[17]

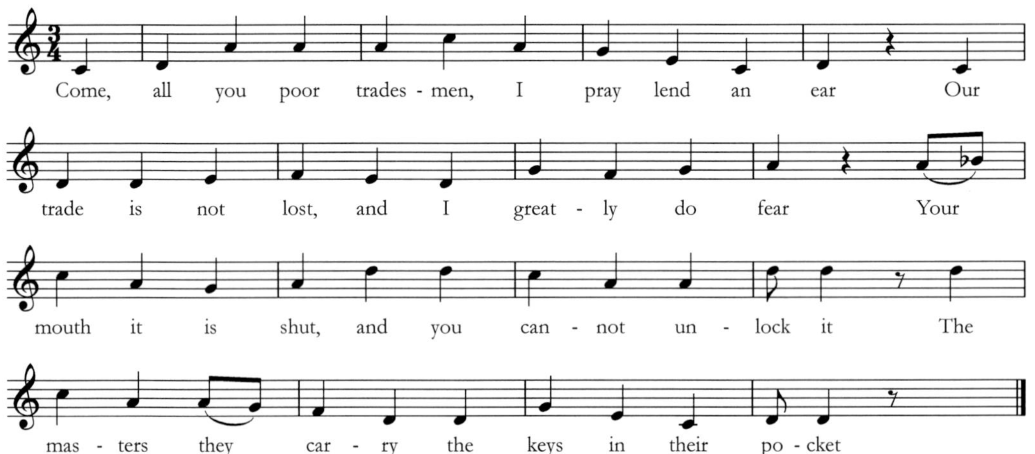

Come, all you poor tradesmen, I pray lend an ear,
Our trade it is lost, and I greatly do fear;
Your mouth it is shut, and you cannot unlock it,
The masters they carry the keys in their pocket.

For many a battle then we have been in,
On board of a ship, thro' France and thro' Spain,
But we settled the job when at WATERLOO,
And now we're come home, and have nothing to do.

When there would be a peace, we did understand,
That the rich and the poor would go hand in hand.
But if you are starving, they'll give no relief,
You may eat what you will, instead of roast beef.

See how the poor tradesmen are treated with scorn,
The times were ne'er worse since ADAM was born;
They say that the poor did suffer of old,
But we're pinch'd in our bellies till our backs double-fold.

Poor journeymen tradesmen have cause for to mourn,
They are paid but one-fourth of what they could earn.

The masters, you see, have got a fresh trick,
They will lock you all out three days in the week.

The ballad was evidently well received, because Marshall twice reprinted it.[18]

The same title served for a slip song issued by John Pitts of Seven Dials, between 1815 and 1819:

The Tradesman's Complaint[19]

Draw near brother tradesmen, listen to my song,
Tell me if you can where our trade is all gone,
For long I have travelled but I can get none
Oh! the dead time in Old England,
In England what very bad times.

If you go to a shop and ask for a job,
The answer is no with a shake of the nob,
'Tis enough to make a poor man turn to and rob,
Oh! the dead time in Old England, &c.

There's many a tradesman you'll see in the street,
Walks from morning to evening employment to seek,
Till he has scarcely any shoes to his feet.
Oh! the dead time, &c.

There are sailors and soldiers returned from the wars,
Who bravely have fought in their coentry's [sic] cause,
To come home to be starved – better staid where they was.
Oh! the dead time, &c.

Provision is pretty cheap it is true,
But if you have no money there's none for you,
What is a poor man with a family to do?
Oh! the dead time, &c.

So now to conclude and finish my song,
Let's hope these dead times they will not last long,
That we may have reason to alter our tone.
And sing O the good times in Old England,
In England what very good times.

The tradesman here is a skilled man who has served an apprenticeship. As a member of a craft, like other travelling brothers he can go on tramp in search of work, and rely on finding financial support and accommodation, thanks to a system dating from pre-industrial times which continued until the late nineteenth century.[20] Even so, he fails to find employment.

The song, thanks to the remarkable Copper Family of Rottingdean, Sussex, lasted in oral tradition until the late twentieth century, and became widely known in the folk revival. Their version remained uncannily close to the broadside original, as a sample verse shows:

Hard Times of Old England[21]

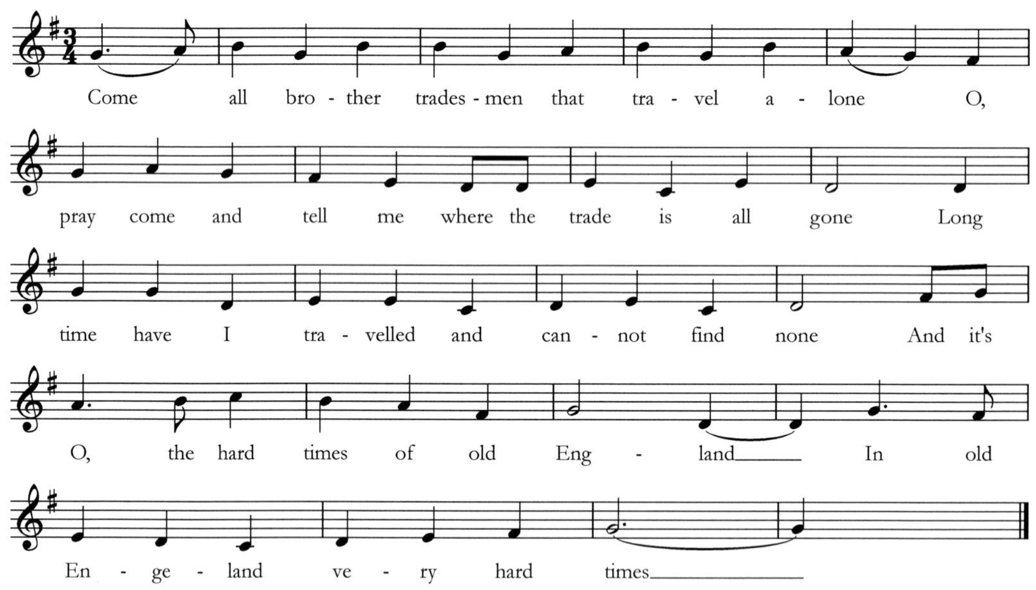

Come all brother tradesmen that travel alone,
O, pray come and tell me where the trade is all gone.
Long time I have travelled and cannot get none,
And it's O, the hard times of old England,
In old England very hard times.

Recession and reform

Exports to Europe and the Americas fell dramatically in 1819 and 1820, causing severe hardship. In a curious prefiguration of the hunger marches of the 1930s, factory workers in the North of England decided to gather in Manchester and march to London with a petition to the Prince Regent, each man carrying a blanket in which to sleep. Many of the leading 'Blanketeers' were arrested before they left Manchester, and the few hundred who set out were harassed by soldiers until they abandoned the venture.

Another response to unemployment occurs in a sheet of that period, 'The World on Credit',[22] printed by Cornelius Croshaw of York. It begins:

The World on Credit[22]

Come all you brisk and jovial blades,
Who'er out of work for want of trade.
Cheer up your hearts, be not dismay'd,
Although there is no working.
Ne'er complain that you are poor,
Drink up your beer, and call for more,
The landlord will run off your score,
When you are paid for working.
Now since we have no work to do,
Let's go to fairs and races too,
And to the statutes let us go,
Since that there is no working.

This may have been a genuine expression of relief, however short-lived, at not having to work; or perhaps bravado, whistling in the dark. Certainly, the writer's mood quickly changes:

There's many a tradesman in the street,
That's scarce got shoes upon his feet,
There [sic] nose and chin do almost meet,
Since they've had nought for working.
Their lanthorn [lantern] jaws grew very thin,
Their mouths are scarcely to be seen,
Pray, don't you think it is a sin,
Men are not paid for working.
Now to the workhouse we must go,
For something to support us through.
Alas! What can poor people do,
Since there's no pay for working.

Then in a further change, hopes are expressed that the Poor Rate will be increased and that trade will revive:

O then the bells shall sweetly ring,
The poor shall all rejoice and sing,
What pleasant days will then be seen,
When we are paid for working.

Croshaw also issued 'The Clothiers' Lamentation on the Badness of Trade',[23] which contrasted the eagerness of workers when business was brisk ('The spinner and the weaver lads, When work was to be had, Rose early in the morning, all, And went with hearts quite glad') with the prevailing unemployment and under-employment ('There's factories that are stopping, Their hands have work to seek; And some that still are going on, Have scarce four days a week'). For good measure, the sheet also includes 'A Petition', beginning 'Sweet Charity, thy aid impart', and 'A Hymn', 'O, God! Our help in ages past'.

One response to the economic crisis of 1819 was a decision to restore the gold standard, which may permit the assignment to that year of a Pitts ballad with this unusual verse: 'The bankers they are at a stand and very well they may, Since flimsey [sic] papers will not stand the great and trying day, 'Tis gold and silver we prefer 'tis that will stand the test, When flimsy are done away and mingled with the dust.' This is 'The New Times',[24] which has an arresting opening:

> Ye working men where'er ye dwell, lend an attentive ear,
> While I in humble verse relate the sufferings that you endure
> Well may the industrious artisan the loss of trade deplore,
> For such distress on English ground was never known before.

In Spitalfields, the narrative continues, 'the weaving tribe' – not a derogatory phrase, but an old-fashioned poetic periphrasis – 'no comfort now enjoy, Some thousands there are as we are told the masters can't employ'. The 'plague' of unemployment has spread across London, 'which makes the Cockneys start, To think that they for want of trade with all their goods must part'. Those who try their luck in country towns 'find with great surprise that sore distress abounds': ''Tis then to crave for charity with tardy steps they go, Asham'd to beg, afraid to steal, their hearts is filled with woe'. Then the perspective broadens: 'In Manchester some thousands there are destitute of work …'; and:

> The Coventry ribbon weavers have nothing for to eat,
> In Leicester town the stocking men now from their frames retreat,
> In Nottingham the working tribe their wages ran so low
> They can't their families maintain which fills their heart with woe.

The extent to which a printer like Pitts sympathised with the plight of the unemployed or merely treated it as a commercial opportunity is a matter for speculation. The position is surely clearer in the case of those of marked radical sympathies, like John Marshall of Newcastle. Thomas Hoggett of Durham may have been of similar stripe. His sheet, 'The Tradesman's Wish for a Better New Year',[25] which, incidentally, neatly provides its own dating ('The year of Nineteen is expiring, And Christmas soon will be here'), laments unemployment:

The Tradesman's Wish for a Better New Year[25]

Our Labourers for want of employment,
Their faces are grown pale and wan,
Likewise the industrious mechanic,
The glory and pride of the land,
And thousands throughout the whole nation,
Are out of employment we hear,
I'm sure we are to be pitied,
God send us a better New Year.

And reports on political action:

'Twas on the thirteenth of December,
A meeting in North Shields town,
Just all for the Rights of Old England,
Reformers they came flocking round.
The meeting took place on the Bank Tops,
Our heroes they all did appear,
We're the glory and pride of Old England,
God send us a better New Year.

A similarly defiant attitude is displayed in another Hoggett sheet, probably of the same period:

Larry's Return to Erin[26]

I am a poor Weaver that's out of employ,
And my name it is Larry O'Broom, sir;
I have no parish my wants to supply,
Nor a web to put in the loom, sir.
To old England I came in the sweet prime of life,
I deserted my country, my friends and my wife,
But now, sir, grown old, and without any strife,
They will send home poor Larry O'Broom, sir.

Just the other day to the parish I went,
And told them of my situation,

They d——'d me and said that no one for me sent,
And they order'd me to my own nation.
They said since the peace, it is very well known,
We're oppress'd by the Irish as much as our own,
But a bill is now past and we'll send them all home,
As well as poor Larry O'Broom, sir.

These words made me smile, and I could not forbear
To spit on my sprig of shelelah;
I twirled it o'er my head in the air,
Crying old Erin will yet flourish gaily,
For as soon as the Parliament we do bring home,
With Paddy Fitzpatrick and brave Wellington
As we oft did with the French, we will yet make them run,
That has banished poor Larry O'Broom, sir.

One of them reply'd, that's treason you speak,
Said I, by my soul you're a liar;
Then the hat on my head it began for to shake,
And my face got as red as the fire.
Then so boldly I stood for old Erin's defence,
And told them they paid us a good recompence;
After gaining your freedom at the dear expence
Of our heart's blood, cry'd Larry O'Broom, sir.

On saying these words they began for to cool,
And they told me the Bill was enacted,
That it had got the voice of the national school,
And likewise the old tool to protect it.
They offer'd me money, but I said them nay,
Since that is the case I'm just going away
To the land of my forefathers Eringobragh;
So away went poor Larry O'Broom, sir.

Now you sons of old Erin, I'd have you repair
With speed to that sweet little Island;
I'll need but instructions I vow and declare
For to make it a great and a high land,
And if Boney should rise to head France & Spain
Don't dare our assistance to ask for again,
For if that you do, you'll meet labour in vain,
And a thumping from Larry O'Broom, sir.

Another Irishman looks forward to returning home in a vigorous narrative, dating from 1826, which again shows resilience in adversity. The lively style and the many telling details give the song a strong sense of genuine experience:

The Weaver's Complaint[27]

I am a brisk weaver it's very well known,
When I was in Ireland I lived in Tyrone,
These five years and better I'll give you to know,
I've wrought in the Calton nigh unto Glasgow.

For the first five years while the trade it was good
I never was short either for drink or for food,
I'd plenty of credit where e'er I did ca',
But since trade got low there's nae credit ava.

My loom now being idle an' mills on half time,
My family an' I we began to repine,
Hundreds of tradesmen as ill off as I,
That ae peck of potatoes or meal couldna buy.

I could get nae money my rent for to pay,
Nor yet raise five shillings to take me away,
Then for a sma' trifle we pawned our claise,
I allow it is true we had hunger and ease.

We all did assemble ae day in the Green,
For nae bad intention 'twas plain to be seen,
'Twas only to let the gentle folk a' know,
That the want of trade was the cause of our woe.

Then with circumspection they viewed our case,
They said it's a pity to see in the place,
So many going idle and good tradesmen too,
Who's willing to work if they had it to do.

They allow'd to the quarry we'd have to repair,
Where all that was married they'd find them work there,
We thank them sincerely we can dae nae less,
They have sav'd many frae want an' distress.

On a Monday morning we march'd away
'Twas the third of April I'll ay mind the day,
With hammer in hand an' green aprons also,
In full uniform to work we did go.

I hadna the art the whin stanes for to break,
Five shillings is all in the week I could make.
There's some I allow that ha' made above nine,
Yet their hands or their banes was nae as sair as mine

I wrought for nine days till my hands grew that sair
I had to resign for I could knap nae mair.
To my old employer my case [I] made known,
But he told me his case was as bad as my own.

Now I hae good news for my countrymen
One shilling will bring you back in the Fiu [Fin (name of ship)]
Was I safe in Ireland nae mair would I roam,
For in good or bad times there's no place like home.

Adieu to the Calton an' Bridgetown also,
An' the lads an' lasses behind in Glasgow,
But I'll ne'er forget while the blood's in my veins
The nine days I spent at the knapping the stanes.

Begging ballads

Seasonal fluctuations in the weather inevitably contributed to unemployment, with boatmen, gardeners and others unable to work in frozen conditions. A slip song entitled 'The Keelmen's Lament for the Frost'[28] provides almost day-to-day information on the progress of a big freeze which began in November 1819 and continued into January 1820. The frozen condition of the Rivers Wear and Tyne made it impossible for keelmen, sailors and carters to move coal, and therefore stopped the pitmen too. The ballad makes no appeal for money, and merely concludes: 'My song for to finish, I've little to say, The poor are lamenting their case ev'ry day. For want of employment we ruin'd shall be, At Sunderland, Shields, and at Newcastle key.'

More commonly, unashamed pleas for help were made in such sheets. For example, a rather later ballad deals with the plight of 'Poor Frozen Out Gardners':[29]

Poor Frozen Out Gardners[29]

We Broken-hearted gardners, and scarce got a bit of shoe
Like Pilgrims we are wandering, & don't know what to do
Our furniture is seized upon, our Togs are up the spout,
Cold winter is come, and we are all froze out.
[Chorus]
O dear we are compel'd for to shout,
We are broken-hearted gardners, and all froze out.

The concluding verse implies that the singers wait outside a house for a response:

> Oh, listen with attention before you close your doors,
> And think upon the state of the languishing poor,
> Our familys are starving we can no longer stay,
> So think upon the poor on a cold winters day.

Of course, there were less than genuine charity seekers. William Gardiner (1770–1853), a Leicester hosiery manufacturer, wrote:

> During a bad trade some of my workmen formed the project of going into the south of England in the character of beggars. One was a comber, who had travelled over the country with his blank [a passport-like document which recorded the journeys of a tramping trade unionist] in search of work, and who led the party. Though all young men, and unmarried, they wrote a ditty describing their wives and children in want of bread. When they returned I questioned them upon their proceedings, and learnt that in the city of Exeter they collected £2 17s. 6d. in one day. The chief delinquent could scarcely keep his countenance when poor women ran across the street to give them a pittance.[30]

Broadside printers saw a way of making money from unemployment, which may explain why sheets entitled 'Leicester Stocking Weavers' Complaint'[31] came to be printed by Hewitt of Glastonbury, and 'Cotton Spinners from Manchester'[32] by James Paul and Company of Seven Dials in London. The latter, with the sub-heading of 'For the Master or Mistress', was presumably left on a doorstep or put through a letter box, prior to a canvass: 'The person who will call for this bill will bring a sample of the very best reels of cotton for sale.' The 'Copy of Verses' featured begins 'We are cotton spinners by our trade; Employ we cannot find: Hundreds are by want compell'd, To leave their friends behind'; and it is full of the usual formulae: the oldest man on the earth cannot remember times so bad, the mother weeps at the plight of her children, we gave to those in distress when we could but now we have no work to do, 'he that giveth to the poor but lendeth to the Lord'. 'There are now four hundred out of employment,' says a note towards the bottom of the sheet; and this, together with the cotton spinners' copy of verses adapted to the needle trade, along with an offer to 'purchase of a few Needles, of our own Manufacture', recurs in a handbill printed in Whitby and headed 'To the Lady of the house'.[33]

'Please deliver this to no person but the Said John Taylor, who left it,' is the message at the foot of another sheet which announces: 'The Occasion of These Verses Being Written Was the Writer John Taylor, Cotton Spinner, Of Manchester, in the County of Lancashire, Being out of Employ, and His Goods Were Sold for Rent.'[34] This may date from the mid-1820s, when a financial crisis in Manchester led to a severe depression there. Miners went on strike there, as did power-loom weavers. Many textile workers in Lancashire were thrown out of work, and some responded by rioting and smashing machinery. It is possible that a further sheet with 'A Blessing', 'A Copy of Verses by a Poor Tradesman' and 'Stanzas'[35] carried the statement 'We are a number of Operatives from Messrs. Firth and Sturdy, Blackburn', in order to provide a guarantee of the authenticity of its distributors.

The use of cliché or commonplace, which continues up to the present time in, say, epitaphs or death notices, does not necessarily mean that those involved do not genuinely grieve; and in a similar way, the conventional pattern followed by begging handbills and songs by no means always indicates fraud. An anonymous customer in a way authenticated 'The Framework-Knitters Appeal' from Leicester by noting on the copy he had purchased: 'Singing in Sunderland streets by two Frame Knitters, June 24th 1826.'[36] In the same year Cobbett reported that throughout the Wiltshire towns of Frome, Bradford and Trowbridge there were 'weavers from the North, *singing . . . ballads of Distress!* They had been doing so at Salisbury, just before I was there. The landlord at Heytesbury told me that people that could afford it generally gave them something.'[37]

Even those in work were sometimes reduced to begging to supplement their income: framework-knitters, for example, of whom E.P. Thompson wrote: 'If there is an episode of the Industrial Revolution more harrowing than that of the handloom weaver, it is that of the stockinger.'[38] The decline in earnings to an average of 4s. 6d. a week in 1840 'was effected', Thompson adds, 'by "free competition" alone, without the introduction of any machinery involving steam or water-power' – 'the frame-rent, on the one side, and a multiplicity of forms of petty exploitation – wage-cutting, "docking" or fining, truck – on the other.'

Paradoxically, it was not until factory production for hosiery came in during the 1860s and later that conditions for the workers improved. Until then, in places as far apart as London and Tewkesbury, but mainly in the Leicester–Nottingham–Derby triangle, the framework-knitters, like the handloom weavers, 'were duly enquired into as they starved'.[39]

'There have been few more inhuman statutes than the Poor Law Act of 1834,' writes Eric Hobsbawm, 'which made all relief "less eligible" than the lowest wage outside, confined it to the jail-like workhouse, forcibly separating husbands, wives and children in order to punish the poor for their destitution, and discourage them from the dangerous preoccupation of procreating further paupers.'[40] The notion of punishing the poor for their poverty not only persisted through Victorian times but lingered until the eve of the First World War. Indeed, it cast a dread shadow long afterwards. My mother (1906–1999) inherited from her Victorian parents a fear of the workhouse, which she, along with millions of others, saw as an abyss into which even a respectable family might fall, given a calamity such as a breadwinner's prolonged incapacity or unemployment.

In 'The Present Condition of British Workmen'[41] the Poor Law is attacked as contrary to 'God's commands, For it parts man and wife'; and as shameful treatment for 'an Englishman, Where they boast of Christianity':

The Present Condition of British Workmen[41]

The parish says they won't relieve
Us without we go in,
Which caused our families for to grieve,
But poverty is no sin.
In the [work]House we are treated worse than slaves,
The truth I will impart,
If we look or speak we're bad behaved,
From our families forced to part.

The writer, observing that 'Trade everywhere is at a stand, The poor man's hopes destroyed', attributes the problems to industrialisation:

Mechanics and poor labourers
Are wandering up and down,
There is nothing now but poverty
In country and in town;
Machinery and steam-power has
The poor man's hopes destroyed,

Then pray behold the numbers of
The suffering unemployed.

The invention of machinery
Has caused many to weep and moan;
It has thrown thousands out of work,
And drove them from their homes.
Where a hundred hands were once employed,
Now there's not more than ten,
And this is through machinery –
God help poor working-men.

This seems to be a remarkably clear-sighted attempt, from a worker's viewpoint, to analyse a problem and to allocate blame for its origin.

To the conventional verses in 'The Staffordshire Nail-makers' Humble Petition',[42] this information is added:

> The reason for our being out of employment is in consequence of the Machines and Foundries, —- They will cast and cut more Nails in one day than 100 men can make in a week.—- Our master, (Mr Woodhall, in Tipton) failed and 100 men were thrown out of employment. We being so many in number were forced to leave our homes, our Parishes being so much oppressed, could not give us employment, there being 500 out of employment there at this present time. [Then comes the request] Good Christians, a small Trifle will be received by us with sincere gratitude. N.B. Please to keep this clean till called for.

Fear and hatred of the new system for poor relief drove people to accept any pittance in order to remain outside it. Framework-knitters, even though they make it clear that they are working, ask for help in a pair of ballads on a single sheet[43] issued by the Nottingham printer Ordoyno in the late 1830s or early '40s. Of these, 'The Miseries of the Framework-knitters' complains of middlemen, low wages, truck ('When we ask for our Money comes paper and string!, Dear and bad Beef or Mutton or some such like thing!!!') and extortion ('Bad Weights and bad Measures are frequently us'd'); then, after the ritual apology ('Pray take no offence tho' we visit this place') makes a tactful request ('We crave your assistance'). From the indication of a chorus ('Derry down &c.') we know at least the family of tunes intended.

In the case of the second ballad, 'The Tear of Pity', 'Written by a poor Framework-knitter' (originally in 1821), the tune is specified as 'Wounded Hussar':[44]

The Tear of Pity[43]

Oh pity dear friends the poor Framework-knitters,
Whose sufferings call for humanity's tear!
Oppression's Iron hand our moments embitter;
And sorrows increase [on us] year after year.

Our old ragged garments be-speak our distress,
Our lank and lean faces be-dew'd with a tear;
Show pity O! pity the poor Framework-knitters,
Our sorrows increase on us year after year.

We've work'd night and day sore pinched with hunger,
And frequently go supperless to our bed!
Tir'd nature at length can bear it no longer;
But drives us abroad thus to beg for our bread!

Our hard-hearted Masters in Luxury live,
Nor feel for their slaves as it plainly appear;
Then pity O! pity the poor Framework-knitters,
Our miseries call for humanity's tear!

May he who does feed the hungry Raven.
And clothes the Lilly that grows in the vale;
Supply all our wants, with blessings from Heaven,
And pardon all those who have caus'd us to wail!

And when we have done with all trouble below,
May our dear friends and us, meet them all where,
Sweet joys are abundant and Riches Redundant,
And the smiles of Philanthropy dries up each tear.

The pious – not to say pie-in-the-sky – protestations were no doubt thought likely to produce a greater volume of contributions. The same approach occurred in many similar sheets, including 'Lament of Two Stocking Makers, from Nottingham', paired with 'O Gracious God'.[45] The latter, headed by a woodcut of Christ on the cross, concludes: 'What prompts that trifle – pray afford, Give to the poor and lend unto the Lord; He will repay thee, for his word is just, And bless thee, if in him thou put thy trust.'

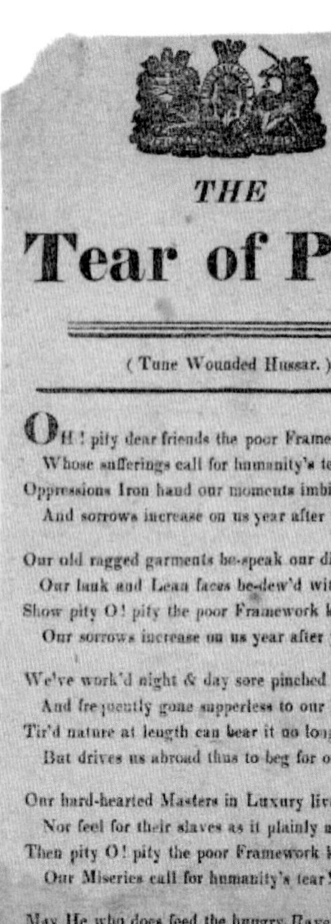

THE

Tear of Pity

(Tune Wounded Hussar.)

OH! pity dear friends the poor Framework-knitte
Whose sufferings call for humanity's tear!
Oppressions Iron hand our moments imbitter;
And sorrows increase on us year after year.

Our old ragged garments be-speak our distress,
Our lank and Lean faces be-dew'd with a tear:
Show pity O! pity the poor Framework knitter,
Our sorrows increase on us year after year.

We've work'd night & day sore pinched with hunge
And frequently gone supperless to our bed!
Tir'd nature at length can bear it no longer;
But drives us abroad thus to beg for our bread!

Our hard-hearted Masters in Luxury live,
Nor feel for their slaves as it plainly appear;
Then pity O! pity the poor Framework knitter,
Our Miseries call for humanity's tear!

May He who does feed the hungry Raven,
And cloaths the sweet Lilly that grows in the vale;
Supply all our wants, with blessings from Heaven,
And pardon all those who have caus'd us to wail!

And when we have done with all troubles below,
May you our dear friends and us, meet them all wh
Sweet joys are abundant and Riches Redundant,
And the smile of Philanthrophy dries up each tear.

Written by a poor Framework-knitter.
SUTTON, April 24th 1821,

Wightman, Printer, Sutton.

'The Tear of Pity' Ballad sheet from the Firth Ballad Collection, reproduced courtesy of the University of Sheffield Library.

Religion and recalcitrance

'The Weaver's Lamentation' and 'The Tradesmen's Lamentation'[46] seek charity in the most abject manner ('We fain would now your mite receive', 'A mite from you, though e'er so small'), and provide the clear intimation that donors will in due course benefit: 'The vineyard of our precious Lord, Before his labourers lies; And lo! We see a vast reward/ Await them in the skies.' Yet the printer, Thomas Dodds of Newcastle, also issued lively and positive sheets dealing with trade union and Chartist activity, and his 'Old Woman and Coal Owner' (see Chapter 5, p. 175) is particularly vigorous. The same is true of another piece, very much intended to be sung, with a title strikingly similar to that of the ballad of 1692 quoted earlier (see p. 288):

The Cries of the Poor[47]

All you distress'd tradesmen in country and town,
Give ear to these few lines that I have penn'd down;
The state of the nation to you I will show,
And the hardships that thousands they do undergo.

My nerves they grow weak and my mind is confus'd,
When I think on the way British subjects are used;
Our Rulers and Statesmen lie snug and secure,
But they shut their ears to the cries of the poor.

They eat and they drink and they wear of the best,
The cares of this life don't disturb them of rest;
They are not afraid when they're sporting up by,
Their children at home they with hunger will cry.

If you are cruel to your beast you'll be fined
But the worst of cruelties they shew to mankind;
For seeking their rights, some the billows has cross'd.
At least it was so with Jones, Williams, and Frost.

There's some have not seen it, but then you have heard
What did befall Wilson, brave Hardie and Baird;
And forty-five more that were banished away,
As exiles for life unto Botany Bay.

The bonny mill lasses to their work they do go,
In the winter season thro' cold, frost, and snow,
From six in the morning till half-past eight at night,
Some do work for fivepence a day, it surely is not right.

In Camlachie, Parknead [Parkhead], Calton and Bridgton,
The weavers and their families are greatly kept down;
Their wages are low and their porridge but thin,
They're working life out here to keep the life in.

The Irish have got no employment at home.
And in search of work they are foreed [forced] to roam;
It's forty years since they lost their parliament.
The wealth of their natton [nation] abroad it is spent.

The poor are distressed in every town,
It's by oppression they are greatly kept down;

You've heard of what tyrants at Rathcormack has done,
They've robbd widow Ryan and murdered her son.

It's some alterations they'll soon have to make,
Or hunger I fear through stone walls it will break;
You feed your dogs well Oh ye great men up by,
While millions in Britain for bread they do cry.

We did live in hopes, but our hopes now are fled,
Begging's not allowed and charity is dead,
Bread to the hungry and freedom to the slave,
It's all that we want, and it's all that we must have.

In Dodds's sheet, instead of piety and cliché we now have politics and clarity, together with some memorable language, simple but telling: 'Their wages are low and their porridge but thin, They're working life out here to keep the life in'; 'It's some alterations they'll soon have to make, Or hunger I fear through stone walls it will break'; 'We did live in hopes, but our hopes now are fled'.

Solidarity is expressed for the Irish, who 'lost their parliament' (by the Act of Union, in 1801) and 'by oppression … are greatly kept down': the events mentioned at Rathcormack, Co. Cork, were the deaths of nineteen people during the forcible collection of 40s. in tithe arrears in May 1834. The Welsh Chartists mentioned, John Frost, William Jones and Zephaniah Williams, were transported after leading the attempt at an armed rising in Newport in 1839, which was put down by troops. Of the Scots radical reformers involved in a skirmish with soldiers at Bonnymuir, near Falkirk, in April 1820, nineteen were transported and three, Andrew Hardie (an ancestor of Keir Hardie), James Wilson and John Baird, were hanged and then beheaded.[48]

Although the campaign against the Corn Laws was essentially middle-class, some working people thought that abolition (which took place in 1846) would improve the economy, hence these verses in yet another 'Tradesman's Complaint',[49] issued probably between 1838 and 1842:

The labourers of England once lived on pudding and good beef,
But now the times are altered, which fills their hearts with grief,
No more the pudding and the beef their dinner tables show,
Tatoes and gruel are their fare now, there's no work to do.

Now let us hope the times will mend, but this is vain, I fear,
For instead of getting better they are getting worse each year,

But if the Corn laws are repealed, and we get work to do,
Then with free trade we will rejoice, and get good wages too.

In the meantime 'lamentations' continued. That of the mechanics, issued by John Harkness of Preston, some time between July 1844 and April 1845, explained:

The labouring poor are starving, you know,
Men are walking the streets with hearts full of woe,
The thoughts of past times make our hearts for to rue,
To see our families starving and have no work to do.

'Ah, England, my country, where now is thy boast, Since thy trade and thy commerce is fled from thy coast?' asked the writer, in sorrow rather than anger, and concluded:

May kind Heaven once more deign on us to smile,
With flourishing trade bless our once happy isle,
Then life's journey so pleasant with joy well pursue,
With our children well fed, and work plenty to do.[50]

'The Poor Threadmaker's Lamentation',[51] from the same printer, reverts to straight begging ('A mite from you tho' e'er so small, Would greatly us befriend, We hope you will no poorer be, but richer in the end'), and it shares a sheet with 'Job, the Patient Man', which reminds the poor that riches are only vanity, and exhorts them to be mindful of their latter end.

However, Harkness, responding no doubt to working-class disillusionment at the absence of any benefit from the repeal of the Corn Laws, published, probably in December 1846, a much more hard-hitting 'New Dialogue and Song on the Times'.[52] Alhough this ended only with a vague expression of hope, it showed a sharply new attitude by castigating the rich in both prose and verse. The dialogue begins on the subject of employment and short time:

BILL. – Good morning, Jack, I'm glad to see you. What's the meaning of all these Spinners, Piecers, Weavers, Winders, Grinders, Strippers, Carders, Doffers, Stretchers, Throstle Spinners, Bobbin Winders, Frame Tenders, and all these folk that works in these places with big chimneys at top of um walking about.

JACK. – Why, if thou recollects, a few months back there wur great talk about the Corn Laws going to come off, and all those big chaps in the Parliament House, and all those Factory Lords of Lancashire, said if the Corn Laws wur repealed that poor people would get plenty of bread for little money, work would be plentiful, and wages would be a great deal higher, but instead of that, bread's dearer, wages is lower, & factories are on short time. . . .

The 'Song on the Times' takes up the theme, with a defiant chorus: 'So arouse you Sons of Freedom the world seems upside down, They scorn the poor man as a thief in country and town'. The stance, though, is the reverse of revolutionary, in that the narrator looks back to 'former times':

Alas! How alter'd are the times rich men despise the poor
And pay them off quite scornful at their door
And if a man is out of work his parish pay is small,
Enough to starve himself and wife, his children and all.

In former times when Christmas came we had a good big loaf,
Then beef and mutton plenty were, and we enjoyed them both,
But now a days such altered ways and different is the times,
If starving and ask relief you're sent to a wig [Whig] bastile.

So to conclude and finish these few verses I have made,
I hope to see before it's long men for their labour paid,
Then we'll rejoice with heart and voice and banish all our woes,
But before we do old England must pay us what she owes.

The big new workhouses brought in by the Whig government under the Poor Law Act of 1834 were known as 'bastilles', after the Parisian prison destroyed at the outset of the French Revolution.

Address and appeal

Three years later, Harkness was still printing ballads of distress. A sheet headed 'Address of Two Unemployed Workmen',[53] issued between January and April in 1849, carries two items: 'The Tradesman's Lamentation' (beginning 'Neighbours, countrymen, and friends') and 'One God has made us all' (beginning 'Come all you worthy Christians'). There were frequent further printings, such as those by J. Ross of Newcastle, J. Duff of Durham and T. Pearson of Manchester, together with several sheets without imprint.[54] Both items, the second doubling as a Christmas carol, remained in oral tradition well into the twentieth century.[55]

After 'The address' came a very similar production, 'The appeal', of which successive editions spanned a period of over fifty years. This dates from the late 1850s or early 1860s:

The Appeal of the Unemployed[56]

Oh list you feeling Christians,
You're aware, where'er you go,
There is thousands of good tradesmen,
Borne down in grief and woe.

Their families are perishing,
Their prospects are destroyed,
Then grant, oh; [sic] grant your sympathy
Unto the unemployed.

It is the want of labour
Causes thousands for to roam,
Their wives and tender children
Do pine for want at home.

Our furniture and clothes are gone,
With grief we are annoyed,
Then assist you feeling christians,
The suffering unemployed.

In every part of this place,
And all the country too,
The tradesman and the labourer
Can get no work to do.

To see our wives and children
For bread, in grief to pine,
Think, what must be our feelings
You Christians good and kind.

Great hardship and privation,
We are compelled to stand,
Then Christians to the unemployed
Pray lend an helping hand.

And heaven will reward you,
That is your Saviour's words,
"He that giveth to the poor,
But lendeth to the Lord."

May trade again soon flourish,
May we see prosperity,
Whatever is bestowed on us
We will most gratefully

Acknowledge every kindness
While our families with joy,
Will bless the hand stretch'd forth to help,
The suffering unemployed.

Then lend, oh! Lend a helping hand,
To the tradesman in distress,
Alleviate his sufferings,
And heaven will you bless.

And when there is a change,
To work we'll go with joy,
And pray for those who did us help,
When we were unemployed.

A note at the foot of the sheet added:

> The Bearers, are a party of unemployed tradesmen, who have been out of work for many weeks past; having large families, we are compelled to throw ourselves at the feet of a sympathising public, hoping they will take our case into consideration, and render us some small assistance, so that we may be enabled to obtain food and shelter for our wives and children till trade mends, and for which we return our sincere and most grateful thanks.

One version is 'Printed for the Vendors', and would have been illegal since it has no printer's name. Others give the author as George Allen, blacksmith, and state the price of one penny. Copies are annotated, presumably with the dates of purchase, as August 1894, 9 March 1896 and 6 July 1909.[57] Two separate impressions of the sheet, which must date from between 1917 and 1929, bear the imprint of W.C. Such, 183–5 Union Street, Borough, London SE 1.[58]

Few of the begging ballads indicate a tune, and sheets left on approval would not need one. Some of those which were sung in the streets might well have received the scornful comments made by an experienced 'griddler' (street singer) to the 'super tramp', W.H. Davies (1870–1940):

> First of all, you sing in too lusty a voice, as though you were well fed, and in good health. Secondly, you are in too much of a hurry to move on, and would get out of people's hearing before they have time to be affected. Try to sing in a weaker voice: draw out the easy low notes to a greater length, and cut the difficult high notes short, as though you has spasms in the side. Your object is to save your voice as much as possible, indifferent to the demands of the music, or the spirit of the song.[59]

Rather more effort would surely have been required with the pair of songs on another Harkness sheet: 'Humanity is Calling', 'The Spinners' Lamentation',[60] which called respectively for 'Red, White and Blue' and 'The Mistletoe Bough'. The former text begins conventionally enough ('We have come to ask your assistance, At home we've been starving too long; And our children are wanting subsistence, Kindly aid us to help them along'), but soon turns to the severe hardship occasioned by the cotton famine caused in this country by the American Civil War:

'Tis no strike, but a greater contention,
That has brought us hunger and pain;
And our laws oppose intervention,
So help us, and honour you'll gain.

Wars, clamour, civil commotion,
Has stagnation brought in its train;
And stoppage brings with it starvation,
So help us some bread to obtain.

The American War is still lasting;
Like a terrible nightmare it leans
On the breast of a country now fasting
For cotton, for work, and for means.

Let us hope that the war will be ended,
And blockades be heard of no more;
But peace and contentment be blended,
As rivals on every shore.

Another ballad on the cotton famine, 'Depression of Trade', was issued jointly, and appropriately, with 'Hard Times Come Again No More'.[61] The latter, written in 1858 by the American Stephen Foster, was widely known on this side of the Atlantic, and continued in oral tradition well into the twentieth century,[62] thanks to its fervent, moving, and almost prayer-like exhortation, 'Oh! hard times come again no more'. 'Depression of Trade' is very different in mood:

Depression of Trade[62]

If the time don't alter soon, I fear
There will be a row in Lancashire;
For the poor, the poor can carry on no longer;
John Bull must give the finishing stroke,
For the American blockade must be broke;
Or the poor, the poor will perish with hunger.
I wish the times would alter, &c.

As I was walking out one day,
And down by Walker-street did stray;
The poor wite [with] jugs and cans were waiting,
Some with tickets green and red,
Some received a loaf of bread;
While others got a quart of soup that was'nt worth eating
I wish the times would alter, &c.

To the pop-shop keepers, Mr. Balls,
Gowns, trousers, petticoats, and shawls,
Victerines and crinolines poor people they keep sending
There's plenty going up the spout,
But very little coming out,
So the pop-shop men they intend to give over lending
I wish the times would alter, &c.

Cheer up your hearts says Sall to Polly,
And drive away all melancholy,
Don't grieve for I believe better days are dawning:
There'll be a star up by and bye,
And everyone will find employ,
Then we'll rejoice both heart and voice, and sing –
noon, night, and morning.
I wish the times would alter, &c.

The pop (or pawn) shop, where items went up the spout (were pledged) against small loans, played a significant role in working-class life and hence lore. Victorines, says the OED, were 'A kind of fur tippet worn by ladies, fastened in front of the neck and having two loose ends hanging down'.

The expression of hope in the final verse of 'Depression of Trade' is shared with many other ballads of unemployment, including 'Ne Wark',[63] by the Tynesider Joe Wilson (1841–1875). His words are refreshingly direct, drawn from his own experience of being out of work as a young man, living with parents who were poor themselves:

Ne Wark[63]

Aw's weary, aw's wretched, aw wander forlorn,
Aw sigh for the neet, an' then wish for the morn;
For neet brings ne cumfort, an' morn little mair,
I' byeth mind an' body aw's worn oot an' sair.

[*Korus* [sic]]
What wretchedness, what misery
Thor's ne one can tell,
Except them that's been oot o' wark, like me-sel.

Aw wander te places, an' try te get wark,
Where "Call back agyen" is the foreman's remark;
Thus hopeless an' cheerless aw pass mony a day,
Tho the pay-week cums roond – it te me brings ne pay.

Ne wark yit! – heart-broken aw bend me ways hyem,
Ne wark yeit! – te tell them aw really think shem;
For dependence is painful, tho it's on yor awn,
Tho te cumfort an' cheer ye they try a' they can.

Thor's nyen can imagine the angwish aw feel
When aw sit doon at hyem te maw poor humble meal
Each bite seems te chowk us, – the day seems full lang,
An' a' that aw de, whey, aw feel tho 'twas rang.

Me fether lucks dull, tho he strives te luck glad,
An' tells us it's nowt te the trubbils he's had;
Me muther smiles kindly, tho sad like the rest,
She whispers, "Cheer up, lad, an' hope for the best!"

It cannet last always! – aw hope afore lang
Wi' wark aw'll be freed from poverty's pang;
For without it hyem's dreary, – the fire's bright spark
Turns gloomy an' dim when at hyem thor's Ne Wark.

Like professional street singers, unemployed workers often favoured the tunes of sentimental, not to say tear-jerking songs. For example, the bilingual 'Ystalyfera Workmen's Appeal to the Public, Cwynfan-Gerdd Gweithwyr Ystalyfera'[64] of 1886 cited 'Just before the Battle, Mother' (see p. 240):

We the men of Ystalyfera,
Are today amidst the storm,
Famine staring in our faces,
Grief in every shape and form,
Trade is gone from our neighbourhood,
Darkness reigns throughout the vale,
Our dear ones are starving!
Listen friends to our tale.

Lleddf yw'r don, a lledf yw'r testyn,
Lleddf yw'n calon dan ein bron,
Cwyno glywir drwy Ystalyfera,
Nid oes son am gywair llon,
Calon masnach wedi methu,
Drws ein cysur wedi'i gloi,
Sel marweidd-dra ar y cyfan,
Hoen a nwyfiant wedi ffoi.

Jobs fit for heroes

The demobilised soldiers of 1918 and 1919, like their counterparts of just over a century earlier, frequently found themselves out of work. '[T]he sight of a blind or maimed ex-serviceman trying to scrape a living by selling matches or bootlaces in the street, or simply by begging, was commonplace throughout the 1920s and 1930s,' wrote Juliet Gardiner.[65] Another expedient was the sale at a penny or twopence of printed sheets such as:

The Men Who Manned the Guns[66]

Where are the lads of the village To-day?
The heroes of the War:
Why – most are in rags drawing no pay,
Wondering what they fought for.

While risking their lives in Khaki,
Fighting their Country's foes,
What were their thoughts of the future?
Not starvation and misery; God knows.

They were promised a better England
Comfort after the strife,
What a rude awakening –
To come back to this miserable life.

When standing knee deep in water –
Facing the treacherous "Huns":
They moulded their Country's future,
As they calmly manned their guns.

Now, in justice give them something
A bit of what they fought for,
If its only a tumbled down cottage,
With a good old oaken door.

The anonymous author would have commissioned copies of the sheet, which clearly states 'Not sold in aid of a Charity'. Another item in similar vein, 'What Price Glory Now?',[67] published by the author, F. Henderson, of 9 Chichester Place, Paddington, W.2, was 'sold exclusively by unemployed ex-service London Territorials'.

On the other hand, when a commercial ballad printer like W.C. Such produced material, one presumes that those doing the selling received no more than any other hawker. His sheet, 'A Copy of Verses on the Unemployed and the Great Distress in England', is prominently marked 'Please buy a Copy from An Unemployed Ex-Serviceman'; and another impression of the same text is specifically entitled 'An Appeal by Unemployed Ex-Service Men', and urges: 'Please purchase a Copy and thus Help.'[68] The former indicates the tune of 'Cast Out', which I have not been able to trace, and they have the same text, which begins:

An Appeal by Unemployed Ex-Service Men[68]
Some thousands in England are starving,
And all through no fault of their own,
The troubles of poverty sharing,
And only to them it is known.

It's hard when the cupboard is empty,
And through the streets the poor men must roam,
And all the week through with nothing to do,
Yet with poor hungry children at home.

[Chorus]
Then pity the unemployed workmen,
Who starve all the week days through,
They don't want to shirk any kind of hard work,
But, alas, they can't get it to do.

The ballad is oddly unspecific, which is not surprising since it precisely reproduces the text of 'Lines on the Unemployed and the Terrible Distress',[69] which Henry Such issued, probably in the 1860s.[70] The 'Copy of Verses' in the Bodleian is annotated 'Purchased in London May 1922', which means that a canny printer achieved a sixty-year run for the piece.

Another printer, this time in Bristol, was still selling 'The Unemployed Ex-Soldier's Appeal' in 1934, with a simple change of title to 'The Unemployed Miner's Appeal'.[71] Apart from adding the words 'No Dole No Relief' at the head, he merely altered at one point 'Ex-Service-Men's' to 'Ex-Miner's' (not quite right, since the men were still miners, even though they were not working).

The worst of times

Coal powered the factories, locomotives and steamships of the Industrial Revolution and became the country's biggest export. Between 1914 and 1918 it also produced £160 million in profit and royalties for shareholders and landowners. Yet between 1921 and April 1926, thanks to short-time working, the average daily pay of a miner fell from 19s. 2d. to 9s. 4d. In 1931 over 400,000 miners were out of work, on an average dole of 32s. a week, subject to means testing (see p. 323). By the following year the 19.9% of the British workforce unemployed included one third of all miners.

Such circumstances help to account for the grovelling nature of some of the printed appeals, and also the sympathy expressed by writers such as Mary Thomason (see Chapter 2, p.69):

A Plea for Unemployed Colliers[72]

With hands in pockets now they stand,
But who would say they were a band
Of lazy men who live on dole?
That were foul slander! On my soul
They'd rather all be getting coal
A thousand times than have the dole!

Miners with lamp, pickaxe and spade,
Of death and danger ne'er afraid,
Oft naked to the skin will slave
Where needs the bravest of the brave.
'Tis wage they'd have, and not the dole,
They long for work with all their soul.

What can they do till trade revives,
They, little kiddies and true wives?
Should foreign foe menace our land,
The colliers then, intrepid band,
As stubborn as their native coal
Would show the greatness of their soul.

Then trades and government combine
While jobs grow fewer in the mine,
To help the men now sick of soul
To supplement the meagre dole;
When times improve (they will at length)
Be sure we'll need the colliers' strength.

Picking for coal on the slag heaps during the Great Depression of the 1930s

The unemployed themselves were not invariably passive: far from it. The Industrial Workers of the World, affectionately known as the IWW or the 'Wobblies', founded in Chicago in 1905, sought to organise the unskilled, and as late as the 1970s still believed in continuing to struggle until 'the workers of the world organise as a class, take possession of the earth and the machinery of production, and abolish the wage system'.[73] So as 'to fan the flames of discontent' the IWW issued in 1908 a song card with just a few items, which later became a book including not only texts but some tunes. My own copy, a reprint of the thirty-fourth edition, published in 1974 at 75 cents, is entitled *Songs of the Workers*.[74]

In Britain, sections of unemployed workers were unwilling to suffer in silence. Out-of-work miners marched from South Wales to London in 1927. Hunger marchers from all over the country converged on the capital in 1922–23, 1932 and 1936. In addition there were local marches in many towns and cities, including Belfast, Birkenhead and Liverpool.[75] William Woodruff recalled: 'Throughout the spring and summer of 1932, there were pitched battles between unemployed workers and the police in London, Manchester, Birkenhead and Glasgow. In Belfast demonstrators had been shot and killed. In Rochdale the army had been called out. Street fights were common.'[76]

In October of that year Woodruff and his friend watched hunger marchers assembling in Blackburn to set off to London, their ranks swelled by a group from Jarrow, which was given tea, and hunks of bread and potato hash, and entertained by a man with a banjo who sang:

> I'm a four loom weaver as many a one knows;
> I've nowt to eat and I've worn out me clothes.
> Me clogs are boath broken and stockings I've none.
> Tha'd scare gie me tuppence for a' I've gotten on.[77]

Still in 1932, Woodruff's father, who had been a tackler, was given the task of breaking up with a sledgehammer the looms which he had tended. 'I watched him destroy his idols – some of them a hundred years old, and thanks to people like him, still in first-class condition. … A hundred years earlier in Lancashire they'd hung people for smashing the first power looms. Now they paid them to do it.'[78]

A Salvation Army soup kitchen providing meals for the unemployed, (John Gorman Collection). Courtesy of the People's History Museum, Manchester

The bitterness and anger of the unemployed found their way into songs such as this, to the tune of 'Marching through Georgia', which refers to the silver jubilee of George V in May 1935:

Hurrah, hurrah, we've had a jubilee;
Hurrah, hurrah, but not for you and me,
Only for King Georgie and the bloody bourgeoisie,
Bringing us war and starvation.[79]

Others sang, to the tune of 'My Bonny Lies Over the Ocean':

We're spending our nights in the dosshouse[80]

We're spending our nights in the dosshouse,
We're spending our days on the street.
We're searching for work but we find none,
We wish we had something to eat.

[Chorus]
Soup, soup, soup, soup, They gave us a big plate of soup.
Soup, soup, soup, soup, They gave us a big plate of soup.
We went and fought for our country,
We went out to bleed and to die.
We thought that our country would help us,
And this was our country's reply.[80]

The song may well have come from America, where Seeger and Reiser attribute it to Maurice Sugar, and print more verses, including this:

> I fell on my knees to my maker;
> I prayed every night to the Lord.
> I swore to be faithful for ever,
> And now I've received my reward.[81]

In Australia a version featured 'a big plate of loop-the-loop' (rhyming slang for soup), and it may well have arrived there thanks to the IWW songbook.[82]

Unemployed marchers, many of them ex-servicemen, prided themselves on swinging along with military precision, and their songs needed suitable rhythms. According to Wal Hannington 'the favourite song of the Scottish contingent was … composed on the road to the tune of the 'Youthful Guardsman':

> From Scotland we are marching, from shipyard, mill and mine,
> Our scarlet banners raise on high, we toilers are in line.
> For victory we'll fight: we'll show the enemy our might.
>
> [Chorus]
> We are the hunger marchers of the proletariat,
> We are the hunger marchers of the proletariat.

'As the lines of the last verse were sung,' he wrote, 'the marchers would all raise their heavy walking sticks in the air, as a mark of defiance against the government. It was a striking sight when hundreds of ash sticks shot above the heads of the marchers as they sang their battle song':

> Now comes the day of reckoning, no longer we'll endure
> Starvation – we will conquer now, our victory is sure.[83]

Another song popular 'amongst all the contingents of marchers' was sung to 'the [unfortunately unspecified] refrain of a military march':

Hunger Marchers of the Proletariat[84]

> Now the unemployed are on the march,
> Marching forward on to London Town,
>
> [Chorus]
> Marching forward on to victory, give us your help, boys,
> We're fighting the battle for you.

Men and women are starving in their homes,
We're their standard bearers on the road.

Millions of workers are starving in revolt,
With our flag of red, we blaze the trail.

With the N.U.W.M. we fight,
As the storm troops of the unemployed.

Victory is certain for our cause,
We call to arms the workers of the land.

'These songs were not only sung on the roads,' added Hannington, 'but in the big halls, at the demonstrations and at impromptu concerts. They always received an enthusiastic response from the workers, and many times the local workers learned the words and sang the songs with the marchers.'[84]

The National Unemployed Workers' Committee Movement was launched in 1921 by three Communists, Percy Hayes, Jack Holt and Wal Hannington. The word 'Committee' was later dropped, and the body became known as the NUWM. Hannington (1896–1966), 'a meticulous organiser, a good platform speaker, and an activist with a flair for publicity',[85] became national organiser, and within a few years claimed 100,000 members in three hundred towns and cities across Britain. Some historians suggest it as probable that the 'membership was half that number and was under 20,000 for most of its [the NUWM's] history'.[86] After a ten-fold decline in the aftermath of the General Strike, numbers rose again thanks to the publicity generated by the marches, the last of which, in 1936, achieved a measure of respectability when C.R. Attlee and Aneurin Bevan addressed its final rally in London, though 'even this success was overshadowed by the publicity attracted by the apolitical Jarrow crusade at the same time, the one hunger march in which the NUWM was not involved'.[87] The movement's last conference took place in 1937; its activities were suspended from the outbreak of war, and it was wound up in 1943.

The *agitprop* flavour of the lyrics quoted by Hannington recurs in the 'Song of the Hunger Marchers',[88] written by Randall Swingler and set by Alan Bush. The sentiments expressed are unexceptionable but the music is ponderous and dirge-like:

Song of the Hunger Marchers[88]

We march from a stricken country, from broken hill and vale,
Where fact'ry yards are empty and the rusty gear for sale.
Our country will not thrive again, our strength is not for use,
The bubble of prosperity has never come to us.

[Chorus]
Then rouse to our tread when you hear us marching by,
For servility is dead and the Means Test too shall die!
Though they think our spirit's broken because we're under fed,
We will stamp the Starvation Government beneath the workers' tread!
Stamp, stamp, stamp,
We will stamp the Starvation Government beneath the workers' tread!

In 1931 Ramsay MacDonald, the first Labour prime minister, abandoned his own party and entered into an alliance with the Tories. After the ensuing election the coalition came to power, calling itself the National Government. It was soon widely known as the 'Starvation Government', when it proceeded to cut unemployment benefit by 10% but to institute a household means test under which all the assets and earnings of members of a family could be assessed in determining the relief given when benefit ran out after twenty-six weeks. For example, a father's dole could be stopped if a son living with him were working, or vice versa. A family could be told to sell a clock or a piano before being considered for benefit, and such intrusions on privacy were particularly resented.

'If somebody had a decent home [and became unemployed],' said a miner from Caerphilly, 'the man from the Means Test came and made a list of what you had. Then you were told to sell a wardrobe this week, some chairs next week, some pictures the week after, until you perhaps only had your bed, two chairs and a table left. Only then would you be able to claim something off the Public Assistance.'[89] To the tune of 'Why are we waiting?', hunger marchers sang: 'Why are we marching?', followed by the emphatic final line of: 'The Reason is the Mean Test.'[90]

In 1934 the Unemployed Assistance Board (UAB) was set up in an effort to prevent the more generous treatment given to the unemployed by Public Assistance Committees in Labour areas. Neville Chamberlain was Chancellor of the Exchequer from 1931 until 1937, when he succeeded Stanley Baldwin as Prime Minister.

Demonstrators in Brighton sang, to the tune of 'The Policeman's Holiday':

Who starves kiddies on the U.A.B.?
Who puts twopence on the workers' tea?
Who wants war because they'd like to see
Swollen profits sweated out of you and me?
Who's laid plans upon conscription bent?
No one but the National Government!

Women marching against the Household Means Test introduced in 1931 by the 'Starvation Government' (Daily Herald Archive) Reproduced by permission of the National Media Museum, Bradford.

That is why the ranks of Labour all united shout:
"Take your cards and beat it, Neville,
Clear out!"[91]

The nose-thumbing, demotic idiom here is close to that of 'Hallelujah, I'm a Bum',[92] one of only a handful of American labour songs to take root on this side of the Atlantic. (Others were 'The Soup Song' (see p. 320) and 'Joe Hill'.[93]) This is the version well known in British left-wing circles from the 1930s until at least the 1960s, when I remember hearing and singing it myself:

Alleluia, I'm a Bum[94]

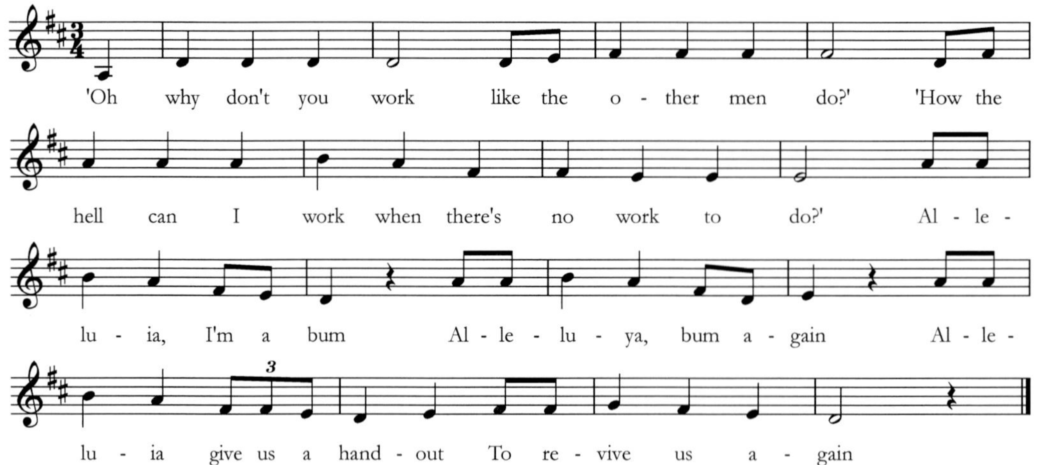

'Oh why don't you work like the other men do?'
'How the hell can I work when there's no work to do?'

[Chorus]
Alleluia, I'm a bum, Alleluia, bum again.
Alleluia, give us a handout, To revive us again.

A lady came out when I knocked at the door:
'You'll get nothing here, for I've seen you before.'

I do love my boss, he's a good pal of mine,
And that's why I'm starving out in the breadline.

'Oh why don't you pray for your daily bread?'
'If that's all I did I should damn soon be dead.'

[Last chorus]
Alleluia, I'm a bum; Alleluia, bum again.
Alleluia, give us a handout, For Christ's sake, amen.

The variant chorus was 'saved to the last in obedience to an artistic recognition of the emotional force of blasphemy'.[95] The song, a parody of the hymn 'Revive Us Again', apparently dates from the late nineteenth century. In 1908 it appeared on the 'Wobbly' song card, and by 1926 had become known in America 'from coast to coast'.[96]

A defiant attitude also comes to the fore in a lively song from Dundee, to the tune of the much parodied 'Bye, Bye, Blackbird', beginning 'We're the lads fae the tap o' the hill, We never worked, we never will, We're on the Bureau'.[97] While they were eligible for benefit the unemployed drew it from the Bureau of Employment, but once it ran out they had to apply to the hated Unemployed Assistance Board, hence the song's conclusion:

> We went down ae Thursday for oor money,
> The cash clerk said, 'Noo, lads, youse think you're funny.
> You're oot o' here, ye see, for noo ye're on the U.A.B.'
> Bureau, bye bye!

From Northern Ireland, equally spirited in its way, comes another song of the 1930s, known as 'The Dream'[98] or

The Labour Boroo[99]

> Last night on my bed as I lay dreaming,
> I dreamt that I stood by the Labour Boroo.
> The clerk he came out and he says,
> 'I am sorry for keeping you so long in the queue.'
> He says, 'Take a seat, for I am sure you are tired,
> Just give me you form and I'll sign it for you,
> And if you feel hungry just call for the waiter.'
> I murmured, 'Good heavens. Is this the Boroo?'

The manager asked, 'Would I have a small brandy?
And we have,' said he, 'whisky and porter and gin,
And if you're teetotal I'll make you a shandy,'
Then he tucked a white serviette under my chin.
'We've cigars, cigarettes, all kinds of tobacco;
Just sit where you are and I'll light one for you,
And if you feel lonesome just switch on the wireless.'
I murmured, 'Good heavens. Is this the Boroo?'

The manager said, 'Will you take notes or silver?
If you haven't enough, just ask for some more!'
I tipped him my hat as I bade him good morning;
Says he, 'There's a taxi for you are the door.'
And when I got home my wife did embrace me,
A thing she's not done for this past fifteen years:
'I don't want your money,' she says, 'you can keep it,
You'll need it for horses,' she said through her tears.

But when I awoke I heard my wife bawling:
'Have you had a nightmare, I've been hearing you scream.
That's all that you're good for, drinking and gambling!'
I murmured, 'Good heavens, 'twas only a dream.'

The reality of Labour Exchanges is described in many accounts of working-class life. John Burnett quotes one man who complained of 'Staff with little or no knowledge of life or work outside the dole office. Their main concern, it seemed, was to cut you down and pay out as little as possible, not even your entitlement, to keep you at arms length by humiliation, by assuming you guilty of wilful idleness before you even opened your mouth.' Several writers mentioned 'physical attacks on clerks by infuriated men whose benefit was cut or disallowed: police were normally on duty inside the Exchange and outside to regulate the queues and to observe the public meetings which the NUWM often called on pay days.'[100]

The experience of the 1930s left a deep mark on the national psyche, expressed in some of the poems of W.H. Auden, the essays of George Orwell, including *The Road to Wigan Pier* (1937), and the novel by Walter Greenwood, *Love on the Dole* (1933), together with much other writing. There were also numerous working-class authors, including lyricists like Mary Thomason (see above) and Harry Whitehead (1890–1966), who spent his entire working life from the age of thirteen until retirement as a mill worker near Oldham. This is his retrospective view of the 1930s:

Hard Times[101]

Yoh munnut come agen hard times;
We thowt those days were done,
When th' dust lay think i' th' jinny-gate [alley],
Where the wheels no longer run;
When th' yed-stocks stood like silent ghosts,
And th' straps and ropes were still;
Where a abeawt 'em seemed to say,
'There's nowt to do i' th' mill.'

Yoh munnut come agen hard times,
For Owdham's had its share,
When th' purse were thin, and times were bad,
And ther' weren't mich to spare;
When nob'dy axed, or seemed to care,
Heaw were its troubles met?
Thoose wounds lie deep, the scars remain,
The folk remember yet.

Yoh munnut come to haunt these streets,
Where once yoh left your mark;
Where care and want together walked,
Wi' thousands eawt o' wark;
Where daycent men, fro' daycent whoams,
Wi' brocken heart an soul,
Went trudgin' deawn that hopeless road,
To th' means test and the dole.

Simply redeployed

When the Second World War began in September 1939 there were still a qurter of a million long-term unemployed men in Britain, with 440,000 dependants. By the end of the war, more or less no one was out of work, and between 1948 and 1966 unemployment averaged only 1.7% of the workforce. As the post-war dream of work for all gradually faded, unemployment rose by fits and starts until in 1986 it stood at 11.2%, or more than three million people.[102]As early as 1966 the new euphemisms for unemployment – redundancy and redeployment – aroused both the anger and the laughter of Bob Cooney, then working in Birmingham. He was an Aberdonian veteran (born 1907) of the International Brigade, which had fought against Franco in the Spanish Civil War. His song 'Simply Redeployed',[103] (tune, 'Tramp, Tramp, Tramp, the Boys are Marching'), which I often heard him sing in the Partisan Folk Club at Birmingham, begins:

Simply Redeployed[103]

I worked at the BMC till the gaffer said to me,
'You've got to go but please don't be annoyed;
You're no longer wanted here but you needn't have a fear:
You're not unemployed, you're simply redeployed.'

Thank you kindly, Mr Wilson, you have made me so content,
For I'm really overjoyed, knowing I'm just redeployed,
But please tell me how to pay the bloody rent.

No, I am not unemployed, I am simply redeployed,
But deployed to where I haven't got a clue,
For at every gate try they refuse to let me by,
Saying, 'Sorry, chum, there's thousands more like you.'

First I tried at BSA but they told me straight away:
'A thousand men we've redeployed you see.
Where they've gone we cannot tell but we really wish them well;
We've advised them all to try the BMC.'

The BMC was the British Motor Corporation, one of the incarnations of British Leyland at Longbridge in Birmingham, the scene of frequent industrial disputes up to the 1970s. Harold Wilson was the Labour Prime Minister from 1964 until 1970 and again from 1974 until 1976.

Among the causes of redeployment was the decline in heavy industry. Between 1966 and 1982, for example, the workforce engaged in metal manufacture declined by a half. At Shotton steelworks in Flintshire (now Clwyd), the workers' campaign to resist the closure proposed in 1973 by the nationalised British Steel Corporation included, in time-honoured fashion, songs. These – 'The Men Who Make the Steel', 'Steel Workers' Dream' and 'Shotton Steel Men' – no longer came in the form of printed ballads but of a 45 rpm record, *Save Shotton!*.[104] This was not available commercially, but I became aware of it thanks to seeing a newspaper article by the MP Ann Clwyd, in which she mentioned that she had come across steelworkers from Shotton selling their record of protest songs during the Welsh National Eisteddfod.

One of the choruses runs: 'To take away the right to earn a decent living wage, The furnaces they'll soon be closing down; The sky no more will glow and six thousand jobs must go, For the men who make the steel in Shotton Town.' 'Like the men who work the coal they too will soon be on the dole,' said another line, but lest the song seem acquiescent, the concluding verse stated 'The steelmen know their cause is right, they won't give up without a fight.'[105]

The campaign achieved a measure of success, in that production continued, and in 1977 the BSC decided to retain and modernise the steelworks at Shotton. However, only two years later the decision was taken to phase out iron- and steelmaking on the site. As a result, 8,000 workers were made redundant. In the meantime, other steelmaking sites had already been shut down.

Ted Edwards lost his job in 1974 when the steelworks at Irlam in Lancashire closed. 'If you can imagine a long shed,' he wrote, 'nearly half a mile long. For sixty years in this shed there's been nothing but noise. There's been furnaces blasting, diesels bombing up and down, clogs clattering, whistles blowing, all manner of noise … then all of a sudden, one day, the entire pitside is quiet.'

The Pitside Is Quiet Today[106]

The ladles are old and they're all growing cold,
And the red it is turnin' to grey.
The roar of the furnace is finished for good,
For today is redundancy day.
The grind of the diesel is over and done,
The drivers have all gone away,
And the cats in the cabins, they don't understand
Why the pitside is quiet today.

For sixty long years in the rumble and roar
Men sweated the night and the day,
A-hammerin' cotters or burnin' the scrap,
Or cleanin' the moulds on the bay.
The clogs were a-clatterin' over the stage,
The whistles were blowin' away,
But you don't have to shout to be heard any more,
'Cause the pitside is quiet today.

There's been laughin' and cryin' and thrutchin' [messing] about,
And words that were better unsaid,
And now everywhere you can feel on the air
The ghosts of the livin' and dead.
Tomorrow the burners and wreckers'll come
To take all the metal away,
And there's some that are glad but we're all a bit sad
That the pitside is quiet today.

The steel strike of 1980 (see also Chapter 7, p. 272) was directed at securing a pay increase and at stopping the government's programme of closures. In one town the movement to defend employment went well beyond the steelworkers themselves, and led to the formation of a pressure group, the Campaign for the Retention of Steelmaking at Corby. This enlisted the support of the Banner Theatre in Birmingham, which responded with *Steel! A Show about the Steel Industry in the Words of Steelmakers Themselves.* The production included songs, one of which began: 'The people of Corby Town are all out and marching. The pitside is quiet, there'll be no work today; The roadway is crammed with workers, marching with banners blazing: "Save steel and save Corby, that's what they say".'[107] Another song started:

Come all you steel workers who use your strength and skill
To work the white hot metal in the pitside and the mill,

I'll tell you of our industry and the struggle to survive,
And the fight to save the Corby works and keep the town alive.

[Chorus]
We've the power to crush the ore and make the furnace glow,
We've the skill to teem it right and keep the steel on flow.
We can forge it round or cast it square,
Roll it out fine as a human hair:
Steel for industry, to make the world go round.[108]

Ian MacGregor (see Chapter 7, p. 271) became chairman of the BSC in 1980, the Conservative government having paid, to use soccer terminology, a transfer fee of £1.8 million to buy him from Lazard Brothers in America. Within three years he had reduced the workforce from 166,000 to 71,000 without loss of overall productivity, thus preparing the industry for the privatisation which followed in due course. Meanwhile, the 85,000 workers displaced potentially became unemployed, the costs of which were to be borne by the taxpaying public. Although MacGregor then became chairman of the National Coal Board, steel closures continued.

In January 1986 a group of steelworkers from Gartcosh, near Glasgow, spent ten days on a march to London through snow, strong winds and freezing rain. They carried a petition asking for the reversal of the decision to close their rolling mill. In the style of the hunger marchers of half a century earlier, they sang on the way: 'The Braes of Killiecrankie' and their own composition, 'The Gartcosh Commandos', which had this chorus, referring to their shop steward, Tommy Brennan:

We're the Gartcosh commandos, we're doon from old Gartcosh,
We haven't got a gaffer, wee Tommy is the boss;
And we'll cause the biggest rally you ever come across;
Just remember we're the Gartcosh commandos.[109]

Although a Scottish Tory MP welcomed the marchers to the House of Commons, the Prime Minister, Margaret Thatcher, announced that she saw 'no purpose' in meeting them. The closure went ahead, and the 700 workers were obliged to seek redeployment or redundancy.

'Coal, not dole' was the main slogan of the miners during their epic strike of 1984–85, the defeat of which was followed by the ruthless contraction of the industry (see below, and also p. 284). One traditional song expressed the pain of a man excluded from pit work as being too old ('I am an old miner, aged fifty and six, If I could get lots, I would raffle my picks, I'd raffle them, sell them, I'd give them away, I can't get employment, for my hair it's turned grey'[110]).

How much more painful was the extinction of mining itself, together with its cultures and communities. Pits had always been abandoned when they were deemed to be exhausted. The Montague Colliery at East Walbottle, to the west of Newcastle-upon-Tyne (after operating since 1750), was deemed to be unviable by the NCB and closed in 1959 during an alleged rationalisation of mining, even though it seemed to pitmen that plenty of workable coal remained. Johnny Handle, who at the time was a surveyor in the pit, wrote a wryly affectionate valediction when a campaign to save it failed.

Farewell to the Monty[111]

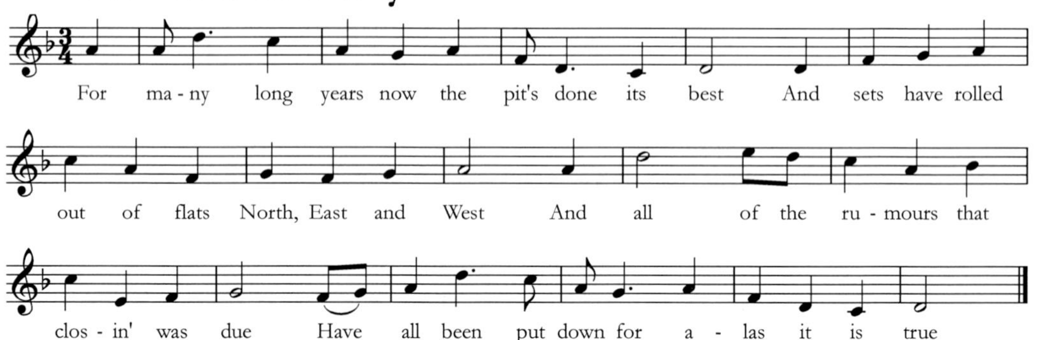

For many long years now the pit's done its best
And sets have rolled out of flats north, east and west,
And all of the rumours that closin' was due
Have all been put down for alas it is true.

A meeting was held to discuss the affair
And the manager said to us, right then and there,
'We'll have one last go before this pit is done
To show a good profit on each single ton'.

But though profits were made, though the stock's pilin' high
The Coal Board decided the pit has to die,
And as output gans doon we get transferred away
Te pits te the south for the rest of wer days.

A've filled in the Fan Pit, a've cut in the Seam,
In the Newbiggin Beaumont since aa wes fifteen.
A've worked at the Sections and in the Main Coal.
It's hot doon the Monty, she's a dorty black hole.

So farewell te ye Monty and aa knaa ye roads well,
And ye work it's been good and yer work it's been hell.
Ne mair te yer dorty owld heap will aa come
For yer workin' is finished, and yer life it is done.

There was sadness in another farewell, anger in another, both of them in 1965. 'The Albert Pit at Abram, near Wigan, ... had retained much of the atmosphere of the old family pits, common in this area before the days of nationalisation,' wrote Keith Roberts, whose song is entitled 'Lament for Albert':

Owd Albert's gone; His days are done;
His gates are shuttered fast. He lies in peace,
Through summers warm, And winter's storm,
There's no one to disturb his blackened sleep.[112]

When Harraton Colliery in County Durham closed, 366 years of mining there came to an end. The pit was known as 'Cotia, a contraction of the nickname Nova Scotia, from a time when many Scotsmen worked there. Jock Purdon worked there as a deputy, having come into mining as a Bevin Boy during the Second World War. He commented: 'Aa knew the pit was closin' and that a lot of lads would be movin' away to pits down south, so ah wrote "Farewell to 'Cotia" for them, and put it up in the pit head baths.'[113]

In fact, the 'Cotia men who remained in the industry, including Purdon himself, moved to Dawdon or Vane Tempest on the coast, but many from the North-East did go to Nottinghamshire, Staffordshire, South Yorkshire or South Wales. The singing of the song, which went to the tune of 'Tramps and Hawkers', came to be a kind of ceremony at the farewell parties when a group of colliers were being transferred from the north-east to the Midlands or South Wales: [114]

Farewell to 'Cotia[115]

Ye brave bold men of 'Cotia the day is drawing near,
Ye'll have to change your lodgings, lads,
you'll have to change your beer,
But leave your picks behind you, you'll ne'er need them again:
Off you go to Nottingham, join Robens' merry men.

Ye brave bold men of ’Cotia, the day is drawing near,
You’ll have to change your language, lads,
you’ll have to change wha cheer,
But leave your picks behind you, you’ll ne’er need them again:
Off you go to Nottingham, join Robens’ merry men.

Ye brave bold men of ’Cotia, the day is drawing thus,
You’ll have to change your banner, boys, and join the exodus,
But leave your cares behind you, your future has been planned:
Off you go to Nottingham, Lord Robens’ promised land.

Ye brave bold men of ’Cotia to you I say farewell,
And maybe someone will someday the ’Cotia story tell,
But leave it all behind you, the death knell has been tolled:
’Cotia was a colliery, her men were stout and bold.

Ye brave bold men of ’Cotia, the time is drawing thus,
You’ll have to change your banner, lads, and join the exodus,
But leave your cares behind you, your future has been planned,
And off you go to Nottingham, to Robens’ Promised Land.[115]

Alfred (later Lord) Robens presided over a whole series of pit closures, as chairman of the NCB.

As late as the 1990s, song writers were still campaigning in defence of individual pits. In 1993 women of the North Staffordshire Miners’ Wives Action group occupied the pithead of Trentham Colliery. A play on the event by Peter Cheeseman, with songs by Dave Rogers, was staged at the New Victoria Theatre in Stoke-on-Trent.[116]

The previous year John Tams expressed his own anger and bitterness at the treatment of the miners in a song loosely based on the experience of his grandfather:

Harry Stone (Hearts of Coal)[117]

Harry Stone was a miner born,
He worked to win his wages.
Riding down the cages
And raging at the seams,
He worked his stall from dusk till dawn,
Sweet sweat and raw endeavour,
Black diamonds bound together
By a strong and simple means.

He met a girl from Ironville;
He promised he would love her,
Put no one above her.
At last they went to town;
He promised he would love her
Till the blackbirds stopped their singing,
The mission bell stopped ringing,
And they closed the coal pit down.

[Chorus]
Where are you tonight now we need you?
Left out in the cold, cold.
Where are you tonight now we need you?
They broke the hearts of coal,
Hearts of coal.

They raised their children chapel-proud,
The lamb and the flag to guide them.
They each strove to provide them
With a sense of right from wrong;
And when the strikes and lock-outs came,
And barefoot hunger tried them,
All hopes were denied them,
Their unity held strong.

Forty years of coaldust
Is a lot of pain to carry;
It made a cripple out of Harry,
But his family came and took up his tools,
And they faced the Orgreave cavalry.
While the world looked on and wondered,
Their right to work was plundered
By the statesmanship of fools.

The 'Enemy Within', they cried,
And the bony finger pointed,
Dripping gold from the anointed
At the beggar and her bowl;
And just like the union said he would,
The axeman came in dancing:
His psychopathic prancing
Chopped out the hearts of coal.

He promised he would love her
Till the blackbirds stopped their singing,
The mission bell stopped ringing,
And they closed the coal pit down.

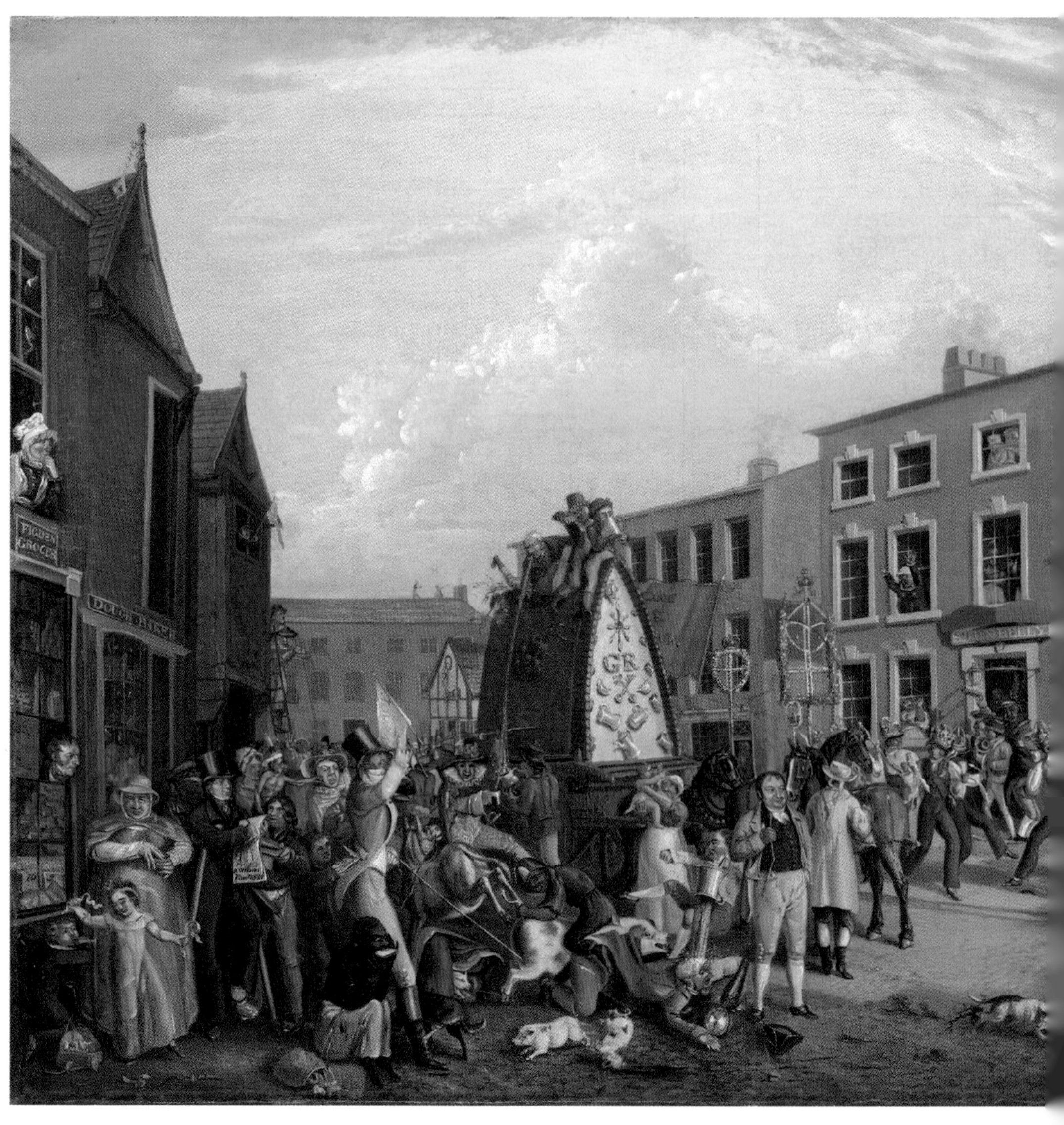

'Rushbearing', oil painting (1821) by Alexander Wilson (1803-1846). The rushcart is shown in Long Millgate, Manchester, as it passes the Manchester Arms public house. Wilson, who was both an artist and a song writer, has depicted himself (left) with crutches and bandaged foot. Private Collection

9 Time to spare

The right to be lazy

The right to work was first enshrined in law in 1793 by the French revolutionary government in Paris. It remained an aspiration in the Europe-wide revolutions of 1848 and a hundred years later it featured in the United Nations' Declaration of Human Rights. Yet what of the right not to work: that is, to have leisure, to play, or simply to refrain for working at all? The socialist Paul Lafargue (1842–1911) famously argued for *Le Droit à la Paresse* in an article of 1880, translated into English three years later as *The Right to be Lazy,* and still in print. He 'practised what he preached', tartly commented Tristram Hunt, referring to Lafargue's habit, after the death of his father-in-law, Karl Marx, of frequently appealing to Frederick Engels for money.[1]

The Labour Movement fought long and often bitter campaigns, backed by both industrial and political action, not only to foster and safeguard employment, but also to decrease the working day and the working week, and to institute, then expand paid holidays. Alongside formally organised trade union and political activity there were traditional ways of resisting discipline imposed by others, and of retaining a measure of control over patterns of work and leisure. Shropshire miners took a holiday called a Gaudy Day or a Cuckoo Morning, signalled by hearing the first cuckoo in spring. Blacksmiths on St Clement's Day exploded some gunpowder on their anvils, and then took the day off. They also resolutely refused to work on a Good Friday, as did Derbyshire lead miners. Keeping up Saint Monday, that is, not working on a Monday, was a significant tradition. Charles Shaw of Tunstall in Staffordshire, referring to the 1850s, described 'This saint [as] the most beneficent patron the poor pottery children ever knew'.[2] To the fury of foremen and managers, factory and pit owners, workers took unofficial holidays for fairs and wakes, and even on occasion simply when they felt like it. When miners in the newly-nationalised pits of the late 1940s were reproached for absenteeism by an exasperated manager and asked why they only worked four shifts a week (out of the five possible), they replied: 'Because we can't live on three.'[3] Such an attitude – essentially, that work was a means of sustaining life rather than the purpose of life – would not have been out of place before the Industrial Revolution.

Saint Monday

George Davis (1768–1819) was born in Birmingham to 'miserably poor' parents. Thanks to a benefactor he attended the grammar school in New Street for four years before becoming an apprentice printer at the age of fourteen. His mother died before he became a journeyman, and soon after he did, his father also died. On the day in 1792 fixed for their wedding his intended wife died, too, and in despair he took to drink, eking out a living as a writer and seller of ballads before spending his last years in the workhouse.[4] It is ironic that he had reproved topers in an Augustan-style poem, *Saint Monday; or, Scenes from Low-Life*, published in 1790:

Saint Monday[5]

When, in due course, SAINT MONDAY wakes the day,
Off to a *Purl-house* straight they haste away;
Or, at a *Gin-shop*, ruin's beaten road,
Offer libations to the tippling God:
And, whilst the gen'rous liquor damps their clay,
Form various plans for saunt'ring out the day. . . .
Perhaps at work they transitory peep,
But *vice* and *lathe* are soon consign'd to sleep;
The shop is left untenanted awhile,
And a cessation is proclaim'd from toil.

'Purl', a mixture of hot ale and sugar, with added wormwood, was a favourite morning drink. 'Clay' indicates a clay pipe.

The devotees of Saint Monday, Davis tells us, spend the day in eating and drinking, some of them in playing at marbles, quoits or 'five-balls'. In the evening they frequent the theatre for an opera or a play, or go to a 'free and easy' for 'song and sentiment' (and also drink), or even 'By mad intoxication led away, In a vile brothel . . . complete the day'. Celebrations might continue beyond the Monday:

Doubtless you know the *Fox* in *Castle-street*; –
There all the scum of creation meet;
For days together at the liquor stick,
And keep ST MONDAY up for a whole week.
Hawkers and *Ballad-singers* here repair,
Sworn foes to dull sobriety and care;
And, yielding to tumultuous noise the sway
Guzzle an hundred gallons in a day.[6]

On his title page, Davis, who well knew that keeping up St Monday had a long history, quoted from an 'old ballad':

> Of all the *red-letter-days*, which th' almanack teaches
> Should rigidly be kept by man in sackcloth and ashes,
> Not one of them all, whether *Saint's-day* or *Sunday*,
> Is half so well attended to, as that great day – ST. MONDAY.

In Sheffield, cutlers loyally honoured the saint, though their wives sometimes objected. According to tradition, a lively song, 'The Jovial Cutlers', was written in 1780 to the tune of 'Cease, rude Boreas' by an old cutler nicknamed 'Boneheft', after the bone-handled knives he made. It features an indignant wife who interrupts men who have settled down in the workshop to a non-working session:

The Jovial Cutlers[7]

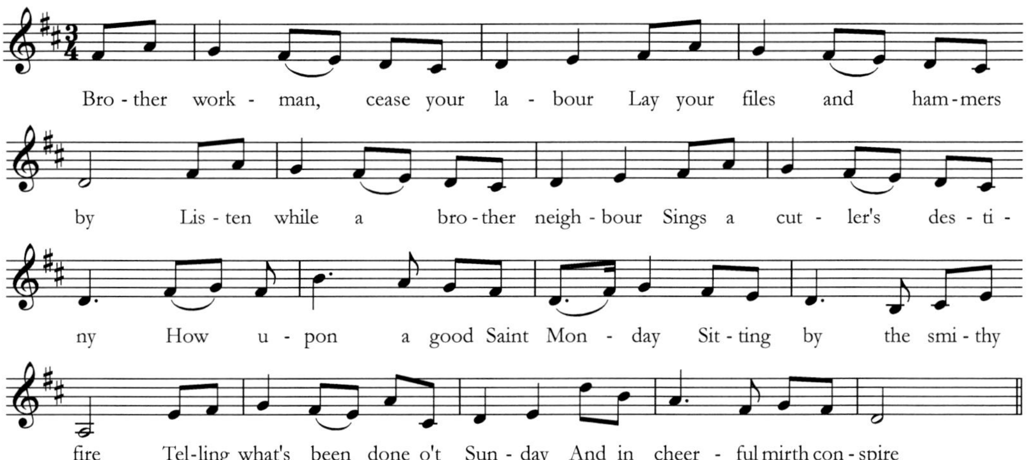

> Brother workmen, cease your labour, Lay your files and hammers by;
> Listen while a brother neighbour sings a cutler's destiny.
> How upon a good Saint Monday, sitting by the smithy fire,
> Telling what's been done o't Sunday, and in cheerful mirth conspire.
>
> Soon I hear the trap-door rise up, on the ladder stands my wife:
> 'Damn thee, Jack, I'll dust thy eyes up, thou leads a plaguy drunken life;
> Here thou sits instead of working, wi' thy pitcher on thy knee;
> Curse thee, thou'd be always lurking, and I may slave myself for thee.'

The wife then complains that her clothes are in a poor state ('See thee, look what stays I've gotten, See thee, what a pair o' shoes; Gown and petticoat half rotten, Ne'er a whole stitch in my hose'), and in a fury seizes her husband's beer and throws it all over him, announcing: ''Od burn thee, Jack, forsake thy barrel, Or never more thou'st lie with me.' She then presumably sweeps out, leaving her husband to reflect:

For her foul tongue, Oh! fie upon her,
Shall we our pleasures thus give o'er?
No! we will good Saint Monday honour,
When brawling wives shall be no more.

Marital discord over a husband's drinking during time taken from his work also features in a song widely printed as a street ballad during the early nineteenth century. To a man's complaint at the discomfort he experiences in the house on washing day, a woman responds, using the same tune, 'Nae luck about the house', with:

The Fuddling Day; Or, Saint Monday[8]

Each Monday morn before I rise, I make a fervent prayer,
Unto the Gods my Husband might, from tip[p]ling keep quite clear,
But, Oh! when I his breakfast take, to shop without delay,
What anguish do I feel to hear, it is a Fuddling day.

[Chorus]
For 'tis drink, drunk, smoke, smoke, drink, drink away,
There is no pleasure in the house, upon a Fuddling day.

St Monday brings more ills about for when the money's spent,
The children's clothes go up the spout, which causes discontent,
And when at night he staggers home, he knows not what to say,
A fool is more a man than he, upon a Fuddling day.

My husband is a workman good, no man can be more civil,
Except upon a Fuddling day, and then he is a devil,
For should I thwart his humour then, the claret's sure to fly,
And I have cause to dread his look, upon a Fuddling day.

A friend of mine came in one day, 'twas cold and foggy weather,
'To comfort you,' says she, 'we'll have a drop of max [gin] together.'
My husband came in at the time, I knew not what to say,
But she'll not come again I'm sure, upon a Fuddling day.

E.P. Thompson, who was prominent in the rediscovery of Saint Monday, observed that it 'appears to have been honoured almost universally wherever small-scale, domestic, and out-work industries existed; was generally found in the pits; and sometimes continued in manufacturing and heavy industry'.[9] The strongholds of Saint Monday were in London, the West Midlands and Sheffield, and the custom lingered in many parts of the country until the third quarter of the nineteenth century.

Handloom carpet weavers at Kidderminster in Worcestershire insisted on making Monday a day of leisure. 'Entertainments were frequently on a Monday, as were many trade union and political (particularly Chartist) meetings. Even after [the strike of] 1828, when wages had fallen and demand for labour was depressed, the practice of keeping St Monday continued. Despite their poverty the weavers carried out the custom, partly to assert their independent artisan status.'[10]

Even though it sometimes meant their working from three in the morning till ten at night to catch up, the men stubbornly clung to the custom. Charles Walters of Birmingham, a small manufacturer of wood screws, complained in 1832: 'Sunday appears to indispose the people on Monday, being a sort of Saint Holiday – among the working classes of the town Thursday generally arrives before all are capable of moving on – one day is a day of exertions, Friday and the quantity set is exceeded – some steady ones approximate daily.'[11]

Still in Birmingham, it was customary in the 1850s for men to play cricket on Monday afternoons in fine weather, and devotion to Saint Monday waned only in the following decade, with the introduction of half-day working on Saturdays.[12] Again during the 1850s, in parts of Lancashire large numbers of miners were idle on Mondays, and Saint Monday was kept up, largely by hewers, into the twentieth century. According to a report of 1872 from the Forest of Dean:

> The mouth of every [pit] manager is full of complaints respecting the irregularity of the men, and the repeated advances of 10 per cent. that have been conceded during the last few months, so far from promoting the industry and comfort of the miners, for whereas they used to be satisfied with "Saint Mondays", Tuesday and Wednesday are now habitually canonised.[13]

Fairs and Wakes

With mediaeval origins, fairs (originally for buying and selling) and wakes (originally church celebrations) attracted various forms of entertainment, which eventually came to predominate. They were undoubtedly one of the high points of the year, eagerly awaited and avidly enjoyed. They often drew large crowds of industrial workers to small places, and in the end many were suppressed not for lack of custom but because they were deemed too popular. The authorities complained of drunkenness, disorder and immorality, and they clearly were uncomfortable that workers should assert their right to be lazy.

The impulsion to attend wakes was so strong that even Josiah Wedgwood, who was committed to a disciplined system of production in his pottery, had to give ground. In the summer of 1776 he despairingly wrote: 'Our men have been at play 4 days this week, it being Burslem Wakes. I have rough'd, & smooth'd them over, & promis'd them a long Xmas [on which they, incidentally, were not keen], but I know it is all in vain, for Wakes must be observ'd though the World was to end with them.'[14]

Joseph Hatherton, an underlooker during the 1840s at Messrs Fosters' mill at Ringley Bridge in Lancashire, was even more unhappy with his workers:

> They have a fortnight at Christmas, a full week at Whitsuntide, three or four days at Ringley Wakes, about the same time at Ratcliff [Radcliffe] Wakes, and at odd times besides. The wages are paid every fortnight; and they are never expected to come on the Monday after pay ... and when they come on a Tuesday they are not fit for their work. Christmas and New Year's-Day are universal holidays in the district, and generally the wakes and feasts of the different villages, and the races in their respective neighbourhoods – for example, at Worsley, Eccles Wakes, at St Helen's and Haydock, the Newton Races, the Manchester Races also, which occur during Whitsuntide, attract an immense number of colliers from Clifton, Bolton, Leigh, Outwood, Middleton, Worsley and the whole surrounding district.[15]

Robert Poole, while noting the connection 'between a prosperous craft-based economy and a strong attachment to customary leisure', pointed out that 'in Lancashire, where the factory system developed so early and so intensively, the wakes developed into a mass industrial holiday faster and farther than anywhere else in the country'. He added: 'It might, then,

The Wakes fair at Shaw near Oldham. The roundabouts and funfair are set up in the shadow of the mill in the background.

broadly be argued that the county's early and rapid industrialisation tended not so much to obliterate the customary holiday as to incorporate it within the new order.'[16]

The fun of the fair – and of hoppings, feasts and wakes – provided ideal subject matter for ballad sheets, which were no doubt hawked to the crowds, which attended. The 'hopping' at Winlaton, just outside Newcastle-upon-Tyne, was celebrated in 1813 by a local man, John Leonard, and subsequently printed by John Marshall:

> You sons of glee, come list to me,
> You who love mirth and toping, O,
> You'll ne'er refuse to hear the muse
> Sing of Winlaton fam'd hopping, O.
> To Tenche's Hotel let's retire,
> To tipple away so neatly, O;
> The fiddle and song you'll sure admire,
> Together they sound so sweetly, O.
> Fal de dal la, fal the dal la,fal the dal the didee, O,
> Fal the dal la, fal the dal la,fal the dal the didee, O.

Although there were 'spice and nuts' to eat, 'toys for girls and boys' to buy, and roundabouts to sample, the main entertainments were singing, dancing and drinking:

Winlanton Hopping[17]

The night came on, with dance and song, each public house did jingle, O;
All ranks did swear to banish care, the married and the single, O;
They tript away till morning light, then slept sound without rocking, O;
Next day got drunk in merry plight, and jaw'd about the hopping, O.

A sheet issued by John Pitts in London between 1802–1819 (and reprinted by Fortey between 1858 and 1885) runs through the sort of people who attended the Whitsun Fair at Greenwich: jolly tars, flashy girls, journeymen, undertakers, shipwrights, fops, beaus, a barber, captains, watermen, women, children, servant girls and prentice boys:

Coachmen, carmen, stabling grooms,
And weavers too [who] had left their looms ...

It also lists the food and drink available to them: nuts and gingerbread, rolls and polonies, sausages, beef and ham, gin, strong and small beer. It concludes with a comment frequent on such sheets:

And some in nine months I declare,
Will see the fruits of Greenwich fair.[18]

'Mottram Wakes'[19] was written in about 1817 by a spinner from Stalybridge called Samuel Cottrell (1799–1837), who also played and taught the violin. The tune, one assumes, must have been 'Kelvin Grove'.

Mottram Wakes[19]

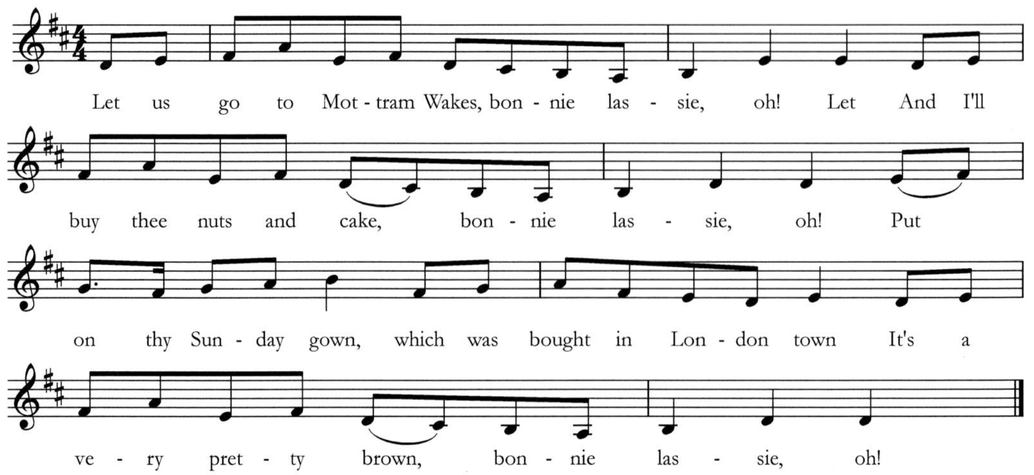

Let us go to Mottram Wakes, Bonnie lassie, oh!
And I'll buy thee nuts and cake, Bonnie lassie, oh!
Put on thy Sunday gown, which was bought in London town:
It's a very pretty brown, Bonnie lassie, oh!

The attractions proposed are 'a foaming gill', 'the standings all in rows', 'the shows', including 'Mr Punch and his big nose'; and then a tour of the churchyard to 'See the verses on th' tombstone', followed by dancing at the 'church-steel' (? stile). Finally:

When the church-bells they do ring, Bonnie lassie, oh!
And the jolly boys do sing, Bonnie lassie, oh!
Some fighting there will be, just to finish up the spree,
It's a jolly sight to see, Bonnie lassie, oh!

There is a very similar approach in 'A New Song, or A Visit to Knott Mill Fair',[20] which indicates as melody 'The Cork Leg' (written by Jonathan Blewitt or Blewett in c. 1835). The ballad describes a day out by people from 'Ashton', which could have been either Ashton upon Mersey – the visitors, who travel by train, describe themselves as 'country Johnnies' – or Ashton-under-Lyne. Knott Mill Fair was held from 1823 at an open space in Manchester known as Campfield, near Deansgate. The sheet describes stands of toys for sale, 'flying boxes', plentiful eating and drinking, and among the shows, that of George Wombwell (1778–1850):

A Visit to Knott Mill Fair[20]

First Wombwell, with his brazen band,
Had taken up the western stand,
And when that band began to play,
All other music died away.

His canvass [sic] pictures spreading far,
Like sails upon a man-of-war,
To tell what ne'er has been denied,
What living wonders are inside

There wax-work figures catch the eye,
And "Walk in, gents," was all their cry,
While pictures on the outside tell,
How Nelson at Trafalgar fell.

Ballads on wakes normally confine themselves to celebrating the joys of the occasion, but here a sequence describes the sort of political argument which may well have featured on such occasions. In response to a pub landlord's complaint that 'the whole British nation, Is in a state of pure starvation', an interlocutor praises 'the Anti-Corn Law League', remarking 'if their point they could obtain, Things would go all right again'. The landlord, expressing a widely held view that the repeal of the Corn Laws would not benefit the working class, replies:

> Give folks good wage, 'tis all they want,
> And not your Anti-Corn Law cant;
> And when in Peter Street I call,
> I'll s**t upon their Free Trade Hall.

The Free Trade Hall was erected in 1843, and the Corn Laws repealed in 1846, which neatly dates the ballad. Its narrator at one point marvels at the 'Oysters, Nuts and Cakes' on sale, which, he muses, are 'Enow to furnish Ashton Wakes'.

During the 1840s Isaac Cottrill, chief constable of Newcastle-under-Lyne in the Potteries, was anxious to promote the wakes because he believed they would provide a counter-attraction to Chartism. Under a charter of 1590 the wakes were held on 1 September (St Giles's Day) until 1753 when, perhaps because of the change in the calendar, they moved to the Monday on or after 11 September.

A specially written (and rather laboured and self-conscious) song of 1841 sought to whip up enthusiasm:

Newcastle Wakes[21]

> To Newcastle Wakes let's go! Let's go!
> To Newcastle Wakes let's go!
> For fun and cakes, the best of Wakes,
> As every one shall know.
>
> To our Town Field then we will repair,
> Where our Fathers drank their wassail,
> And proclaimed the Charter of the wakes,
> The Birthright of Newcastle.
>
> [Chorus]
> Then to Newcastle Wakes, &c.

Cottrill's drunkenness led to his being dismissed in 1849, though the wakes continued, and were listed in the local council's year book until 1951.

Other towns were less fortunate in maintaining such events.

'Eccles was long celebrated for its wakes and its cakes', wrote Alfred Burton in 1891.[22] The elaborate wake, which attracted workfolk in large numbers, including from Manchester, four miles to the east, started on the first Sunday in September, and continued for three more days. A handbill set out the programme for 1830, which included three days of bull-baiting, cock-fighting and foot-racing, starting on a Monday. A race in which women competed for a smock was a particular attraction on the Wednesday, and the wake ended with 'a fiddling match, by all the fiddlers that attend, for a piece of silver.[23]

> ECCLES WAKE. – On Monday morning, at eleven o'clock, the sports will commence with the most ancient, loyal, rational, constitutional, and lawful diversion, BULL-BAITING, in all its primitive excellence, for which this place has long been noted. At one o'clock there will be a foot-race; at two o'clock, a bull-baiting, for a horse-collar; at four, donkey-races, for a pair of panniers; at five, a race for a stuff hat; the day's sport to conclude with baiting the bull 'Fury', for a superior dog-chain. The animal is of gigantic strength and wonderful ability, and it is requested that the Fancy will bring their choice dogs on this occasion. The bull-ring will be stumped and railed round with English oak, so that
>
> The timid, the weak, the strong,
> The bold, the brave, the young,
> The old, friend, and stranger,
> Will be secure from danger.
>
> On Tuesday the sports will be repeated; also, on Wednesday, with the additional attraction of a smock-race by the ladies. A main of cocks to be fought on Monday, Tuesday and Wednesday, for twenty guineas, and five guineas the byes, between the gentlemen of Manchester and Eccles. The wake to conclude with a fiddling match, by all the fiddlers that attend, for a piece of silver.[24]

A big oil painting of 1808 by Joseph Parry, now in Manchester Art Gallery, shows the scene. A church and the 'Old Original Red Lion' provide a background against which bull baiting is taking place. Single-stick fights are in progress, and a prize-fighting ring is shown. A man races on a donkey. Women prepare to run for a smock or shift, laced and ribboned, which is prominently displayed, hanging from a frame. Morris dancers also feature and, inevitably, a man selling Eccles cakes.[24]

Some of these activities are reflected in a ballad sheet printed between 1834 and 1841 by William Ford of Sheffield. The shape of the verses, with their short sixth line, seems to point to the tune of 'John O' Greenfield' (for which, see p. 85).

Photograph of workers ready to go on the annual Wakes week holiday.

Eccles Wakes[25]

In August last, it being holiday time,
And being myself a young lad in my prime,
To see Eccles wakes it was my intent,
So I dressed in my best and away then I went,
With Ned & a few men, & Robert the ploughman,
And Sally, and Ally, and Moll.

Each had hugged his lass as we passed along,
And when we came there it was a wonderful throng
There were some buying Eccles, some Banbury cakes
For the lasses and lads that attend at the wakes,
For Ned treated Sally, and Bob treated Ally,
And I bought a Banbury for Moll.

Your fine dress work folk from Manchester town,
They strutted as if all the wake was their own;
Putters-out and warpers, yet [yes] cutters and all,
Dressed like master & dame, jeered both me & Moll,
I ne'er saw their fellows in spreading their umbrellas
Ere rain from the elements fall.

There were filberts as large as the eggs of our poot, [? pullet]
And gingerbread jannock [oatbread] as big as my foot,
We eat and we crack'd, and did both stuff and eat,
Till I thought we should burst 'twas so good and so sweet,
Thus me and my love ranged all the wake over,
Partaking of all in the street.

The bellart [bullward] ere long tied the bull to the stake,
The dogs were set on, some pastime to make,
He jostled about gave a terrible roar,
Tossed the dogs in the air, and the folks tumbled o'er.
Such shouting and bawling, such pushing and hauling,
I ne'er in my days saw before.

Mrs. Rice in the dirt spoiled her muslin gown,
Mrs. Warpingmill had her new petticoat torn,
Their spouses (poor creatures) in quitting the mob,
Had their coats torn to spencers [jackets] robbed Stitch of a job,
Rent aprons and shawls which they got in their falls,
Made many poor wenches to sob.

But too my good folks the fun ended not here,
A Banbury merchant attended the fair,
Crying buy now or toss – the bull chanced him to spy,
Gave his basket a toss, but chose not to buy,
I thought to the wakes they were coming with cakes
Confectioners down from the sky.

Next followed the race for the leathern prize,
Tits [nags] entered the field amidst bustle and noise,
Now Dobbin, now Short, now Ball was the cry,
Though Dobbin beat Short, Ball passed both by,
Disputing who won, to fighting they ran,
And the winner came off with black eyes.

When racing and betting were both at an end,
To a [public] house each went, with his sweetheart or friend,
Some went to Shaw's, others Philip's chose,
But me and my Moll to the Hare and Hounds goes,
With music and cakes to finish the wakes,
Among wenches and country beaux.

When morning approached, quite willing and glad,
I went with my Moll to her mammy and dad,
Unwilling to part with my joy and delight.
I gave her a ball [?] and then bade her goodnight,
What before we'd been doing, you're not to be knowing,
But time will bring all things to light.

There were wakes in the Lake District, and in the Lancashire textile district. 'Almost everywhere the parish church anniversary, the summer "rushbearing" or "wakes", formed the climax of the recreational year.'[26] Of associated songs only one, 'Droylsden Wakes', seems to have lasted long in oral tradition. The earliest printed text, under the title of 'The Greenside Wakes'[27] (after an area of Droylsden) dates from 1857, and is pretty much in standard English. In 1859 a local historian, John Higson, gave what he considered to be 'the original idiomatic and more spirited version', dating from the second half of the eighteenth century, and beginning:

It's Dreighlsdin wakes, un we're commin to teawn,
To tell yo' o' somethin' o' great reneawn;
Un iv this owd jade ull lemmi begin,
Aw'l show yo heaw hard un heaw fast aw con spin.
[Chorus]
So it's threedyweel, threedywell, dan, don, dill, doe.[28]

Then in 1908 the Lancashire folk song collector and scholar, Anne Gilchrist (1863–1954), noted from J. Allan Bates of Prestwich the version which he had heard in Droylsden in 1844 and subsequently. He could remember no more words, but referred her to Higson for three more verses and also the explanation that two men dressed as women sat on a cart, singing the song, spinning and collecting money from bystanders.[29] (The female dress may have been because spinners were often women.)

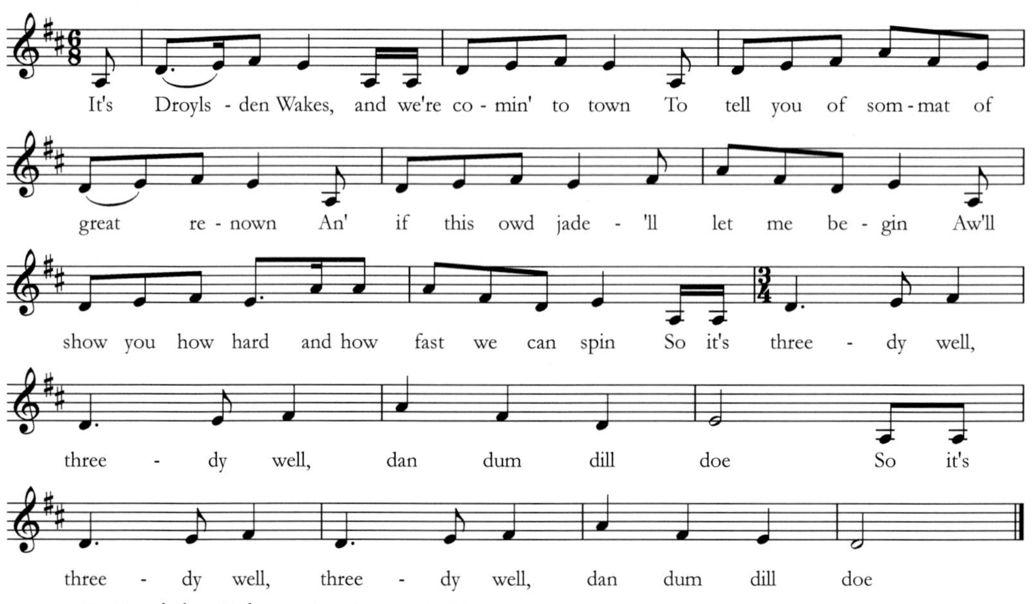

It's Droylsden Wakes, an' we're comin' to town,
To tell you of sommat of great renown;
An' if this owd jade'll let me begin,
Aw'll show you how hard an' how fast we can spin.

[Chorus]
So it's threedy well, threedy well, dan dum dill doe,
So it's threedy well, threedy well, dan dum dill doe.

Woman:
Thou brags of thyself, but aw dunno' think it's true,
For aw will uphold thee, thy faults aren't a few,
For when thou has spun, an' spun very hard,
Of this aw'm well sure, thy work is ill-marred.

Man:
Thou saucy owd jade, thou'd best howd thy tongue,
Or else aw'll be thumpin' thee ere it be long,
An' if 'at aw do, thou'rt sure for to rue,
For aw can ha' mony a one's good as you.

Woman:
What is it to me who you can have?
Aw shanno' be long ere aw'm laid i' my grave,
An' when 'at aw'm dead, an' ha' done what aw can,
You may find one 'at'll spin as hard as aw've done.

Sowerby Bridge Rushcart procession, the first weekend in September. The tradition was revived in the '70s and has now become an event for the whole community. Photo courtesy of Chris Coe

The Lord's Day Observance Society, founded in 1831, campaigned against secular activities on Sundays. The Society for the Prevention of Cruelty to Animals, established in 1824 and becoming the RSPCA in 1840, objected to blood sports. The churches reproved what they saw as immorality and excess. It is clear that in addition to religious and moral concerns the urge to control was strong, as with employers concerned at workers' escape from industrial discipline, their assertion of independence, and their gathering in large and confident numbers. One commentator on the Black Country wrote in 1863:

> A wake, a fair, or a race empties the pits of all but the steadiest hands. No bribe would induce these votaries of pleasure to remain. The great difficulty of employers is to induce their men to go regularly to their work, especially when they are most wanted, when the trade is good and wages rise. Every Monday [fortnightly] after pay-day is devoted by many to jollity. On such occasions the pit is said to be at 'play'; and so entirely is the word 'play' associated with the idea of idleness only, that a poor invalid may sometimes be heard to complain how hard it is to be kept at play for so many weeks, lying on his back, and unable to turn in his bed without help.[31]

After pressure from local clergy the fair at Eccles Wakes was suppressed in 1877 by the local authority. Powers conferred by a Parliamentary act of six years earlier simplified the legal procedure for such action.

As shown in 'A Visit to Knott Mill Fair' (see p. 347), railways brought large numbers of people to the fairs and wakes, which in some cases became steadily more popular. 'Excursion trains from all directions brought thousands of visitors into the town,' wrote the *Birmingham Post* of the great Michaelmas Onion Fair in 1874. Despite – or because of – such success the town council banished the fair from the town centre the following year.[34] It finally expired in the 1930s.

Changes in the patterns of leisure militated against fairs and wakes. They included: the slow movement to reduce hours of work (the Act of 1850 brought in a Saturday half-day holiday for factory workers, extended to all workers in 1878); the arrival of Bank Holidays in 1871; and the opening of public parks and libraries.

The trains in Lancashire, which took workers and their families to the wakes, also conveyed them to the seaside, first on day excursions, then for a week's stay. By 1896, writes Robert Poole, some eighty thousand people

Waiting for the excursion train to 'Oldham-by-the-Sea' (Blackpool).

from Oldham spent their wakes week at Blackpool, which became 'Oldham-by-the-Sea'.[33] Other Lancashire towns evolved a similar routine. 'Going away' clubs, present in most cotton towns between 1880 and 1930, were established to fund annual holidays during wakes or fair weeks.

People made a weekly contribution to clubs in a variety of settings: churches, workplaces, the Co-op. By the mid-1930s some £300,000 was paid out each year in the week leading to a town's annual holiday in June.[34] The mill girls of Leigh said:

> Soon our money will be spent, we shall be without a cent,
> But on pleasure now we're bent, and we know it is not lent.
>
> In the mill we'll work for more just as we have done before;
> Work to us is not a bore though we're glad when it is o'er.[35]

But Glasgow's July fair survived into the twenty-first century, chronicled during the 1850s and 60s by a series of ballad sheets – 'Humours of Glasgow Fair', 'Jock Clarkestone's Description of Glasgow Fair' and 'The Sights of Glasgow Fair'. 'The Day We Went to Rothesay-O', dealing with a seaside outing during the Glasgow Fair holiday, and the equally uninhibited 'Rawtenstall Annual Fair' remained popular until the late twentieth century.[36]

We want no work

Photograph courtesy of the Royal Photographic Society, National Museum of Science and Industry

In the words of an epigrammatic song: 'We want no wark to do, we want no wark to do. We want some cash to cut a dash, but we want no work to do.'[37] The singer, Bert Dobson of Todmorden in the West Riding of Yorkshire, added: 'Quite a number of men used to gather in the pub on Monday morning and drink till dinner time, and then they threw their caps up. And if they stayed up they went to work; if they fell, they stopped where they were. It was usually that kind of man who sang "We want no work to do".'[38]

The cap trick was widely practised by miners, including those of Glamorgan and Monmouthshire, who were often not keen to work on Mondays, when some potential danger might have emerged during their absence from the pits on Sundays. A group of men would nominate one of their number to throw his cap into a tree. If it stuck in the branches they would go to work; if it fell they would go home. It usually fell. At Rhymney, as it went up these words were said: 'Un, dau, tri. Cap lawr i mi.' (One, two, three. Cap down for me.)[39] Boilermakers in Lancashire had a similar custom, with a more predictable outcome: they used a brick. Edward Thompson was told by 'an old Yorkshire miner' that 'in his youth it was a custom on a bright Monday morning to toss a coin in order to decide whether to work or not'.[40]

Another celebration of the non-work ethic comes from Norfolk, in the days of fishing under sail:

The Candlelight Fisherman[41]

Oh me dad was a fisherman bold,
And he lived till he grew old,
For he opens the pane and he pops out the flame,
Just to see how the wind do blow.

If the flame don't flicker 'e'd know
That there's not enough wind to blow,
But if that silly old flame blow out
There's too much wind to go.

The fishermen of Mevagissey in Cornwall had the same jocular story, though apparently not the song.

A more elaborate hymn to work-avoidance, dating from the 1850s, clearly called for the tune of 'There was a jolly miller once lived on the River Dee':

The Jolly Grinder![42]

There was a jolly Grinder once.
Lived by the river Don,
He work'd and sang from morn to night,
And sometimes he'd work none;
But still the burden of his song
Forever used to be –
''Tis never worthwhile to work too long,
For it doesn't agree with me!'

He seldom on a Monday work'd,
Except near Christmas Day;
It was not the labour that he'd shun,
For it was easier far than play;
But still the burden of his song
For ever used to be –
''Tis never worthwhile to work too long,
For it doesn't agree with me!'

A pale teetotaller chanc'd to meet
Our grinder one fine day,
As he sat at the door with his pipe and his glass,
And thus to our friend did say:
'You destroy your health and senses too';
Says the grinder 'you're much too free,
Attend to your work, if you've ought to do,
And don't interfere with me.

There's many like you go sneaking about,
Persuading beer drinkers to turn!
'Tis easier far on our failings to spout,
Than by labour your living to earn;
I work when I like, and I play when I can,
And I envy no man I see;

Such chaps as you won't alter my plan,
For I know what agrees with me!'

Of the same period or a little later – and perhaps, surprisingly, for the height of the Victorian era – is the light-hearted:

Drunkard's Friend[43]

To work on a Monday I think it's not right,
That day ought to be spent in some other delight –
In pitching and tossing, or some other game,
And at night to the alehouse a-carding the same.

On Tuesday morning, when I rise from my bed,
I am sadly afflicted with a pain in my head;
But I will go to the alehouse, to get another draight [draught]
For to cure those old ones that I got last night.

On Wednesday morning it runs hard in my side,
To think on my work I can hardly abide;
But I go out in the fields for to take some fresh air,
And there I view the hounds in quest of a hare.

On Thursday morning I am forced to begin,
When my meat's nearly done, and my money's growing thin,
For I have nothing to eat in the house, neither bit nor bite,
And I am forced to box Harry till Saturday night.

On Friday morning I'll whistle and sing,
And I'll go to my work as content as a king;
All the day long you shall scarce see my face,
And all that dark night I shall stare through a blaze.

On Saturday evening when my work is done,
Saying I am the lad that can carry it home,
I'll throw it over my shoulder, and away I will sling,
And at night with a jug of brown beer I will sing.

'Boxing Harry' was to do without a meal, or, at the time the sheet appeared, to take afternoon tea and lunch together.

A similar survey of a week appears in condensed form in the 'Idle Song':[44]

The Idle Song[44]

On Monday I never go to work,
On Tuesday I stay at home;
On Wednesday I don't feel inclined,
Work's the last thing on my mind.
Thursday, half holiday, and Fridays I detest.
Too late to make a start on Saturday,
And Sunday is my day of rest.

Soldiers enjoyed singing and hearing songs in praise of desertion, but this on the whole did not make them into deserters: their pleasure was vicarious. Indeed, paradoxically, the cathartic effect might have made them more able to bear their burdens, and therefore less likely to desert. The same kind of equation might well have been present in workers' songs about shirking work. In some cases, though, these could well have expressed a genuine intention to escape from work.

'If a man can support his family with three days' labour, he will not work six,' wrote William Hutton, the historian of Birmingham, in 1781.[45] A century later: 'Wayvers 'd go what they call on t' rant – and doffers. I've heard my father say he'd seen more ale on taproom floor on a Monday dinner time than's supped now. … They'd never go into t' work o' t' Monday. They'd rather go drinking, and then it'd last all t' wik sometimes.' So said Jack Ingham, who was born in the early 1900s at Midgley in West Yorkshire's Calder Valley, where his father kept the Lord Nelson Inn.[46]

Even in the 1930s, when work was at a premium, there were bitter-sweet songs like:

The Dole Boys[47]

We are two jolly scroungers, belong to the sons of rest,
We dinnet intend to look for work and at that we'll do our best,
And as we travel round the world we'll not take another man's job,
We'd rather scrounge a pint of beer or a lend of a couple of bob,
And our union is the oldest ever since the world began,
We pay nowt in, we get nowt out, but we'll stick to it like a man.

An anonymous author from Worcester must have written or adapted this song, which mentions several nearby villages:

The Out of Work Song[48]

I've just got off the sofa,
Like the boys of the Old Brigade;
We share each other's troubles
But they all burst into bubbles
When we handle all the rhino,
What a cert, money for dirt.
They say that work for all
Is a step in the right direction,
But I know one who will sign on
Till the day I draw my Old Age pension.
I've looked for work at Kempsey,
And at Fernhill Heath as well,
I've even been to Powick by the sea.
I've seen the lighthouse keeper down at Whittington,
But he hasn't got a job for me.
I've stayed in bed till I'm fed up
Looking for work in the Sporting Buff.

[Chorus] *As before, except for the final couplet:*
But I know one who will sign on
Till the day of the resurrection.

The same spirit surfaced in the 1960s, with a joke about becoming unemployed so as to avoid particularly arduous work: 'Never work for Wimpey's, MacAlpine's or John Laing, Just pop your cards in the Labour, and join the dosser gang.'[49]

In contrast, this was also a time when some workers felt impelled by acquisitiveness to put in very long hours. The working-class ethic, which condemned the work-shy, also reproached the selfish and greedy. The irresistible Matt McGinn (1928–1977) of Glasgow pursued the latter point in a funny and angry song:

Three Nights and a Sunday[50]

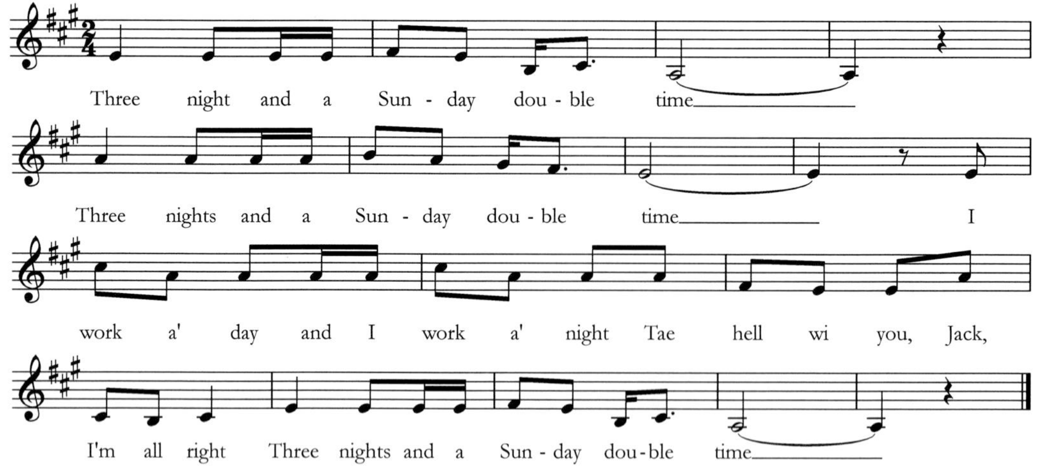

[Chorus]
Three nights and a Sunday double time.
Three nights and a Sunday double time.
I work a' day and I work a' night,
Tae hell wi' you, Jack, I'm all right.
Three nights and a Sunday double time.

There's a fella doon the road that I avoid,
He's wan o' them they call the unemployed.
He says it's all because of me,
He canny get a job and I've got three.
Three nights and a Sunday double time.

The wife came tae the work the ither day.
Says she, 'We've anither wee one on the way'.
Says I, 'No wonder you can laugh.
I've no' been hame for a year and a half.'
Three nights and a Sunday double time.

I never miss the pub on a Friday night,
And there you'll always find me gay and bright.
You'll see me down at the Old Bay Horse:
I'm a weekend waiter there, of course.
Three nights and a Sunday double time.

There's some will head for heaven when they die
Tae find a Dunlopillo in the sky,
But I'll be going to the ither place,
For an idle life I couldny face.
Three nights and a Sunday double time.

After two years in an approved school, Matt McGinn started work at the age of fourteen. In 1959 he won a trade union scholarship to Ruskin College in Oxford, and he then trained as a teacher in Huddersfield. During the latter period he won a newspaper competition for a song in the folk idiom with 'The Foreman O' Rourke', about a worker due to be hanged in Barlinnie Gaol for murdering his gaffer by plunging his head in a lavatory bowl. The judges were A.L. Lloyd, Charles Parker and Peggy Seeger. After teaching for a time in Glasgow, McGinn became a full-time songwriter and entertainer.

Another singer-songwriter, Dave Goulder (born 1939), left school in

Nottinghamshire at fifteen and worked for British Railways as station porter, engine cleaner and general labourer, then fireman. No doubt he would have become an engine driver, but for the defect in his eyesight which in 1961 caused him to leave the service. He subsequently became well known as a writer and singer of songs about railways, particularly steam railways. 'Father Doesn't Fancy Work At All', particularly with its reference to the Crimean War, feels rather like a pastiche of the nineteenth-century music hall, but it was written in the 1960s:

Father Doesn't Fancy Work At All[51]

Well, the family all work at what they fancy,
But father doesn't fancy work at all.
Oh we've got a little railway house not very far from town;
The windows and the doors are painted green.
When everyone gets down to work things really do get done,
But the folks at home they number seventeen.

Oh the family they all work at what they fancy,
But father doesn't fancy work at all.
Oh my eldest brother, Sam, he makes loganberry jam,
And Uncle Henry sells it on his stall.
Grandma's knitting sweaters for the army,
For the lads out in Crimea, so she said;
And while me sister carries coal
Father comes home from the dole
And wanders up the stairs and into bed.

Oh from Monday until Friday when me brother's at the sheds
Me mother digs the garden until three,
Then she puts away the shovel and lights up the kitchen fire,
And goes to wake up father for his tea.
Well the family all work at what they fancy,
And father doesn't fancy work at all.

Even grandpa you will see keeps the sewers running free,
And auntie works behind a prison wall,
But father never wanders from the fireside,
He doesn't even answer when I call,
So to get a crust of bread I just have to leave my bed,
Oh father doesn't fancy work at all,
Oh father doesn't fancy work at all.

Well, the fam-'ly all work at what they fan - cy But Fa-ther does-n't fan-cy work at
all Oh we've got a lit - tle rail-way house not ve-ry far from town The
win-dows and the doors are pain-ted green When ev - 'ry one gets down to work things
real - ly do get done But the folks at home they num-ber se - ven - teen Oh the
fam - 'ly they work at what they fan - cy But Fa - ther does - n't fan - cy work at
all Oh my el - dest bro - ther Sam he makes lo - gan - ber - ry jam And
Un - cle Hen - ry sells it on his stall Grand-ma's knit-ting swea-ters for the
ar - my For the lads out in Cri - me - a so she said And while me
sis - ter car - ries coal Fa - ther comes home from the dole And wan-ders up the stairs and in - to
bed Oh from Mon-day un - til Fri - day when me bro-ther's at the sheds Me
Mo-ther digs the gar - den un - til three Then she puts a - way the sho-vel and lights
up the kit-chen fire And goes to wake up Fa - ther for his tea Well the
fam' - ly all work at what they fan - cy But Fa - ther does - n't fan - cy work at

The clever sting in the tail signals that the son is going to follow in his father's footsteps.

Yet work, with all its demands, was (and is) understandably the central feature of most people's lives. 'Men and women were not judged so much by what they did at home but by what they did in the mill,' wrote William Woodruff. 'People respected skill. Pride of work meant a lot. Work was everything.'[52] Some were deprived of such status, paradoxically, by injury or ill health deriving from their employment. Others, anxious to work, suffered from a lack of opportunity caused by political or economic circumstances. Freed at last from the tyranny of time on reaching retirement age, some were too poor or too enfeebled to enjoy the leisure that beckoned.

But others felt a deep sense of satisfaction at what they had achieved in their working life. Lucy Berry, who started work at the age of twelve as a half-timer in a Lancashire cotton mill, looked back with pride at having been 'a gradely lass and one o' t' best there were in t' factory'.

'one o' t' best that were in t' factory' Weavers and tacklers in Stuttard's Mill, West Yorkshire 1930. Photo: Roger Birch

I'm a Poor Old Weaver[53]

When I were but a youngster, that's many years ago,
And factories they were very scarce and trade were bad an all,
And folks they had to work like slaves from morning until neet,
To get their childer clothing and summat for to eat,
As soon as I could knock about me father said to me,
'You'll have to go to t' factory, lass, a weaver for to be.'
So of course I had to buckle to, for I durst not tell him nay,
Wi' pullbacks, floats and rotten wefts for many a weary day.

[Chorus]
I'm a poor old weaver and gradely out of tune,
I haven't strength to pick a cop nor yet set on a loom.
I'm growing old and feeble, my factory days are o'er;
I'll never weave no coloured sides nor beams any more.

I soon went on to tenting for a chap that liked his ale,
And how he used to treat me, eh, I could tell a tale;
And often on a Monday afore day's work were o'er,
Wi' kicks and clouts and knocking-abouts me head and feet were sore.
But I persevered and did me best and tackler liked me well,
And very soon he put me on to two looms by mesel,
But time revolved and I became, and I became to be
A gradely lass and one o' t' best there were in t' factory.

Notes

For abbreviations used, see page 385.

Introduction

1. Hobsbawm (1999), p. xi.
2. Gammon, p. 10, and citing John Case, *The Praise of Musicke* (Oxford, 1586), p. 11.
3. Keith Rees of the Welsh National Museum quoted in the *Guardian* (24.02.2007), 16.
4. 'Moch an diugh', recorded from Mrs Flora Boyd and waulking chorus, Barra, recorded in 1967 by Thorkild Knudsen; translation by John MacInnes (*Tocher*, no. 6 (1972), 182-183).
5. Henderson (1992), p. 130. See also Various Artists (2006).
6. Terry (Jan. 1920), p. 35.
7. Lloyd (1967), p. 297.
8. Grainger (1908), pp. 229 and 241.
9. As note 6.
10. Quoted Rose, p. 201.
11. Quoted Hughes, p. 49; and Holt, p. 39.
12. Styles, p. 109.
13. Quoted in Jenkin, pp. 102-103.
14. Ford, p. 200. See Roud 374.
15. Seeger and MacColl (1960), p. 37.
16. 'A new Song, in Praise of the Coal-miners': Harding, Garlands, A3 no. 25, p.3. The first two pages are wanting, so there is no imprint, but the typography and the whole tenor of the piece indicate that it is probably eighteenth century.
17. 'Colliers of wear & of Tyne', by J.M. Clarke (Harker (1985), pp. 91-93).
18. 'Collier's Rant': Ritson, pp. 88-89. Roud 1366.
19. Dave Harker has found a broadside copy pasted within a decorative border of later date in the BL, Roxburghe Collection, no. 352 (transcribed in Harker (1999), pp. 82-83.
20. Wood, p. 201.
21. See Wood; and the performances by Jack Elliott and Johnny Handle (Various Artists (1969) and (1975) respectively).
22. Harker (1999), pp. 120 and 266.
23. Ibid. pp. 240, 268 and 303.
24. Allan, pp. 143-145.
25. Ibid., pp. 363-366.
26. Harker (1999), pp. 202 and 213.
27. Harland (1839), no. 1.
28. Williams (1982), p. 53.
29. 'Steam-Loom Weaver' (see chap. 1).
30. 'The Factory Bell' (see chap. 1).
31. 'Jone o' Grinfield' (see chap. 3).
32. 'The Jute Mill Song' (see chap. 3).
33. 'Striking Times' (see chap. 6).
34. 'The Cotton Lords of Preston' (see chap. 6).
35. 'Durham Strike' (see chap. 6).
36. 'Trimdon Grange Explosion' (chap. 3).
37. 'Freddie Mathews' (chap. 7).
38. Harker (2007), P. 168.
39. See Wood, appendix 1.
40. Harker (1999), p. 155; Lloyd (1978), p. 45 (tune).
41. Quoted Harker (2007), p. 167.
42. Gregory (1970), p. 16. For songs from Lloyd's Australian repertoire, see Lloyd (2008), disc 2.
43. Lloyd (1998), tracks 12, 8, 1 and 6.
44. 'The Plodder Seam': song by Ewan MacColl (Seeger (2001), p. 161).
45. Harker (2007), p. 109.
46. Various Artists (1963), leaflet insert.
47. See Bibliography, under MacColl, Parker and Seeger.
48. *The Ballad of the Miners' Strike*, broadcast on BBC Radio 2, September 2009.
49. Lloyd (1978), p.6.

Chapter 1

1. Gilchrist, p.313.
2. Thompson's paper of 1967 was reprinted as chapter 6 in his book *Customs in Common* in 1991. But see critique by Glennie and Thrift (2009).
3. Thompson (1991), p.394.
4. The 'Law Book' is in the British Library, Add. MSS 34555. See also Price on Crowley in ODNB.
5. See McKendrick.
6. 'Rules to be Observed By the Hands Employed in This Mill': poster dated 'Water-foot Mill, Near Haslingden, September, 1851', printed by J. Read, Haslingden (facsimile on sale at Hebden Bridge, Yorkshire, in the autumn of 2008; location of original unknown).
7. From the document reproduced in Shellard, p.13. For a further set of factory rules, see Dodd, pp.259–263.
8. 'The Factory Bell / The Ashes of Napoleon': street ballad without imprint (Kidson, vol. 2, fol. 38; first item transcribed, with suggested tune ('The Labouring Man') added in Palmer (1974a), p.11).
9. 'Factory Bells of England': street ballad printed (1856–1861) by J.O. Bebbington, 26 Goulden Street, Oldham Road, Manchester (Harding B 16 (83b); transcribed Hepburn, pp.231–32). 'The Merry Bells of England' was written by Joseph Edward Carpenter (1813–1870), and set to music by John Edney. A text printed by Bebbington can be seen among the broadsides held in the Edwin Ford Piper Collection in the University of Iowa Library.
10. 'The Factory Bell': poem by Edwin Waugh (Hollingworth, pp.87–88). For two more poems on the same subject, by William Barron (1865–1927), see ibid., pp.93–94 and 91–92) :'Six o'clock at morning'

and 'Hawf past five at neet'. The latter begins: 'For fooak at's slaves to t'factory bell, Life's noan so breet nor gay; For every morn they start at six, An' wark like foo's [fools] o't [all the] day. Bud when id geds tort stoppin' time, Ther sinkin' hearts grow leet; An' sich a change comes o'er 'em o, At hawf past five at neet'.

11. 'A Dialouge . . .': sheet printed by J. Hobson, Swan Yard, Huddersfield (London University Broadside Collection, 7.104; transcribed Palmer, with suggested tune (1974b), pp.218–20).
12. Cooke, p.25.
13. 'The morn is black . . .' and 'Oh the whistle . . .': texts noted by Raymond Kellett of Knapton, North Yorkshire (*English Dance and Song* (Autumn, 1969), p.93; reprinted with suggested tunes Palmer (1974a), p.12).
14. Messenger, p.57.
15. Woodruff, pp.15 and 9.
16. Harker (2007), p.8.
17. Dodd, p.108.
18. Griffiths (2007), p.137.
19. Quoted by Emsley, p.125.
20. 'Four o' clock at Sullivan's . . .': sung by Mrs Kathleen Lyons (born 1933) of Batley, Yorkshire; recorded in 1965 by A.E. Green (published under the title of 'The Knocking-up Song', in Dawney, p.24). The original recording is in the Dialect and Folklife Archive of the University of Leeds.
21. 'A pal of mine . . .': as note 13 (Palmer (1974a), p.13).
22. 'Wake up . . .': Lloyd (1967), p.404.
23. 'Stop that clock . . .': sung by Mrs E.M. Turner (aged 77) of Wednesbury, Staffordshire; recorded by Roy Palmer, August 1966 (Palmer (1972), p.92). The recording can be heard in the BL Sound Archive: Roy Palmer Collection, C 1023/61 C 2.
24. 'On a Monday . . .': song of 1962 by Cyril Tawney (Tawney (1972), side 2, track 2).
25. Greenwood.
26. Hewitt, p.119, from Beggs's poem, 'The Auld Wife's Address to Her Spinning Wheel'.
27. 'The Weaver and the Factory Maid': Palmer (1974b), pp.133–34. The song's earliest known ancestor dates from c. 1670–80: see Palmer (1977), p.274. Roud 17771.
28. 'Hand-loom *v.* Power-loom': Harland (1882), pp.188–89. No tune is indicated, but there are a number of performances on record with adapted melodies, including Boardman (1978), side 1, track 1, and Dowding (2004), track 7.
29. Harland (1839).
30. 'Owd Ned . . .': Palmer (1988), pp.60–61; Moorman, pp.17–18; Hudleston, pp.276–78. The tune commonly used is 'The Fine Old English Gentleman', written in 1826 by Henry Russell.
31. 'Oldham Workshops / Betty Martin, or the Steam Loom Lass': street ballad without imprint, but bearing the stock number, 752, of John Harkness of Preston, and therefore presumably issued by him (Firth c 14, fol. 255). A version printed by J. Cadman of Manchester, who was at work from 1850 to 1857, is reproduced in facsimile in Boardman and Palmer, no. 22. Hollingworth (pp. 83–85) prints a very similar text under the title of 'Rambles in Owdham, and Peep into the Workshops'.
32. 'Steam-Loom Weaver / The Lady's Bustle': ballad sheet without imprint, but bearing the stock number, 584, of John Harkness of Preston (Madden 18/1119). I date this at 1848–49. Vicinus ((1974), pp.289–90), who prints an almost identical text, suggests c. 1830 (p.321, note 3), but I doubt whether engine drivers would have been widespread enough by then to have featured as protagonists in songs.
33. 'The Old Cock Crows': Palmer (1979a), p.46. The original words were byby Harry Linn (1846-90). See Roud 1572.
34. 'I like to be there . . .': sung by Eliza Bolton, Oldham; collected by Joan Littlewood (MacColl (1954), p.5).
35. Dodd, pp.108–109.
36. 'The Factory Lad / On the Q-T': street ballad without imprint (Kidson, vol. 9, fol. 110; transcribed and adapted in Palmer (1974a), pp.34–35, and set to the music of 'Jim the Carter Lad'.
37. Davies (1972), pp.90–91.
38. 'The Collier's Ragged Wean': poem by David Wingate (Maurice, p.123, from Wingate's *Selected Poems and Songs* of 1890).
39. Benson, p.48.
40. Children's Employment Commission, *Reports and Evidence* (1842).
41. Burt, p.55.
42. 'The Driver': poem by Alexander Barrass (Barrass).
43. Reece Elliott's version is quoted in Lloyd (1978), pp.51–52. On the Elliott family, see Wood.
44. 'The Pony Driver': sung by William Will, miner, of Castleford, Yorkshire; collected by A.E. Green (Lloyd (1967), pp.386–87; Palmer (1974a), p.41).
45. 'The Best Little Doorboy': sung by Jack Randall; collected by Alan Lomax (MacColl (1954), p.25). For details of versions of the tune 'Villikins', see Roud 271.

Chapter 2

1. George (1953), p.23, quoting Defoe, *A Plan of English Commerce* (1728).
2. As note 1. For lacemakers' songs, known as 'tells', see: Wright; Porter (1994); and Pinchbeck, pp.232–35.
3. Defoe (1971), p.493.
4. Cole and Postgate, pp.207–08.
5. Thompson (1963), pp.311–32.
6. Pollard, pp.259–60.

7. Quoted in *The Penny Magazine*, 5 (1836), 30.
8. Dodd, p.38.
9. 'The White Slave . . .': street ballad no. 63 [A], printed by T. Ford, Chesterfield (Ford (2001)). The original collection is in Derby City Library.
10. 'The Factory Girl' ('Who is she with pallid face?'): street ballad printed by E. Willan, Dewsbury (Bradford Central Library, Scruton Collection); transcribed in James (1976), p.330.
11. 'The Factory Child's Complaint': street ballad printed by H. Wardman, Bradford (Scruton Collection). I owe the suggestion on Miss Strickland to Hepburn (his p.404), who transcribes a printing, c. 1853, of the same ballad by Harkness of Preston, under the title of 'The Factory Child'.
12. 'There's Nowt Loike . . .': Hollingworth, pp.89–90, from Joseph Burgess, *A Potential Poet? His Autobiography and* Verse (Ilford: Publications, [1927]), pp.58–59. See also Vicinus (1974), pp.218–20.
13. Engels, pp.213–14.
14. Boardman (1973), side 2, track 1.
15. Weaver, ODNB.
16. Ibid.
17. 'A New Song . . . / Lowland Caroline': street ballad sold by W. Midgley, Russell Street, Halifax (Scruton Collection). Cf. 'Oastler is Free! Oastler is Welcome' (London University Library,Broadside Collection, no. 609).
18. 'Oastler and the Factory . . .': street ballad printed by J. Lister, a little above the gas works, near Halifax (Broadside Collection, London University Library).
19. Quoted by Hoppen, p.96.
20. Ibid., pp.102–93.
21. As note 18. I am indebted to Dr Michael Honeybone for information on half-timers.
22. Pollitt, pp.26–28.
23. Holt, pp.31, 33 and 40.
24. 'The Half-Timer': song of 1974–75 by Henry Boot and Bernard Wrigley (Wrigley (1976), pp.18–19; and Wrigley (2005), track 11). Bernard Wrigley informed me (November 2008) that 'the words were by the late Henry Boot, and the song was jointly written.' See website www.bernardwrigley.com
25. Burton (1976), p.79.
26. 'The Collier Lass / A New Song in Praise of George Donaldson': street ballad no. 134 printed by Harkness, Preston (Madden 5/664; transcribed, and suggested tune added in Palmer (1974a), p.44).
27. Quoted in Palmer (1974a), p.43, from *First report of the Commissioners on the Employment of Children*, vol. XV (1842), p.108.
28. 'The Testimony of Patience Kershaw': song of 1967 by Fred Higgins (Wales (1970), pp.32–34, from *Club Folk* 3:3 (May–June, 1970), 7–8).
29. Littlewood, p.386.
30. 'Fourpence a Day': sung by John Gowland, Middleton-in-Teesdale (MacColl (1954), p.6). Recording: Megson, track 5.
31. Durham Record Office, d/HH 10/17/523. I am indebted for this reference to Henry Peacock.
32. 'Mother wept . . .': poem of 1878 by Skipsey (quoted Vicinus (1974), p.60).
33. Langton, ODNB.
34. 'Get Up': poem by Skipsey (Maurice, p.142, from Skipsey's *Poems* of 1971).
35. 'The Taunton Maids delight . . .': black-letter street ballad printed for P. Brooksby at the Golden Ball in West Smithfield, London (1670s?) (Harvard University Library, Houghton Collection, EBB65H, volume 2). The original is in eight-line stanzas, with a four-line chorus. The tune nominated, 'I have a good mother at home', is lost.
36. 'The Lucky Factory Boy / The Merry Haymakers': street ballad no.775, printed by J. Harkness, Preston (Harding B 11 (2414)). For 'The Farmer's Boy', see Roud 408.
37. 'The Pretty Factory Boy / The Factory Girl': street ballad no. 353, printed by J. Harkness of Preston, probably c. 1840 (Madden 18/889). The former is transcribed, with added tune, in Palmer (1974a), p.19. For 'The Pretty Ploughboy', see Roud 186.
38. 'The Factory Girl': see previous note.
39. 'Mary and the Handsome Factory Boy / I am a Rover': street ballad no. 329, printed by J. Harkness, Preston (Madden 18/865).
40. 'The (Fortunate) Factory Girl': see Roud, Broadside Index. I quote here from the Jacques version, dating probably from between 1840 and 1845, which is reproduced in facsimile in Vicinus (1975), p.36. The original is in the Harris Library, Preston, Harkness Collection.
41. See Roud 1659.
42. 'The Factory Lasses. . . / The Flower of Bonny Banchory': street ballad printed by Stephenson, Gateshead (Madden 1/801).
43. 'Campbell's Mill': Henry, p.368.
44. 'The Flower . . .': Kennedy (1999), track 1. Roud 2928.
45. 'The Handsome Factory Lass / Spider and Fly': street ballad no. 151, printed by J. Harkness, Preston (Madden 18/681).
46. 'Dashing Steam Loom Weaver / Greatest Lie out of London': street ballad no. 381 printed by J.O. Bebbington, Printer, 31 Oldham Road, Manchester, and sold by John Beaumont, 176 York Street, Leeds (Manchester Central Library, Language and Literature Section, Q 398.8 S.9, vol. 2, fol. 356). The original text of the former is in eight-line stanzas.
47. 'My Collier Laddie': Kinsley, pp.500–501.
48. See Roud 3787.

49. 'My mither sent ...': Herd, vol. ii, p.208. Roud 506.
50. 'Sailor Lads ...': Harker (1985), p.202.
51. 'Colliery lads ...': sung by a Burslem potter to Paul Johnson (born 1929), who was brought up in Tunstall (Johnson, p.113).
52. 'Collier lads ...': sung by an unknown Yorkshire singer (Hudleston, p.23).
53. From poem, 'Kiss, Kiss', by Mary Thomason (Thomason, p.247).
54. 'A Factory Lassie': poem by Mary Thomason (ibid., p.56).
55. See Roud Broadside Index.
56. 'The Brave Collier Lads / Down by the Spanish Shore', street ballad printed by W. Harris, 179 Deritend, Birmingham (BL, Baring Gould Collection, LR 271 a 2, vol. 1.1, fol. 176). Harris was in business from 1828 until 1861. Another Birmingham printer, William Jackson, working from 1839 until 1851, issued a very similar text under the title of 'Brave Collier Boys' (Madden 21/549). Harris's sheet is headed by a woodcut of a miner wearing a round hard hat and holding some sort of pick. A tall chimney smokes in the background. No tune is indicated, but the penultimate verse points indubitably to 'We shepherds are the best of men', for which see Roud 1470.

Chapter 3

1. 'The Poor Man Payes for All': street ballad 'printed at London for H[enry] G[osson]' (Roxburghe, vol.I, fols 326, 327; reprinted in Chappell and Ebsworth, vol.II, p. 334; and in Pinto and Rodway, pp.102-105).
2. 'All things be dear ...': street ballad printed for J. Clark at the Bible and Harp, [London] (before 1674) (Bodleian, Wood, E25, 119). 'Troubles of this World...': street ballads printed for P. Brooksby, J. Deacon, J. Blare and J. Back (1675-1696) (Magdalene College, Cambridge, Pepys Ballad Collection, VI, 273).
3. Macaulay, chapter III.
4. 'The Clothiers Delight ...': street ballad printed for F. Coles, T. Vere, J. Wright and J. Clarke (between 1674 and 1679), London (Chappell and Ebsworth, vol. VII, pp.7-9, from Roxburghe, vol. IV, fol. 35). A further copy: Firth c. 23(72). Tune, 'Packington's Pound': Chappell, p. 124.
5. 'Weavers' Crime': street ballad 'Printed and Sold Wholesale & Retail by G Jacques Oldham Road Library, Manchester (BL, 1876 d 41, vo. 2.2, fol. 1332-1333). I am indebted to Jim Hepburn for turning up this sheet, which seems to be unique.
6. 'Hand-loom v. *Power*-loom': Harland and Wilkinson (1882), pp. 188-189. Recordings: Boardman (1978), side 1, track 1; Dowding (2004), track 7.
7. 'The Hand-loom Weavers' Lament': Harland and Wilkinson (1882), pp. 193-195. Recordings: Boardman (1968), side 1, track 1; Dowding (2004), track 1.
8. Dodd, p. 218.
9. Messenger, pp. 235-237.
10. 'A Weighver's Song': Hollingworth, pp. 90-91. Recording: Wrigley (2005), track 10.
11. Woodruff, p. 261.
12. 'The Factory Girl': street ballad without imprint (Middle Tennessee State University, Center for Popular Music, Kenneth S. Goldstein Collection of American Popular Music); reproduced in facsimile and discussed in Cohen. Tune: Lomax, pp. 331-332. The song appears under the title of 'Pity Me, My Darling', in Seeger and Reiser, pp. 27-28. Roud 15534.
13. Messenger, pp. 27, 135, 136 and 35.
14. Ibid., p. 30.
15. Kindly communicated by Gordon Cox, 1983.
16. Quoted Addy and Power, p. 14, from Richard Guest, *Compendious History of the Cotton Trade* (1828).
17. 'Jone o' Grinfield/ Sally Sly': street ballad no. 32, printed by J.O. Bebbington, Goulden Street, Manchester (Axon). Tune: Derby, p. 93. The Bebbington sheet is reproduced in facsimile inn Vicinus (1975), p. 34, and also partially in Boardman and Palmer, No. 5. though unfortunately with the erroneous ascription as a broadside from the Language and Literature Library, Manchester Public Libraries. Recording: Dowding (2005), CD 1, track 5. Roud 937.
18. Harland and Wilkinson (1882), p. 162.
19. 'The Four Loom Weaver': MacColl (1954), pp. 4-5.
20. Ibid, p. 3.
21. These were: 'Poaching Song', 'Mowing Match Ballad', 'Owd Towler', 'A-begging' and 'Jim the Carter's Lad' (BBC Archive no. 18136; recorded 24.5.1952).
22. 'Bowton's Yard' and 'Welcome, Bonny Brid': Laycock, pp. 3-4 and 41-42 respectively. Recordings: Dowding (2004), tracks 14 and 9.
23. 'The Shurat Weaver's Song': Laycock, pp. 51-52. The text with a suggested tune is in Palmer (1974b), pp. 226-229. Recordings: Boardman (1973), side 1, track 1; Dowding (2004), track 17.
24. 'The Jute Mill Song': written and sung by Mary Brooksbank; recorded in 1968 by Hamish Henderson, and published in the periodical *Tocher*, no. 50 (1995), p.44. It appears, together with others of Mary Brooksbank's songs, in Gatherer. Roud 2585.
25. Daniel, p.3.
26. Woodruff, p.271.
27. 'Poverty Knock', 'as sung by an unknown singer, Leeds', appears in Hudleston, pp.27–28. A note adds: 'It is unfortunate that we have lost the identity of the singer of this prize piece, who sang it to us in a West Riding dialect. He accompanied himself on a ukulele banjo, and it is certainly the same singer as "Old Jim Slack's Horse".' (p.306). Tom Daniel played the same instrument, and is the only known source of the latter

song (see Daniel, pp.4–6), so he must have been the 'unknown singer'.

28. Quoted by Dawney, p.16.
29. 'Poverty Knock': sung by Tom Daniel; recorded by A.E. Green, 1964 (Palmer (1974a), pp.34–35). Daniel apparently did not always sing the same number of verses, nor keep to the same order. A further verse included in Dawney (p.15), runs: 'This weaving; shed is so old, We're nearly frozen with cold. When we are wheezin', And coughin' an' sneezin', It meks us grow feeble and old.' Roud 3491.
30. *Preston Guardian*, 24 June 1848. I am indebted for this reference to Henry Peacock. An earlier report appeared on 17 June 1848.
31. '*A Copy of Verses ... / Roger the Miller and the Gray Mare*': street ballad no. 564, printed by Harkness, Preston (Madden 18/1099). A different edition of the same sheet is in the Harris Library, Preston, Harkness Collection.
32. 'Marco and Pedro / Five in the Morning': street ballad no. 665, printed by T. Pearson, [Chadderton Road], Manchester (Axon). The title appears in the supplement, no. 2 (? 1872), to Pearson's catalogue. A very similar text, 'The Miner's Song, or, Five in the Morning', from the sheet printed by H. Such, London, together with suggested tune, is in Palmer (1974a), p.48.
33. Benson, p.39.
34. 'The Hartley Calamity': poem by Skipsey (Maurice, pp.217–20, from Skipsey's *Poems, Songs and Ballads* of 1862). Lloyd (1978), pp.170–71, gives a text with marginal differences.
35. Duckham, pp.202–207.
36. Benson, pp.41 and 43.
37. Harrison (1971), p.134.
38. 'The Submissive Petition ...': street ballad without imprint (Johnson; facsimile: Palmer (1988), p.113).
39. Palmer (2007), pp.100–102.
40. Ibid., pp.102–103.
41. 'The Collier's Hymn': street ballad no. 735 printed by H. Such, London (Harding). Another version, printed by W.S. Fortey of London, is in the Norfolk Rural Life Museum, reference GRSM: 1981.151.4a.
42. 'The Collier's Hymn': street ballad printed by Thomas Thomas, 25 Church Street, Oswestry (Harvard College Library, 2521/2.10.5.f.46).
43. Derby, p.91.
44. The late Colliery Explosion ...': street ballad printed by D. Thomas, Wallcroft, [Lancashire] (Sheffield University Library, Firth Collection). 'Copy of Verses ... ': street ballad printed by H. Disley, 57 High Street, St Giles, London (BL, LR 271 a 2, vol. 1/1, fol. 160). See also Roud Broadside Index.
45. 'Truly Descriptive Lines ...': street ballad without imprint (Cardiff Central Library, Ballads and Fugitive Pieces, W 7.162, vol. 1, p.24). Tune, 'Teddy O'Neale', from an untraced Irish source. Roud 5207.
46. 'Terrible Explosion ...': street ballad without imprint (as note 46).
47. 'A Copy of Verses ...': street ballad without imprint (Sheffield University Library, Firth Collection). 'Tanchwa ...': booklet without imprint (NLW, 1569/3).
48. 'Trimdon Grange ...': song of 1882 by Tommy Armstrong (Armstrong (1930), pp.1–2; and (1987), p.20). These sources have text only. Lloyd (1952), p.129, and (1978), p.183, gives the 'come-all-ye' style tune, which is used in all recordings to date, including Various Artists (1977 and 1987), side A, track 6, and (1997), track 13. For 'Go and leave me ...' see Roud 459.
49. 'Lines on the Dreadful Explosion ...' and 'Lines on the Terrible Colliery Explosion ...': street ballads without imprint. The former, which gives the incorrect date of 30 April instead of 30 August, was in private hands when I saw it but is now in the NLW. The latter, which has a prose preamble referring to earlier disasters of 1849 and 1862, is in Harding.
50. 'Fearful Colliery Explosion ...': broadside without imprint (Kidson , vol. I, p.125). Of the six verses, Lloyd (1978, p.182) omits three, and also the chorus.
51. 'Appalling Colliery Accident ...': broadside without imprint (BL, Crampton Collection, vol. 8, fol. 297).
52. 'The Sorrowful Lamentation ...': slip song without imprint, but with the attribution: 'By John Wilson, B.S., G.' (NLS: www.nls.uk/broadsides/broadside.cfm/id/ 14972/criteria/Blantyre accessed 12/07/2007). The song is closely related to 'The Lover's Lament for John Sneddon, a Collier. By John Wilson, B.S.': slip song without imprint (Firth Collection, Sheffield .
53. The Blantyre Explosion': sung by John Maguire and noted by Robin Morton (Morton (1970), pp.9–10). Roud 1014. Recordings: Gaughan, side 2, track 3; Harte and Lunny, track 6.
54. See the chapter on Lofthouse in Renwick, pp.185–230.
55. 'The Lofthouse Colliery Disaster': song of 1973 by Sam Richards (Richards and Stubbs (1979), pp.187–88).
56. Richards (1992), pp.94–95.
57. 'The Gresford Disaster': Lloyd (1952), pp.80–81 and 130 (tune).
58. Ibid., p.136.
59. MacColl (1954), pp.11–12.
60. Various Artists (1968), side 1, track 9.
61. For some of the letters, see Palmer (1974a), pp.57–58.
62. Private communication, 27.12.1974.
63 See Bailey, p.79.
64. Davies (1972), p.16.
65. Elliott (1969), side 2, tracks 2 and 1.
66. Wood, p.203.

67. *English Dance and Song* 27:4 (1965), 115.
68. 'Jowl . . .': Lloyd (1978), pp.70–71. Roud 3191.
69. 'I remember . . .': Elliotts (1969), side 2, band 1. For the Elliotts, see also Wood.

Chapter 4

1. Quoted in Palmer (1974b) p.275.
2. Horden (1993), p.6. See also Horden on Freeth in ODNB; and Hobday.
3. 'The Colliers March': song by John Freeth (Freeth (1790), pp.60–61). For an edited version of the text, with a tune (reproduced here) by Pam Bishop, see Palmer (1974b), pp.274–75.
4. Thompson (1963), p.63.
5. Thompson (1991), p.229.
6. 'The Dudley Boys': one version was published in Palmer (1974a), p.58, with a tune later discovered to be by Wilf Darlington, though based on 'The Bold Benjamin'. (For an oral version of the latter, under the title of 'The Benjamin's Lamentation', see Williams and Lloyd (2003), p.10. Cf. Roud 2632). The second version of 'The Dudley Boys' appeared in Palmer (1972), p.88, with a tune by Pam Bishop.
7. 'The Dudley Boys': as last entry in previous note.
8. Thompson (1991), p.64
9. See Palmer (2007), Chap. 7.
10. Bennett and Elton, vol. 3, pp. 284 and 286, *History of Corn Milling* (4 vols, Liverpool, 1898–1900); vol. 3, pp.284 and 286.
11. Quoted by Thompson (1963), p.67.
12. 'The Baker's Glory . . .': slip song without imprint (Derby Public Library, Derby Broadsides, reference 8672; another copy in Madden 4/80).
13. 'The Albion Mills . . .': engraved sheet 'Publish'd, March 10th, 1791, by C. Sheppard, N°. 19 Lambert Hill, Doctors Commons', London (facsimile in Shellard, no. 4). Shellard gives the source simply as 'British Museum', but in fact it is BL 1876 e 20. Partly transcribed by Henderson (1937), p.139, who gives no hint as to why he includes it in a collection of Victorian street ballads.
14. Cole and Postgate, p.112.
15. Hunt on Edmund Cartwright, ODNB.
16. 'Grimshaw's Factory . . .': Harland and Wilkinson (1882), pp.202–204.
17. Ibid., p.202.
18. As note 15.
19. OED.
20. Palmer (1985), pp.90 and 92.
21. Fletcher, pp.3–4.
22. 'A Dialogue . . .': Fletcher, p.7, from a street ballad printed by Cotes, Loughborough.
23. *Leicester Mercury*, 15 August 2006.
24. 'An Ode . . .': poem by Byron (Pinto and Rodway, p.117). There are two more verses.
25. Thompson (1963), p.570.
26. 'Boney's Disappointment / Hunting a Loaf': street ballad without imprint, identified by a manuscript note as having been printed by G. Coates, Alfreton (Firth c 16 (9)).
27. 'Hunting a Loaf': slip song without imprint (Derby PL, Broadsides 8672), but probably cropped from the sheet listed in note 26; transcribed, with some minor changes, and with the addition of a tune, in Palmer (1974b), pp.289–90.
28. Burnett (1969), p.209.
29. Quoted here from Binfield, pp.229–30. There are two more verses.
30. The probable identification of the handwriting was made by Binfield (p.98).
31. 'General Ludd's . . .': manuscript formerly in the Home Office, now in the National Archive (H.O 42/119). Transcribed, with tune added, in Palmer (1974b), pp.286–87. 'Poor Jack' was composed in 1788 for Dibdin's one-man show, *The Whim of the Moment*, and published in various collections of his, including *Sea Songs* (1823). I am indebted for this information to Jeremy Barlow.
32. Hammond (1919), pp.260–61.
33. Binfield, pp.228–29.
34. Hammond (1919), p.307.
35. Ibid., p.301.
36. 'Taking a hearty swig . . .': Peel (1895), pp.241–42; Peel (1880), pp.47–48.
37. Titles include 'The Poacher's Fate' and 'The Gallant Poachers'. See Roud 793.
38. Hammond (1919), p.303.
39. 'The Croppers' Song': Peel (1895), p.47; reprinted with some small amendments of text and an appropriate tune in Palmer (1988), pp.105–106.
40. Hammond (1919), pp.329–30.
41. 'Horsfall's Mill': Peel (1893), pp.259–259.
42. 'Foster's Mill': Peel (1895), p.218. The tune is of uncertain provenance.
43. Palmer (1974a), p.9.
44. Peel (1895), pp.119–20.
45. Ibid., p.120.
46. Binfield, p.226.
47. Wrigley (1912), pp.140–41.
48. Hobsbawm and Rudé, appendix 2.
49. Hammond (1948), vol. 2, p.84.
50. Quoted by Gretton, p.68.
51. Roach, pp.97–98. I am indebted for this reference to Bob Bushaway.
52. The tune given here is that of 'The Owslebury Lads', sung by James Stagg, Winchester; noted by G.B. Gardiner, 1906 (VWML, MS. H 204). Stagg's text, which is very similar to that of M.H., was published in Reeves, pp.203–204, and his text and tune in Palmer (1972b),

p.25. Recording: sung by Roy Palmer, Various artists (1972), side 1, track 6. Roud 17212.

53. I am indebted to Keith Chandler for information from the 1891 census (Morestead and Owslebury, Hampshire). See also Chambers.
54. W.H. Hudson in *A Shepherd's Life* (1910).
55. Gretton, p.69.

Chapter 5

1. *OED*, *s.n.* 'strike', *v*, 17, quoting *Annual Register*. For a study of the strike of 1768, which also affected Sunderland, North Shields, Bristol and London, see Charlesworth, pp.12–17.
2. Dobson, p.19
3. George (1966), p.166.
4. *OED, s.n.* 'strike', *v*, 24, and 'strike', *sb*, 9.
5. Dobson, p.20.
6. 'General Distress': street ballad without imprint (VWML, Cecil Sharp Broadside Collection).
7. 'The Complaints of the Poor': slip song without imprint (BL, Broadside Collection 1876 e 20, fol. 13).
8. On Mather, see Palmer in ODNB and also the works by Hobday, Paul Smith and John Wilson.
9. 'The File Hewer …' Wilson (1862), p.1. Missing line in verse 3 from Smith (2001), p.274. Tune, for which I am indebted to W. G. Shepherd, from *The Compleat Tutor for the Common Flute* (1770).
10. 'W—'s THIRTEENS': street ballad without imprint (Sheffield Central Library, MP 141 S). Text also in Wilson (1862), pp.63–65; and, with possible tune, in Palmer (1974b), pp.281–83.
11. Wilson (1862), pp.63–64.
12. Ibid., p.65.
13. Lonsdale, p.741.
14. Cole and Postgate, p.173.
15. Ibid., pp.173–74.
16. Wilson (1843), preface.
17. Cole and Postgate, p.178.
18. N. Rogers (2008), p.122.
19. Ibid., p.124.
20. Quoted ibid., p.124.
21. 'The Seamen['s] Complaint': Harker (1985), pp.6–8. Roud 8975. Harker points out that the manuscript version he quotes is very similar to a broadside entitled 'The Seamen's Complaint; A New Song, written by a Sailor who was present at the Battle of the Nile' (UNTL, Bell Broadside Collection).
22. 'Little P.D.': Thomson, nos 61, 229, 230, 473, 474 and 546.
23. Ritson, pp.90 and 91; see also Allan, pp.1 and 4. See also Roud 33059 and 9021.
24. See Metcalfe, pp.13–14.
25. 'The Keelman's Lamentation': pp.3–4 in twelve-page booklet, *The Newcastle Songster*, part V, printed by J. Marshall, Old Flesh Market, Newcastle (UNTL, Special collections; listed as no. 478 in Thomson). Tune. 'Lancashire Dick': under the title of 'Gee ho Dobbin' (Chappell, p.691).
26. 'The Keelmen's Stick' (beginning 'Smash! Jamie'): pp.2–3, as in note 25.27. 'The Keelmen's Stick' (beginning 'One day wi' surprise'): slip song printed by [W.] Stephenson, Gateshead (Johnson, 1717b; Madden 1/439). Tune: 'Chapter of Donkies', variant title for 'The Chapter of Kings' (Kidson and Shaw, p.164).
28. 'The Keelmen's Trial …': slip song printed by W. Stephenson, Gateshead (Johnson 1717a).
29. Rowe, p.254.
30. Charlesworth, p.4.
31. Cole and Postgate, p.234.
32. 'A Word of Advice / The Weavers' Turn-out': street ballad printed by Bonner & Henson, 3 Narrow Wine Street, Bristol (Madden 23/170). Bonner and Henson were in business at that address from 1825 until 1830.
33. 'The Carpet Weavers' True Tale': street ballad without imprint (reproduced in quasi-facsimile in Smith (1979), pp.34–35; transcribed and provided with a tune in Palmer (1974a), p.21).
34. 'The Carpet Weavers' Lamentation': street ballad without imprint (transcribed in Smith (1979), pp.38–39).
35. Weavers Never Will Be Slaves': street ballad printed by J. Bromley, Blackhall Street, Kidderminster (transcribed in Smith (1979), pp.46–47).
36. 'The Carpet Weaver's New Song': street ballad without imprint (transcribed in Smith (1979), pp.36–37).
37. 'The Carpet Weaver's Determination': street ballad printed by J. Bromley, Kidderminster (reproduced in quasi-facsimile in Smith (1979), pp.46–47).
38. Smith (1986), p.135.
39. Thompson (1963), p.203.
40. 'The Tommy Note': street ballad printed by T. Bloomer, High Street, Birmingham (Birmingham Central Library; facsimile in Palmer (1979b), no. 7; transcribed in Raven (1977), pp.53–54.
41. 'The Truck Master': street ballad without imprint (Stoke-on-Trent Library).
42. 'The Truck Man's Wife …': as note 41.
43. Hammond (1919), p.19.
44. Ibid., p.35.
45. 'First Drest Man …': street ballad printed by J. Marshall, Newcastle (UNTL, Bell Collection; facsimile in Vicinus (1975), plate 20; transcribed in Harker (1999), pp.117–20). Abridged, with suggested tune, in Palmer (1974b), pp.306–308; text also in Lloyd (1978), pp.218–20.
46. 'The Oppressions …': street ballad printed for the author, Joseph Hall, Collier, Sheriff Hill, by Douglas and Kent, Newcastle (Harker (1999), pp.120–22, from

UNTL, Bell/White Collection).

47. 'Grievances . . .': street ballad printed by J. Beckwith, Houghton (Harker (1999), pp.126–27, from Newcastle Central Library, Thomas Allan Collection).
48. The Pitman's Complaint' (beginning 'O Lord hear the poor pitmen's cry'): street ballad printed for the author by W. Fordyce, 48 Dean Street, Newcastle (Harker (1999), pp.126–27, from UNTL, Bell Collection; and in Vicinus (1974), pp.63–65).
49. 'The Pitmen's Complaint. A New Song. By J. Knox' (beginning'Ye Collier Lads, I pray attend'): street ballad printed by J. Marshall, Newcastle (Harker (1999), pp.128–29, from Newcastle Central Library, Thomas Allan Collection).
50. 'The Pitmen's Stick. A New Song by Jeremiah Knox': street ballad printed by Douglas and Kent, 50 Quayside, Newcastle (Harker (1999), pp.131–33, from UNTL, Bell Collection; also in Lloyd (1978), p.230).
51. 'The Pitmen's Union': street ballad printed by Stephenson, Gateshead (Harker (1999), p.134, from UNTL, Bell Collection; and Lloyd (1978), pp.226–27).
52. Cole (1948), p.85.
53. 'The Operative Builders': street ballad printed by T. Birt, 39 Great St Andrew Street, Seven Dials (Madden 7/1793). Birt was in business at this address from 1833 until 1841.
54. 'The Derby Strike . . .': street ballad printed by W. Horsley, Derby (Derby Public Library, Derbyshire Anthology, MSS. 8225).
55. Thompson (1984).
56. 'The Cotton Spinners' Farewell': street ballad printed by W. & T. Fordyce, Dean Street, Newcastle (BL, A Collection of Ballads, 1876 e 3, fol. 375; transcribed and tune added in Palmer (1979), p.115).
57. 'Jamie Raeburn's Farewell': Ford, pp.243–44. Roud 600.
58. 'Whaur wad nae . . .', 'Saw ye the cotton spinners . . .' and 'Wha saw the 42nd': recording by Hamish Henderson in programme about him broadcast on BBC Radio 4 on 14.10.2008. Henderson sent me variant versions on the last two items (private communication, undated). For another version of the first item, words and tune, under the title of 'Wha Wadna Fecht for Charlie', see Davidson (1847), vol. 1, p.397.
59. See Hepburn, pp.49 ff.
60. 'The Reported Strike of the Policemen': street ballad printed by W. Taylor, 14 Waterloo Road, 'near the Victoria theatre', London (Madden 7/235). Cf. by the same author and printer, 'They're all Striking. A Most Famous Hit at the Times' (Madden 7/235). Having previously been the Coburg Theatre, the Victoria Theatre was so called only from 1837, in which year Taylor gave up business (Hepburn, p.513).
61. Thompson (1984), p.295.
62. 'A New Song on the Great Lock-out . . .': street ballad without imprint (from a volume of broadsides formerly belonging to Sabine Baring-Gould, and now in the NLW; listed in Johnson and Thiedeman as G274). I was allowed to photograph the sheet in the late 1970s while the volume was in the possession of a friend.
63. 'The Factory Workers' Song': Mortimer, pp.61–62. The first three verses are in Hollingworth, p.86.
64. 'The Miners' Philanthropic . . .': Smethurst (nd), p.31; also in Harker (1999), pp.179–80, who prints several other songs on the Philanthropic Society (pp.174–79).
65. Engels, p.289.
66. Burt, pp.33–34.
67. Ibid.
68. 'A Song to the Blacklegs . . .': MS. (Harker (1999), p.272, from Picton Library, Liverpool; also, under the title of 'The Durham Strike', in Lloyd (1978), p.252).
69. 'A New Song on the Pitmen's Grievances': street ballad without imprint (Harker (1999), pp.240–41, from Newcastle Central Library; also, with some alterations, in Lloyd (1978), p.261).
70. Burt, pp.36–37.
71. 'Munkwaremouth . . .': street ballad without imprint (Harker (1999) p.264, from Wigan Archives).
72. 'A New Song' ('Come all you Colliers in this place'): MS. and also street ballad (Harker (1999), pp.241–43, from Picton Library and Wigan Archives respectively; also Lloyd (1978), p.250).
73. 'The Colliers' Appeal . . .': broadside without imprint (Harker (1999), pp.245–49, from Wigan Archives).
74. 'The Old Woman and the Coal Owner': street ballad without imprint (Wigan Archives). Original not divided into stanzas, and lacking chorus, which has been added from MS. version, entitled 'A New Song (Harker (1999), pp.293–94, from Picton Library).
75. 'The Coalowner and the Pitman's Wife': Lloyd (1952), pp.93–95; Lloyd (1978), pp.235–55; Lloyd (1967), pp.344–46. Recording by Tommy Gilfellon (Various Artists (1975), side 3, track 4).
76. 'Fish Betty' and 'A New Song' (beginning 'Now Jobson'): Harker (1999), pp.297 and 307.
77. Ibid., pp.240, 266 and 255.
78. 'The Collier Boy': Harker (1999), pp.219–20. 'The Chartist Mother's Song', by George Binns, appeared in the Sunderland-published Chartist newspaper, *Northern Liberator* (29 Feb. 1840). 'The Rose of Allandale' was by Charles Jefferys (words) and Sidney Nelson (music).
79. Colls, p.97.
80. Lewis (1981).
81. Derby, p.90.

Chapter 6

1. 'Exhibition of All Nations / Kendal Fair': street ballad no. 667 printed by J. Harkness, Preston (Madden 18/1204).
2. 'Chrystal Palace': street ballad printed by E. Hodges, 31 Dudley Street, Seven Dials (Johnson 485). Another ed.: printed by W. Pratt, 82 Digbeth, Birmingham (Johnson 1434).
3. Cole and Postgate, p.328.
4. Ibid., p.330.
5. Samuel (1977), p.16.
6. As note 2.
7. Morton and Tate, p.105.
8. Samuel (1977), p.15.
9. 'The Sailors' Strike': street ballad printed by Luckway, Broadway, Westminster (Harding B.13, 303). I am indebted to James Hepburn for drawing my attention to this.
10. Anon (1851). I am indebted to the National Maritime Museum for providing copies of these articles.
11. White, p.181.
12. 'Strike of the London Cabmen': street ballad printed by E. Hodges, 31 Dudley Street, Seven Dials (Madden 5/376).
13. 'The General Strike' ('To pass dull care away'): street ballad printed by Hodges, as in note 85 (London University Library, Broadside Collection, no. 626).
14. 'Striking Times': street ballad printed by Hodges, as in note 85 (Madden 5/376 and BL 11621 k 5, fol. 308; abridged text and tune added in Palmer (1974b), pp.309–11).
15. See Roud 1696.
16. 'A New Song on the Stockport Strike': street ballad without imprint (Madden 18/1309 and 1310, two editions).
17. Perkin, p.399.
18. Jenny Uglow, introduction (p.xv) to 2008 ed. of *North and South.*
19. Dickens (1854); Lowe (1853).
20. Lowe, p.347. A copy of the original ballad sheet of 'Ten Per Cent!' is in Madden 18/1343.
21. Madden 18/1313–1345 (Preston) and 18/1306–1308 (Stockport).
22. 'The Preston Steam-Loom Weavers / Auld Robin Gray': street ballad no. 696 printed by J. Harkness, Church Street, Preston (Madden 18/1231; abridged with tune added in Palmer (1974a), p.22). Another copy: BL 1876 d 41, vol. 2.2, fol. 1332. I owe this reference to James Hepburn. Once the strike had begun Harkness issued, without imprint but with his stock number 752, 'Oldham Workshops / Betty Martin, or the Steam-Loom Lass' (Madden 18/1275).
23. 'Preston Throstle Spinners' Strike / Uncle Ned . . .': street ballad without imprint (Madden 18/1302).
24. 'The Haslingden Strike / The Ten Per Cent Question': street ballad without imprint (facsimile in Aspin, p.74).
25. Hewitson, p.179.
26. 'The Cotton Lords . . .': street ballad without imprint (Madden 18/1312; with some minor changes and added tune in Palmer (1974b), pp.313–15). Recording: Boardman (1978), side 2, track 1.
27. Madden 18/1311, 1318, 1330, 1334, 1340.
28. 'Betty Martin . . .': see note 94. Tune: O Lochlainn (1965), p.120, from Joyce's *Old Irish Folk Music and Songs* (1909).
29. Hobsbawm (1975), p.221.
30. Scott, p.183.
31. 'New Song on the Strikes': street ballad printed by W.S. Fortey (Madden 5/869). I am again indebted to James Hepburn for drawing my attention to this. Another version, shorn of two verses, is entitled 'We are on the Strike' (Firth c. 16 (267). Cf. 'A New Song on Trades' Strikes': street ballad printed by H.P. Such, 177 Union Street, Borough, London (Harding B 13 317).
32. I am indebted to Jon Hurley for information on Mace and Goss.
33. 'A New Song on the Turn-Out': street ballad printed by McCall, 81 Cheapside, Liverpool (Liverpool Record office, Ballad Collection, fol. 233; facsimile in Palmer (1979), pp.146–47).
34. 'Work Boys Work, and be Contented': sheet music song by Harry Clifton, published by Hopwood & Crew, 43 New Bond Street, London [1867] (Bodleian Mus. 5c. C 3, 8).
35. Tressell, p.563.
36. 'The Collier's Eight Hours . . .': street ballad without imprint (Sheffield University Library, Firth Collection, A 15). Lloyd (1978), pp.274–75, has a slightly different version.
37. Quoted in Wilson, OND article on Bass.
38. 'A new Song on the Carters' . . .': street ballad without imprint (Harding c. 16, 270). The tune, 'Britannia, the Pride . . .' is by J.W. Cherry (1824–1889).
39. Charlesworth, p.90.
40. 'Perseveer . . .': song by Matthew Dryden (Allan, pp.494–95). The tune indicated, 'Nelly Ray', was probably 'Nelly Gray', which is given here. I am indebted to Johnny Handle for this insight.
41. 'The Strike!': song by Joe Wilson (Wilson (1970), pp.324–25). The tune indicated is 'The Gallowgate Lad', an alternative title for 'Sally Gray'.
42. 'Young Women's dreams / A New Song . . .': street ballad without imprint (Kidson, vol. 9, fol. 186).
43. 'Stick up for the Women . . .': street ballad without imprint, price one penny (Firth c. 16, 262). The tune, 'Act on the Square', was 'sung with immense success by the Great Vance' (sheet music copy in my possession, with no publisher or date indicated). The song was written in 1866 by Alfred Lee (died 1906). Alfred Vance

was the stage name of Alfred Glanville (1838–1888).

44. Hoppen, p.70.

45 & 46. 'Strikes of 1872' and 'the Strike of Laundresses': street ballads printed by Henry Disley, High Street, St Giles, London (Firth c.16, 259 and 264). The former, under the title of 'Nine Hours a Day' is transcribed, with tune added in Henderson (1979), pp.128–29.

47. 'The Strike Alphabet': street ballad printed by Disley, as in previous note (Firth c 16, 260).

48. Charlesworth, p.90.

49. See Evans.

50. 'The Fine Old English Labourer' and 'My Master & I': street ballads printed by H.P. Such, Union Street, Borough, London (Kidson, vol. 9, fol. 253, and vol. 10, fol. 164; transcribed, with music added, in Palmer (1972b), pp.44 and 49). Recording of second item: Various Artists (1972), side 1, track 5.

51. 'Success to the Farm Labourers . . .': street ballad printed by H.P. Such, 177 Union Street, Borough (Harding b.13, 310).

52. 'Oh, dear . . .': Richards and Stubbs (1979), pp.188–89, from Frederick Clifford, *The Agricultural Lockout of 1874* (1875).

53. 'A New Song on the General Trades' Strike / I'm Going to Join the Army': street ballad without imprint (Harding b 13, 316).

54. 'Father's On the Strike': slip song without imprint (Firth c 16, 267). My dating of 1872 is conjectural.

55. 'South Yorkshire Lock-out . . .': handbill without imprint; 'The Great Lock-out . . .': handbill marked 'These sheets are Sold to Miners only, at Whitham's, New Street'; 'The Barnsley Miners' Lock-out /A Miners' Hymn': street ballad printed by Elliott, Barnsley (facsimiles from Barnsley Library in Vicinus (1975), plates 26, 27 and 27).

56. 'A New Song on the Lock Out . . .': street ballad printed by J.T. Morgan, Workman's Advocate Office, Merthyr Tydfil (Cardiff Central Library, Ballads and Fugitive Pieces, vol. 1, fol. 88). The song 'Shy Robin' was written by Talhaiarn, with tune by John Owen, the composer of the Welsh national anthem.

57. Quoted in Palmer (2004), p.212.

58. See Armstrong (1930).

59. 'The Row . . .': song by Tommy Armstrong (Armstrong (1930), pp.34–36; with tune, Lloyd (1978), pp.326–28). Recordings: Various Artists (1997), track 2; and (1987 and 1997), side B, track 5.

60. 'South Medomsley . . .' and 'Oakey's . . .': songs by Tommy Armstrong (Armstrong (1930), pp.34 and 25; Lloyd (1978), pp.278–79 and 280–81). Recordings: Various Artists (1997), tracks 14 and 18; and (1987 and 1997), side A, track 3, and side B, track 3.

61. Quoted in Lloyd (1967), pp.376–77.

62. 'Lines on the Shropshire Strike': handbill printed at the office of the *Labour Tribune*, West Bromwich (Brown, p.11).

63. Charlesworth, p.68, drawing on John Burnet, *Report on the Strikes and Lock-outs of 1888* (1889).

64. 'When they went on strike . . .': recorded from Samuel Webber (born 1874) in 1971 (Palmer (1974a), p.35). Tape now in the BL Sound Archive (Roy Palmer Collection).

65. Letter to Kautsky, quoted in Hunt, p.333.

66. Letter to Bernstein, quoted in Hunt, p.333.

67. 'Strike for Better Wages': Buchan (1980), pp.175–76. Cf. Richards and Stubbs (1979), pp.174–76, and Benn, p.149 (first three verses, under the title of 'The Dockers' Tanner').

68. Leeson (1973), p.13.

69. 'Durham Strike': Armstrong (1930), pp.3–4. Tune: 'Castles in the Air': sheet music (words, James Ballantine; music, Robert Adams), published by David Swan (Edinburgh, Glasgow, London, nd), price 2/6 (Bodleian Mus. 5 c. A 7, 2). Recordings (to different tune): Various Artists (1997), track 6; (1977), side 3, track 1.

70. 'The Miners' Lock-Out': ballad sheet without imprint, by Burnett O'Brien, Wigan (Smethurst (nd), pp.33–34; Lloyd (1978), p.285). Recording: Dowding (2004), track 6.

71. Charlesworth, p.119.

72. 'The Miners' Great Struggle': on a sheet priced one penny, headed 'The Day of Progress', which also contains a second ballad, 'How to Prevent Strikes!', both written and composed by E. Allen, miner, Featherstone, printed by J.W. Fawbert, Featherstone (Johnson).

73. 'A Bitter Cry . . .': handbill without imprint (Cardiff Central Library, Ballads and Fugitive Pieces (W 7.162), vol. 1, fol. 94).

74. 'A Song On the present Lock-Out . . .': handbill without imprint (Cardiff Central Library, Ballads and Fugitive Pieces, W 7.162, vol. 1, fol. 95).

75. Benson, pp.39 and 41.

76. Davies (1972), p.223.

77. Palmer (2004), p.214

78. 'Working today . . .': Davies (1972), p.122 (text); Palmer (1974a), p.39 (with tune supplied in sol-fa by Davies).

79. 'Billy Fair Play': version from Gilfach Goch (private communication of 18.12.2008 from Ceri Thompson, Curator (Coal Collections), Big Pit, National Coal Museum, Blaenafon).

80. 'Cân [Song] "Billy Fair Play"': pp.1–3 in booklet of songs printed by Joseph Williams, Merthyr Tydfil (Cardiff University, Arts and Social Studies Library, Special Collections, TJ 3891). I am grateful to Peter Keelan for drawing my attention to this item, and to Ceri Thompson and his colleagues for the translation.

Chapter 7

1. I am drawing here on Raphael Samuel's introduction to Samuel *et al.* (1986), p.2.
2. This is the subtitle of Milne (2004).
3. 'The chain masters . . .' and 'Strike, strike . . .': Henderson (1979), p.166. 'Rouse, ye women': Palmer (2007), p.142, from cuttings in Dudley Reference Library relating to the chainmakers' strike.
4. 'Holly Ho': Palmer (2007), pp.143–44.
5. 'Idris Strike': Henderson (1979), pp.166–67. Recording: Chumbawamba (2003).
6. 'We are out . . .': Gatherer, p.92.
7. 'Description of a Scab': Mulcahy and Fitzgibbon, p.172, from *The Irish Worker*, 10 June 1911.
8. Quotations and 'O claddwch . . .': Davies (1972), pp.71–72; with tune and translation: Palmer (1974a), p.59.
9. David Gilbert, in Charlesworth, p.141.
10. Cole and Postgate, p.383.
11. As note 9, p.144.
12. 'The Case . . .': Sassoon, p.137.
13. 'Song. On behalf of the victimised men of Clydach Vale', by Moses Blake (NLW, Baledi a cherddi, vol. 8, fol. 73).
14. 'Locked out at Clydach Vale': printed sheet in private hands; text contributed by Janice Howells Fehribach to website *http://welshcoalmines.co.uk/htm/poems*. The version in Lloyd (1978), p.292, is identical, except that for the final verse it substitutes: 'We have fathers, mothers, sisters, Now in need this very day, O kind friends if you will help us, God above will surely pay.' This was previously printed in the *Labour Monthly* (April 1962), with the incorrect date of 1910–11.
15. Cole and Postgate, p.578.
16. 'The Strikers' Alphabet': Benn, pp.166–67.
17. See Thompson on Joynson-Hicks in ODNB.
18. 'Meditations . . .': Benn, p.168.
19. 'Promises': poem by Eleanor Farjeon, first published under the title of 'Stand By' in *The British Worker*, no. 4 (8.5.1926). I am indebted to Jim Clayson for this information.
20. 'We had a wonderful summer . . .': Tim Greeney, recorded by Tony Conron, who kindly communicated a copy of the tape.
21. Quoted in Bailey, p.248.
22. Davies (1993), pp.6 and 37.
23. Ibid., p.54
24. Francis on Cook in ODNB.
25. Ashraf, p.364, from Idris Davies, *Gwalia Deserta* (1938).
26. 'Where the Trouble lies', by Fred Stott, on sheet headed 'Poems written during the General Strike April, 1926' (typewritten copy of unknown provenance, in my possession).
27. Elsbury, foreword.
28. Quoted in Leeson (1973), pp.117–18. The song, which is entitled 'Stick Togther', is also in Elsbury, pp.9–10.
29. 'The Rego Strikers': Elsbury, p.7.
30. See, for example, 'We are the First Herts Boys': Palmer (1990), p.41.
31. 'The Rego Girls': Elsbury, p.9. The tune indicated is 'Mary had a little lamb', which presumably applied to a popular song, rather than the nursery rhyme. The title is recorded as being in the repertoire of Queenie Leighton (1872–1945), but I have not been able to trace a copy.
32. 'The Busted-hearted Boss': Elsbury, pp.23–24.
33. 'The Koff Drop': ibid., p.22. Tune, 'Constantinople': transcribed from the singing of Harold Wirdnam (1998) by Pat Palmer (BL Sound Archive, Roy Palmer Collection).
34. 'Solidarity for Ever' (tune, 'John Brown's Body') and 'The Union Banner' (tune, 'The Scarlet Banner – Banderossa [sic])': Elsbury, pp.13–14 and 25 respectively. The first verse of 'Bandiera Rossa' runs: 'Avanti popolo, alla riscossa, Bandiera rossa, bandiera rossa. Avanti popolo, alla riscossa, Bandiera rossa trionferà [ter], Evviva il socialismo e la libertà.' ('Forward the people in revolt, Red banner, red banner, Forward the people in revolt, Red banner will triumph, Long live socialism and liberty.') See also Straniero. Recording: Laggan, track 11.
35. 'The Picket Song' (tune, 'What'll we do') and 'Only Playing at Scabbing' (tune, 'John Brown's Body'): Elsbury, pp.8 and 20 respectively.
36. 'Song for the Blacklegs': ibid., p.12.
37. 'Bye-bye Blacklegs': ibid., p.22. The song is also given by Richards and Stubbs (1979), p.175, who change the final phrase to the more felicitous 'Blacklegs, bye-bye'.
38. David Gilbert in Charlesworth, p.174.
39. 'Harry was . . .': Pinto and Rodway, p.435, with some amendments from my own recollection of the song. Recording: Various Artists (1981), track 40.
40. See version on recording in previous note.
41. Chris Wrigley in Charlesworth, p.205.
42. Ibid., p.202.
43. Quoted ibid., p.207.
44. 'The Tyre Fitter': song by Alasdair Clayre (Clayre (1968); Palmer (1971), pp.4–5).
45. 'Motor Trade Workers': song by Don Perrygrove (recording: Various Artists (1971), side 2, track 8). For 'Birmingham Lads', see Palmer (1974b), pp.28–30, under the title of 'The New Navigation'.
46. 'The Docker's Lament': song by Brian Jacques (Jacques, unpaginated). Tune,'Dark as a Dungeon': Fowke and Glazer, pp.49–50.
47. Chris Wrigley, in Charlesworth, p.197.
48. 'Dock Strike 1970': song by Rod Shearman, who died in 2001 (kindly communicated by his executors, Dave

Webber and Anni Fentiman).
49. 'Freddie Mathews': song by Ron Elliott (Richards and Stubbs (1979), p.112, from *Garland* (Oct. 1974). For 'Famous Flower of Servingmen' see Roud 199.
50. Arthur Scargill, quoted in *www.marxist.com/hbtu/chapter_20.html* (accessed 09.08.2008).
51. 'Saltley Gate': song by Dave Rogers (Rogers, pp.15–16). For the tune, 'Ye Jacobites by Name', see Roud 5517.
52. Arnison, p.24.
53. Ibid., p.17.
54. Ibid., p.26.
55. Ibid., p.63.
56. Tomlinson, p.130.
57. 'The Shrewsbury Three': song by Joe Kay (recording: Various Artists (1981), track 44). Transcribed by Pat Palmer.
58. 'Song for the Trico Women Workers': *The Labour Party Song* Sheet (nd), p.6; Henderson (1979), pp.169–70
59. Dromey and Taylor, p.25.
60. 'Union Woman II': song by Peggy Seeger (Seeger (1998), pp.144–45).
61. Beckett, pp.370–71.
62. Quoted in *Steel Strike: An Illustrated Review* (published in Rotherham by the Yorkshire and Humberside Strike Committee, 1980), p.20. I am indebted for this reference to Georgina Boyes.
63. Rogers (2005), p.34.
64. 'The Ballad of Kevin Casey': song by Dave Rogers (Rogers (2005), p.35); reprinted in *Steel Strike*... (as in note 62).
65. 'I belong ...': *Steel Strike* ..., p.17.
66. Quoted in Milne, p.8.
67. Chris Wrigley in Charlesworth, p.219.
68. Goodman.
69. 'Yorkshire Picket Song': quoted Palfrey (not paginated).
70. 'You are our heroes': Boyes, p.282.
71. 'A Hundred Thousand ...': ibid., p.279. Tune: from personal recording kindly supplied by Georgina Boyes. Transcribed by Pat Palmer.
72. Wood, p.119.
73. 'For it's early ...': personal communications from Angela Tuckett, 23 and 28 June 1984.
74. 'Miner's Lifeguard': Boyes, p.279. Recording: Gaughan, side 1, track 1. Original song: Fowke and Glazer, pp.65–67; Lloyd (1978), p.290; Seeger and Reiser, p.90. The tune is the Welsh, 'Calon lân' ('Pure heart'). Roud 3510.
75. 'Which Side ...': Gaughan, side 2, track 1; text and tune in *NCS [New City Songster]*, no. 20 (April 1985), p.38. Original song of 1931, by Elizabeth Reece: Fowke and Glazer, pp.54–55; Seeger and Reiser, pp.132–33. Roud 15159.
76. McVicar, p.50.
77. 'Auchengeich Disaster': ibid., p.51; Buchan (1962), p.130 (tune, 'Skippin' Barfit Thro' the Heather'); Lloyd (1978), pp.194–95.
78. Bragg, p.11.
79. Rogers (2005), p.46.
80. Ibid., pp.46, 48, 52 and 50.
81. Harker (2007), pp.242–43, referring to 'Only Doing their Job', 'Holy Joe of Scabsville', 'The Media' and 'Daddy, What did you do in the strike?' (Seeger (2001), pp.290, 94, 346 and 96 respectively).
82. MacColl and Seeger (1984).
83. 'Daddy, What did you do in the Strike': song by Ewan MacColl (as previous note; published in *NCS [New City Songster]*, no. 20 (Apr. 1985), pp.12–13).
84. 'Mr Nesbit': Boyes, p.281.
85. Ibid.
86. 'The Laughing Policeman': song by Ian Campbell; communicated by him in October 2008. Punctuation as in original, which is in eight-line stanzas. The song was recorded by Mike Elliott on the LP *Which side are you on?* (Which Side Records, WSR 1), and it featured in the film of the same title, commissioned from Ken Loach during the strike by London Weekend Television but not broadcast because of 'lack of balance' (see *www.screenonline.org.uk/tw/id/530268*). I am indebted to Georgina Boyes for the information in the last sentence.
87. Milne, p.ix.
88. Hattersley, pp.296–97.
89. Quoted Samuel *et al* (1986), p.236.
90. 'Picket Line': poem by J.H. Smith (*www/welshcoal mines.co.uk/htmpoems/PicketLine.htm*, accessed 02.06.2008).
91. Quoted in Bell, p.114.
92. Ibid, p.115.
93. 'The Dirty Thirty': poem by Dave Barker in Bell, p.67.
94. Communication from Georgina Boyes, 29.07.2008.
95. 'Coal not Dole': poem by Kay Sutcliffe (*Red and Green Songs*, no. 2 (nd), pp.40–41). The tune, by Paul Adams, is from the recording by Eve Bland of the 7:84 Theatre Company on the record *Which side are you on?* (see note 86). Later recordings with different tunes were made by Coope, Boyes and Simpson; and by Chumbawamba on the double cassette *Undefeated: A Benefit for the Miners* (Fuse Records M100 (1993).

Chapter 8

1. Engels, pp.120–21.
2. Burnett (1994), p.1.
3. Dobson, p.112.
4. White, p.185.
5. Quoted in Hoppen, p.79.
6. Beier, p.3.
7. Hobsbawm (1975), p.221.

8. 'The Poor Man's Complaint . . .': street ballad 'Printed for C. Bates, next Door to the Crown-Tavern, in West-Smithfield', London (Rollins (1929–1932), no. 411).
9. 'The Gentle Craft's Complaint. . .': white-letter ballad without imprint, which from internal evidence must have been issued during the reign of Queen Anne (1702–1714) (Roxburghe III, fol. 662 (Chappell and Ebsworth, vol. 7, pp.35–36); Bodleian, Douce III, fol. 38 verso; Chetham's Library, Manchester, Halliwell–Phillips Collection; Madden, Garlands F-N, no. 340). Tune: 'Now comes on the glorious year' (Simpson, p.521).
10. 'A New Song On the loss of the Beef of Old England': slip song without imprint (Madden, Slip Songs H-N, no. 1383).
11. 'The Weavers' Garland . . .': street ballad cropped so that the imprint reads simply 'Printers, Manchester'; indicated by internal evidence to date from 1793 (Manchester Central Library, Ballad Collection, F 821.04 Ba 1, fol. 29).
12. 'Admiral Parker's Engagement with the Dutch Fleet / A New Song called The Tradesman's Lamentation': street ballad printed and sold by J. Rusher, Banbury (Birmingham Reference Library, Ballads (Broadsides), 119932, fol. 55). The admiral in question, Hyde Parker (1714–1782), fought a battle with Dutch ships in 1781. The Rusher dynasty was printing at Banbury from 1808. T. Hoggett, printing at Durham from 1816 until 1843, issued a version of the second Rusher text under the title of 'A New Song, called Times as they are; or The Tradesman's Lamentation' (Harding B25 (1907)).
13. 'Medley's Remarks . . . / The Sailor's Wedding': street ballad printed by Edmunds (no further details) (as previous note, fol. 41).
14. 'A New Song on the Times': street ballad without imprint (as note 12, fol. 54).
15. Cole, pp.44–45 and 43.
16. 'Waterloo Times . . .': in 'Four New Songs', an eight-page garland printed by J. Morren, Edinburgh (Harding, A 12, no. 25). For an abbreviated version, printed under the title of 'Waterloo Fashions' by J. Pitts, 4 Great St Andrew Street, Seven Dials, London, see Madden 8/1378; transcribed in Holloway and Black (1979), p.273.
17. 'The Tradesmen's Complaint': slip song printed by J. Marshall, Newcastle, originally in stanzas of eight lines (Johnson 1955); transcribed in Palmer (1977), pp.253–54, with the addition of an appropriate tune.
18. 'Forestalling Done Over. A New Song / The Tradesman's Complaint. A New Song / Remember the Poor. A Favourite Song' and 'Forestalling Done Over. A New Song / The Tradesman's Complaint. A New Song': street ballads printed by Marshall, Newcastle (Harding B 11 (1242) and B 25 (674) respectively).
19. 'The Tradesman's Complaint': slip song printed and sold by J. Pitts, 14 Great St Andrew Street, Seven Dials (Harding B 17 (321). In the original there are no divisions between verses.
20. See Leeson (1979).
21. 'The Hard Times of Old England': Copper (1971), pp.6 and 204–205; Kennedy (1975), p.505. Roud 1206. Recording: Copper Family (2001), track 17.
22. 'The World on Credit': street ballad printed by C. Croshaw, Coppergate, York (Firth b. 25 (123)). A different copy by the same printer is transcribed by Hepburn (pp.103–104) from Firth c. 16 (243).Croshaw was in business from 1816 until 1849, though after 1828 he was at addresses other than Coppergate.
23. 'The Clothiers' Lamentation . . .': street ballad printed by C. Croshaw, York (BL, York Publications, 1870 c 2, fol. 701). For a reworking, see 'The Mechanic's Lamentation on the Stagnation of Trade', printed by W. Armstrong, Liverpool (Bodleian 2806 c 17 (267); transcribed Hepburn, pp.108–109).
24. 'The New Times / A New Song called No Go. Or, Dapper H—-b, and the Little Dress Makers Daughter': pair of slip songs on a single sheet, printed by Pitts, Wholesale Toy and Marble Warehouse, [6] Great St Andrew Street, Seven Dials (Harding 2690). The second title provides the house number, omitted by the first, to which Pitts moved in 1819. The London rival of Pitts, James Catnach, also issued 'The New Times' (Bodleian 2806 c. 17 (305).
25. 'The Tradesman's Wish . . .': slip song printed by Hoggett, Durham (Harding B 25 (1942).
26. 'Lary's [sic] Return . . .': slip song printed by T. Hoggett, Durham (Harding B 25 (1073)). In the original text the word Larry is spelled throughout as Lary. Another version under the title of 'Larry O'Broom' was issued by W. Armstrong (at work from 1820–24) of Banastre Street, Liverpool (Harding B 28 (45).
27. 'The Weaver's Complaint': pp.4–5 in 'Sandy's Reflections On the Times. / Lamentation of the Four Men that were drowned, at Portsmouth [in fact, Portrush]. / The Weaver's Complaint', 8 pp. booklet printed in 1826 by Joseph Smyth, Belfast (NLS, L.C.2902 a. 8). The printing is rather chaotic, and I have produced an edited version. Another copy, from the National Library of Ireland (I 3998864: Belfast 1807:137H17), was kindly communicated by John Moulden.
28. 'The Keelmen's Lament . . .': slip song without imprint (Harding B 25 (1020). A manuscript note has the print order and date: 500/ January 22, 1820.
29. 'Poor Frozen Out Gardners': street ballad printed by Sharp, 30 Kent Street, Borough, London (Nottingham University Library, r PR 1181 B2; transcribed and supplied with tune in Palmer (1974b), pp.230–31). J. Sharp was in business from the mid-1830s to the mid-1850s.

30. Gardiner, p.586.
31. 'Leicester Stocking Weavers' ...': slip printed by Hewitt, Glastonbury (Harding B 25 (1092).
32. 'Cotton Spinners ...': sheet printed by James Paul and Co., 2 & 3 Monmouth Court, Seven Dials, 1838–1845 (Johnson 646).
33. 'To the Lady ...': sheet printed by Horne and Richardson, Whitby (Johnson 2068).
34. 'The Occasion of These Verses ...': sheet without imprint (Johnson 2994); transcribed in Hepburn, pp.287–89.
35. 'A Blessing ...': sheet without imprint (Harding B 13 (269)). Thomas Firth and J.B. Sturdy, cotton spinners and manufacturers, erected Bankfield Mill, Copy Nook, Blackburn, in 1852–54. I am indebted for this information to Jeff Cooper.
36. 'The Framework-Knitters...': slip printed by E. Smith, Leicester (Johnson 1850). The same text, under the title of 'Frame Work Weavers Petition', printed by Robson, is annotated '1826' (Johnson 2511); and in another issue without imprint, 'Singing in Sunderland ...' (Johnson 2509).
37. Cobbett, p.316.
38. Thompson (1963), p.551.
39. Ibid., p.341.
40. Hobsbawm (1999), p.67.
41. 'The Present Condition ...': street ballad without imprint (source untraced).
42. 'The Staffordshire Nail-makers' ...': street ballad printed by Woodward, Tipton (Madden 8/5). I have unfortunately been unable to date either the printer or the Mr Woodhall mentioned.
43. 'The Miseries ... / The Tear of Pity': sheet printed by Ordoyno, Nottingham (Madden 20/72; BL 1876 e 3), probably in the late 1830s or early '40s. The first item is transcribed in Palmer (1974a), p.204, with tune added. The second, printed by Wightman of Sutton, Nottinghamshire (listed Carnell C87 (1)), was attributed to 'a poor framework-knitter, Sutton, April 24th, 1821'.
44. Tune, 'The Wounded Hussar': Davidson, vol. 2, p.200. The second strain of the tune has a very wide compass, and 'The Tear of Pity' may well have been sung to the first strain only. 'The Wounded Hussar' was a poem by Thomas Campbell (1777–1844), set to the Irish tune 'Captain O'Kain', previously used by Robert Burns for the song beginning 'The small birds rejoice, on the green leaves returning' (Kinsley, p.328, where the tune is given as 'Captain Okean').
45. 'Lament ... / O Gracious ...': street ballad no. 363 printed between July 1844 and March 1845 by Harkness, Church Street, Preston (Madden 50/899; Harding B 20 (89).
46. 'The Weaver's Lamentation': street ballad no. 37, printed by T. Dodds, 43 Head of the Side, Newcastle (Madden 83/35); transcribed Harker (1999), pp.164–65.Dodds was at that address between 1841 and May/June 1843, when he moved to 77 Side. 'The Poor Tradesmen's Lamentation': street ballad without imprint, but ascribed to Dodds; transcribed in Harker (1999), pp.165–66, from a copy in the Wigan Archives. Harker (ibid., p.23) suggests that in the latter sheet 'the appeal is widened so as to highlight the insecurities of the self-employed', but it seems clear to me that the tradesman of the title is 'One who is skilled in and follows one of the industrial arts; an artificer, an artisan, a craftsman' (*OED*).
47. 'The Cries ...': street ballad printed by T. Dodds, 43 Head of the Side, Newcastle (Madden 1/37); transcribed in Harker (1999), pp.167–68. See also another version printed under the title of 'The Distressed Tradesmen' by A.C. Brander, Elgin (in scrapbook of broadsides once belonging to Baring-Gould and now in the NLW).
48. For a separate ballad on Bonnymuir, see 'The Radical Convict' (Freshwater, pp.55–57).
49. 'The Tradesmans' [sic] Complaint (beginning 'You Englishmen wherever you be, come list to what I say') / He Loves and he Rides away': street ballad printed by J. Plant, 6 Clare Street, Nottingham (Madden 20/84); first item transcribed, with music added, in Palmer (1974b), p.214).
50. 'Mechanics' Lamentation / Nature's Gay Day': street ballad no. 362 printed by Harkness, 121 Church Street, Preston (Madden 18/898). 'The Spinner's Lamentation', no. 439 by the same printer (Madden 18/975), is identical, save for the change of title and the omission of the last verse.
51. 'The Poor Threadmakers ... / Job, the Patient Man': street ballad no. 448, printed by Harkness, Preston (Madden 18/984).
52. 'New dialogue ... / The Crook and Plaid': street ballad no. 507 printed by John Harkness, 121 Church Street, Preston (Madden 18/1042); transcribed, and music added, in Palmer (1974b), pp.218–20.
53. 'Address ....: The Tradesmen's Lamentation / One God has made us all'': street ballad without imprint, though clearly printed by Harkness of Preston, and bearing his stock number 592 (Madden 18/1127). Harkness's imprint does appear on another issue of the same sheet, stock no. 593, without the 'Address ...' heading (Madden 18/1128).
54. For Ross, Pearson and some sheets without imprint, see Roud Broadside Index. For Duff and more versions without imprint, see Bodleian Ballads. For a sheet without imprint, with the note 'Hymns 7 and 8' at the foot, see Norfolk Rural Life Museum, Broadside Ballad Collection, GRSRM: 1981.151.10b.
55. See Roud 21211 ('Tradesman's Complaint') and 815

('One God . . .').

56. 'The Appeal of the Unemployed': street ballad without imprint (Harding B 13 (266); verses in original in double column. The sheet is attributed to Harkness. The note 'Sec. 25' at the head and the stock number 868 at the foot compare with 'Sec. 26' and 889 on another sheet, also attributed to him: 'Humanity is Calling / The Spinners' Lamentation' (Harding B 11 (1594), the first item of which refers to the cotton famine consequent on the American Civil War of 1861–1865.
57. Other copies: Printed for the Vendors; giving author as Allen; annotated 1909: Firth c. 16 (362). Giving author as Allen; without imprint; annotated 1894; priced one penny: Firth b. 27 (515). Ditto, but annotated 1896: Firth c. 16 (322).
58. Johnson 1159 and 1160.
59. Davies (1942), p.214.
60. 'Humanity . . . / The Spinners' . . .': street ballad attributed to Harkness (see note 56, above); reproduced in facsimile in Boardman and Palmer, no. 28, with the appropriate tunes. 'Red, White and Blue' dates from the 1850s, 'The Mistletoe Bough' from the 1830s.
61. 'Depression. . . / Hard Times . . .': street ballad printed by J.B. Hodge, 74 High Street East, Sunderland. 'Hawkers and Shops supplied on reasonable terms'. (Harding B 11 (866)).
62. See Roud 2659.
63. 'Ne Wark': Wilson (1970), pp.7–8. For the tune, 'Pretty Polly Perkins', see Kilgarriff, pp.414 and 554; Roud 430.
64. 'Cwynfan-Gerdd Gweithwyr Ystalyfera / Ystalyfera Workmen's Appeal to the Public. January 1886': 4 pp.booklet printed by E. Rees, Ystalyfera (Cardiff University, Arts and Social Studies Library, Llyfr Baledi WG 16.11.L). Cf., possibly from the same period, 'O! Cynorthwywch Ni / Help Us, Oh! Help Us. An Appeal from the Needy Tinworkers of Briton Ferry': sheet without imprint (Cardiff Central Library, Gaianydd Williams Collection, Ballads and Fugitive Pieces, W 7.421, fol. 14).
65. Gardiner (2010), p.13.
66. 'The Men Who Manned . . . ': sheet 'To be obtained from the Printers, 204, Hammersmith Road' (Johnson 1368).
67. 'What Price . . . ': sheet printed by W.G. Chapman, 86 Richmond Road, London SW5 (Johnson 1248).
68. 'A Copy of Verses . . . ' and 'An Appeal by Unemployed . . . ': street ballads printed by W.C. Such, 183 and 185 Union Street, Borough, London SE1 (Harding B 13 (276) and Johnson 1158 respectively). The latter is in facsimile in Palmer (1988), p.295.
69. 'Lines on the Unemployed . . . ': street ballad printed by H.P. Such, 183 and 185 Union Street, Borough, London SE (Johnson 1178).
70. In H.P. Such's catalogue, *Songs Constantly Kept in Stock* (BL 271 a 2, vol. 1–2), issued in the mid-1860s, 'The Unemployed', no. 660, may be 'Lines on the Unemployed'.
71. 'The Unemployed Ex-Soldier's Appeal' and 'The Unemployed Miner's Appeal': handbills printed by F. Dando, 62a Paddock, Bristol (Johnson 1523 and Firth C 14 (345) respectively). For another version of the former, without imprint, see Johnson 2942.
72. 'A Plea . . .': Thomason, p.58.
73. Front cover of songbook, for which see next note.
74. Anon. (1974).
75. Hobsbawm (1999), p.187.
76. Woodruff, p.382.
77. Ibid. The text cited is almost word for word, save for the omission of one verse, the unique version given by MacColl (1954), pp.4–5. One wonders whether Woodruff had only a vague recollection of the song heard some seventy years earlier, and checked with a published text.
78. Woodruff, p.353.
79. Communicated by Dorothy Thompson, 1 July 2008. There were other verses, which she did not recall.
80. 'Soup Song': in my collection, from a scribbled text of unknown provenance.
81. Seeger and Reiser, pp.130–31.
82. Fahey, p.131.
83. Hannington, pp.190–91.
84. Ibid., p.191.
85. Stevenson, article on Hannington in ODNB..
86. David Gilbert in Charlesworth, p.159.
87. Ibid., p.162.
88. Bush and Swingler, pp.53–55.
89. Quoted in Gray, p.36.
90. Quoted in Gardiner (2010), p.158.
91. Trory, p.121. The tune, 'Policeman's Holiday', was written by Montague Ewing in 1911.
92. 'Hallelujah . . .': Anon. (1973), p.9. See also Seeger and Reiser, pp.68–69; Fowke and Glazer, pp.126–27.
93. 'Joe Hill': Seeger and Reiser, p.111; Fowke and Glazer, pp.20–21. See also Richards (1983) for the song in Britain. Recording: Laggan, track 10.
94. 'Alleluia . . .': from my memory of singing and hearing it sung in the 1950s and '60s.
95. Nettel, p.222.
96. Fowke and Glazer, p.127.
97. 'The Bureau': Gatherer, pp.93–94.
98. 'The Dream': Morton (1970), pp.40–41.
99. 'The Labour Boroo': Hammond (1978), pp.46–47. Roud 2886.
100. Burnett (1994), p.261.
101. 'Hard Times': Hollingworth, p.95, from H.B. Whitehead, *Rhymes of a Village Poet* (1963). See also Boardman (1973a), p.7, where it appears with a tune written by Harry Boardman, who also sings the song

on Boardman (1978), side 2, track 2.
102. Burnett (1994), pp.266–67.
103. 'Simply Redeployed': song by Bob Cooney, communicated in manuscript, 1966.
104. Various Artists (1973).
105. 'The Men Who Make the Steel': song by Ian Chesterman (Various Artists (1973), side 1, track 1; transcribed in Palmer (1979), p.182).
106. 'The Pitside': song by Ted Edwards (*New City Songster*, no. 12 (1985), 23).
107. 'People of Corby Town': song of 1980 by Dave Rogers (Rogers (2005), p.37).
108. 'Song of Steel': song of 1980 by Dave Rogers and Pete Yates (Rogers (2005), p.39).
109. 'Gartcosh Commandos': Palmer (1988), p.84.
110. 'The Banks of the Dee': sung by Jack Elliott (Elliott (1969), side B, track 5; text and tune: Wood, p.197; cf. Lloyd (1978), p.143). Roud 3484.
111. 'Farewell to the Monty': song by Johnny Handle, with tune by Louis Killen; sung by Handle (Various Artists (1975), side 1, track 7). Text and tune in Lloyd (1978), pp.130–31.
112. 'Lament for Albert': song by Keith Roberts (Roberts, pp.18 and 20). Cf. Lloyd (1978), pp.302–303).
113. Quoted in Wood, p.108.
114. Quoted in Gregory (1970).
115. 'Farewell to 'Cotia': song by Jock Purdon; sung by him (Purdon, (nd)). Another recording: Gaughan (nd), side 1, track 3. Published in Purdon (1977) and (nd), p.12, and Lloyd (1978), pp.304–305).
116. 'Promised Land', 'And it rolls on', 'The Trentham Occupation' and 'Belly of the Beast': songs of 1993 by Dave Rogers (Rogers (2005), pp.92–99).
117. 'Harry Stone . . .': Song of 1992 by John Tams (*www.mysongbook.de/msb/songs/f/fairfiel.html*). Recording: Tams (2000), track 8.

Chapter 9

1. Hunt, p.269.
2. Shaw, p.16.
3. Quoted in Palmer (1991a), p.174.
4. Palmer (1999), pp.78 ff.
5. Davis (1790), pp.7–8.
6. Ibid., p.11.
7. 'The Jovial Cutlers': Wilson (1862), pp.88–90, in an appendix entitled 'Miscellaneous Songs relating to Sheffield'. For an abridged version of the words, together with a version of the tune, see Palmer (1974a), p.7. The tune, by G.A. Stevens, was originally published in 1754 (Chappell, p.598 and note, p.786).
8. 'The Fuddling Day . . .': slip song printed by R. Walker, near the Duke's Palace, Norwich (Douce 4 (52); transcribed, with tune, 'Nae luck about the house', added: Palmer (1974b), pp.144–45. Other copies printed by Pitts of London, Bloomer of Birmingham and Armstrong of Liverpool: see Roud Broadside Index.
9. Thompson (1991), p.375.
10. Smith (1986), p.60.
11. Quoted in Behagg, p.63.
12. Ibid., p.123.
13. Quoted in Benson, p.58
14. Quoted in McKendrick, p.46.
15. Quoted in Cunningham, p.96.
16. Poole (1983), p.72.
17. 'Winlaton Hopping': Allan, pp.130–32, with chorus added from *The Monthly Chronicle* (1890), p.6, which also includes the tune. For Marshall's copies, see Madden 1/795 and Frances Thomson, no. 476. Thomson also has five listings for 'Swalwell Hopping'.
18. 'Fun of the Fair': slip song printed by J. Pitts, 14 Great St Andrew Street, Seven Dials (Harding B16 (99d). Fortey sheet: Firth c 19 (145).
19. 'Mottram Wakes': song by Samuel Cottrell (Hill, pp.16–17).
20. 'A New Song, Or A Visit . . .': street ballad printed by George Booth, Hyde (Harding B 11 (2014); reproduced in facsimile, with tune, in Boardman and Palmer, no. 17).
21. 'Newcastle Wakes': slip song, to the tune of 'With Wellington we'll go', printed by Bayley, Newcastle (Newcastle-under-Lyne Public Library, 68125; transcribed, and tune added, in Palmer and Raven, p.19).
22. Burton (1891), p.163.
23. Ibid. pp.162–63.
24. The painting, *Eccles Wakes*, is reproduced in part in Styles, p.246.
25. 'Eccles Wakes / Unfortunate Wife': street ballad printed by W. Ford, York Street, Sheffield (BL LR 271 a, vol. 1-1, fol. 168. An abridged text under the title of 'The Humours of Eccles Wakes', from 'a copy of an old song sung at Eccles wakes some thirty or forty years ago', in *Manchester Notes and Queries* (13 April, 1878), no. 203, is reprinted, with a tune by Jon Raven, in Palmer and Raven, pp.8–9.
26. Walton and Poole, p.101.
27. Bell (1856), pp.187–88.
28. John Higson, *Historical and Descriptive Notices of Droylsden, Past and Present* (Manchester, 1859). Can now be read online at GoogleBooks.
29. Harland and Wilkinson (1882), pp.147–50.
30. 'Droylsden Wakes': sung by J. Allan Bates; noted by Anne Gilchrist, 1908 (JFS 5:19 (1915), 204); repr. Williams and Lloyd (2003), pp.19–20. Roud 3290: no other oral version.
31. Quoted in Palmer (2007), p.115
32. Quoted in Palmer (2004b), pp.200–201.
33. Poole (1983), pp.87–88.

34. Griffiths (2001), p.212.
35. Thomason (1961), p.49.
36. Bodleian 2806 c. 11 (218), 208 c. 11 (217) and Harding B 17 (284b) respectively. 'Rothesay-O': Buchan (1962), pp.104–105. 'Rawtenstall': Palmer (1979), pp.172–73.
37. 'We want no work': sung by Bert Dobson, Todmorden (Hudleston, p.34).
38. Ibid. p.307.
39. Palmer (1998), p.217.
40. Thompson (1991), p.375, note.
41. 'The Candlelight Fisherman': sung by Phil Hamond, Morston, Holt, Norfolk; recorded by Peter Kennedy, 1952 (Kennedy (1975), p.499). Hamond can be heard singing the song on Various Artists (1968), side A, track 3. For a different version, see Palmer (2001), p.286. Roud 1852.
42. 'The Jolly Grinder / The First Rose of Summer': street ballad printed by Joseph Ford, 70 Pinstone Street, Sheffield (Sheffield City Libraries; facsimile in Vicinus (1975), p.27). Vicinus ascribes the date of c. 1835 to the ballad (Vicinus (1974), p.321), but it seems more likely that the printer, Joseph Ford, was at work during the 1850s. For the tune, 'There was a jolly miller', see Chappell (1859), p.668.
43. 'Peter and Peggy / Drunkard's Friend / Rose, Shamrock and Thistle': street ballad no. 404, printed by J. Bebbington (who was at work from 1856–1861), 31 Oldham Road, Manchester (Harding B 11 (3334)).
44. 'Idle Song': *Red Songbook*, p.38. Cf. Keeping, pp.64–65.
45. Quoted in Reid (1976), p.78.
46. 'Wayvers 'd go . . .': recorded in 1977 from Jack Ingham by Bob Pegg, and kindly communicated by him.
47. 'The Dole Boys': sung in 1976 by Bert Draycott, Fishburn, Cleveland; recorded by Ian Scott Massie (Beamish Museum Collection, in Richards and Stubbs (1979), p.19).
48. 'The Out of Work Song': collected from J. Pratt of Worcester by Bill Gwilliam (Worcester History Centre, Gwilliam Collection Microfiche, Worcestershire Folk Songs, 1, p.7).
49. 'Never work . . .': learnt from Sheila Dawson of Armley, Leeds, in 1967 by Bob Pegg, and kindly communicated by him.
50. 'Three Nights . . .': song of 1964 by Matt McGinn (McGinn, p.169).
51. 'Father Doesn't Fancy. . .': song of the 1960s by Dave Goulder (Goulder, track 38).
52. Woodruff, p.161.
53. 'I'm a Poor Old Weaver': sung by Lucy Berry; collected by Alison McMorland, 1974 (Henderson (1979), pp.155–56, and reproduced with her permission.

Bibliography and Discography

Abbreviations

Axon: Axon Collection, Lancashire and Cheshire Antiquarian Society, held in Chetham's Library, Manchester, and available on the CD-ROM, *Manchester Ballads* (2003)
BL: British Library
Douce: Douce Collection, Bodleian Library, Oxford*
Firth: Firth Collection, Bodleian Library, Oxford*
FMJ: Folk Music Journal
Harding: Harding Collection, Bodleian Library, Oxford*
JFS: *Journal of the Folk Song Society*
Johnson: Johnson Ballads, Bodleian Library, Oxford*
Kidson: Kidson Broadside Collection, M9526, Mitchell Library, Glasgow
Madden: Madden Collection, Cambridge University Library
ODNB: *The Oxford Dictionary of National Biography* (Oxford: Oxford University Press, 2004)
NLS: National Library of Scotland, Edinburgh
NLW: National Library of Wales, Aberystwyth
Roud: Steve Roud, Folk Song Index, available through the Vaughan Williams Memorial Library, Cecil Sharp House, London (www.efdss.org).
Roxburghe: Roxburghe Ballads, British Library
UNTL: University of Newcastle Upon Tyne, Robinson Library
VWML: Vaughan Williams Memorial Library, Cecil Sharp House, London

Books published in London unless otherwise stated.

Addy, J. and Power, E.G. (eds) (1976) *The Industrial Revolution*

Allan, Thomas (ed.) (1972) *Allan's Tyneside Songs*, with an introduction by Dave Harker (Newcastle: repr. of 6th ed. of 1891; first ed., 1862)

Anon. (nd) *Old Songs Sung in Bedfordshire* (Bedford)

Anon. (1851) 'The Sailors' Strike in the North', *The Times* (29 Jan., 2; 31 Jan., 8; 1 Feb., 2; 3 Feb., 8; 10 Feb., 5; 15 Feb., 8; 17 Feb., 8; 18 Feb., 6; 19 Feb., 4; 22 Feb., 5)

Anon. (1863) 'The Black Country', *Edinburgh Review* (April), 406–43

Anon. (1935) 'The Collieries', nos. 1 and 2, *The Penny Magazine*, 121–28 and 161–68

Anon. (1974) *IWW Songs. Songs of the Workers to Fan the Flames of Discontent* (Chicago: 2nd printing of 34th ed.; first ed. 1909)

Armstrong, Tommy (1930) *Song Book containing 25 Songs of the late Tommy Armstrong* (Chester-le-Street)

Armstrong, Tommy (1987) *Polisses and Candymen. The Complete Works of Tommy Armstrong, the Pitman Poet*, ed. Ross Forbes (np)

Arnison, Jim (1974) *The Shrewsbury Three. Strikes, Pickets and 'Conspiracy'*

Arnot, R. Page (1949) *The Miners. A History of the Miners' Federation of Great Britain, 1889–1910*

Ashraf, Mary (ed.) (1975) *Political Verse and Song from Britain and Ireland*

Ashton, T.S. (1972) *An Economic History of England: The Eighteenth Century*

Aspin, Chris (1995) *The First Industrial Society. Lancashire, 1750–1850* (Preston)

Auden, W.H. (1933) *Poems*

Bailey, Catherine (2007) *Black Diamonds. The Rise and Fall of an English Dynasty*

Bamford, Samuel (1843) *Walks in South Lancashire*

Barrass, Alexander (1897) *The Pitman's Social Neet* (Consett)

Beckett, Andy (2009) *When the Lights Went Out. Britain in the Seventies*

Behagg, Clive (1990) *Politics and Production in the Early Nineteenth Century*

Beier, A.L. (1985) *Masterless Men* (Oxford)

Bell, David (2009) *The Dirty Thirty: Heroes of the Miners' Strike* (Nottingham)

Bell, Robert (ed.) (1856) *Early Ballads*

Benn, Tony (ed.) (1984) *Writings on the Wall. A Radical and Socialist Anthology, 1215–1984*

Bennett, Margaret (2007) '"History, Heartbreak and Hope": Recording the Story behind the Song', in Anne Clune (ed.), *Dear Far-voiced Veteran: Essays in Honour of Tom Munnelly* (Co. Clare)

Bennett, R., and Elton, J. (1898-1900) *History of Corn Milling* (4 vols, Liverpool)

Benson, John, 'Thomas Burt (1837-1922)', ODNB

Benson, John (1980) *British Coalminers in the Nineteenth Century: A Social History*

Binfield, Kevin (ed.) (2004) *Writings of the Luddites* (Baltimore and London)

Boardman, Harry (singer) (1973) *A Lancashire Mon. Ballads, Songs and Recitations*, Topic Records LP 12TS236

Boardman, Harry (singer) (1978) *Golden Stream. Lancashire Songs and Rhymes*, AK Records LP AK7813

Boardman, Harry et al. (singers) (1968) *Deep Lancashire. Songs and Ballads of the North-West*, Topic Records LP 12T188

Boardman, Harry, and Lesley (eds) (1973a) *Folk Songs and ballads of Lancashire* (London and New York)

Boardman, Harry, and Palmer, Roy (eds) (1983) *Manchester ballads. Thirty-five Facsimile Street Ballads* (Manchester)

Boyes, Georgina (1986) 'The Performance and Creation of Vernacular Songs in a Contemporary Urban Culture. A classification of songs associated with the National Union of Miners' Strike, 1984–85', pp. 273–84 in Hugh Shields (ed.), *Ballad research: The Stranger in Ballad Narrative and other Topics* (Dublin)

Bracegirdle, Cyril (1974) 'The Great Cotton Famine', *International History Magazine*, no. 21, 90–97

Bragg, Billy (2009) 'Protest and Survive. Twenty-five years on, Billy Bragg remembers lending his voice to the miners' strike', *Observer Music Magazine* (March), 11

Bridson, D.G. (1950) *The Christmas Child*

Brown, I.J. (1977) 'Shropshire Tragedies. A collection of old ballads commemorating industrial tragedies in the Shropshire coalfields', *Shropshire Mining Club Journal* (Dec.), 1–14

Buchan, Norman (ed.) (1962) *101 Scottish Songs* (Glasgow and London)

Buchan, Norman (1980) 'Folk and Protest', pp. 165–90 in Edward J. Cowan (ed.), *The People's Past* (Edinburgh)

Burnett, John (1969) *A History of the Cost of Living* (Harmondsworth)

Burnett, John (1994) *Idle Hands. The experience of Unemployment, 1790–1990* (London and New York)

Burt, Thomas (1924) *Pitman & Privy Councillor. An Autobiography*, with supplementary chapters by Aaron Watson (repr.1984)

Burton, Alfred (1891) *Rush-Bearing: An Account of the Old Custom of Strewing Rushes…* (Manchester)

Burton, Anthony (1976) *The Miners*

Bush, Alan, and Swingler, Randall (eds) (1938) *The Left Song Book*

Bushaway, Bob (1982) *By Rite. Custom, Ceremony and Community in England, 1700–1880*

Cameron, David Kerr (1998) *The English Fair* (Stroud)

Carnell, Peter W. (1979) *Ballads in the Charles Harding Firth Collection* (Sheffield)

Chambers, Jill (1996) *Hampshire Machine Breakers – The Story of the 1830 Riots* (Letchworth, 2nd ed.)

Chaplin, Sid, 'Jack Elliott of Birtley', sleeve note on LP record, q.v. under Elliott

Chappell, William (1859) *Popular Music of the Olden Time*

Chappell, William, and Ebsworth, J.W. (eds) (1871–1899) *The Roxburghe Ballads*, 9 vols (Hertford)

Charlesworth, Andrew, Gilbert, David, Randall, Adrian, Southall, Humphrey and Wrigley, Chris (1996) *An Atlas of Industrial Protest in Britain, 1750–1990* (Basingstoke and New York)

Chumbawamba (singers) (2003) *English Rebel Songs, 1381–1984*, Mutt Records CD, Mutt CD 004

Clayre, A. (ed.) (1968) *100 Folk Songs and New Songs*

Cobbett, William (2001) *Rural Rides*, ed. Ian Dyck (orig. 1830)

Cohen, Norm (2005) 'Where is the Lowell Factory Girl? A Tangled Yarn from the Textile Mills', Fund for Labor Culture & History Occasional Paper, no. 5 (May)

Cole, G.D.H. (1948) *A Short History of the British Working-Class Movement, 1789–1947*

Cole, G.D.H., and Postgate, Raymond (1946) *The Common People, 1746–1946*

Colley, Linda (2009) 'Rank and File', *Guardian Review* (16 May), 16–17

Colls, Robert (1977) *The Collier's Rant. Song and Culture in the Industrial Village*

Cooke, Anthony (2008) *Stanley Mills. The Official Souvenir Guide* (Edinburgh)

Copper, Bob (1971) *A Song for Every Season. A Hundred Years of a Suffolk Farming Family*

Copper Family (singers) (2001) *Come Write Me Down. Early Recordings of the Copper Family of Rottingdean*, Topic Records CD TSCD534

Costello, Cecilia (singer) (1975) *Cecilia Costello*, Leader LP LEE 4054

Cox, Harry (singer) (2002) *What Will Become of England?* Rounder CD 1161-1839-2

Craig, David (1973) *The Real Foundation: Literature and Social Change*

Cunningham, Hugh (1980) *Leisure in the Industrial Revolution, c. 1780–1880*

Daniel, Tommy (nd) *Yorkshire Broadsheet. Folk Songs Collected, Revised or Rewritten by Tommy Daniel* (Batley)

Dataller, Roger [Arthur Eaglestone] (1925) *A Pitman's Notebook*

Davidson, G.H. (ed.) (1847) *Davidson's Universal Melodist*, 2 vols

Davidson, Peter (1971) *Songs of the British Music Hall* (New York)

Davies, Idris (1993) *The Angry Summer. A Poem of 1926*, with an introduction by Tony Conran (Cardiff; orig. 1943)

Davies, W[illiam] H[enry] (1942) *The Autobiography of a Super-tramp* (orig. 1908)

Davies, Walter Haydn (1972) *The Right Place – the Right Time. Memories of Boyhood Days in a Welsh Mining Community* (Llandybie)

Davis, George (1790) *Saint Monday; or, Scenes from Low-life. A Poem* (Birmingham)

Dawney, Michael (ed.) 1974) *The Iron Man. English Occupational Songs* (

Defoe, Daniel (1971) *A Tour through the Whole Island of Great Britain*, ed. Pat Rogers (Harmondsworth; orig. 1724–1726)

Denselow, Robin, 'MacColl, Ewan (1915–1989)', ODNB

Derby, Thomas (1913) 'Folk Songs of Lancashire', Manchester Literary Club Papers, 79–99

[Dickens, Charles] (1854) 'On Strike', *Household Words* (11 Feb), 551–59

Dobson, C.R. (1980) *Masters and Journeymen: a Prehistory of Industrial Relations, 1717–1800*

Dodd, William (1842) *The Factory System Illustrated in a Series of Letters to the Right Hon. John Murray, Lord Ashley* (repr. 1968)

Douglass, Dave (1977a) 'The Durham pitman' and 'Pit talk in county Durham', pp. 205–96 and 297–348 respectively in Samuel (1977a) , q.v.

Dowding, Mark (singer) (2004) *A Mon like Harry. The Songs of Harry Boardman*, Cock Robin Music CD, CRM 097

Dowding, Mark, and Harvey, Chris (singers) (2005) *Manchester Ballads*, Cock Robin Music double CD, CRM 143/4

Dromey, Jack, and Taylor, Graham (1978) *Grunwick: The Workers' Story*

Duckham, Helen and Baron (1973) *Great Pit Disasters. Great Britain, 1700 to the Present Day* (Newton Abbot)

Dunn, George (1984) *George Dunn, The Minstrel of Quarry Bank*, ed. Roy Palmer (Dudley)

Dutton, H.I., and King, J.E. (1981) *'Ten Per Cent and No Surrender'. The Preston Strike, 1853–1854* (Cambridge)

Ebsworth, J.W. (ed.) (1876–1878) *The Bagford Ballads*, 2 vols (Hertford)

Elbourne, Roger (1980) *Music and Tradition in Early Industrial Lancashire, 1780–1840* (Woodbridge)

Elliott, Brian (2009) *Yorkshire Miners* (Stroud)

Elliott, Jack (singer) (1969) *Jack Elliott of Birtley. The Songs and Stories of a Durham Miner*, Leader LP, LEA 4001

Elliotts of Birtley, The (singers) (1969) *The Elliotts of Birtley, a Musical Portrait of a Durham Mining Family*, comp. and ed. by Ewan MacColl and Peggy Seeger, Transatlantic LP, XTRA 1091

Elsbury, A.B. (ed.) (1929) *Rego and Polikoff Songs*

Emsley, Clive (2009), *The Great British Bobby. A History of British Policing from the Eighteenth Century to the Present*

Engels, Frederick (1845) *The Condition of the Working Class in England*, in *Karl Marx and Frederick Engels on Britain* (Moscow and London, 1953)

Evans, Howard (ed.) (nd) *Songs for Singing at Agricultural Workers' Meetings*

Fahey, Warren (1989) *The Balls of Bob Menzies. Australian Political Songs, 1900–1980* (North Side (New South Wales) and London)

Fletcher, W.G. Dimmock (1883) *Chapters in the History of Loughborough* (Loughborough)

Ford, Robert (ed.) (1904) *Vagabond Songs and Ballads of Scotland with Many Old & Familiar Melodies* (Paisley; orig. 2 vols, 1899 and 1901)

Ford, Thomas (printer) (2001) *Thomas Ford's Ballads. A Collection of Sheets published by Thomas Ford of Chesterfield in the 1830s*, with an introduction by Roy Palmer (Felinfach)

Forshaw, C.F. (ed.) (1892) *Holroyd's Collection of Yorkshire Ballads* (repr. Wakefield 1974)

Francis, Hywel, 'Cook, Arthur James', ODNB

The Freemen (1971) *On the One Road*, Emerald Records LP GES1050

Freeth, John (1790) *The Political Songster; or, A Touch on the Times, on Various Subjects, and Adapted to Common Tunes*, 6th ed. (Birmingham)

Freshwater, P.B. (ed.) (1991) *Sons of Scotia, Raise your Voice. Early 19th century Scottish Broadsides* (Edinburgh)

Frow, Edmund and Ruth (eds) (1994) *Radical and Red Poets and Poetry* (Salford)

Gallop, Alan (2003) *Children of the Dark: Life and Death Underground in Victorian England* (Stroud)

Gammon, Vic (2008) *Desire, Drink and Death in English Folk and Vernacular Song, 1600–1900* (Aldershot)

Gardiner, Juliet (2010) *The Thirties. An Intimate History*

Gardiner, William (1838) *Music and Friends*, vol. 2

Gatherer, Nigel (ed.) (1986) *Songs and Ballads of Dundee* (Edinburgh)

Gaughan, Dick (singer) (nd) *True and Bold. Songs of the Scottish Miners*, Scottish TUC LP, STUC2

George, Dorothy (1953), *England in Transition* (orig. 1931)

George, Dorothy (1954) *England in Transition. Life and Work in the Eighteenth Century* (Melbourne, London, Baltimore; orig. London, 1931)

George, Dorothy (1966) *London Life in the Eighteenth Century* (Harmondsworth; orig. London, 1925)

Gilchrist, Alexander (2005) *Life of William Blake. Pictor Ignotus* (orig. 1863)

Gioia, Ted (2006) *Work Songs* (Durham and London)

Glennie, Paul, and Thrift, Nigel (2009) *Shaping the Day: A History of Timekeeping in England, 1300–1800* (Oxford)

Gomme, G.L. (1885) 'Labour Songs and Cries', *The Antiquary*, 12 (Jul.-Dec.), 145–49

Goodman, Geoffrey (2006) 'Betty Heathfield' (obituary), *Guardian* (22 Feb.), 32

Goose, Nigel (ed.) (2007) *Women's work in Industrial England*

Gorman, John (1976) *Banner Bright. An Illustrated History of the Banners of the British Trade Union Movement* (Harmondsworth)

Goulder, Dave (singer) (2008) *The Golden Days of Steam. The Railway Songs of Dave Goulder*, Fellside CD FECD221

Grainger, Percy (1908) 'Collecting with the Phonograph', JFS 3:12, 170–242

Gray, Nigel (1985) *The Worst of Times. An Oral History of the Great Depression in Britain*

Green, Archie (ed.) (1993) *Songs about Work. Essays in Occupational Culture* (Bloomington, Indiana)

Green, Tony (1965) 'Some Notes on the Popular Song of the West Riding', *ABE* 3: 4-5 (June), 17–34

Greenwood, Joseph (1909) 'Reminiscences of Sixty Years Ago', *Todmorden Advertiser,* 10 Sept.

Gregory, E. David (1997) 'A.L. Lloyd and the English Folk Song Revival, 1934-44', *Canadian Journal for Traditional Music,* 25, 14–28

Gregory, Mark (1970) 'A.L. Lloyd Interviewed, 1970', *http://mustrad.org.uk/articles/lloyd.htm* (accessed 13.11.2009)

Gregory, Mark (2006) 'Sixty Years of Australian Union Songs', MA thesis, Macquarie University, Sydney

Gretton, M. Sturge (1922) *Some English Rural Problems*

Griffin, Emma (2005) *England's Revelry. A History of Sports and Pastimes, 1660–1830*

Griffiths, Bill (comp.) (2007) *Pitmatic: The Talk of the North-East Coalfield* (Newcastle-upon-Tyne)

Griffiths, Trevor (2001) *The Lancashire Working Classes, c. 1880–1930* (Oxford)

Grose, Francis (1981) *Dictionary of the Vulgar Tongue* (London and Basingstoke; reprinting ed. of 1811)

Groves, Reg (1949) *Sharpen the Sickle! The History of the Farm Workers' Union*

Halliwell, James O. (1851) *A Catalogue of Proclamations, Broadsides, Ballads, and Poems presented to the Chetham Library, Manchester* (privately published)

Hamer, Fred (1973) *Green Groves. More English Folk Songs collected by Fred Hamer*

Hammond, David (ed.) (1978) *Songs of Belfast* (Skerries, Co. Dublin)

Hammond, J.L. and Barbara (1919) *The Skilled Labourer, 1760–1832*

Hammond, J.L. and Barbara (1948) *The Village Labourer*, 2 vols (orig. 1911)

Handle, Johnny (1965) 'Industrial Folk Music & Regional Music Hall in the North East. 2. Growth and Extent of the Music Hall' Oct., 138–41

Handle, Johnny (1966) 'Industrial Folk Music & Regional Music Hall in the North East. 3. Music of the Miners', *English Dance and Song,* New Year, 6–9

Handle, Johnny (1976) 'Industrial Folk Music & Regional Music Hall in the North East. 1. Established Traditions and the New Era', *English Dance and Song,* Aug., 106–108

Hannington, Wal (1936) *Unemployed Struggles, 1919–1936. My Life and Struggles among the Unemployed*

Harker, Ben (2007) *Class Act. The Cultural and Political Life of Ewan MacColl*

Harker, D.I. (ed.) (1985) *Songs from the Manuscript Collection of John Bell* (Gateshead)

Harker, Dave (1980) *One for the Money. Politics and Popular Song*

Harker, Dave (1985) 'The Original Bob Cranky?', FMJ 5:1, 48–82

Harker, Dave (ed.), (1999) *Songs and Verse of the North-East Pitmen, c.1780–1844* (Gateshead)

Harland, John (1839) 'Songs of the working Classes', nos. 1 and 2, *Manchester Guardian* (respectively 4 and 12. Dec.)

Harland, John (ed.) (1865) *The Songs of the Wilsons; with a Memoir on the Family* (Manchester, nd [1865]; orig. 1839)

Harland, John, and Wilkinson, T.T. (1870–1) 'An Essay on Songs and Ballads', *Transactions of the Historical Society of Lancashire and Cheshire* 11, 87–118

Harland, John, and Wilkinson, T.T. (eds) (1882) *Ballads and Songs of Lancashire, Ancient and Modern*, 3rd ed. (Manchester and London; orig. Harland only, 1865)

Harrison, J.F.C. (1971) *The Early Victorians, 1832–51*

Harrison, J.F.C. (1990) *Late Victorian Britain*

Harte, Frank, and Lunny, Donal (singers) (2007) *There's gangs of them digging: Songs of Irish labour*, Daisy Label CD DLCD022

Harvey, Jane (1841) *Fugitive Pieces* (Newcastle)

Hattersley, Roy (1997) *Fifty Years On: A Prejudiced History of Britain since the War*

Henderson, Hamish (1992)*Alias MacAlias. Writings on Songs, Folk and Literature* (Edinburgh)

Henderson, Kathy, with Armstrong, Frankie, and Kerr, Sandra (eds) (1979) *My Song is my Own. 100 Women's Songs*

Henderson, W. (ed.) (1937) *Victorian Street Ballads*

Henry, Sam (coll.) (1990) *Sam Henry's Songs of the People*, ed. Gale Huntington (Athens, Georgia, and London)

Hepburn, James, (2000 and 2001) *A Book of Scattered Leaves. Poetry of Poverty in Broadside Ballads of Nineteenth Century England*, 2 vols. (Lewisburg and

London)
Herd, David (coll.) (1973) *Ancient and Modern Scottish Songs*, 2 vols. (Edinburgh; reprint of 1776 ed.; orig. 1769)
Hewitson, A. (1883) *History of Preston*
Hewitt, John (ed.) (1974) *Rhyming Weavers and Other Country Poets of Down and Antrim* (Belfast)
Hickling, A.J.R. (1989) *Black Country Pits* (Sedgley)
Hill, S. (1898) *Old Lancashire Songs and their Singers* (Stalybridge)
Hobday, Charles (1975) 'Two sansculotte poets: John Freeth and Joseph Mather', chap. 4 in Hobsbawm, Eric, *The Age of Capital, 1848–1875*
Hobsbawm, E.J., and Rudé, George (1969) *Captain Swing*
Hobsbawm, Eric (1975) *The Age of Capital, 1848–1875*
Hobsbawm, Eric (1999) *Industry and Empire*
Holden, Triona (2005) *Queen Coal. Women of the Miners' Strike* (Stroud)
Hollingworth, Brian (1977) *Songs of the People. Lancashire Dialect Poetry of the Industrial Revolution* (Manchester)
Holloway, John, and Black, Joan (eds) (1975 and 1979) *Later English Broadside Ballads*, 2 vols
Holt, William (1942) *I Haven't Unpacked. An Autobiography* (orig. 1939)
Hoppen, K. Theodore (1998) *The Mid-Victorian Generation, 1846–1886* (Oxford)
Horden, John (1993) *John Freeth (1731–1808), Political Ballad-writer and Innkeeper* (Oxford)
Horn, Pamela (1971) *Joseph Arch (1826–1919). The Farm Workers' Leader* (Kineton)
Hornsby, Malcolm (nd) *The Loughborough Job. The Incident at Heathcoat's Mill* (Loughborough)
Howes, Frank (1969) *Folk Music of Britain – and Beyond*
Howkins, Alun (2005) 'Bob Copper (1915–2004)', FMJ 8:5, 683–86
Hudleston, Mary and Nigel (coll.) (2001) *Songs of the Ridings. The Yorkshire Musical Museum* (Scarborough)
Huggins, Mike (2004) *The Victorians and Sport* (London and New York)
Hughes, Glyn (1975) *Millstone Grit*
Hunt, David, 'Cartwright, Edmund', ODNB
Hunt, Tristram (2009) *The Frock-coated Communist. The Revolutionary Life of Friedrich Engels*
Hutton, Guthrie (comp.) (2005) *Coal not Dole. Memories of the 1984/85 Miners' Strike* (Catrine)
Hutton, William (1781) *The History of Birmingham*
Jackston, T.A. (1947) *Ireland her Own. An Outline History of the Irish Struggle*
Jacques, J.B. [Brian] (1972) *Yennoworrameanlike* (Liverpool)
James, Kevin J. (2007) *Handloom Weavers in Ulster's Linen Industry* (Dublin)
James, Louis (ed.), (1976) *Print and the People, 1819–1851*
James, Steven G. (1988) *Sport, Politics and the Working Class. Organised Labour and Sport in Inter-war Britain* (Manchester)
Jefferys, James B. (1945) *The Story of the Engineers, 1800–1945*
Jenkin, A.K. Hamilton (1972) *The Cornish Miner* (Newton Abbot)
Jenkins, Jess, (2005) *The Plight of Leicestershire's Framework Knitters in the 1840s* (Leicester)
Jenkins, Mark (1980) *The General Strike of 1842*
Johnson, C.R., and Thiedeman, C.P. (comp.) (1980) *Street Literature* (Altrincham)
Johnson, Paul (2004) *A Vanished Landscape. A 1930s Childhood in the Potteries*
Jolly Fine Company (singers) *The Old Lamb and Flag*, Dragon Records CD DRGN921
Joyce, Patrick (1994) *Visions of the People: Industrial England and the Question of Class, 1848–1914* (Cambridge; orig. 1991)
Keeping, Charles (ed.) (1975) *Cockney Ding Dong. A Song Book* (Harmondsworth and London)
Kennedy, John (singer) (1999) *The Girls along the Road*, Veteran CD VT137CD
Kennedy, Peter (ed.) (1975) *Folksongs of Britain & Ireland*
Kidson, Frank, and Shaw, Martin (1913) *Songs of Britain*
Kilgarriff, Michael (1998) *Sing Us One of the Old Songs. A Guide to Popular Song, 1860–1920* (Oxford)
King, Steven, and Timmins, Geoffrey (2001) *Making Sense of the Industrial Revolution: English Economy and Society, 1700–1850* (Manchester)
Kinsley, James (ed.) (1971) *Burns. Poems and Songs*
Kirby, M.W., 'MacGregor, Sir Ian Kinloch (1912–1998)', ODNB
Lafargue, Paul (1880) *Le Droit à la Paresse* (Paris; translated into English in 1883 as *The Right to be Lazy*)
Laggan, The (singers) (2002) *I am the common man*, Lochshore CD CDLDL 1311
Langton, John, 'Skipsey, Joseph', ODNB
Laycock, Samuel (1893) *Warblin's fro' an Owd Songster* (Oldham and London)
Leeson, R.A. (1973) *Strike. A Live History, 1887–1971*
Leeson, R.A. (1979) *Travelling Brothers. The Six Centuries' Road from Craft Fellowship to Trade Unionism*
Leigh, J.S. (2008) *Preston Cotton Martyrs* (Lancaster)
Lewis, Brian (1971) *Coal Mining in the Eighteenth and Nineteenth Centuries*
Lewis, Richard, 'Macdonald, Alexander (1821-1881)', ODNB

Littlewood, Joan (2003) *Joan's Book. The Autobiography of Joan Littlewood* (orig. 1994)
Lloyd, A.L. (1944) *The Singing Englishman. An Introduction to Folksong* (nd [1944])
Lloyd, A.L. (1951) 'Folk-songs of the Coalfields', *Coal* (May), 26–27
Lloyd, A.L. (1952 and 1978) *Come All Ye Bold Miners*
Lloyd, A.L. (1967) *Folk Song in England*
Lloyd, A.L. (1978) 'The Meaning of Folk Music', chap. 1 (pp.5–28) in Robert Leach and Roy Palmer (eds), *Folk Music in School* (Cambridge)
Lloyd, A.L. (singer) (1998) *Leviathan! Ballads & Songs of the Whaling Trade*, CD Topic Records TSCD497 (orig. 1967)
Lloyd, A.L. (singer) (2008) *Ten Thousand Miles Away*, CD disc 2, *The Australian Songs*, Fellside Recordings (recordings originally made in the 1950s)
Lloyd, E.M., 'Vane, Charles William, 3rd Marquess of Londonderry (1778–1854)', ODNB
Lomax, John A. and Alan (eds) (1934) *American Ballads and Folk Songs* (New York)
Lones, T.E. (1898) *A History of Mining in the Black Country* (Dudley)
Lonsdale, Roger (ed.) (1984) *The New Oxford Book of Eighteenth Century Verse* (Oxford)
Loosley, John (1993) *The Stroudwater Riots of 1925* (Stroud)
[Lowe, J.,] 'Locked Out' (1853) *Household Words* (10 Dec.), 345–48
Lucas, John (ed.) (1996) *Writing and Radicalism*
Macaulay, Lord (1849–1855) *History of England* (and later editions)
MacColl, Ewan (ed.) (1954) *The Shuttle and Cage. Industrial Folk-Ballads*
MacColl, Ewan (singer) (1958) *Steam Whistle Ballads*, LP record, Topic Records 12T104
MacColl, Ewan, Parker, Charles, and Seeger, Peggy (1999) *The Ballad of John Axon,* TSCD 801; *The Big Hewer*, TSCD 804; *The Body Blow*, TSCD 805; *The Fight Game*, TSCD 807; *On the Edge*, TSCD 806; *Singing the Fishing*, TSCD 803; *Song of a Road*, TSCD 802; and *The Travelling People*, TSCD 808 (all Topic Records CDs)
MacColl, Ewan, and Seeger, Peggy (singers) (1984) *Daddy, What Did You Do in the Strike?* Blackthorne audio cassette BS1
MacDougall, Ian (ed.) (1985) *Labour in Scotland. A Pictorial History from the Eighteenth Century to the Present* (Edinburgh)
McCarthy, Terry (ed.) (1988) *The Great Dock Strike 1889: the story of the Labour Movement's First Great Victory*
McDonnel, John (ed.) (1986) *Songs of Struggle and Protest* (Cork and Dublin; orig. 1979)
McGinn, Matt (1987) *McGinn of the Calton. The Life and Works of Matt MacGinn (1928–1977)* (Glasgow)
McKendrick, Neil (1961) 'Josiah Wedgwood and Factory Discipline', *The Historical Journal* 4:1, 30–55
McNaughtan, Adam (19??) 'A Century of Saltmarket Literature, 1790–1890' in Peter Isaac (ed.), *Six Centuries in the Provincial Book Trade in Britain* (Cirencester)
McVicar, Ewan (1990) *One Singer, One Song. Songs of the Glasgow Folk* (Glasgow)
Magpie Lane (singers) (2002) *Six for Gold*, Beautiful Jo records CD BEJOCD-42
Mann, F.O. (ed.) (1912) *The Works of Thomas Deloney* (Oxford; repr. 1969)
Mann, Tom (2008) *Tom Mann's Memoirs* (Nottingham; orig. London, 1923)
Marr, Andrew (2007) *A History of Modern Britain*
Martin, E.W. (1965) *The Shearers and the Shorn*
Marx, Karl (1930) *Capital*, with an introduction by G.D.H. Cole, 2 vols (orig. 1867)
Maurice, William (comp) (2004) *A Pitman's Anthology*
Megson [Stu Hanna and Debbie Hanna-Palmer] (singers) (2008) *Take Yourself a Wife*, EDJ Records CD EDJ015
Messenger, Betty (1980) *Picking Up the Linen Threads. A Study in Industrial Folklore* (Belfast)
Metcalfe, W. Stanley (1937) 'History of the Keelmen and their Strike in 1822', *Archaeologia Aeliana*, 4th ser. 14, 1–16
Milne, Seumas (2004) *The Enemy Within. The Secret War Against the Miners* (orig. 1994)
Moorman, F.W. (ed.) (1916) *Yorkshire Dialect Poems, 1673–1915*
Morgan, Kevin, 'Pollitt, Harry (1890–1960)', ODNB
Mortimer, John (1890) 'Some Lancashire Rhymes', *Manchester Literary Club Papers*, 55–65
Morton, A.L. (1965) *A People's History of England* (orig. 1938)
Morton, A.L., and Tate, George (1979) *The British Labour Movement, 1770–1920. A History* (orig. 1956)
Morton, Robin (comp.) (1970) *Folk Songs Sung in Ulster* (Cork)
Moulden, John (ed.) (1979) *Songs of the People. Selections from the Sam Henry Collection*, part 1 (Belfast)
Mulcahy, Michael, and Fitzgibbon, Marie (1982) *The Voice of the People. Songs and History of Ireland* (Dublin)
Nettel, Reginald (1969) *A Social History of Traditional Song* (orig. as *Sing a Song of England,* 1954)
Neuburg, Victor (1977) *Popular Literature. A History and Guide* (Harmondsworth)
Newsome, David (1997) *The Victorian World Picture*
O'Hagan, Andrew (2009) 'The Age of Indifference',

Guardian Review (10 Jan.), 2–4
O Lochlainn, Colm (ed.) (1965) *More Irish Street Ballads* (Dublin)
O Neill, Dennis, and Meazey, Peter (eds) (1973) *Topical Songs of Wales* (Cardiff)
Palfrey, Sammy (nd) 'Writing on the Miners' Strike, 1984–5', *www.wcml.org.uk/culture/miners.htm* (accessed 29.09.08), from *Working Class Movement Library Bulletin*, no. 12
Palmer, R.E. (1770-2) 'The funny rigs of good and tender-hearted masters in the happy town of Kidderminster. Anno 1828', *Transactions of the Worcestershire Archaeological Society*, 3rd ser. 3, 105–13
Palmer, Roy, 'Armstrong, Thomas ('Tommy') (1848–1920)', ODNB
Palmer, Roy, 'Corvan, Edward (1830–1865)', ODNB
Palmer, Roy, 'Cox, Harry (1885–1971)', ODNB
Palmer, Roy, 'Mather, Joseph (1737–1804)', ODNB
Palmer, Roy (ed.) (1971) *Room for Company. Folk songs and ballads* (Cambridge)
Palmer, Roy (ed.) (1972) *Songs of the Midlands*, music eds Pamela Bishop and Katharine Thomson (East Ardsley)
Palmer, Roy (ed.) (1972b) *The Painful Plough. A portrait of the agricultural labourer in the nineteenth century from folk songs and ballads and contemporary accounts* (Cambridge)
Palmer, Roy (ed.) (1974a) *Poverty Knock. A picture of industrial life in the nineteenth century through songs, ballads and contemporary accounts*
Palmer, Roy (ed.) (1974b) *A Touch on the Times. Songs of Social Change, 1770–1914* (Harmondsworth)
Palmer, Roy (1977) 'The Weaver in Love', FMJ 3:3, 261–74
Palmer, Roy (ed.) (1977b) *The Rambling Soldier* (Harmondsworth)
Palmer, Roy (ed.) (1979) *A Ballad History of England*
Palmer, Roy (ed.) (1979a) *Everyman's Book of English Country Songs*
Palmer, Roy (ed.) (1979b) *Birmingham Ballads. Facsimile Street Ballads* (Birmingham)
Palmer, Roy (ed.) (1980) *Everyman's Book of British Ballads*
Palmer, Roy (1983) 'Canti della Rivoluzione Industriale', *Movimento Operaio e Socialista*, NS Anno 6, no. 2, 259–81
Palmer, Roy (1985) *The Folklore of Leicestershire and Rutland* (Wymondham)
Palmer, Roy (1986) 'A.L. Lloyd and Industrial Song', pp. 133–44 in Russell, q.v.
Palmer, Roy (1988) *The Sound of History. Songs and Social Comment* (Oxford and New York)
Palmer, Roy (ed.) (1990), *What a Lovely War. British Soldiers' Songs from the Boer War to the Present Day*
Palmer, Roy (1991) 'Welsh Ballads and Broadsides', *Poetry Wales* 26:4, 6–8
Palmer, Roy (1991a) *Britain's Living Folklore* (Newton Abbot; reprinted Felinfach, 1995)
Palmer, Roy (1998), *The Folklore of (Old) Monmouthshire* (Almeley)
Palmer, Roy (ed.) (2001) *Boxing the Compass. Sea Songs and Shanties* (Todmorden)
Palmer, Roy (2004) *The Folklore of (Old) Monmouthshire* (Almeley)
Palmer, Roy (2004a) *The Folklore of Worcestershire* (Almeley)
Palmer, Roy (2004b) *The Folklore of Warwickshire* (Stroud)
Palmer, Roy (2007) *The Folklore of the Black Country* (Almeley)
Palmer, Roy, and Raven, Jon (eds) (1976) *The Rigs of the fair. Popular sports and pastimes in the nineteenth century through songs, ballads and contemporary accounts* (Cambridge)
Peace, David (2004) *GB84*
Peel, Frank (1893) *Spen Valley: Past and Present* (Heckmondwike)
Peel, Frank (1895) *The Risings of the Luddites*, 3rd ed. (Brighouse; orig. 1880)
Perkin, H.J. (1969) *The Origin of Modern English Society, 1780–1880*
Pickering, Michael, Robertson, Emma, and Korczynski, Marek (2007) 'Rhythms of Labour: The British Work Song Revisited', FMJ 9:2, 226–45
Pike, E. Royston (1966) *Human Documents of the Industrial Revolution in Britain*
Pinchbeck, Ivy (1930) *Women Workers and the Industrial Revolution, 1750–1850*
Pinto, Vivian de Sola, and Rodway, Allan Edwin (eds) (1957) *The Common Muse. An Anthology of Popular British Ballad Poetry, XVth–XXth Century*
Pivato, Stefano (2005) *Bella Ciao. Canto e Politica nella Storia d'Italia* (Bari)
Pollard, Sydney (1963) 'Factory Discipline in the Industrial Revolution', *Economic History Review* 16:2, 254–71
Pollitt, Harry (1940) *Serving My Time*
Poole, Robert (1983) 'Oldham Wakes', chap. 5 in Walton and Walvin, q.v.
Porter, Gerald (1981) 'The Significance of the Transmission, Variants and Distribution of Jone o'Grinfilt Jr', *Proceedings of the University of Vaasa: Research Papers*, no. 80, 70–79
Porter, Gerald (1992) *The English Occupational Song* (Umea)
Porter, Gerald (1994) '"Work the old Lady out of the Ditch": Singing at Work by English Lacemakers', *Journal of Folklore Research* 31:1–3, 35–55

Porter, Gerald (1995) 'Cobblers All: Occupation as Identity and Cultural Message', FMJ 7:1, 43–61

Porter, Gerald (1998) '"The World's Ill-Divided": the Communist Party and Progressive Song', chap. 10 in A. Croft (ed.), *A Weapon in the Struggle*

Power, Rosemary (2008) '"After the Black Gold": A View of Mining Heritage from Coalfield Areas in Britain', *Folklore* 119:2, 160–81

Price, Jacob M., 'Crowley, Sir Ambrose (1658–1713)', ODNB

Purdon, Jock (nd) *The Echo of Pit Boots. Pitwork, Politics & Poetry. The Collected Songs and Poems of Jock Purdon* (North Shields)

Purdon, Jock (singer) (nd) *Pitwork, Politics and Poetry. The Songs and Poetry of Jock Purdon*, audiocassette PLP 001

Purdon, Jock (1977) *Songs of the Durham Coalfield*

Raven, Jon (ed.) (1977) *The Urban and industrial Songs of the Black Country and Birmingham* (Wolverhampton)

Reach, Angus Bethune (2007) *Fabrics, Filth and Fairy Tents. The Yorkshire Textile districts in 1849*, ed. Chris Aspin (Mytholmroyd; orig. as articles in the *Morning Chronicle*, Dec. 1849)

Rediker, Marcus (1987) *Between the Devil and the deep Blue Sea. Merchant Seamen, Pirates, and the Anglo-American Maritime World, 1700–1750* (Cambridge)

Reeves, James (ed.) (1960) *The Everlasting Circle. English Traditional Verse*

Reid, Douglas A. (1976) 'The Decline of Saint Monday, 1766–1876', *Past and Present,* no. 71 (May), 76–101

Reid, Douglas A. (1996) 'Weddings, Weekdays, Work and Leisure in Urban England, 1791–1911: The decline of Saint Monday Revisited', *Past and Present,* no. 153 (Nov.), 135–63

Reid, Robert (1986) *Land of Lost Content. The Luddite Revolt, 1812*

Renwick, Roger de V. (1980) *English Folk Poetry. Structure and Meaning*

Richards, Sam (1983) 'Joe Hill: A Labour Legend in Song', FMJ 4:4, 367–84

Richards, Sam (1992) *Sonic Harvest. Towards Musical Democracy* (Charlbury)

Richards, Sam, and Stubbs, Tish (eds) (1979) *The English Folksinger* (Glasgow and London)

Ritson, Joseph (ed.) (1793) *The Northumberland Garland* (Newcastle)

Roach, T. (1896) 'The Riots of 1830', *Hampshire Notes and Queries* 12, 97–98

Roberts, Keith (1970) *On the Road to Wigan Pier and Back* (Wigan)

Rogers, Dave (2005) *Singing the Changes. Songs by Dave Rogers for Banner Theatre* (Coventry)

Rogers, Nicholas (2008) *The Press Gang. Naval Impressment and its Opponents in Georgian Britain*

Rollins, Hyder E. (ed.) (1929–1932) *The Pepys Ballads*, 8 vols (Cambridge, Mass.)

Rollins, Hyder E. (1967) *An Analytical Index to the Ballad-Entries (1557–1709) in the registers of the Company of Stationers of London* (Hatboro, Pennsylvania; orig. 1924)

Rose, Jonathan (2001) *The Intellectual Life of the British Working Classes* (New Haven and London)

Roud, Steve, *Folk Song Index* and *Broadside Index*, available through website of VWML

Russell, Ian (ed.) (1986) *Singer, Song and Scholar* (Sheffield)

Salzman, Paul, 'Deloney, Thomas', ODNB

Samuel, Raphael (1977) 'The Workshop of the World: Steam Power and Hand Technology in mid-Victorian Britain', *History Workshop Journal,* 3, 6–72

Samuel, Raphael (ed.) (1977a) *Miners, Quarrymen and Saltworkers*

Samuel, Raphael, Bloomfield, Barbara, and Boanas, Guy (eds) (1986) *The Enemy Within. Pit Villages and the Miners' Strike of 1984–5*

Sassoon, Siegfried (1984) *Collected Poems, 1908–1956*

Scargill, Arthur (2009) 'We could surrender – or stand and fight', *The Guardian* (7 Mar.), 26–27

Scott, Derek B. (1989) *The Singing Bourgeois. Songs of the Victorian Drawing Room and Parlour* (Milton Keynes and Philadelphia)

Seeger, Peggy (1998) *The Peggy Seeger Songbook: Forty Years of Songmaking* (London and New York)

Seeger, Peggy (ed.) (2001) *The Essential Ewan MacColl Songbook: Sixty Years of Songmaking* (London and New York)

Seeger, Peggy, and Ewan MacColl (eds) (1961) *Songs for the Sixties*

Seeger, Pete, and Reiser, Bob (eds) (1986) *Carry it on! A History in Song and Picture of the Working Men and Women of America* (Poole)

Seng, Peter J. (ed.) (1978) *Tudor Songs and Ballads from MS Cotton Vespasian A-25* (Cambridge, Mass., and London)

[Sharp, Cuthbert] (ed.) (1969) *The Bishoprick Garland* (Newcastle; orig. London, 1834)

Shaw, Charles (1979) *When I Was a Child* (Firle, Sussex; orig. as by An Old Potter, 1903)

Shellard, Peter (ed.) (1970) *Factory Life, 1774–1885*

Shepard, Leslie (1986) 'A.L. Lloyd – A Personal View', pp.125–32 in Russell, q.v.

Simonin, L. (1868?) *Mines and Miners; or, Underground Life*, trans. and ed. by H.W. Bristow

Simpson, Claude M. (1966) *The British Broadside Ballad*

and its Music (New Brunswick, New Jersey)
Simpson, Jacqueline, and Roud, Steve (2000) *A Dictionary of English Folklore* (Oxford)
Smethurst, J.B. (nd) *Ballads of the Coalfields*, duplicated typewritten pamphlet (Eccles)
Smethurst, John B. (1967) *Strikes and Strike Breakers in Worsley Coalfield*, duplicated typewritten pamphlet (Eccles)
Smith, Alan (1969) *Discovering Folklore in Industry* (Tring)
Smith, L.D. (1986) *Carpet Weavers and Carpet Masters. The Hand Loom Carpet Weavers of Kidderminster, 1780–1850* (Kidderminster)
Smith, Len (ed.) (1979) *The Carpet Weavers' Lament. Songs and ballads of Kidderminster in the Industrial Revolution* (Kidderminster)
Smith, Paul (2001) 'Joseph Mather: filesmith and ballad-monger', pp. 271–323 in Malcolm Jones (ed.), *Essays in Lore & Language presented to John Widdowson* . . . (Sheffield)
Spencer, J.H. (1948) *A Preston Chap Book and its Printer* [John Harkness], *Preston Herald* (2 Jan.), 2
Spiegl, Fritz (ed.) (1966) *Genuine Liverpool Street Songs and Broadside Ballads*, folder (Liverpool)
Stephens, Meic (ed.) (1986) *The Oxford Companion to the Literature of Wales* (Oxford)
Stevenson, John, 'Hannington, Walter ('Wal')', ODNB
Storch, R.D. (ed.) (1982) *Popular Culture and Custom in 19th Century England*
Straniero, Michele (1991) 'Ciao, Bandiera Rossa', *Guardian* (27 Dec.)
Strawhead (singers) (1993) *Victorian Ballads*, Dragon Records CD DRGNCD941
Stuart, Marie W. (1948) 'Lowland Hand-Workers' Songs', *The Countryman* 37:1, 96–97
Styles, John (2008) *The Dress of the people: Everyday Fashion in 18th Century England* (New Haven and London)
Tams, John (singer) (2000) *Unity*, Topic Records CD TSCD508
Tawney, Cyril (singer) (1972) *Cyril Tawney in Port*, Argo LP ZFB28
Tennant, Charles, 'Kinloch, George (1775–1833)', ODNB
Terry, R.R. (1920) 'Sailor Shanties', I and II, *Music and Letters* 1:1 (Jan.), 35–44, and 1:3 (July), 256–68, respectively
Thomason, Mary (1938) *Warp and Weft. Cuts from a Lancashire Loom* (Leigh)
Thomason, Mary (1961) *The Poetry of Mary Thomason* (Leigh)
Thompson, Dorothy (1984) *The Chartists*
Thompson, Dorothy (1990) *Queen Victoria. The Woman, the Monarchy and the People* (New York)
Thompson, E.P. (1963) *The Making of the English Working Class*
Thompson, E.P. (1967) 'Time, Work-discipline and Industrial Capitalism', *Past and Present*, no. 3 (Dec.), 56–97
Thompson, E.P. (1991) *Customs in Common*
Thompson, E.P. (1995) *Making History. Writings on History and Culture* (New York)
Thompson, F.M.L., 'Hicks, William Joynson-', ODNB
Thomson, Frances M. (1969) *Newcastle Chapbooks in Newcastle upon Tyne University Library* (Newcastle)
Thomson, George, (1946) *Marxism and Poetry* (New York)
Tolmie, Frances (coll.) (1997) *One Hundred and Five Songs of Occupation from the Western Isles of Scotland*, ed. and annotated by A.G. Gilchrist and Lucy Broadwood (Felinfach: Llanerch Publishers; orig. JFS 4: 16, 1911)
Tomlinson, Ricky (2003) *Ricky*
Tressell, Robert (2004) *The Ragged Trousered Philanthropists*, with an introduction by Tristram Hunt (orig. 1914)
Trory, E. (1974) *Between the Wars* (Brighton)
Urfey, Thomas d' (ed.) (1959) *Wit and Mirth: or, Pills to Purge Melancholy*, 6 vols, (New York; orig, London, 1719–20)
Various Artists (singers) (1963) *The Iron Muse. A Panorama of Industrial Song arranged by A.L. Lloyd*, Topic Records LP 12T86 (orig. 1956)
Various Artists (singers) (1968) *Jack of All Trades*, Topic Records LP 12T159
Various Artists (singers) (1971) *The Wide Midlands*, Topic Records LP 12TS210
Various Artists (singers) (1972) *The Painful Plough. Songs and Ballads of the Agricultural Labourer*, Topic Records LP IMP-A 103
Various Artists (singers) (1973) *Save Shotton! Songs for the Shotton Steelworks Campaign*, Sound News Productions 45 rpm record SNP/SH 01/B
Various Artists (singers) (1975) *The Bonny Pit Laddie. A Miner's Life in Music and Song*, Topic Records double LP 12TS271/2
Various Artists (singers) (1977) *Tommy Armstrong of Tyneside*, Topic Records CD TSCD484
Various Artists (singers) (1981) *An English Folk Music Anthology*, recorded by Sam Richards and Tish Stubbs, Folkways 4 LP set FE 38553
Various Artists (singers) (1987) *Polisses and Candymen. The Songs of Tommy Armstrong*, Redrow records audio cassette RR1
Various Artists (singers) (2006) *Gaelic Songs of Scotland: Women at Work in the Western Isles*, recorded by Alan

Lomax, Rounder CD 11661-1785-2
Vicinus, Martha (1973) 'Literary Voices of an Industrial town. Manchester, 1810–70', chap. 31 in H.J. Dyos and Michael Wolff, *The Victorian City: Images and Realities*, vol. 2
Vicinus, Martha (1974) *The Industrial Muse. A Study of Nineteenth Century British Working Class Literature*
Vicinus, Martha (ed.) (1975) *Broadsides of the industrial North* (Newcastle-upon-Tyne)
Voth, Hans-Joachim (2000) *Time and Work in England, 1750–1830* (Oxford)
Wales, Tony (ed.) (1970) *Folk Song Today*, no. 4
Walton, John K., and Poole, Robert (1982), 'The Lancashire Wakes in the Nineteenth Century', chap. 5 in Storch, q.v.
Walton, John K., and Walvin, James (eds) (1983) *Leisure in Britain, 1780–1939* (Manchester)
Walton, Thomas H. (1885) *Coal Mining Described and Illustrated* (Philadelphia and London)
Ward, J.T. (ed.) (1970) *The Factory System*, 2 vols (Newton Abbot)
Watson, Ian, (1983) *Song and Democratic Culture in Britain* (London and New York)
Weaver, Stewart A., 'Oastler, Richard (1789–1861)', ODNB
Weightman, Gavin (2007) *The Industrial Revolutionaries*
White, Jerry (2008) *London in the 19th Century*
Williams, Ned (1989) *Black Country Folk at Werk* [sic] (Wolverhampton)
Williams, Ralph Vaughan, and Lloyd, A.L. (eds) (2003) *Classic English Folk Songs*, revised by Michael Douglas (orig. *The Penguin Book of English Folk Songs*, 1959)
Williams, W.H.A. (1982) 'The Broadside Ballad and Vernacular Culture', *Irish Folk Music Studies* 3, 45–60
Wilson, A.N. (2002) *The Victorians*
Wilson, Joe (1970) *Tyneside Songs and Drolleries, Readings and Temperance Songs* (East Ardsley; orig. Newcastle-upon-Tyne, nd [1890?])
Wilson, John (ed.) (1862) *The Songs of Joseph Mather...* (Sheffield)
Wilson, Thomas (1843) *The Pitman's Pay* (orig. 1830)
Wolmar, Christian (2007) *Fire & Steam. How the Railways transformed Britain*
Wood, Pete (2008) *The Elliotts of Birtley* (Todmorden)
Woodruff, William (2000) *The Road to Nab End. An Extraordinary Northern Childhood* (orig. as *Billy Boy*, Halifax, 1993)
Woods, Fred (1980) *The Observer Book of Folk Song in Britain*
Woods, Fred (ed.) (1983) *The Oxford Book of English Traditional Verse* (Oxford)
Woollard, Richard (nd) 'Albion Mill', *www/vauxhallsociety.org.uk/Albion%20Mill.html*
Wright, Thomas (1982) *The Romance of the Lace Pillow*, 2 vols. (Bedford; orig. 2 vols, Olney, 1919)
Wrigley, Ammon (1912) *Songs of a Moorland Parish* (Saddleworth)
Wrigley, Bernard (nd) *Fables to Frighten your Frog. 12 Songs and Stories* (Daventry, [1976?])
Wrigley, Bernard (singer) (1974) *Rough & Wrigley*, Topic Records LP 12TS241
Wrigley, Bernard (singer) (2005) *God's Own County*, Loofy Records CD 019CD
Young, Robert (2002) '"A Dialogue I'll Tell You as True as me Life...": Vernacular Song and Industrial Archaeology in Northern England', *Industrial Archaeology Review* 34:1

Index of Songs

Text with music — **Chapter Ref.**
Text only — Chapter Ref.
First lines — *Chapter Ref.*

Index

Acknowledgements

For permission to include songs (full details in the Notes), both words and tunes (unless otherwise specified):

Pam Bishop, 'Colliers' March' and 'Dudley Boys' (tunes), Lesley Boardman, 'Handloom v. Powerloom' (tune), Georgina Boyes, 'Hundred Thousand Heroines', Bucks Music Group, 'Three Nights and a Sunday', by Matt McGinn, Ian Campbell, 'The Laughing Policeman' (words), Gordon Cox, 'Doffers of Old Whittam's Mill', Ted Edwards, 'The Pitside is Quiet', Dave Goulder, 'Father Doesn't Fancy Work at All', A.E. Green, 'Four o' clock at Sullivan's door', 'Pony Driver' and 'Poverty Knock', Johnny Handle, 'Farewell to Monty', the late Hamish Henderson, 'Saw ye the cotton spinners', Brian Jacques, 'The Docker's Lament', Sandra Kerr, 'Freddie Matthews', by Ron Elliott, Alison McMorland, 'I'm a Poor old Weaver', Keith Roberts, 'Lament for Albert', Dave Rogers, 'The Ballad of Kevin Casey' and 'Saltley Gate', School of Scottish Studies Archives, University of Edinburgh, and *Tocher*, 'The Jute Mill Song', sung by Mary Brooksbank and recorded by Hamish Henderson, John Tams, 'Harry Stone (Hearts of Coal)', Third Party Ltd., and Rosemary Tawney, 'On a Monday Morning', by Cyril Tawney, Dave Webber and Anni Fentiman, 'Dock Strike 1970', by Rod Shearman, and Bernard Wrigley, 'Half Timer'.

For permission to include poems:

Barbara Levy Literary Agency, 'The Case for the Miners', by Siegfried Sassoon
David Higham Associates, 'Promises', by Eleanor Farjeon

For permission to reproduce documents and illustrations

Aberdeen Art Gallery & Museums Collections,
Roger Birch,
Bodleian Library, University of Oxford,
Bolton Museum & Archive Service,
Burnley Community History Library,
Cardiff Council Library Service,
Chris Coe,
Derby City Library,
Firth Ballad Collection, University of Sheffield Library
Gallacher Memorial Library, Glasgow Caledonian University Research Collections Harris Museum & Art Gallery,
Hebden Bridge Local History Society Archive,
Malcolm Hornsby,
Kirklees Image Archive,
Kyzyl Tan Consultants Ltd, 'Rush Bearing', by Alexander Wilson,
Laing Art Gallery,
National Library of Scotland,
National Library of Wales,
National Media Museum (Daily Herald Collection), Bradford,
National Railway Museum, York,
Pat Palmer,
People's History Museum,
Perth Museum and Art Gallery,
Potteries Museum and Art Gallery, Stoke-on-Trent,
Record Office for Leicestershire, Leicester & Rutland,
Peggy Seeger,
South Wales Coalfield Collection, Swansea University,
Rod Stradling,
Topic Records,
Vaughan Williams Memorial Library,
John Wardroper,
Wigan Heritage Service,
Worcester Record Office,

For assistance from the staffs of these institutions:

BBC Sound Archive,
Birmingham Central Library,
Birmingham University Library,
Bodleian Library,
Bradford Central Library,

Bristol City Library,
British Library,
Calderdale Library, Todmorden,
Cambridge University Library,
Cardiff Central Library,
Cardiff University Library,
Chetham's Library, Manchester,
Derby City Library,
Durham Record Office,
Glasgow University Library,
Harris Library, Preston,
Harvard University, Houghton Library,
Helmshore Textile Museum, Rossendale,
Lancashire County Council Reference and Information Service,
Leeds University Dialect and Folklore Archive,
Liverpool Record Office,
London Metropolitan University (TUC Collection),
London University Library,
Manchester Central Library,
Middle Tennessee State University (Kenneth S. Goldstein Collection of American Popular Music),
Mitchell Library, Glasgow,
National Coal Mining Museum for England,
National Coal Mining Museum for Wales,
National Library of Ireland,
National Library of Scotland,
National Library of Wales,
National Maritime Museum,
Newcastle-upon-Tyne Libraries & Information Service,
Newcastle-upon-Tyne University Library,
Norfolk Museum of Rural Life,
Nottingham University Library,
Picton Library, Liverpool,
Rotherham Archives & Local Studies Service,
Ruskin College College, Oxford,
Sheffield University Library,
Somerset County Record Office,
Stoke-on-Trent City Archives,
Vaughan Williams Memorial Library,
Victoria & Albert Museum,
West Yorkshire Archive Service,
Wigan Archive Service,
Worcester History Centre,
Worcestershire Libraries,
Worcestershire Record Office.

For generous help from these colleagues and friends:

Dawn and Hugh Anderson, Jeremy Barlow, Margaret Bennett, Pam Bishop, Georgina Boyes, Bob Bushaway, Keith Chandler, Jim Clayson, Tony Conran, the late Bob Cooney, Jeff Cooper, Mark Dowding, Martin Graebe, Mark Gregory, Johnny Handle, the late Hamish Henderson, Michael Honeybone, Jon Hurley, Sandra Kerr, Louis Killen, Emily Lyle, Adam McNaughtan, John Moulden, Bob Pegg, Robert Poole, Gerald Porter, Domenico Rischitelli, W.G. Shepherd, Rosemary Tawney, Roger Thomas, Dorothy Thompson, the late Angela Tuckett, the late Eric Twigg, Jean Moorcroft Wilson, Pete Wood.

I should like to offer particular thanks to:

Jim Hepburn, for information and insight on broadside ballads, as well as transcriptions and photocopies; Henry Peacock, for tireless ferreting in the Internet; Steve Roud, for extraordinary generosity in helping me to install successive versions of his invaluable indexes; David Eckersley, my publisher, and his wife, Erica, for their unstinting hard work and a host of suggestions; everyone at Herron Publishing, Ali Burns for the music layout, Ali Crann for proof reading, Kit Eckersley for website design and internet marketing, and Bryan Ledgard for the book design, layout and the striking cover; and the National Folk Music Fund for grants for research (2005) and reproduction fees (2009);

and above all,

My wife, companion of well over fifty years, best friend and harshest critic, Pat Palmer, whose support, tolerance and musical skills have been fundamental.